Promoting Inclusive Growth in the Fourth Industrial Revolution

Sheryl Beverley Buckley
University of South Africa, South Africa

A volume in the Advances in
Business Strategy and Competitive
Advantage (ABSCA) Book Series

Published in the United States of America by
    IGI Global
    Business Science Reference (an imprint of IGI Global)
    701 E. Chocolate Avenue
    Hershey PA, USA 17033
    Tel: 717-533-8845
    Fax: 717-533-8661
    E-mail: cust@igi-global.com
    Web site: http://www.igi-global.com

Library of Congress Cataloging-in-Publication Data

Names: Buckley, Sheryl, 1959- editor.
Title: Promoting inclusive growth in the fourth industrial revolution /
  Sheryl Beverley Buckley, editor.
Description: Hershey, PA : Business Science Reference, [2020] | Includes
  bibliographical references and index. | Summary: "This book focuses on
  the role of formal education in preparing students for uncertain futures
  and for societies that are changing at great speed in terms of their
  abilities to drive job creation, economic growth, and prosperity for
  millions in the future"-- Provided by publisher.
Identifiers: LCCN 2020004156 (print) | LCCN 2020004157 (ebook) | ISBN
  9781799848820 (hardcover) | ISBN 9781799852766 (paperback) | ISBN
  9781799848837 (ebook)
Subjects: LCSH: Labor supply--Effect of education on. | Labor
  supply--Effect of technological innovations on. | Technical education. |
  Vocational education.
Classification: LCC HD5706 .P756 2020 (print) | LCC HD5706 (ebook) | DDC
  331.11--dc23
LC record available at https://lccn.loc.gov/2020004156
LC ebook record available at https://lccn.loc.gov/2020004157

This book is published in the IGI Global book series Advances in Business Strategy and Competitive Advantage (ABSCA) (ISSN: 2327-3429; eISSN: 2327-3437)

British Cataloguing in Publication Data
A Cataloguing in Publication record for this book is available from the British Library.

All work contributed to this book is new, previously-unpublished material.
The views expressed in this book are those of the authors, but not necessarily of the publisher.

For electronic access to this publication, please contact: eresources@igi-global.com.

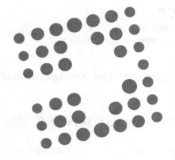

Advances in Business Strategy and Competitive Advantage (ABSCA) Book Series

ISSN:2327-3429
EISSN:2327-3437

Editor-in-Chief: Patricia Ordóñez de Pablos, Universidad de Oviedo, Spain

MISSION

Business entities are constantly seeking new ways through which to gain advantage over their competitors and strengthen their position within the business environment. With competition at an all-time high due to technological advancements allowing for competition on a global scale, firms continue to seek new ways through which to improve and strengthen their business processes, procedures, and profitability.

The **Advances in Business Strategy and Competitive Advantage (ABSCA) Book Series** is a timely series responding to the high demand for state-of-the-art research on how business strategies are created, implemented and re-designed to meet the demands of globalized competitive markets. With a focus on local and global challenges, business opportunities and the needs of society, the **ABSCA** encourages scientific discourse on doing business and managing information technologies for the creation of sustainable competitive advantage.

COVERAGE

- Strategic Alliances
- Balanced Scorecard
- Small and Medium Enterprises
- Competitive Strategy
- Tacit Knowledge
- Value Creation
- Economies of Scale
- Customer-Orientation Strategy
- Cost Leadership Strategy
- Adaptive Enterprise

IGI Global is currently accepting manuscripts for publication within this series. To submit a proposal for a volume in this series, please contact our Acquisition Editors at Acquisitions@igi-global.com or visit: http://www.igi-global.com/publish/.

Titles in this Series

IGI Global
PUBLISHER of TIMELY KNOWLEDGE

701 East Chocolate Avenue, Hershey, PA 17033, USA
Tel: 717-533-8845 x100 • Fax: 717-533-8661
E-Mail: cust@igi-global.com • www.igi-global.com

This book would not have been possible without the support to all those with whom I have had the pleasure to work with during this project and I am grateful. I am especially indebted to Nicky Lucas who assisted with proofreading. Most importantly, I wish to thank my loving and supportive husband who provides unending inspiration.

Table of Contents

Detailed Table of Contents

Chapter 1
Implications of Digital Transformation on the Strategy Development Process
for Business Leaders 1

> *Theunis Gert Pelser, University of KwaZulu-Natal, South Africa*
> *Garth Gaffley, University of KwaZulu-Natal, South Africa*

What the internet with its connectivity did to facilitate the third industrial revolution, cloud computing and artificial intelligence have done for the fourth industrial revolution. Technology is changing the world at an alarming rate, which includes products and services that require scale to manage the growing demands of an ever-changing and increasing population. Digital transformation is enabled through cloud technology where human comprehension cannot cope with the size and speed of data required to manage a business in the digital economy. Artificial intelligence and machine learning assist in activities to overcome human limitation, using algorithms to develop predictive and simulation models and scale to provide data for decision making. The technologies employed to run and execute these require skill and resource. The challenge for the modern-day CEO is that the use of technology and its demand in the digital economy of the Fourth Industrial Revolution is not fully understood by them due to their digital skill level and managing the generational skill sets in their structure.

Against the background of promoting inclusive growth in the context of the Fourth Industrial Revolution (4IR), the purpose of this chapter is to introduce Industry 4.0 in terms of the impact of Unified Communication and Collaboration (UC&C) technologies on productivity and innovation within a global automotive enterprise. To provide readers with a further overview of, and summarize, the content of the chapter, issues, controversies, problems, and challenges related to Industry 4.0 adoption, including, for example, Cyber-Physical Systems (CPS), are discussed. Solutions and recommendations for dealing with the issues, controversies, and/or problems are presented, and the chapter will also discuss future research directions and emerging trends, together with providing insight about the future of the book's theme from the perspective of the chapter focus on the impact of UC&C technologies on productivity and innovation. The last section will provide discussion of the overall coverage of the chapter and concluding remarks.

The last 20 years have brought significant developments to digital fabrication technology, known as additive manufacturing (3D printing), and it has finally started to shed its prototyping mantel in favor of an industrial one. Yet its innovations are in danger of being subsumed into existing commercial practices, as society arguably continues to underestimate its ability, in conjunction with data collection, analysis, and communication tools, to disrupt current systems and enable a more equitable distribution of manufacturing wealth, capability, and capacity. This chapter highlights the potential of emerging industrial technologies to support a shift towards a more human-centered, responsible society where social and environmental problems are addressed through systems that maximises cyberspace and physical space integration, through the reframing of higher education engineering curriculum and pedagogy for manufacturing in Society 5.0.

The rapid industrial and technological development of the last years has transformed the human society to its current form of knowledge and globalization. As a result, the formal education is nowadays faced with the big challenge of preparing students for a new way of life in the forthcoming fourth industrial revolution. This new revolution could be characterized as the era of the internet of things and energy and of the cyber-physical systems. The present chapter focuses on the role that computers and artificial intelligence could play in future education and the risks hiding behind this perspective. It is concluded that it is rather impossible that computers and the other "clever" machines of artificial intelligence will reach to the point of replacing teachers for educating students in future, because all these devices have been created and programmed by humans and therefore it is logical to accept that they will never succeed to reach the quality of human reasoning. However, it is certain that the role of the teacher will be dramatically changed in the future classrooms.

The purpose of this chapter is providing readers with an overview of the content promoting the growth of the Fourth Industrial Revolution (4IR) and the implications for information and communication technology (ICT) open distance e-learning (ODeL) students. Preparing students for the 4IR presents important and complicated opportunities towards changing higher education. Education should be about content design and delivery for teaching, learning, and assessment, with the profile of ODeL ICT students at the core. This chapter reports on issues, controversies, and problems arising from the 4IR. The mixed-method research approach adopted involved collecting and analyzing quantitative and qualitative data obtained from first-year courses at a Southern Africa institution. The emerging picture cautions concerning students' real biographic information and digital literacy in a developing world context. The conclusion summarizes the content and informs instructors to examine their perceptions of student profiles regarding teaching, learning, and assessment in preparation for the 4IR.

Chapter 6

The Fourth Industrial Revolution (41R) era requires industries to adopt the use of technology and specialised study accomplished with digital knowledge. This has contributed to the high rate of unemployment and job loss of people, especially the youths without digital knowledge. The objective of this study is to understand how ICTs can be used for the sustainable development of youth employability. The youths are among the low-income populations that require access to information on industry requirement for improved employability and the provision of digital skills training will allow them to have the knowledge to use ICTs to access information on the relevant job skills needed in the labour market. The sustainable livelihood theory was used to guide the study. Recommendations for the study will allow the government, ICT policymakers, and stakeholders to use ICTs for the sustainable development of youths and improve employability.

Chapter 7

Education 4.0 is an education model aligned with future trends in order to develop and enhance individualized education that will eventually go on to define the manner in which youngsters of the future will work and live. Since youth are the main asset of any nation, education becomes the most powerful tool for social transformation. India's demographic structure is changing; while the world grows older, the Indian population is becoming younger, and by 2025, about two-third of Indians will be in its workforce. A few issues addressed in this study are to identify the drivers of Education 4.0, to identify and understand the role of disruptive technologies, to study the transition from Education 1.0 to Education 4.0 and its relevant impact on the higher education system.

Chapter 8

Industry 4.0 is a key activity as of late presented by the German government. The objective of the activity is a change of mechanical fabricating through digitization and misuse of possibilities of new advancements. An Industry 4.0 generation framework is in this way adaptable and empowers individualized and modified items. The point of this chapter is to introduce and encourage a comprehension of Industry 4.0 ideas, its drivers, empowering influences, objectives, impediments. Building squares are depicted and a keen industrial facility idea is displayed. An architecture model and job of institutionalization in the future execution of Industry 4.0 idea are addressed. Also, sure contextual investigations of organizations, for example, Bosche and Siemens case studies, have been mentioned. These case studies emphasize on practical implementation of Industry 4.0 and future challenges to deal with successful adoption of Industry 4.0. The current status of Industry 4.0 availability in the German organizations is introduced and remarked.

Chapter 9

    Kesavan Dhanapal, Hindustan College of Arts and Science, Chennai, India

Considering the breathtaking changes in global business models, all entities foresee to develop new markets and products for survival in the economy. Increasing pollution levels at major cities around the globe, changing climatic conditions, and global warming makes a cloud bubbling thought of making safer and environmentally friendly products. This agenda leads to generate ideas that may create innovative products or practices may bring a competitive advantage for the new establishments. We all know that energy production constitutes to majority of the pollution in the environment. In order to tackle this situation, fostering entrepreneurs can think of ideas that are relating to renewable energy generation. Recently the rise of electric vehicles market seems to be a playground for new technology breakthroughs. This segment has huge potential for the next two decades. New entrepreneurs can take advantage of the renewable energy in making new business prospects.

Chapter 10

    Selma Leticia Capinzaiki Ottonicar, Sao Paulo State University (UNESP), Brazil
    Jean Cadieux, Université de Sherbrooke (UdeS), Canada
    Elaine Mosconi, Université de Sherbrooke (UdeS), Canada
    Rafaela Carolina da Silva, Sao Paulo State University (UNESP), Brazil

Industry 4.0 contributes to the increase in technological production and the use of environmental resources. Because of that, researchers need to discuss circular economy issues in the context of I4.0. To understand the circular economy, people need to know how to access, evaluate, and use the information (information literacy). The purpose of this chapter is to discuss how information literacy has been studied for the development of the circular economy. The methodology implies a review of the literature on circular economy, information literacy, and Industry 4.0. Subsequently, the document connects the information literacy and BNQ21000 standard (Québec) focusing on sustainability. The review showed that there are only a few documents that analyze the circular economy in the context of Industry 4.0. In addition, the information literacy needs to be studied in the circular economy and Industry 4.0 so that managers, students, and researchers can contribute to that revolution in a critical and sustainable way.

Two conceptual platforms meet in the use of technologies: the technological milieu and the ethical principles that underlie every human action. The interface, called "use," imposes a change of attitude in the behavior developed by humankind throughout centuries of mental evolution. This interface connects the two platforms although this is invisible to the naked eye. Using complex system analysis, it is possible to identify the components of the two platforms and understand the influences of their characteristics, providing a meaningful perspective of how technologies can contribute to the development of a secure and positive society in the future. The development and use of technologies can influence the developer/user in a positive or damaging way. Neuroscience's contributions point in this direction. The concern for the welfare of people affected by technologies is a must in the next era. The author intends to prove in an extensive way that for safety, ethic regulations should be considered for industry, health, and education.

Foreword

Every industrial revolution brought with it benefits and challenges to the socioeconomic status of the countries that have engaged in such transformation. For instance, Great Britain led the first industrial revolution with the invention of the commercial steam engine, which revolutionized communication and transportation and led to many other industrial developments (Mokyr, 2018). In the second industrial revolution, the United States was primarily in the lead, with the telephone revolutionizing communication this time (Zimmerman, 2017). In the third industrial revolution, the Internet was the key factor and succeeded because it was conceived as a public infrastructure technology rather than a proprietary technology. The Internet transformed the world economic landscape, and this transformation is expected to continue with the Internet of things (IoT). Rifkin (2014) confirms this trend in his concept of zero marginal cost, which emphasizes connectivity in his anticipation of a collaborative economy that will replace the capital system in its current form – with the IoT as the main driver. The rapid progress of smart cities is also paving the way to a more collaborative world (Mora, Deakin, & Reid, 2017).

All these industrial revolutions have resulted in economic growth, increased productivity, and advanced welfare in the countries that managed to reap most of its positive impact, including from high-quality goods and services. However, the wealth distribution within the developed countries who led the industrial revolution was not equitable, certainly not at the global level, where inequality has become one of the key challenges along with climate change and other sustainability issues. The rapid depletion of Earth's resources at the expense of the future of the society and environment has created an epic global challenge. Concepts such as sustainability and social innovation have surfaced and have rapidly attracted global attention as potential resolutions. The United Nations global initiative towards sustainable development goals (SDGs) has sent a strong message committing to inclusive social and economic development (United Nations, 2016). Innovative efforts in using, for example, the sustainable livelihood approach to link socioeconomic and environmental issues are also relevant endeavors (Laeis & Lemke, 2016).

The exponential change which we are just beginning to recognize and live with the Fourth Industrial Revolution, though, provides enormous challenges. Will we succeed in bending the arc of change driven by exponential technology towards the benefit of mankind, all mankind, and to the planet? What would it take for all of us to proactively and concretely contribute to that? What is certain is that we will fail unless we tackle what has become untenable levels of inequality.

According to the 2017 edition of the Global Wealth Report published by Credit Suisse (Credit Suisse Research Institute (CSRI) (2017), total global wealth increased 27% over the course of the prior decade, and slightly more than half of all of the household wealth in the world was owned by just 1% of the global population (when the current millennium had begun, 45.5% of total global wealth was owned by the top 1%, according to the report). Even within the member countries of the Organization for Economic Co-operation and Development, as of 2011 the average income of the richest 10% of their populations was about nine times that of the poorest 10%. Inequality within most countries is getting worse, even in places that have enjoyed rapid economic growth across income groups and corresponding declines in poverty.

This book brings together some of the most interesting and relevant voices within their fields to highlight new directions in contemporary research in the book's core theme, wealth inequality.

With scholars from a dozen different countries and an editorial board spanning much of the globe, this book provides a broad and heterogeneous view covering topics including, the consequences of digital transformation, the impact of unified communication and collaboration (UC&C) technologies, re-framing of higher education engineering curriculum and pedagogy for manufacturing in Society 5.0, preparing students for the forthcoming era, the implications for open and distance e-learning, the sustainable development of youth employability, the future of learning with disruptive technologies, a practical approach to Industry 4.0, opportunities for entrepreneurs in the renewable energy segment, the development of the circular economy and innovations redefining what it means to be human.

The editor and contributors provide an eye-opening assessment of the Fourth Industrial Revolution and related emerging technologies, and a sobering look at the potential negative impacts of transforming systems, matched by a hopeful call to action.

Moses John Strydom
University of South Africa, South Africa
Lyon, France, May 2020

REFERENCES

Credit Suisse Research Institute (CSRI). (2017). *Global Wealth Report 2017: Where Are We Ten Years after the Crisis?* https://www.credit-suisse.com/about-us-news/en/articles/news-and-expertise/global-wealth-report-2017-201711.html

Laeis, G. C. M., & Lemke, S. (2016). Social entrepreneurship in tourism: Applying sustainable livelihoods approaches. *International Journal of Contemporary Hospitality Management, 28*(6), 1076–1093. doi:10.1108/IJCHM-05-2014-0235

Mokyr, J. (2018). *The British Industrial Revolution: An Economic Perspective.* Routledge. doi:10.4324/9780429494567

Mora, L., Deakin, M., & Reid, A. (2017). *Smart and Sustainable Planning for Cities and Regions. SSPCR 2017. Green Energy and Technology.* Springer.

Rifkin, J. (2014). *The Zero Marginal Cost Society: The Internet of Things, the Collaborative Commons, and the Eclipse of Capitalism.* New York: St. Martin's Press.

United Nations. (2016). https://www.un.org/sustainabledevelopment/sustainable-development-goals/

Zimmerman, C. (2017). Albert Kahn in the Second Industrial Revolution. *AA Files, 2017*(75), 28–44.

Preface

The Fourth Industrial Revolution (4IR) feels like the ghost in the machine. We have a sense about it. It seems to be all around us. However, there isn't a common understanding of what 4IR means.

There are many names and definitions for the 4IR. 4IR is the naming convention used as it's a widely communicated definition from the World Economic Forum (WEF). WEF positions the First Industrial Revolution to be that of mechanisation and steam and waterpower. The Second Industrial Revolution looks at mass production, division of labour, assembly lines, and electricity. The third is seen as electronics, ICT, and automated production.

The 4IR is about the emergence of cyber-physical systems, network and artificial intelligence (AI). Cyber-physical systems involve new ways of embedding technology within larger societies, communities, and even in the human body. Artificial intelligence and robots are already replacing many more routine jobs, and while technology may create many, yet unimagined jobs, teachers and professors are in the position of having to educate for the unknown. How then do we respond effectively to uncertain futures by repurposing education? How do we reimagine teaching, lecturing, nurturing, mentoring, and the curation and transmission of knowledge? How do we prepare for students to thrive when confronted with the unexpected? How do we plan for yet unknown disruptive change?

There is a lot of controversy around mining for example. At the same time, people use products and materials from mines just to live… from housing to technology. This tension ramps up further when we face the near future. As we look to reduce carbon output and environmental impact, we focus on green energy sources and the 4IR. The latter needs minerals from the earth to operate. It seems we have much to investigate. Currently, there are debates around whether what is happening is, actually the 4IR. There are numerous frameworks available, ranging from this being an extension of the Third Industrial Revolution to Society 5.0. Suddenly, AI and machine learning are mainstream, the 'amplification' of everything is becoming a reality, and 5G and even 6G are on the horizon. New technologies have the potential to revolutionise manufacturing industries. What are the challenges to realising the rich potential of 4IR technologies in manufacturing? The irony is that we are on the brink of a brave new 4IR world in which life could potentially be made better for all the world's people.

The book will concentrate on the role of formal education in preparing students for uncertain futures, and for societies that are changing at great speed terms of its ability to drive job creation, economic growth and prosperity for millions in future. It aims to unpack some of the issues around 4IR, with reference to science, engineering, technology and innovation. We all need to become more agile and find time to keep on learning, to master new technologies. Change management will have to be the new normal across all IT departments. And now, more than ever before, we must keep our fingers on the pulse of change – sharing knowledge with our peers and colleagues. Exciting times lie ahead for industry, and by working together, we will be able stay ahead of the changes, overcome challenges to be more competitive globally.

This book consists of serious research, conscientious studies, and tumultuous debates. The collective experience that has gone into writing this book has come from many authors, as their writing endeavours are embedded in different cultures and societies. The themes of the book and the abstracts preceding each chapter reflect our awareness of 4IR practitioners' needs. An attempt has been made to indicate how the original approach to identify, create, represent, distribute, and enable the adoption of 4IR can empower students, managers, and educators to become innovative in all aspects of 4IR, resulting in measurable economic benefits to society as a whole. The book is intended to serve as a guide to the 4IR discipline. In fact, the book is one of the few detailed resources available on 4IR and innovation. The combination of a primary emphasis on theory and practice with applications to interdisciplinary education as well as organizational environments make this book unique among the burgeoning literature on 4IR.

The book is proposed for both students and practitioners, retaining its appeal as a guide for the educational and organizational professionals, and as a comprehensive introduction for the student at the upper-level undergraduate level. The intended audiences for this book, then, are teachers, researchers, students, and 4IR professionals, who are interested in understanding and applying 4IR theory and practice. One will notice that we are not presenting this book as a research text only, as an academic artefact, but we are instead presenting it as a personal route into a depth of 4IR and innovation. In addition, 4IR general points and issues are often illustrated, when appropriate, with reference to specific educational and/or educational contexts.

There are 11 chapters in the book. Each chapter concentrates on a particular point of 4IR and innovation. Chapter 1 presents the implications of digital transformation on the strategy development process for business leaders. Chapter 2 introduces Industry 4.0 in terms of the impact of Unified Communication and Collaboration (UC&C)

technologies on productivity and innovation within a global automotive enterprise. The chapter will also discuss future research directions and emerging trends, together with providing insight about the future of the book's theme from the perspective of the chapter focus on the impact of UC&C technologies on productivity and innovation. Chapter 3 highlights the potential of emerging industrial technologies to support a shift towards a more human-cantered, responsible society where social and environmental problems are addressed through systems that maximises cyberspace and physical space integration, through the reframing of higher education engineering curriculum and pedagogy for manufacturing in Society 5.0. Chapter 4 focuses on the role computers and Artificial Intelligence could play in future education as well as the risks hiding behind it. Chapter 5 provides readers with an overview of the content promoting the growth of Fourth Industrial Revolution (4IR) Information and Communication Technology (ICT) students and the implications for Open and Distance e-Learning (ODeL). Chapter 6 introduces how ICTs can be used for the sustainable development of youth employability. Chapter 7 presents issues: a) To identify the drivers of Education 4.0 b) To identify and understand the role of disruptive technologies c) To study the transition from Education 1.0 to Education 4.0 and its relevant impact on Higher Education System. Chapter 8 highlights a practical change of mechanical fabricating through digitization and misuse of possibilities of new advancements. Chapter 9 discusses how new entrepreneurs can take advantage of the renewable energy in making new business prospects. Chapter 10 presents how information literacy has been studied for the development of the circular economy. Chapter 11 discusses ethical concerns for the welfare of people affected by technologies.

OVERVIEW OF THE CHAPTERS

Synopses of chapters are described in the following paragraphs.

Chapter 1: Implications of Digital Transformation on the Strategy Development Process for Business Leaders

What the internet with its connectivity did to facilitate the third industrial revolution cloud computing and artificial intelligence has done for the fourth industrial revolution. Technology is changing the world at an alarming rate which includes products and services that require scale to manage the growing demands of an ever changing and increasing population. Digital transformation is enabled through cloud technology where human comprehension cannot cope with the size and speed of data required to manage a business in the digital economy. Artificial intelligence and machine learning assist in activities to overcome human limitation, using algorithms to develop predictive and simulation models through advanced analytics requiring size and scale to provide data for decision making. The technologies employed to run and execute these require skill and resource. The challenge or problem for the modern day chief executive officer, (CEO), is that the use of technology and its demand in the digital economy of the Fourth Industrial Revolution is not fully understood by them due to their digital skill level and managing the generational skill sets in their structure.

Chapter 2: The Impact of Unified Communication and Collaboration Technologies on Productivity and Innovation – Promotion for the Fourth Industrial Revolution

Against the background of promoting inclusive practice and growth in the context of the Fourth Industrial Revolution (4IR), the purpose of this chapter is to introduce Industry 4.0 in terms of the impact of Unified Communication and Collaboration (UC&C) technologies on productivity and innovation within a global automotive enterprise. To provide readers with a further overview of, and summarize, the content of the chapter, issues, controversies, problems and challenges related to Industry 4.0 adoption, including e.g. Cyber-Physical Systems (CPS), are discussed. Solutions and recommendations for dealing with the issues, controversies and/or problems are presented, and the chapter will also discuss future research directions and emerging trends, together with providing insight about the future of the book's theme from the perspective of the chapter focus on the impact of UC&C technologies on productivity and innovation. The last section will provide discussion of the overall coverage of the chapter and concluding remarks.

Chapter 3: Manufacturing Education for Society 5.0 – Reframing Engineering and Design

The last twenty years have brought significant developments to digital fabrication technology, known as additive manufacturing (3D printing), and it has finally started to shed its prototyping mantel in favor of an industrial one. Yet its innovations are in danger of being subsumed into existing commercial practices, as society arguably continues to underestimate its ability, in conjunction with data collection, analysis and communication tools, to disrupt current systems and enable a more equitable distribution of manufacturing wealth, capability and capacity. This chapter highlights the potential of emerging industrial technologies to support a shift towards a more human-cantered, responsible society where social and environmental problems are addressed through systems that maximises cyberspace and physical space integration, through the reframing of higher education engineering curriculum and pedagogy for manufacturing in Society 5.0.

Chapter 4: New Challenges for Education in the Forthcoming Era of the Fourth Industrial Revolution

Rapid industrial and technological development of the last 100-150 years has caused radical changes to traditional human society, transforming it into a modern society of knowledge and globalisation. As a result, formal education at all levels, from elementary to university/tertiary, faces the great challenge of preparing students for the forthcoming era of a new but not yet well-known industrial revolution. This new era could be characterised as the era of the Internet of Things and Energy and Cyber-Physical Systems. This chapter focuses on the role computers and Artificial Intelligence could play in future education as well as the risks hiding behind it. It concludes that it is highly unlikely for computers and other "clever" Artificial Intelligence machines to replace teachers in the future, because all these devices were created and programmed by humans. It is therefore logical to accept that they will never be able to achieve the quality and independence of human thought. However, it is certain that the role of the teacher will dramatically change in future classrooms.

Chapter 5: Promoting the Growth of Fourth Industrial Revolution Information Communication Technology Students – The Implications for Open and Distance E-Learning

The purpose of this chapter is providing readers with an overview of the content promoting the growth of Fourth Industrial Revolution (4IR) Information and Communication Technology (ICT) students and the implications for Open and Distance e-Learning (ODeL). Preparing students for the 4IR presents important and complicated opportunities towards changing higher education, which should be about content design and delivery for teaching, learning and assessment, with the profile of ODeL ICT students at the core. This chapter reports on issues, controversies and problems arising from the 4IR. The mixed-method research approach adopted involved collecting and analyzing quantitative and qualitative data, obtained from first-year modules at a Southern Africa institution. The emerging picture cautions concerning students' real biographic information and digital literacy in a developing world context. The conclusion summarizes the content and informs instructors to examine their perceptions of student profiles regarding teaching, learning and assessment in preparation for the 4IR.

Chapter 6: Impact of ICTs for Sustainable Development of Youths Employability – 4IR and Sustainable Development of Youths

The Fourth Industrial Revolution (41R) era requires industries to adopt the use of technology and specialized study accomplished with digital knowledge. This has contributed to the high rate of unemployment and job loss of people especially the youths without digital knowledge. The objective of this study is to understand how ICTs can be used for the sustainable development of youth employability. The youths are among the low-income populations that requires access to information on industry requirement for improved employability and the provision of digital skills training will allow them to have the knowledge to use ICTs to access information on the relevant job skills needed in the labour market. The sustainable Livelihood Theory was used to guide the study. While, recommendations for the study will allow the government, ICT policy makers and stakeholders to use ICTs for the sustainable development of youths and improve employability.

Chapter 7: Education 4.0 – Future of Learning With Disruptive Technologies

A disruptive system, Education 4.0 is an education model aligned with future trends, in order to develop and enhance individualized education that will eventually go on to define the manner in which youngsters of the future will work and live. Since youth are the main asset of any nation, education becomes the most powerful tool for social transformation. India's demographic structure is changing, while the world grows older, the Indian population is becoming younger and by 2025, about two-third of Indians will be in its workforce. Few issues addressed in this study which also happens to be its learning objectives are:a) To identify the drivers of Education 4.0 b)To identify and understand the role of disruptive technologies c) To study the transition from Education 1.0 to Education 4.0 and its relevant impact on Higher Education System.

Chapter 8: Industry 4.0 – A Practical Approach

Industry 4.0 is a key activity as of late presented by the German government. The objective of the activity is a change of mechanical fabricating through digitization and misuse of possibilities of new advancements. An Industry 4.0 generation framework is in this way adaptable and empowers individualized and modified items. The point of this Chapter is to introduce and encourage a comprehension of Industry 4.0 ideas, its drivers, empowering influences, objectives, impediments. Building squares are depicted and a keen industrial facility idea is displayed. An Architecture Model and job of institutionalization in the future execution of Industry 4.0 idea are addressed. Also, sure contextual investigations of organizations, for example, Bosche and Siemens case studies have been mentioned. These case studies emphasize on Practical implementation of Industry 4.0 and future challenges need to deal with successful adoption of Industry 4.0 The current status of Industry 4.0 availability of the German organizations is introduced and remarked. At long last, it is talked about if Industry 4.0 is extremely a challenging idea or essentially a characteristic steady advancement of mechanical generation systems. The key target of Industry 4.0 is to drive assembling forward to be quicker, progressively effective, and client-driven while pushing past computerization and streamlining to find new business openings and models. By installing present-day innovation into manufacturing, we basically accomplish Industry 4.0 goals.

Chapter 9: Emerging Opportunities for Entrepreneurs in Renewable Energy Segment

Considering the breath-taking changes in global business models, all entities fore see to develop new markets and products for survival in the economy. Increasing pollution levels at major cities around the globe, changing climatic conditions, and global warming makes a cloud bubbling thought of making safer and environment friendly products. This agenda leads to generate ideas that may create innovative products or practices may bring a competitive advantage for the new establishments. We all know that, energy production constitutes to majority of the pollution in the environment. In order to tackle this situation, fostering entrepreneurs can think of ideas that are relating to renewable energy generation. Recently the rise of electric vehicles market seems to be a playground for new technology breakthroughs. This segment has the huge potential for the next two decades. New entrepreneurs can take advantage of the renewable energy in making new business prospects.

Chapter 10: Information Literacy and the Circular Economy in Industry 4.0

Industry 4.0 contributes to the increase in technological production and the use of environmental resources. Because of that, researchers need to discuss circular economy issues in the context of I4.0. To understand the circular economy, people need to know how to access, evaluate and use information (information literacy). The purpose of this chapter is to discuss how information literacy has been studied for the development of the circular economy. The methodology implies an exploratory, qualitative and quantitative review of the literature on circular economy, information literacy and Industry 4.0. Subsequently, the document connects information literacy and the BNQ21000 learning standard (Québec) focusing on sustainability for a company. A review of publications showed that there are only a few documents analyzing the circular economy in the context of I4.0. In addition, the role of information literacy needs to be studied in relation to circular economy and I4.0 so that managers, students and researchers can contribute to that revolution in a critical and sustainable way.

Chapter 11: When Ethics Meets Technology

Two conceptual platforms meet in the use of technologies: the technological milieu and the ethical principles that underlie every human action. The interface, called "use", imposes a change of attitude in the behavior developed by humankind throughout centuries of mental evolution. This invisible interface connects the two platforms. Using complex system analysis it is possible to identify their components and understand the influences, providing a meaningful perspective of how technology can contribute to the welfare of society in the future. The responsible development and use of technologies can influence the developer/user in a positive or damaging way. Neuroscience contribution to these aspects offers a mean to evaluate the consequences of the use of technology. The concern for the welfare of people affected by technologies is a must in the next era. We intend to prove in an extensive way that for our safety, ethic regulations should be considered in industry, health and education.

The book, *Promoting Inclusive Growth in the Fourth Industrial Revolution,* is a collection of a broad array of resources that has been written and edited to provide flexibility and depth of 4IR innovations, strategies and practices.

Sheryl Buckley
University of South Africa, South Africa

Acknowledgment

A big thank you to those whose chapters are included, as well as to those whose work was not included in the book.

The primary aim of this book is to provide relevant theoretical frameworks and the latest empirical research findings in the area of promoting growth in the fourth industrial revolution. It will grapple with complex value and governance issues that arise as a consequence of the fourth industrial revolution phenomenon and will ambitiously provide relevant scholarly work, the latest research findings, as well as, examples of best practices found in organisations concerning teaching and learning in academia and the business-industrial environment.

The book will additionally investigate the potential for making faster advances in many scientific disciplines and improving the profitability and success of different enterprises and provide for interesting reading. Moreover, the book will provide insights and support executives concerned with the management of expertise, knowledge, information and organizational development in different types of work communities and environments in the fourth industrial revolution.

These chapters represent truly global research, from 6 countries, from Australia to South Africa, Brazil to Greece, and India to Israel. The high standard of the book is derived from the independent treble blind peer review process. We would like to thank the 21 reviewers from 12 countries, again spanning the globe – Australia, Brazil, France, Greece, India, Israel, Jordan, South Africa, Sweden, Switzerland, and Zimbabwe, who have critically evaluated the chapters. Special thanks go to Moses Strydom from France for writing the foreword.

Acknowledgment

Finally, we hope that the chapters will stimulate further progress in the fourth industrial revolution discipline and can give rise to a more global collaborative approach to fourth industrial revolution management, underpinned by innovation. In a fast-changing world, it is only though innovation that we keep ahead of time.

Sheryl Buckley
University of South Africa, South Africa

Chapter 1
Implications of Digital Transformation on the Strategy Development Process for Business Leaders

Theunis Gert Pelser
University of KwaZulu-Natal, South Africa

Garth Gaffley
University of KwaZulu-Natal, South Africa

ABSTRACT

What the internet with its connectivity did to facilitate the third industrial revolution, cloud computing and artificial intelligence have done for the fourth industrial revolution. Technology is changing the world at an alarming rate, which includes products and services that require scale to manage the growing demands of an ever-changing and increasing population. Digital transformation is enabled through cloud technology where human comprehension cannot cope with the size and speed of data required to manage a business in the digital economy. Artificial intelligence and machine learning assist in activities to overcome human limitation, using algorithms to develop predictive and simulation models and scale to provide data for decision making. The technologies employed to run and execute these require skill and resource. The challenge for the modern-day CEO is that the use of technology and its demand in the digital economy of the Fourth Industrial Revolution is not fully understood by them due to their digital skill level and managing the generational skill sets in their structure.

DOI: 10.4018/978-1-7998-4882-0.ch001

INTRODUCTION

The Fourth Industrial Revolution has manifested itself in the modern era, sparked by artificial or machine intelligence enabled through cloud technology which is having an unprecedented impact on businesses where embracing it is essential to corporate survival in the digital economy, Kaldero (2018). Mell and Grance (2011) define cloud computing as, *A model for enabling ubiquitous, convenient, on-demand, network access to a shared pool of configurable resources and released with minimum management effort or service provider interaction.*

Cloud technology has facilitated digital disruption of traditional business which has seen the rise of technology businesses in a short period of time dominating their industry sectors, such as, Amazon, the world's most important retailer, and Uber, dominating digital transportation, through cloud technology having no limitation to the size and speed of data and software development. Digital transformation is all about software, where hardware without software has no value at all and software developers are and have become the most important people in the world Chappell (2015).

Meffert and Swaminathan (2018) define digital transformation simply as driving the business forward by leveraging the opportunity offered by technology. Westerman, Bonnet, and McAfee (2014) offer an alternative definition whereby the use of technology radically improves the performance and reach of the business where executives are transforming their businesses in three areas, customer experience, operational processes and business models. Gruman (2016) finds meaningful common ground between these definitions by stating that all aspects of business and society are impacted on with the application of digital technologies. Balachandran and Prasad (2017) share that big data analytics and cloud computing are two of the most significant developments in the information technology industry in recent times.

Kane, Palmer, Phillips, Kiron, and Buckley (2015) in their 2015 Digital Business Global Executive Study and Research Project by MIT Sloan Management Review and Deloitte concur with Pyle and San Jose (2015), identified the key driver in the digital transformation process as strategy, and not technology. A repeat study in 2017 showed 63% of respondents were over 45 years old. Most of these business leaders are familiar with strategy, strategic direction, and strategy development processes but are not technically astute in the digital parameters associated with digital strategy fluency and competing in the digital economy. If not digitally astute or competent and there is hesitation on the part of business leaders to take risk, invest in technological innovations, minimise the impact of digital disruption, and delegate key decisions to more technologically astute individuals the strategic direction of the business could be impaired. It is essential that business leaders have the confidence to make these decisions off an informed platform through having the correct data available in the right format at the required time.

This view is supported by Andriole (2017), of the opinion that it is imperative for business leaders to become fully proficient in cloud computing which enabled the Fourth Industrial Revolution and that in leading the organisations digital transformation, one must not be seduced by the hype, but that the first step is to grasp the realities of digital transformation.

The aim of the chapter is to source meaningful content as input to develop a unique framework and model for business leaders to better understand digital transformation and technological innovation for inclusion as an integral component of their strategy development process to meet the digital demands of business in the 21st century. Also to determine if human limitations, Ross et al. (2016), by business leadership is the contributing factor to the lack of digital transformation in the strategy development process for their businesses. The objectives to realise the aim would include:

- Determine the importance of data to the industry sector under review
- Understand the societal influence of the digital economy and level of digital capability
- Determine of the threat of digital disruption limits investment and risk
- Investigate human limitations of business leaders and human capital investment

BACKGROUND

Strategy as a concept and aligning traditional with the digital strategy development process is understood from various authors as demonstrated in the theory by Grant (2016) who defines the term strategy as originating from the Greek word, "Strategia" which means, from the office of the general and interprets the strategic position of the organisation where strategy is the plan for deploying resources to establishing a favourable position. This explanation is concurrent with Binedell (2015) who aligns strategy with warfare where "Strategos", is the art of the general, chief executive officer or business leader.

In terms of a traditional strategy development process Kaplan and Norton (2008), developed a four dimensional measurement model known as the Balanced Scorecard comprising financial, customer, internal business process, learning and growth segments (Figure 1). After thirty years of application Kaplan and Norton (2008) advise that strategy focussed organisations have transferred from the Balanced Scorecard as a performance management tool into a strategic tool. This model is in line

Figure 1. The Balanced Scorecard
Source: Kaplan and Norton (2008)

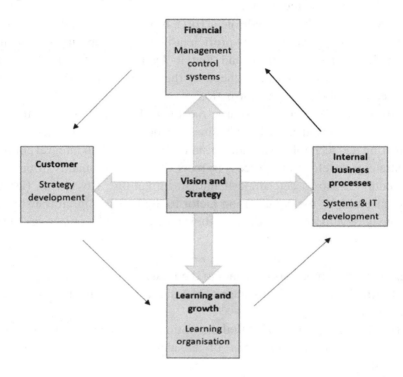

with modern digital thinking strategy processes as advocated by Ross et al. (2016), (Figure 2), where less measurement and more creative innovation is encouraged.

For each of these four parameters the question asked of the organisation is; "To achieve our vision, succeed financially, satisfy our shareholders and customers, appear to our customers, and how will we sustain our ability to change and improve?" Within each of the parameter's objectives, measures, targets, and initiatives are developed for strategy implementation. It is important to note that the parameters of being a learning organisation, customer strategy development, change and improvement of business processes are linked with a digital strategy model such as Ross et al. (2016) and Sebastian et al. (2017), (Figure 2), with strategic choice either through digitised solutions that transform the business model, or the customer engagement that transforms the go to market, enabled through the operational backbone that facilitates operational excellence.

With these definitions and interpretations of strategy, the researcher will seek to explore in the literature survey how best the traditional strategic development process can be aligned with the rapidly changing technological innovations experienced in

Figure 2. Digital Strategy Basics model
Source: Ross et al. (2016) and Sebastian et al. (2017)

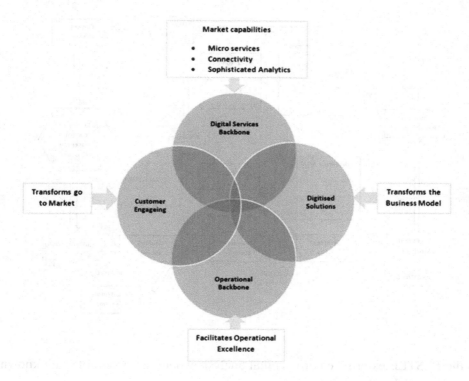

the digital strategy in a model that enables the chief executives and their teams to better understand digital transformation.

Traditional Strategy Process Development and The New Digital Economy

Sondhi (2008), differentiates the integrative strategy development process where key activities such as the analytical, creative, evaluative, and pragmatic steps are developed as thinking styles and can be included in a digital strategy model (Figure 3). The components of this model will be expanded on to include digital age considerations for 21st century digital strategy development processes.

The *analytical thinking style*, focusses on the external and internal environments from which the opportunities and threats are extracted, with strengths and weaknesses, internally identified. The external drivers that impact the position of a business include; political, economic, social, technological, environmental, and legal known

Figure 3. The Sondhi strategy process model
Source: Sondhi (2008)

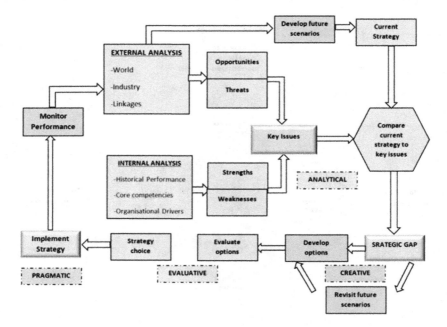

as the PESTLE external environmental analysis where these variables are known as uncontrollable variables.

Traditional strategy and digital strategy commonality have technology as the common key external variable which has direct linkage to the technological innovations of the digital age with the rise of the Third Industrial Revolution through the worldwide web, www, birth of the internet in 1994, giving rise to the internet of things, IOT, with the impact of cloud computing the key driver of disruptive technologies and birth of the Fourth Industrial Revolution, Chappell (2015), with big data and machine learning as some of the key external parameters for consideration, identified from these opportunities.

Threats according to Lloyd (2015) would include digital disruption, cyber security, hacking and virus attacks. In line with the external environment the industry five forces analysis developed by Porter and Millar (1985) for analysing industries and competitors was revised by Lloyd (2015) to include the digital considerations impacting on the digital age industry analysis, (Figure 4).

Figure 4. Lloyd's digital adaptation of Porter five forces model
Source: Lloyd (2015)

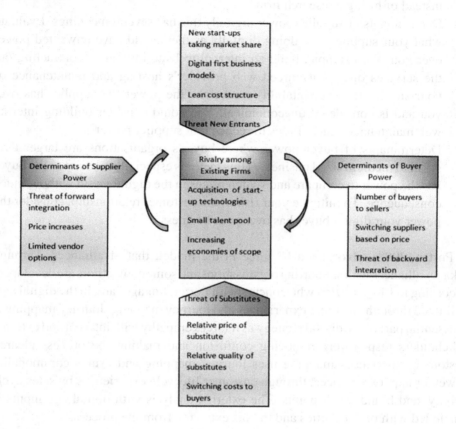

Lloyd (2015) explains the adaptation as:

- Rivalry among existing firms - where direct competitors are considered with an understanding the things, they are doing in their digital programs today, capturing these, which could include building applications, apps, acquiring start-up technologies, or leveraging new software
- Threat of new entrants should encompass thinking about start-ups that could become threats where the many small companies and technologies that could through digital disruption, potentially ruin you at scale are identified
- Threat of substitutes here thinking around and identifying what companies in the marketplace with their products and services that are typically substitutes to your offer. Continually be on the lookout for new business models, for

example, use survey monkey and internalise it through a monthly subscription instead of hiring a research firm

- Determinants of supplier power digitally this has several meanings. Evaluate what your suppliers are doing digitally as they could have unwanted power over you. For example, build an internal website instead of contracting out the services of an outsourced web provider's hosting and maintenance of your site if little accountability outweighs the power the supplier has over you and is considered uneconomical. You could consider building internal web maintenance capabilities to reduce that supplier power
- Determinants of buyer power where buyer's organisations are larger than small to medium sized businesses this factor is especially relevant as the buyer has the power to compare and switch prices in the digital world without much consequence. To mitigate your risk in the customer relationship, consider the power your digital buyer has over your business

Porter (2008) advocates a 6th force in the model, that of alliances. Through linkages alliances with supporting organisations and some competitors are developed. According to Lloyd (2015) who concurs with Porter, linkages are, in the digital age, facilitated through customer experiences and journey mapping. Journey mapping is an essential part of the digital strategy as it forces empathy with internal and external stakeholders respectively removing confusion and making the process clearer. Customer experiences mapping uses journey mapping and brings commonality of web or app, experiences, through customer lifecycle experiences by sales cycle activity, and brand touch points. The external analysis with digital age inputs is concluded with opportunities and threats extracted from the process.

The internal analysis considers the controllable variables those over which the organisation has control. These are evaluated through application of the Porter value chain, Porter and Millar (1985), where the value chain is introduced as the tool for systematically examining all activities a business performs, their linkages and interaction as a source of competitive advantage. The value chain comprises the primary, functional activities with the support activities common to the functions (Figure 5).

The value chain breaks the business into strategically relevant activities for the business to better understand cost and financial implications of product development, marketing, selling, delivering and support of its products with a view to enhance competitive advantage. Porter and Millar (1985) over thirty years ago identified information as a source of competitive advantage, developments at that stage are shown in italics (Figure 5).

Porter and Heppelmann (2015) add that the value chain of a business is part of a bigger stream of activities; the value system. The ability to gain and sustain

Figure 5. The Porter value chain and technological advances
Source: Porter and Millar (1985)

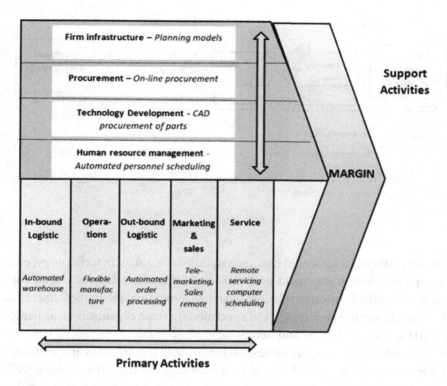

competitive advantage is co-dependent on understanding the businesses existing value chain with that of its customer or their buyers. This is seen in the retail sector where competitors supply multiple brands and line items to crowd or block competitors from being able to list their brands. Kaplan and Norton (2008) concur with Porter and Heppelmann (2015) through their internal business process perspective (Figure 6).

The relationship between the supply chain and value chain (Figure 6), is seen with focus on production, marketing, sales and after service elements of the operations process as the supply chain, while the value chain includes the innovation processes of product development and design incorporated as time to market. The areas of speciality within these lead to core competencies for the business and become internal organisational drivers. The value chain and supply chain evaluation of each internal business component and linkage enables the identification of strengths and weaknesses within the business.

Strengths inclusive of digital inputs would be, effective data management, system data flow, cloud capability, appointment of data management specialists, seamless operational spine, website interactivity, customer engagement and feedback, and

Figure 6. The internal business process value chain perspective
Source: Kaplan and Norton (2008)

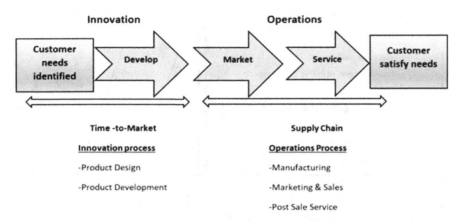

blog content. Weaknesses would encompass, little investment in technology, cost of system updates, non-engagement of social media platforms, lack of search engine optimisation, limited customer relationship management and incomplete operational services backbone, not becoming a data and model driven organisation, as per Ross et al. (2016), Kaldero (2018) and Sebastian et al. (2017).

When combining the opportunities and threats with the strengths and weaknesses key issues are extracted which are in turn compared to the current strategy. The current strategy comprises the vision, mission, strategy, and objectives currently set for the business. This completes the analytical phase of the Sondhi (2008) strategic development process and leads into the creative phase.

The *creative phase* of the Sondhi (2008) strategic process (Figure 3), starts with the development of future scenarios leading into the current strategy. From a digital perspective these scenarios could include; paired technologies such as blockchain, 3D and 4D printing, augmented and virtual reality, biometric identity, data analytics, cloud computing, autonomous systems for cars and drones, robotics, and nanotechnology, Binedell (2015) and Bordignon (2017). Each of these contribute to the creative thinking of future scenarios for the business and will be expanded on.

Once evaluated for inclusion in the current strategy and compared with key issues from the strengths, weaknesses, opportunities and threats, or SWOT, the analytical phase with the creative phase identifies the *strategic gap* for the business (Figure 3). Options around the strategic gap are developed for evaluation which leads into the *evaluative phase* with subsequent option selection for strategic implementation. Finally, the *pragmatic phase* (Figure 3), calls for implementation, measurement, and control as advocated by the parameters of the balanced scorecard of Kaplan and

Norton (2008). What has been uncovered is that digital parameters can be overlaid into the traditional strategy development process as per the Sondhi (2008) traditional strategic process some of which date to the mid 1980's and are still relevant today. The resultant strategy implementation is accompanied by change of which the impact must be considered.

Change and the Strategy Development Process

According to Binedell (2015) the South African dynamic today can be equated to Toffler (1980), "The Third Wave", written after his best seller, "Future Shock" in 1979. Toffler predicts the future is going to come in forms and shapes that will impact us at a personal, family, social, and organisational level. Thirty years ago, predictions as to the impact of new technologies which would facilitate the rise of new industries in information technology, space science, electronics, genetics, and ocean ecology. Changes in industrial output and production would be facilitated by data processing and computers. Media would move away from mass media to specialised interest formats. Binedell (2015) believes this has arrived where disruption is the order of the day and the digital economy is changing the rules daily. Against this disruption the South African economy, a small economy by global standards, is a 'Rule Taker' not a 'Rule Maker', is going through economic, psychological, and sociological change at an unprecedented pace.

Binedell (2015) claims that mature institutions and organisations are inclined to turn inward and drive an internal mind-set, which is wrong. Good strategy starts from the outside where markets dictate the way forward. Binedell states that the most important strategic insight for South African business leaders is to encourage innovation, entrepreneurship, and creativity in their organisations.

Balogun, Hope Hailey, and Gustafsson (2015) propose four types of strategic change, these are; adaptive, reconstructive, and revolutionary when weighed against realignment and transformation on one axis with incremental and big bang on the other, (Figure 7). Digital transformation would be accompanied by reconstructive and revolutionary change as disruptive technologies cannot be predicted or anticipated with the level of resultant change having major impact on the business sustainability going forward.

The integrative strategy process development from Sondhi (2008) with its four thinking styles shows affinity with the digital parameters associated with digital strategy development as per Ross et al. (2016). Change accompanies traditional and digital strategy development and implementation and is manifested through disruptive technologies enabled by cloud computing, impacting on the direction of the strategy development process as shown by Balogun et al. (2015) which when aligned with digital processes the resultant change is revolutionary and reconstructive.

Figure 7. Strategic change
Source: Balogun et al. (2015)

End Result

	Transformational	Realignment
Incremental	**Evolution** transformational change gradual interrelated initiatives planned, forced or emergent	**Adaptation** change in current paradigm incremental realigning of operations
Big Bang	**Revolution** simultaneous change on different fronts in a short period of time called crisis management	**Reconstruction** change with upheaval not changing paradigm but improving efficiency

Nature

This shows that traditional strategic development processes can accommodate the digital strategy basics which leads to understanding how a traditional business can be completely digitally transformed.

From Porter and Millar (1985) and Porter (2008), understanding the value chain analysis aspect of the supply chain is essential for the success of the business in that adding value to its service is ultimately achieved through its people. In revisiting the Kaplan and Norton (2008) supply chain, value chain relationship a global traditional business in the beauty sector and market leader has been wholly digitally transformed against this relationship (Figure 6).

DIGITAL TRANSFORMATION AND THE FOURTH INDUSTRIAL REVOLUTION

How does a traditional global business in the beauty sector transform itself to meet the demands of the Fourth Industrial Revolution to remain competitive and dominate its industry sector?

A Global Traditional Business Digitally Transformed the L'Oréal Case Study

Rochet (2017) the chief digital officer at L'Oréal in a lecture at the SAID Business School at Oxford titled, "Leading the digital transformation process at L'Oréal", advises that to win in e-commerce there are three ways; become a product services company, become a data driven business, and reinvent your marketing methods.

Rochet (2017) advises that L'Oréal, by way of company background, competing in the beauty sector, has 34 international brands, such as Garnier and Vichy, valued at €26 billion and a 13% global market share, the company is an ecologically and socially responsible company with strong ethical values, gender equality in pay structures, a unique people company, decentralised with people above process, encompassing an entrepreneurial approach through a big group with start-up mentality with some 90000 employees worldwide. L'Oréal is the first Fortune 500 company to appoint a chief digital officer at executive or c-level which demonstrates the importance of digital capability to market in the digital age.

Bordignon (2017) concurs with Rochet (2017) that digital will change the operating of your organisation from augmented reality to a new reality where if you are in marketing you must up your game as the Facebook kids are now a significant consumer segment. Rochet (2017) emphasises that some 3,5 billion people daily are not on, but live on the internet, the universe is detailed in (Table 1), an essential part of the digital consumer journey. E-Commerce accounts for €1,7 billion or 8% of L'Oréal's business and is growing at around 20% per annum compared with traditional offline growth channels at 5% per annum. Interestingly China is an identified growth market which accounts for 25% of e-Commerce revenue of which

Table 1. The online universe in 2017

Audience	Number
Internet users	3,5 billion
Mobile internet users	2,1 billion
Social networks	2,3 billion
Facebook	1,9 billion
WeChat	700 million
Online shoppers	1,6 billion
Live streaming and watching	900 million
e-Commerce spends	€1500 billion

Source: Rochet (2017)

75% is generated from mobile internet users. L'Oréal is the third largest advertiser worldwide of which 32% is spent on digital marketing.

To understand how digital transformation has changed the way of L'Oréal doing business consider the traditional strategy development processes followed:

- Big media spends with the logic being, more spend more prescriptions
- Product driven research into big molecules and formulations
- Distribution and supply chain at mass marketing scale is no longer the norm

Rochet (2017) claims that this strategy development approach is dated, digital transformation is a consumer revolution in certain market sectors such as beauty, with digital disruption a daily challenge. Start-up companies use e-commerce and smaller integrated supply chains for versatility. They have accounted for the rise of Digital Native Vertical Brands, DNVBS, which are small brands with zero media, no product development, and no supply chains selling directly to the consumer via digital, not retail.

L'Oréal is acquiring these brands in the beauty sector such as NYX, referred to as a love brand, as consumers love them and there have been no costs attached to developing them, consumers love their content and if aligned with an influencer these brands have huge potential to grow. Learning from these brands enables development of consumer engagement content from their consumers, in so doing providing needs specific targeted brands, thereby creating competitive advantage.

Consumers want to buy their beauty requirements online and building brands in the digital era, says Rochet (2017), is enabled through good content, which in turn produces analytics or data of which there are over a billion consumer records available to marketing to build brands. L'Oréal is producing content for Facebook, Instagram, YouTube, and WeChat internally as owned media. Lines are becoming blurred with media agencies as L'Oréal is becoming a content factory. Good data signals precious time spent on a brand building competitive advantage.

This data is instantaneous, available in real time, unlike past marketing models where data was provided on a weekly basis. The product development process at L'Oréal today is not driven by product push from big molecules and formulations but by engaging consumers on Facebook, YouTube, Instagram, and social media platforms to understand trends. Data is important to move from mass marketing to precision targeted marketing.

In the new marketing model's precision targeting is referred to as tribal, horizontal, and fast in other words, the tribe is targeted using social media from which information is gained from the tribe which is hot real-time data.

Rochet (2017) adds that marketing models and methods must be reinvented as consumers want services on how to use their product. In this regard L'Oréal has built applications such as Makeup Genius where you can apply various makeup looks to your lipstick, or eye liners, decide on what suits you and order online. The move from conceptual to visual marketing through social media gives consumers what they want.

Marketing adverts traditionally have employed 30 seconds with tease, talk and reveal of the product. In digital this is too long; it is 6 seconds where you reveal then talk. AdBlock, a piece of software designed to prevent adverts on a web page, is used by 30% of online users with up to 50% of millennials which does not necessarily mean consumers do not want to engage with your content as consumers continually engage and share new types of content. Digital marketers according to Rochet (2017) must build content platforms sharing these through, videos, live streaming, messaging, short content, long form deep dive contents and fun contents.

Rochet (2017) has shown and presented an argument as to how the value chain is optimised in the digital age and adds, supply chain initiatives from now follow trends derived from Facebook, Snapchat, YouTube, and the website. From these research and development, product development, social media content and product launch are within six months as opposed to nine months in the past.

In a digital era, an organisation cannot function in isolation and partners need to be built up. Strategically, where trade channels have limited beauty knowledge partnerships have been developed, both direct with traditional retail channels and indirect e-Commerce channels such as Amazon and Ali Baba to create beauty category trade traffic. L'Oréal have partnered with Partech a global services financier with regular feedback from them on financial services.

Rochet (2017) further states that digital transformation is, at its core, a people and talent transitional transformation and ways to upskill all employees must be found. In this regard to realise these changes and ensure digital fluency in the organisation L'Oréal has had to focus on people, starting at the top with the appointment at the executive level the chief digital officer role, an additional 1600 industry best digital talents were employed to lead digital transformation. Upskilling of 14000 employees at considerable investment in human capital has taken place. Success in a volatile, uncertain, complex, and ambiguous world or VUCA is understood through a simple formula:

$$M + L = S$$

where;

M= Millennials
L= Leadership
S = Success

This formula developed by Rochet (2017) is driven by:

- An understanding that the digital revolution is a consumer driven one
- You land in a new country with nothing, work hard and build something, therefore take the view of an immigrant
- Learn, do not be a "Know-it-All", be a; "Learn-it-all"
- In digital do not do benchmarks as everything changes so fast
- You must be prepared to pivot from your North
- Competition kills creativity, do not monitor your competition too closely your product will resemble theirs, focus on consumers and you will succeed, be naïve
- To encourage creativity, ensure there are soft experimentation places for yourself and your teams
- Be agile, fail fast and recover by scaling faster

In sum, Rochet (2017) concludes, with the scaling of this digital transformation at L'Oréal, (Figure 8), the vision is having as its infusion by 2025 everyone upskilled as functional beauty specialists in the digital age working alongside digital experts.

Figure 8. Scale of digital transformation
Source: Rochet (2017)

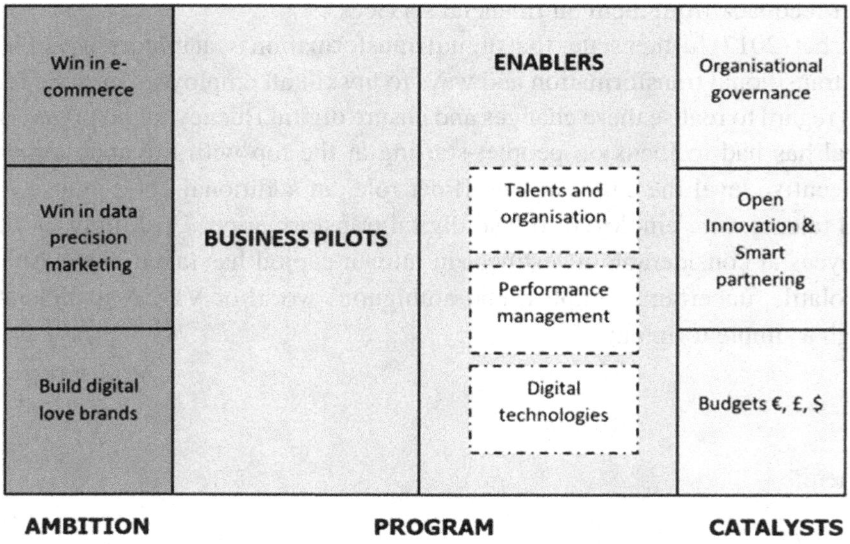

Benchmarks as advised by global consultancies such as McKinsey are no longer relevant as change is taking place at an unprecedented rate. It is about new ways of working such as Hackathons where cross functional teams debate scenarios and outcomes. In conclusion Rochet (2017) has shown how L'Oréal embraced digital transformation enabling competitive differentiation and making it an industry leader in the beauty sector. Value chain and supply chain optimisation are realised through skill development and a move to digital infusion of all staff. A new culture has emerged capable of addressing any form of digital disruption through people upskilling and introducing different ways of working. Having seen how a traditional organisation is digitally transformed to compete in the Fourth Industrial Revolution some of the pitfalls and challenges in this journey must be examined.

Digital Disruption and Transformation of Your Business in The Digital Economy

Supporting Lloyd (2015), Ross et al. (2016) defines digital strategy as nothing more than a business strategy inspired by the capabilities of technology. This is accompanied and brought about by a barrage of technologies influencing businesses which include: social, mobile, analytics, cloud, and the internet of things, IoT. This is referred to as SMACIT, (derived from the first letter of each technology influence) because it feels as if one is continually being hit behind the head with the constant barrage of technology.

Boag (2013) concurs with Ross et al. (2016) and Lloyd (2015) in that a digital strategy is not as intimidating as it sounds. It is just a document outlining how your company or client should handle the different aspects of digital from the website and mobile to email, social media, and digital marketing. It does not need to cover everything in huge depth but instead should establish some general approaches to these different areas. Boag continues, creating a digital strategy is a chance to bring some order to the chaos that most organisations approach to digital. What these authors tell us is that digital strategy is enabled through a consideration of all technological innovations impacting on a business.

Sebastian et al. (2017) and Ross et al. (2016) have built these into their digital strategy development model (Figure 2) with a focus on human limitations, not the technologies behind utilising the social, media, analytics, cloud, and the internet of things as components for competitive advantage. They continue that information reacts to SMACIT by simply adding new technologies such as:

- Mobile strategies
- Social media strategies
- Internet of things strategies
- Biometrics strategy
- Cloud strategy
- Big data
- Cognitive computing, and
- Bring your own device, BOYD strategy

These do not create competitive advantage but integration of these through a digital strategy does. A digital strategy is an integrated business strategy inspired by the capabilities of powerful, readily accessible technologies like SMACIT and responsive to constantly changing market conditions. Sebastian et al. (2017) and Ross et al. (2016) advocate two types of strategy in their digital strategy model (Figure 2), these are; customer engagement and digitised solution strategies, where they caution that only one is used at a time, not both.

- The customer engagement strategy is built on trust, creating value and passion as seen in the approach of USAA Bank promoting passion through focussing on life events, such as the purchase of a home or car. Drone technology is used in areas of natural disaster damage through tornadoes or hurricanes. The disaster area is surveyed by drones with damage impact assessment conducted through aerial interpretation and compensation made available to homeowners before their claim applications are submitted.
- The digitised solutions strategy identifies customer needs and problems and how these are addressed and fixed. Here General Electric have moved away from financial services into big asset management for their customers. This is enabled by using an eco-system of partners to develop solutions for their customers using PREDEX Cloud for data storage and retrieval.

In making either of these strategies work, Sebastian et al. (2017) and Ross et al. (2016) advocate a strong operational backbone is non-negotiable where a seamless end-to-end reliable service provides data flow across functions negating the silo effect of the Porter value chain. Through the digital services backbone enablement of power for big data analysis, social media platforms, customer engagement and feedback amongst other services are possible. Whilst SMACIT disrupts one's business and the way it is run, it also redefines business opportunities. There are no longer limitations to the amount of processing, size of data required or how much data can be sourced and the time in which to source data this is enabled through cloud technology. Vendor driven technologies offer no competitive advantage, but integration of these does.

Ross et al. (2016) concurs that, these challenges are gone, the biggest challenge is human limitations in the Fourth Industrial Revolution, this leads to exploring human limitations.

Human Limitation and Generational Influence Impacting on the Digital Era

No other issue has the potential to divide the generations as much as their adoption, or not, of technology at work Codrington and Grant-Marshall (2011). Care should be taken in organisations with a one for all communication approach with their older customers and work colleagues not adept at the use of technology in communication such as SMS, Whatsapp or texting let alone office communication and planning systems such as Trello or Slack. The human element and generational leadership styles and influences are explained (Table 2).

Table 2. Leading the generations

Generation	Leaders	Birth	Generational Leadership Traits
GI	Sam Walton, Nelson Mandela	1900 to 1920	Principled, tough but fair, authoritarian, stoic, civic minded, visionary, gentlemanly
Silent	Jack Welch, Desmond Tutu	1920 to 1940	Pragmatic, stable, hardworking, low key, loyal balanced, formal, hierarchical
Boomers	Bill Gates, Richard Branson, Steve Jobs	1940 to 1960	Visionary, idealistic, workaholic, enthusiastic, energetic, bossy, passionate, principled, loud, reward driven
Xers	Jeff Bezos, Barack Obama	1960 to 1980	Cautious, creative, pragmatic, realistic, low key, innovative, flexible, independent, adaptable
Yers or Millennials	Mark Zuckerberg, Rodger Federer	1980 to 2000	Civic minded, visionary, confident, optimistic, moralistic, principled, values driven, networked, and connected
iFacebook	None yet	2000 onwards	Will be fair, hardworking, loyal, structured, entrepreneurial, innovative, environmentally friendly, team driven

Source: Codrington and Grant-Marshall (2011)

Codrington and Grant-Marshall (2011) continue with regards boomers and social media platforms, boomers who lead most businesses today, might have a smug feeling of having embraced technology as most have smart phones, tablets and other gadgets and are on one or more social media platforms. In spite of having the latest devices and being on one or two social media platforms they do not understand the benefit of technology which is evidenced in some behavioural traits such as:

- Banning Facebook at work or limiting its use
- Most Boomer's do not understand the business uses of Twitter and its analytical tool associated with target marketing
- Their opinion of LinkedIn is as a means of getting a new job with their suspicions raised when staff update their LinkedIn status
- Should they venture into social media they often get it wrong as they treat it as another channel in doing what they are already doing

Boomers believe in vision, mission, strategy, tactics, and encourage annual teambuilding strategy workshops where the team must overcome challenges and obstacles. In not as driven an approach, Xers as opposed to boomers find individual strengths in the team to improve its output whist Yers are still migrating into the managerial ranks. This dichotomy of approach is cause for divergent views and outcomes in strategic direction. The Yers and iFacebook find the boomer strategy detail too much and in line with boomers need to understand that social media is not about teenagers chatting but reflects a new approach to engaging others. It is a whole new way to connect, interact, converse, contribute and be involved. These can be of great benefit to any business if managed well as is seem with by the approach of L'Oréal in digital age marketing, Rochet (2017).

Generations X and Y (Table 2) are developing and leading the way in finding out how to make the most of these new communication technologies. It is not just a technical issue; it is a mind-set shift. For these reasons the use of technology at work divides the generations. Successful digital transformation has technology at its core, but successful leadership directing culture change is foremost together with new business processes, Heavin and Power (2018) this supports Codrington and Grant-Marshall (2011) who offer further caution in managing the generational divide where the students of today are born into technology and are called digital natives, fluent speakers of the digital languages of computers, video games, and the Internet. Those not born into the digital world but acquire aspects of the new technology are digital immigrants. They continue that as digital immigrants we learn and adapt to our new environment but maintain the digital immigrant accent. Digital natives are used to receiving information very fast, they like to parallel process and multi-task. The appreciation of these skills business leaders who are digital immigrants, from the boomer and Xers generations must consider in managing the Yers and new entrant iFacebook generations, the digital natives.

Boag (2013) adds that senior management lack confidence in digital because they do not really understand it, they need a roadmap to reassure them. The need for improved digital understanding and competence by business leadership will be investigated further.

Disruption in Future Time Against Technological Horizons and Digital Transformation

Digital transformation is the process of transforming a business from one state to another, Benedict (2016), from a time when a business operates in human time to digital time and finally to future time, these time continuums are defined by Benedict and based upon global research conducted by Cognizant Centre for Future work across 18 countries with 2000 executive, 500 managers, 50 futurists and 150 MBA students, as:

- The disruptive transformation era, the period in which disruptive technologies develop and disrupt everything, being governed by our physical, biological, and mental limitations as humans, human time
- The hyper-digital transformation era, time governed by computing, data transmissions speeds, and networking, as digital time, which leaving laggards behind, and operating as close to real time as possible
- The ubiquitous transformation era, time governed by predictive analysis, algorithms, and artificial intelligence, as future time when mature digital technologies are adopted and needed, operating faster than real time and automatically anticipate needs, acts, and delivers content to prepare the future in a manner that adds value

Benedict (2016) adds that human time cannot keep up with digital time in an always connected world. Human time is incapable of delivering the real-time mobile and online commerce speeds required by digital consumers. Benedict (2016) continues that there are some 7.6 billion mobile devices around the world estimated for 2020, 5 billion will be smartphones connected to the internet and will have access to a number of applications. The need for data at increased speed is shaking up the information technology world. In this regard human time cannot respond to mobile search engine queries, or mobile payments, instead optimised information logistics systems, OILS, are needed which are integrated with artificial intelligence, AI, enabled bots responding automatically in digital time. A bot is a device or piece of software that can execute commands, reply to messages, or perform routine tasks either automatically or with minimum human intervention.

The business world is being completely driven by digital transformation which places more emphasis on future strategy development according to Benedict (2016) who summarises the key findings of their research:

- Leaders in the digital era act and think differently, they realise the importance of digital transformation on their business future and strive to get transformation right
- Digital leaders navigate resource constraints by executing the right sequences and actions to negate these
- The business executives interviewed acknowledge the impact of digital technologies on realising opportunity
- Business leaders acknowledge they are in the middle of the hyper-digital transformation era and are intent on understanding the current and future digital trends, investments to be made to align the digital capability with maximising return
- Business leaders must take risk in investing in the correct technology to maximise return and ensure the threat of cybersecurity is minimised
- They must employ a digital map outlining project implementation and roll out with anticipated return on investment, ROI
- They ensure that they have the capable resources in human capital, digital agility to meet the challenges of data requirements and speed of digital flux to matter

Aligned with Benedict (2016) the impact of key technological trends impacting the future time line is shown by Bordignon (2017) (Figure 9). The x-axis the level of technological progress and breakthrough with the y-axis being the technology adoption curve. Levels 1 and 2 (1994 to 2020) are past and current, introduction of the internet giving rise to the third industrial revolution in 1994 and cloud technology introducing the Fourth Industrial Revolution, taken as given, with late adopters embarking. Level 3, (2020) is about exponential breakthrough within the current situation, level 4, (2020 to 2025) requires risk taking and experimentation with future technologies and level 5, (2025 onwards) is the futuristic endeavour with entrepreneurs such as Elon Musk CEO and founder of Tesla and SpaceX, level 5 will not form part of this chapter.

With cloud technology giving rise to the Fourth Industrial Revolution it dictates that business leadership must be technologically competent to lead their businesses into the 21st century. In the next three to five years the technologies of level 4 will

Figure 9. Horizons of technological change the digital enterprise maturity levels
Source: Bordignon (2017)

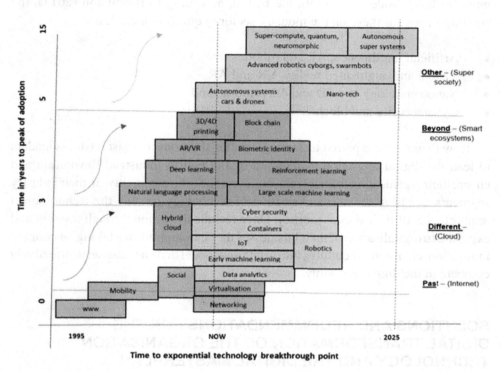

be impacting and become maturing, the impact of these must be understood as risk, innovation and experimentation will be required.

Bordignon (2017) highlights progress made by the Armoury Sports Organisation, (ASO), established in 1903, which supports the Tour de France one of the highest spectator value sports globally, employing level 3 technologies transforming their organisation using cloud, big data analytics, the internet of things, and cybersecurity to become a leader in athlete performance information, analysed in real time, for stakeholders and spectators alike. This was enabled through partnering with Dimension Data as their technology services partner who also sponsor a team in the Tour.

Similarity between the technological time horizons (Figure 9) from Bordignon (2017), with that of Sebastian et al. (2017) and Ross et al. (2016) shows that businesses capable of competing successfully in the 21st century and prosper in the digital economy must be platformed to enable seamless connection of humans with machines and data ensuring secure ecosystem flows enabled through the operational backbone and digital services backbone brought about through the SMACIT technologies of level 3.

In the migration of technologies, from level 3 to 4 in the digital enterprise maturity level model (Figure 9), are paired, according to Bordignon (2017), the pending impact of these on the industry sector in question includes:

- Artificial intelligence, AI, and robotics
- Virtual and augmented reality, VR and AR
- Nanotechnology and 3D and 4D printing, and
- Cybersecurity and blockchain

How then do these paired technologies offer solutions to assist business leaders to lead the digital migration as required by the Fourth Industrial Revolution and ensure their organisations remain relevant, continue to be competitive in their industry segments and have the correct selection of technology to suite the technological requirements of their digital journey. Once technically astute through training and exposure to digitalisation of their businesses they can support risk taking, encourage innovation, change their cultures into a data and model driven mind-set to effectively compete in the digital economy.

SOLUTIONS AND RECOMMENDATIONS FOR THE DIGITAL TRANSFORMATION OF THE ORGANISATION TECHNOLOGY AND THE DIGITAL MASTERPLAN

A consideration of the 4 paired technologies and their role in digitally transforming businesses to be competitive in the Fourth Industrial Revolution that require business leaders understanding will serve as one of a number of recommendations. A model proposed by Kane et al. (2015), the digital masterplan will be recommended as it will house the paired technologies, SMACIT digital technologies and the cultural adaptation to a digitally transformed business with a consideration of ethical standards in the digital era.

Artificial Intelligence and Robotics

The first of the paired technologies which according to Brynjolfsson, McAfee, and Spence (2014) and Kaldero (2018) rate artificial intelligence, (AI), as the most general-purpose technology of the digital era and especially machine learning, (ML) for employment in robotics and the industrial internet of things, (IIoT). Lee and Shin (2019) regard ML as not only the most disruptive technology but also a major source of competitive advantage. Simply, machine learning is the ability to keep improving performance without human intervention on how tasks should be completed. These authors offer two reasons as to why artificial intelligence is becoming so prominent. In the first instance humans cannot articulate everything they know, this makes automation difficult, however this is now possible. Secondly, machine learning is an excellent learner in that a wide range of tasks can be achieved at superhuman performance levels for example in detecting fraud through analysis of big data and medical diagnostic of diseases.

Artificial intelligence will have a major impact on all general-purpose technologies such as the internal combustion engine and associated technologies over the next decade transforming their core processes and business models. Ross et al. (2016) highlighted human limitation as the factor that inhibits digital transformation and agrees with Brynjolfsson et al. (2014) in that the bottleneck for the transformation lies with management, business reimagination and implementation. They continue that two advances in AI are; firstly, voice recognition as evidenced with Siri, provided by Apple iPhone who identify Siri as an intelligent personal assistance that helps you get things done efficiently, can check your diary, place calls, and send messages amongst some duties. Secondly, improvement of facial recognition as employed at Facebook but the subject of confidentiality challenges. They mention additional examples which include Google's Deep Mind team has used ML systems to reduce cooling system efficiency at data centres by some 15%, enhancing performance. Deep Instinct, a security company, uses intelligence agents to detect malware and PayPal to prevent money laundering. Amazon employs ML to optimise inventory, improve its customer interaction and product offer to customers. Music choices such as Apple music's iTunes and movie selection from Netflix can be personalised and based on AI and ML systems which business models can use effectively to boost customer satisfaction.

Brynjolfsson, McAfee, and Spence (2014) conclude that there is risk associated with employment of ML in that machines are taught on statistical approximations which can have hidden bias as opposed to the traditional systems built on explicit linear logic rules of humans. Therefore, if problems in ML systems occur these can be most challenging to diagnose, however they remain adamant that AI and ML remain the most important general-purpose technology of our era. These authors have demonstrated the future technological advances in AI and ML expected in the Fourth Industrial Revolution.

Virtual and Augmented Reality

Sight, of all the sensory capability is the real powerhouse of human absorption, Porter and Heppelmann (2015). Through the internet of things, (IoT) smart connected products, (SCP's), have technologies embedded in them referred to as the fourth wave of augmented reality, (AR), which is upon us, where it is not just about the products but the human interface with products and data, as a result AR will permeate every industry.

Porter and Heppelmann (2015) advise of a deluge of data from 4.4 zettabytes in 2013 to 44.0 zettabytes in 2020. To understand the magnitude of this deluge of data, Whatabyte.com define a zettabyte as; 1024 Gigabytes = 1 Terabyte, 1024 Terabytes = 1 Petabyte, 1024 Petabytes = 1 Exabyte, 1024 Exabyte's = 1 Zettabyte. Humans must take advantage of this data available despite there being a disconnect in that the physical reality is three dimensional with the rich data available trapped in a two-dimensional delivery through an iPad, computer screen or mobile device.

The effort in transposing the digital information into the physical space reduces the cognitive resources available to complete other tasks creating human limitation. Ross et al. (2016) supports this stating that it is not the size or access of data, but human limitation in utilising the data which remains the biggest challenge in the digital era.

Answering the challenge of human limitation in the interpreting and use of data as detailed by Ross et al. (2016), Porter and Heppelmann (2015) show that this is overcome by the breakthrough in AR which enables humans to assimilate, absorb and act on information. Virtual reality, (VR), a distinct, yet complimentary technology used in gaming and entertainment applications can be used for training purposes to replicate physical situations. Holograms of the equipment are used to train technicians by immersing them in a virtual environment using VR which adds a fourth capability of simulation to AR's visualise, instruct, and interact.

Porter and Heppelmann (2015) provide the solution in that AR solves this problem by super imposing digital images onto real objects. In a manufacturing environment these can be retrieved and enabled by pixelated glasses such as the Microsoft HoloLens or Vuzix AR 3000. Smart applications such as the Harvard Business Review AR app available from the App store or Google play offers an AR capability where encrypted images can be embedded into pages, retrieved by pointing a device at these pages launching an AR experience capable of visualisation, instruction, interaction, and simulation.

By combining the strengths of humans and smart machines Porter and Heppelmann (2015) conclude that AR will drastically increase value creation through improving productivity, quality, and training across all functions in the value chain. In over a hundred organisations researched by them a 13% to 19% value chain function improvement is reported by among others, General Electric, and the Mayo Clinic for cancer treatment. AR supported by VR will have a dramatic impact on the manufacturing sector in the Fourth Industrial Revolution.

Nanotechnology and 3D/4D Printing

O'Brien, Lin, Girard, Olvera de la Cruz, and Mirkin (2016) and Roco (2011) define nanotechnology as everything when miniaturised to the sub-100 nanometre scale as having new properties regardless of its origin, source or what it is. This allows and makes nanoparticles the materials of the future where nanoscale materials can be used in various products such as chemical catalysts, anti-bacterial agents, and sunscreen applications. The smaller the particle size the ratio of surface to bulk atoms increases where at a larger scale the surface atoms are largely inconsequential but at nanoscales a particle that is almost all surface is possible where the atoms can contribute significantly to the overall properties of the material. This relationship is applicable to the electronics industry where materials such as graphene and quantum dots find application in small computers and devices for communication to great advantage.

The relationship between nanotechnology with 3D and 4D printing is explained by Bordignon (2017) where new business models are enabled through the revolution of 3D printing with impact on traditional businesses such as retail, manufacturing, construction, other industrial applications and supply chain distribution. The printing of matter for example organic material, changing structures or shape over time is found in the fourth dimension contained in 4D printing. This enables the printing of human transplant tissue able to adapt to body chemistry and structure. This shows how 3D and 4D printing are changing the face of manufacturing in the Fourth Industrial Revolution's digital environment.

Cybersecurity and Blockchain

Security alerts and cyber-attacks are becoming more frequent and malicious, Bordignon (2017) where threats include; private access attempts and exploitation software or phishing, malware, web application attacks, and network penetration. In research conducted by the Nippon Telegraph and Telephone Global Threat Intelligence report, only 23% of organisations can counter these effectively. Organisations can counter these threats through two key areas of innovation, security analytics and biometric identity measurement.

The focus of security analytics is on predicting and preventing breaches through early identification and intervention of such threats, to apprehend intruders enabled through managed services platforms. Biometric security for a more secure, accurate, and convenient form of identification has become the standard for governments in all identification documentation. Biometric fingerprint sensors are the favoured identification method currently in use in commercial access control.

Crosby, Pattanayak, Verma, and Kalyanaraman (2016) and Marr (2017) advocate that more control over personal data ecosystems is now taking place with one of the world's most profound technological advances of the decade being blockchain which will transform financial services and other industrial sectors. Blockchain is a distributed data base, with storage devices for the system not linked to a common processor but containing a list of ordered records called blocks. Each block is linked through a timestamp to a previous one and through cryptography where only users can edit parts of the blockchain they own through processing keys to write a file. This ensures that everyone's copy of the distributed blockchain is kept synchronised.

According to Marr (2017) using the example of a medical file where the information can only be accessed by a doctor who has one private key to the block and patient the other. Only when one of these shares their private key with a specialist or third party can the information be retrieved. Marr (2017) indicates that this formed the origin of blockchain and was introduced in 2008 by the Bitcoin founder, who remains a secret, legendary and unconfirmed figure as reported by the New Yorker in 2016. It was used by the Bitcoin currency in 2009 and serves as the public ledger for all Bitcoin transactions. With the security built into blockchain through the distributed timestamping server and peer to peer network results in a data base that is managed autonomously in a decentralised manner, blockchain are excellent for keeping records, transactions and enabling mass dissemination of trade and transaction processing.

Blockchain can fulfil financial transactions by unlocking financial value in the currency stored at the same time ensuring security through trust and identity because no one can edit a blockchain without having the corresponding keys. Blockchain can have a devastating effect on financial services as it can perform operations performed traditionally by the banks as it effectively blocks out the middleman. The potential of this technology is vast as it improves efficiencies and Marr (2017) predicts most businesses will employ it at some stage in some future stage of the Fourth Industrial Revolution. An examination of the paired technologies and the SMACIT technology advances must be considered in a comprehensive digital strategy the formulation of which should follow the guidelines proposed in the digital masterplan.

The Digital Masterplan

To realise the objectives aligned with the aim of this chapter a digital strategy is essential. Kane et al. (2015) advise that a good digital strategy will exhibit the following characteristics:

- Maturity of the digital strategy is based on a clear coherent strategy
- Technological innovations will add to the growth of the digital strategy as seen with Walmart Stores Inc. who plan for the changing needs of their

customers over the next ten to twenty years which will be radically different to those of today

- Effective communication of the digital strategy to all employees in the business

Lloyd (2015) has identified three key considerations aligned with the changing digital landscapes which are; start-ups are bringing pain to traditional businesses, changing customer experiences are the order of the day and mobile initiatives and expansion initiatives are being impaired by unreliable data security. Lloyd advises there are three additional considerations before starting a digital strategy these are:

- More spend and investment must be assigned to end-to end architecture of customer-facing technology to create end-to-end experiences especially aligned to mobile applications, apps
- Mobile enterprise solutions and apps must be identified to reduce costs
- Business models shift through; technology driving value, enhanced connectivity, manual task automation and consumer needs satisfied through product development at no cost using for example crowdsourcing, a means of funds being raised online from a large audience of people, usually free

The factors highlighted by Kane et al. (2015) and Lloyd (2015) form the basis of the 4 Phase digital masterplan as developed by Lloyd and constitutes understanding:

- Insights and analysis
- Digital framework
- Digital scope
- Execution and governance

Boag (2013) advises that traditional business strategies have been around for many years with well-established formats, these do not fit with digital as their focus is two-fold; a long-term roadmap and budget forecasting neither of which are replicated in a digital strategy. The reasoning by Boag (2013) is that a three to five-year time horizon in digital is populated with too many technological changes and cannot be constant, also the budgeting process needs to move form an external fixed budget to a more fluid internal and experimental one. A digital strategy therefore needs to focus more on creating policies, priorities, and people. Against the insights of Boag (2013) the four-phase digital masterplan from Lloyd (2015) needs to be evaluated in more depth.

Phase One: Insights and Analysis

It is not only about understanding the needs and priorities of people says Lloyd (2015), but also of customers, employees, executives who form the core of your digital evolution but also to understand where the biggest value is through:

- External value analysis
- Customer expectation mapping
- Digital value chain analysis

The external value analysis is about adapting and incorporating the digital parameters into the Porter five forces model as shown and expanded (Figure 4). Customer and journey mapping are covered with the digital value chain (Figure 5). To complement the digital value chain Lloyd (2015) highlights some practical examples, these are:

- The use of dynamic systems to enhance the inbound logistics with suppliers such as the Bosch 4.0 initiative, where the German manufacturer has created inter-connected, self-optimising factories that can automatically adjust machine downtime or supply of incoming raw materials or components to align with demand
- Operations which require optimal software and reads on inventory such as the mobile operators Telefonica and Telenor who created a value ecosystem BlueVia to connect partners with Facebook, Microsoft, Google, and Samsung with a combined 460 million subscribers allowing developers to build a data platform capable of billing and taking payments from their customers
- In outbound delivery systems apps need to be developed to make it easier for customers to plan for deliveries, FedEx SenseAware exposes data about a packages environment, via an app, allowing for the tracking of packages in real time creating a greater mindshare within a customer ecosystem of value
- Content management, e-commerce, business intelligence, lead nurturing are platforms that enhance customer relationship management, CRM, and planning systems. Such customer-facing units are being levered hard with big data systems and should be regularly evaluated
- Lloyd concludes with service that starts after the sale, to create brand loyalty. Target a retailer accepts goods returns without receipts with funds paid straight back into the card used for the payment. People must be equipped with digital tools to ensure optimum service is guaranteed always

Lloyd (2015) has shown how easily traditional strategy models and frameworks can be populated with digital content with Boag (2013) urging a shorter digital planning horizon of six weeks compared with the traditional long-range strategy plans and encourages a more fluid budgeting process.

Phase Two: The Digital Framework

To address digital goals and objectives Lloyd (2015) recommends that the digital framework creates a mechanism for detailing what digital does and means for your business, (Figure 10).

Figure 10. The digital framework
Source: Lloyd (2015)

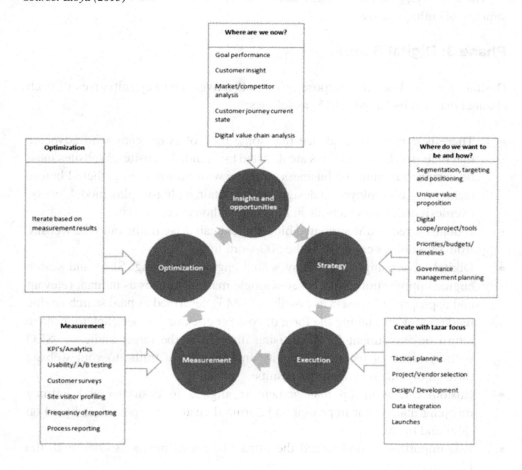

- The mission, vision and values for big data must be summed up into five to seven words, communicated to the business for people to make it their own
- Digital goals are what stakeholders want most for the business when goals are combined with objectives this is what digital will do for your business. This can be referred to as the Bill of Rights for the business where the rules can change so that it becomes key in the digital world to be able to pivot effectively
- The unique value proposition, UVP, is what creates standout for the business and builds perceived value
- Digital planning frameworks and iteration models must be accompanied by a 6-week planning cycle with a single objective focus of updating the evolutionary nature of technological innovation and digital transformation

These 6-week planning sprints must be incorporated into the broader traditional strategy planning framework.

Phase 3: Digital Scope

Digital scope outlines the purpose, goals, objectives, and key initiatives of each channel detailed by Lloyd (2015) as follows:

- There is conclusive evidence that some 69% of Americans who advocate that their purchase decisions are dictated by branded websites. Websites must be designed around the business strategy, with information gathered before technology is employed in design, must contain a plug-in-play model, not be overdesigned, having a built-in blog engine housed on the site
- If done correctly differentiated blog content can drive traffic onto the website from other blogs confined to the 500-word limit
- Digital advertising is driven by search engine marketing, SEM and search engine optimisation, SEO, where Google makes searches as human, relevant and appropriate for users as possible. SEM is described as paid search engine marketing where taking the form of cost per click or pay per click to manage return on investment for advertising directed at the target audience. SEO is the practise of increasing quality and quantity of traffic to your website through organic search engine results
- Customer relationship management is aligned to customer and journey mapping making for improved and nurtured customer experiences based on sales and marketing data
- It is important to understand the impact of social media as done with the L'Oréal case study

Phase 4: Execution and Governance

Lloyd (2015) cautions that timelines, achievement targets and budgets must be aligned with execution through the following considerations:

- Project priorities must be based on profit expectation, employee morale, productivity, brand equity and the assigned customer experience
- Project teams should be drawn up on a cross functional basis, be afforded with a start-up empowerment to address big digital projects accountable to the board
- KPI's and progress reporting must be viewed on a regular basis

These four phases can be effectively overlaid into a traditional strategy development process (Table 3). With execution and review comes ethical practise.

Table 3. Traditional and digital strategy development process alignment

Sondhi 2008 traditional	Kaplan & Norton 2008 traditional	Ross 2016 digital	Lloyd 2015 digital
Creative future scenarios, strategic gap	Finance & management control systems with dashboard	Digital services backbone, sophisticated analytics, micro services	Insights & analysis, goals, digital value chain, customer expectation & competitors
Analytical SWOT and Key issues identified	Internal business processes, systems & IT review and development	Operational backbone, facilitates operational excellence	Digital framework, segment, target, position, UVP, digital scope, budgets, ethics
Evaluative options and decide on strategic choice	Customer strategy, traditional channel and e-commerce platform	Customer engagement strategy, transforms go to market	Digital scope, reviews all customer issues, channel strategy, website capability
Pragmatic learning, implement, review and monitor performance	Learning culture and growth organisation	Digitised solutions which transforms the business model	Execution, measurement, optimisation & governance

Ethics in the Digital era

Shetty (2017) in an article, *"Getting Digital Ethics Right"*, states that organisations are rethinking their codes of ethics and digital ethical strategies because participation in business in the digital era has blurred boundaries between technology capability and business. Information technology has moved from being a support function to an important business enabler.

Sarathy and Robertson (2003) point out that at the heart of online commerce is individualised customer information. The success of one-on-one marketing, e-commerce is dependent on the use of increasing amounts of individualised customer data. The extensive collection of such specific personalised data and use thereof causes alarm over the loss of digital privacy and is the root cause of conflict and confrontation between e-commerce and society. Europe has responded with privacy protection legislation while the United States has allowed companies and industry associations to self-regulate themselves. This tenuous balance is under attack and with the outcome that businesses need to develop strategy to handle and manage digital privacy concerns.

Many professions in accounting, engineering, medicine, legal, scientific have developed strong ethical behavioural codes over many years. In the field of information technology says Shetty (2017) ethical codes are less common, developed, and prominent. The unintended risk and consequences of their effect with amplification of their effects make the need to develop digital ethics very real and must be done very fast.

Shetty (2017) and Porter and Heppelmann (2015) indicate that the digital economy is built on data and that massive streams of data, some 44.0 zettabytes projected in 2020, will have been collected, collated and available to share and use. Current risk migration strategies and traditional governance frameworks are insufficient to deal with this situation. New classes of risk are being identified in the digital economy through unethical use of insights, without consent, from personal data sharing highlighting biases from data that should not be disclosed for the purposes it is being used for creating social anxiety and legal challenge.

Shetty (2017) continues, with the scope of digital ethics is a broad one inclusive of cybercrime, security, privacy, and social interaction many companies and businesses are employing professionals to oversee and pay attention to digital ethics as part of digital risk in the digital era. The digital ethics strategy is being developed around four key areas; values, differentiation, risk, and compliance. Where there is no checklist there is the need to self-regulate and keep alert to the unintended consequences and constantly monitor that the right thing is always being done. Ensure transparency and that all data utilised by the business does not violate the personal privacy of the customer.

Bordignon (2017) cautions that leaders of iconic institutions, governments and communities are aware of the challenges aligned to participating in a twenty-four-seven, always-on-economy. Amid the unprecedented change being experienced in the digital social age, though aware, not all business leaders have a confident, cohesive strategy and the right resources to execute a transformative plan for success in the new digital economy of digital systems, knowledge and associated intangible assets required in the Fourth Industrial Revolution.

FUTURE RESEARCH DIRECTIONS

This chapter has provided the literature content for the development of a digital transformation model for use by business leaders in the Fourth Industrial Revolution. There are two aspects for consideration and further research, the first is the role of data management for digital transformation and the digital capability of the business and its people, secondly is the human element of generational leadership, skill, knowledge and understanding of digital transformation and how to lead such a process with the cultural change and human capital requirements to successfully transform a business.

Lincoln, Lynham, and Guba (2011) and Neuman (2013) share that there are four worldviews framing a research study these are; postpositivism, constructivism, transformative and pragmatism. Tashakkori and Teddlie (2010) support pragmatism as it applies to mixed method research where inquirers draw readily on both qualitative and quantitative insights when they engage in research.

To frame such research a multi method convergent parallel mixed methods approach should be followed as advocated by O'Leary (2017) and Bell, Bryman, and Harley (2018). Here qualitative research by interview and quantitative research by questionnaire are undertaken side by side with a merging of data on conclusion of each method.

The inductive nature of qualitative research Easterby-Smith, Thorpe, and Jackson (2012) should uncover generational aspects, human capital requirements and skill levels at leadership and employee level with the culture change requirements for a digitally transformed business. The deductive nature of quantitative research Bell et al. (2018) involves collection of numerical data better suited to data management, strategy development and digital capability.

The use of mixed method convergent parallel research method through inductive qualitative and deductive quantitative research as advocated by Creswell (2014) is best applied to a specific industry for example manufacturing in South Africa. These will determine how far ahead or behind the manufacturing sector is on the digital transformation migration curve.

CONCLUSION

This chapter has identified the components for content that can to be integrated into a model which in turn can be applied by senior management in their migration from analogue to digital businesses systems. They are encouraged to take risk, invest and know which technology to employ to improve competitiveness, counter digital disruption and cybersecurity in the 21st century.

Traditional strategy process development models such as Sondhi (2008) and Kaplan and Norton (2008) have been in place for a number of years which business leaders are familiar with and are designed for long term implementation. Both models have common integration parameters with the digital models of Sebastian et al. (2017), Ross et al. (2016), Kane et al. (2015) and Lloyd (2015). The Sondhi model shows how in the external environmental analysis the Porter (1980) five forces is upgraded with digital parameters and integrated into the model, similarly with the internal value chain analysis of Porter and Millar (1985) and Porter (2008).

This introduces change as a key element in the strategy development process as advocated by Balogun et al. (2015) where digital disruption leads to incisive revolutionary or reconstructive change that accompanies the fast pace of digital transformation and concurrent disruptive technologies.

Kaplan and Norton (2008) introduced the balanced scorecard as a strategic management measurement tool with four key areas aligned to the vision and strategy; the customer strategy development, financial management and control, internal business processes IT and systems development, and the learning organisation. After thirty years of application of the model Kaplan and Norton (2008) revised the model as a strategic development process tool as opposed to essentially one of measurement of business processes. They emphasize the value chain, supply chain relationship, with the value chain as time-to-market and supply chain as route-to-market. As a benchmark this relationship is developed further as seen in the complete digital transformation of a traditional global business, L'Oréal which dominates the beauty sector in which it competes. The success at L'Oréal was due to recruiting capable people to train and develop all employees in the group to be digitally astute.

Codrington and Grant-Marshall (2011) supported by Heavin and Power (2018) stress the importance of the generational divide in management and highlight behavioural differences with regard digital capability between the generations. Boag (2013) highlights the lack of knowledge and understanding business leadership has of digital transformation. Ross et al. (2016) show that digital transformation is about managing the impact of technological innovations coming from all directions and the human element and its limitations in managing this onslaught that is important as we move into the digital era, not the amount or availability of data.

Review of the balanced scorecard by Kaplan and Norton (2008) from a measurement to strategy development model over the past thirty years, aligns the four key areas of the digital strategy model, SMACIT, of Sebastian et al. (2017) and Ross et al. (2016). Alignment is seen with the four digital parameters (Figure 1) as; the operational backbone with IT development and systems development, customer engagement with customer strategy, digitised solutions with financial management and controls and finally, market capabilities with a learning organisation (Table 3).

Bordignon (2017) in the digital enterprise maturity model shows the time horizon and technology breakthrough points accompanying the technological developments impacting the manufacturing sector. The model considers paired technologies such as artificial intelligence and robotics, virtual and augmented reality, nanotechnology with 3D and 4D printing, and cybersecurity and blockchain as key considerations for the manufacturing sector in the strategy process development. Bordignon (2017) offers the digital societal balance sheet as the means to manage the impact of the digital enterprise maturity model which embraces seven strategic capabilities driving business value, each of these have differing maturity levels enabling a mathematical evaluation of organisational migration from analogue to digital capability.

The consideration of business ethics remains the cornerstone of digital transformation moving into the digital era in the 21st century.

REFERENCES

Andriole, S. J. (2017). *Five myths about digital transformation*. Academic Press.

Balachandran, B. M., & Prasad, S. (2017). *Challenges and benefits of deploying big data analytics in the cloud for business intelligence*. Academic Press.

Balogun, J., Hope Hailey, V., & Gustafsson, S. (2015). Exploring Strategic Change (4th ed.). Academic Press.

Bell, E., Bryman, A., & Harley, B. (2018). *Business research methods*. Oxford University Press.

Benedict, K. (2016). *The Work Ahead 40 months of Hyper - Digital Transformation*. The Center for Future Work.

Binedell, N. (2015). The Fingers of the strategist. *Fingers of the Strategist,* (11), 14-15.

Boag, P. (2013). *So you want to write a Digital Strategy? Smashing Magazine*.

Bordignon, D. (2017). The exponential digital world. *Dimension Data Australia*, 1-67.

Brynjolfsson, E., McAfee, A., & Spence, M. (2014). New world order: Labor, capital, and ideas in the power law economy. *Foreign Affairs*, *93*(4), 44–53.

Chappell, D. (2015). *Introducing Azure Machine Learning. In A Guide for Technical Professionals*. Microsoft Corporation.

Codrington, G. T., & Grant-Marshall, S. (2011). *Mind the gap* (2nd ed.). Penguin Books.

Creswell, J. W. (2014). *Research design qualitative, quantitative, and mixed methods approaches* (4th ed.). SAGE Publications, Inc.

Crosby, M., Pattanayak, P., Verma, S., & Kalyanaraman, V. (2016). *Blockchain technology: Beyond bitcoin*. Academic Press.

Easterby-Smith, M., Thorpe, R., & Jackson, P. R. (2012). Management research. *Sage*.

Gruman, G. J. I. (2016). *What digital transformation really means*. Academic Press.

Heavin, C., & Power, D. J. (2018). *Challenges for digital transformation–towards a conceptual decision support guide for managers*. Academic Press.

Kaldero, N. (2018). *Data Science for Executives: Leveraging Machine Intelligence to Drive Business ROI*. Lioncrest Publishing.

Kane, G. C., Palmer, D., Phillips, A. N., Kiron, D., & Buckley, N. (2015). Strategy, not technology, drives digital transformation. MIT Sloan Management Review, 14.

Kaplan, R. S., & Norton, D. P. (2008). *The execution premium: Linking strategy to operations for competitive advantage*. Harvard Business Press.

Lee, I., & Shin, Y. J. (2019). *Machine learning for enterprises: Applications, algorithm selection, and challenges*. Academic Press.

Lincoln, Y. S., Lynham, S. A., & Guba, E. G. (2011). *Paradigmatic controversies, contradictions, and emerging confluences, revisited*. Academic Press.

Lloyd, H. (2015). *Marketing Essentials, Tech and Design*. Harrison James Co.

Marr, B. (2017). *Data Strategy: How to Profit from a World of Big Data, Analytics and the Internet of Things*. Kogan Page Publishers.

Meffert, J., & Swaminathan, A. (2018). *Leadership and the urgency for digital transformation*. Academic Press.

Mell, P., & Grance, T. (2011). *The NIST definition of cloud computing*. Academic Press.

Neuman, W. L. (2013). *Social research methods: Qualitative and quantitative approaches*. Pearson education.

O'Brien, M. N., Lin, H.-X., Girard, M., Olvera de la Cruz, M., & Mirkin, C. A. (2016). *Programming colloidal crystal habit with anisotropic nanoparticle building blocks and DNA bonds*. Academic Press.

O'Leary, Z. (2017). The essential guide to doing your research project. *Sage (Atlanta, Ga.).*

Porter, M. E. (2008). The five competitive forces that shape strategy. *Harvard Business Review*, *86*(1), 25–40. PMID:18271320

Porter, M. E., & Heppelmann, J. E. (2015). How smart, connected products are transforming companies. *Harvard Business Review*, *93*(10), 96–114.

Porter, M. E., & Millar, V. E. (1985, July). How information gives you competitive advantage. Harvard Business Review.

Pyle, D., & San Jose, C. J. M. Q. (2015). *An executive's guide to machine learning*. Academic Press.

Rochet, L. (2017). *Leading digital transformation at L'Oreal*. SAID Oxford Business School.

Roco, M. C. (2011). *The long view of nanotechnology development: the National Nanotechnology Initiative at 10 years*. Springer.

Ross, J. W., Sebastian, I., Beath, C., Mocker, M., Moloney, K., & Fonstad, N. (2016). *Designing and executing digital strategies*. Academic Press.

Sarathy, R., & Robertson, C. J. (2003). Strategic and ethical considerations in managing digital privacy. *Journal of Business Ethics*, *46*(2), 111–126. doi:10.1023/A:1025001627419

Sebastian, I. M., Ross, J. W., Beath, C., Mocker, M., Moloney, K. G., & Fonstad, N. O. (2017). How Big Old Companies Navigate Digital Transformation. *MIS Quarterly Executive*.

Shetty, A. D. (2017). E-Commerce Industry Significant Factor for the Growth of Indian Economy. *Asian Journal of Research in Social Sciences and Humanities*, *7*(4), 177–183. doi:10.5958/2249-7315.2017.00275.1

Sondhi, R. (2008). Total strategy (3rd ed.). BMC Global Services Publications.

Tashakkori, A., & Teddlie, C. (2010). *Sage handbook of mixed methods in social & behavioral research* (2nd ed.). Sage. doi:10.4135/9781506335193

Toffler, A. (1980). *The third wave*. Bantam Books.

Westerman, G., Bonnet, D., & McAfee, A. (2014). *The nine elements of digital transformation*. Academic Press.

KEY TERMS AND DEFINITIONS

Artificial Intelligence: Or AI, is the most general-purpose technology of the digital era which with machine learning is regarded as the most disruptive technology and is a major source of competitive advantage. The reason why artificial intelligence is becoming so prominent is that humans cannot articulate everything they know which makes automation difficult. With artificial intelligence this is now possible enabled by the internet of things, where continuous processes are captured on an ongoing basis providing data stored and retrieved from the Cloud to be accessed for algorithm development the building block of artificial intelligence.

Augmented Reality: Sight, of all the sensory capability is the real powerhouse of human absorption. There is an immense amount of data around products which the human interface must take advantage of where, in the physical reality is three dimensional but trapped on a two-dimensional delivery through an iPad, computer screen or mobile device. The effort in transposing the digital information into the physical space reduces the cognitive resources available to complete other tasks creating human limitation. Answering the challenge of human limitation in the interpreting and use of data is overcome by the breakthrough in Augmented Reality, (AR), which enables humans to assimilate, absorb and act on information. The solution is seen in that AR solves this problem by super imposing digital images onto real objects in real time. In a manufacturing environment these can be retrieved and enabled by pixelated glasses such as the Microsoft HoloLens or Vuzix AR 3000.

Blockchain: Is a distributed data base, with storage devices for the system not linked to a common processor but containing a list of ordered records called blocks. Each block is linked through a timestamp to a previous one and through cryptography where only users can edit parts of the blockchain they own through processing keys to write a file. This ensures that everyone's copy of the distributed blockchain is kept synchronised. With the security built into blockchain through the distributed timestamping server and peer to peer network results in a data base that is managed autonomously in a decentralised manner, blockchain are excellent for keeping records, transactions and enabling mass dissemination of trade and transaction processing.

Cloud Computing: Digital transformation is enabled through cloud technology where human comprehension cannot cope with the size and speed of data required to manage a business in the digital economy. Storage, size and retrieval of data is no longer a problem to humans. There are no longer limitations to the amount of processing, size of data required or how much data can be sourced and the time in which to source data this is enabled through cloud technology. Cloud technology overcomes these challenges though the storage and access of big data and enables the development of algorithms that drive artificial intelligence and machine learning, both key enables of the fourth industrial revolution.

Cybersecurity: Cybersecurity is seen where security alerts and cyber-attacks are becoming more frequent and malicious, these threats include private access attempts and exploitation software or phishing, malware, web application attacks, and network penetration. Organisations can counter these threats through two key areas of innovation, security analytics and biometric identity measurement. The focus of security analytics is on predicting and preventing breaches through early identification and intervention of such threats, to apprehend intruders enabled through managed services platforms. Biometric security for a more secure, accurate, and convenient form of identification has become the standard for governments in all identification documentation. Biometric fingerprint sensors are the favoured identification method currently in use in commercial access control.

Digital Migration: The migration of key technological trends on the future time line is best explained on a timeline where the horizontal axis has the level of technological progress and breakthrough and the vertical axis with the level of technological adaptation. Level 1 is the time period (1994 to 2020), the past to current, with the introduction of the internet in 1994 that gave rise to the third industrial revolution. Level 2 around the 2000's introduced cloud technology enabling the Fourth Industrial Revolution. Level 3, in and around 2020, is about exponential breakthrough within the current situation. Level 4, (2020 to 2025) requires risk taking and experimentation with future technologies. Level 5, (2025 onwards) is the futuristic endeavour with entrepreneurs such as Elon Musk, CEO and founder of Tesla and SpaceX, developing driverless automation in vehicles, space travel to Mars and drone deliveries amongst some of the futuristic technologies.

Digital Transformation: Is defined simply as driving the business forward by leveraging the opportunity offered by technology. More specifically it is the use of technology to radically improve the performance and reach of the of the business in three areas, customer experience, operational processes and business models. To be competitive in the digital economy going forward business leaders are urged to digitally transform their businesses, using technology to remain competitive and relevant.

Machine Learning: Together with artificial intelligence, machine learning, ML, is being rated as the most general-purpose technology of the digital era, as both a disruptive technology and source of competitive advantage. Simply, machine learning is the ability to keep improving performance without human intervention on how tasks should be completed and is an excellent learner in that a wide range of tasks can be achieved at superhuman performance levels.

Nanotechnology: Nanotechnology is defined as everything when miniaturised to the sub-100 nanometre scale as having new properties regardless of its origin, source or what it is. This allows and makes nanoparticles the materials of the future where nanoscale materials can be used in various products such as chemical catalysts, anti-bacterial agents, and sunscreen applications. The smaller the particle size the ratio of surface to bulk atoms increases where at a larger scale the surface atoms are largely inconsequential but at nanoscales a particle that is almost all surface is possible where the atoms can contribute significantly to the overall properties of the material. This relationship is applicable to the electronics industry where materials such as graphene and quantum dots find application in small computers and devices for communication to great advantage.

Paired Technologies: In the migration of technologies from level 3 to 4, (2000 to 2025), the following technologies work in tandem to establish digital enterprise maturity levels. These include, artificial intelligence and machine learning, augmented and virtual reality, nanotechnology with 3D and 4D printing, blockchain and cybersecurity.

Software: Digital transformation is all about software which employs code used by code writers to develop software. Hardware without software has no value at all and code writers and software developers are and have become the most important people in the world.

Strategy Development: The term strategy originates from the Greek word 'Strategia' meaning, from the office of the general and interprets the strategic position of the organisation where strategy is the plan for deploying resources to establishing a favourable position. Traditional strategy development is normally undertaken annually. Digital strategy is aligned with the employment of technology to digitally transform the business and is defined as nothing more than a business strategy inspired by the capabilities of technology. With the rapid changes in technology digital strategies are short lived and need to be re-evaluated and updated almost every six weeks. The outcomes of the digital strategy form key objectives in the corporate strategy.

Three- (3D) and Four-Dimensional (4D) Printing: The 3D printing process of making a physical product from a three-dimensional model is possible by laying down many fine layers of a material in succession, for example replicating an obsolete motor car part. The printing of matter for example organic material, changing structures or shape over time is found in the fourth dimension contained in 4D printing. This enables the printing of human transplant tissue able to adapt to body chemistry and structure. This shows how 3D and 4D printing are changing the face of manufacturing in the Fourth Industrial Revolution's digital environment.

Virtual Reality: Virtual reality (VR), is a distinct, yet complimentary technology used in gaming and entertainment applications creates an artificial environment but can be used for training purposes to replicate physical situations. Holograms of the equipment are used to train technicians by immersing them in a virtual environment using VR which adds a fourth capability of simulation to AR's visualise, instruct, and interact.

Chapter 2

The Impact of Unified Communication and Collaboration Technologies on Productivity and Innovation:
Promotion for the Fourth Industrial Revolution

Anthony Bolton
 https://orcid.org/0000-0002-1259-7479
University of South Africa, South Africa

Leila Goosen
 https://orcid.org/0000-0003-4948-2699
University of South Africa, South Africa

Elmarie Kritzinger
 https://orcid.org/0000-0002-5141-4348
University of South Africa, South Africa

ABSTRACT

Against the background of promoting inclusive growth in the context of the Fourth Industrial Revolution (4IR), the purpose of this chapter is to introduce Industry 4.0 in terms of the impact of Unified Communication and Collaboration (UC&C) technologies on productivity and innovation within a global automotive enterprise. To provide readers with a further overview of, and summarize, the content of the

DOI: 10.4018/978-1-7998-4882-0.ch002

chapter, issues, controversies, problems, and challenges related to Industry 4.0 adoption, including, for example, Cyber-Physical Systems (CPS), are discussed. Solutions and recommendations for dealing with the issues, controversies, and/or problems are presented, and the chapter will also discuss future research directions and emerging trends, together with providing insight about the future of the book's theme from the perspective of the chapter focus on the impact of UC&C technologies on productivity and innovation. The last section will provide discussion of the overall coverage of the chapter and concluding remarks.

INTRODUCTION

Over the past fifty years, the third revolution in industrial and technical development has enabled humanity to escape the confines of Earth and venture into space, to explore the neighboring planets of the solar system. Within twenty years of launching the first satellite, the Voyager missions extended beyond mere planetary observation, to embark on a "Grand Tour" of space beyond the solar system (Lanius & MCCurdy, 2008, p. 231) and included communication, carrying technology and information about humanity into the cosmos. Digital transformation has propelled humanity towards what Schneider and Friesinger (2011) described as a new horizon of possibilities.

Now, suddenly, it seems to be all around: Artificial Intelligence (AI) and machine learning are mainstream, the 'amplification' of everything is becoming a reality, and 5G and even 6G are on the horizon. New technologies have the potential to revolutionize manufacturing enterprises.

The Fourth Industrial Revolution (4IR), however, feels like the ghost in the machine. Currently, there are debates around whether it is coming, or may it already be here? Is what is happening, actually, the 4IR? There are many names and definitions for the 4IR, as well as numerous frameworks, ranging from this merely being an extension of the Third Industrial Revolution, to Society 5.0. Since there does not seem to be a common understanding of what 4IR means, the 4IR naming convention will be used, as it is a widely communicated definition from the World Economic Forum (WEF).

The 4IR is about the emergence of Cyber-Physical Systems (CPS), AI and networks. Cyber-physical systems involve new ways of embedding technology within larger societies, communities, and even in the human body. Artificial intelligence and robots are already replacing many routine jobs, while technology may create many as yet unimagined jobs. How then can enterprises respond effectively to uncertain futures? How can the curation and transmission of knowledge be reimagined? How can enterprises be prepared to thrive when confronted with the unexpected? How can plans be made for yet unknown disruptive change? What are the challenges to realizing the rich potential of 4IR technologies in manufacturing? The irony is that standing on the brink of a brave new 4IR world, life could potentially be made better for all the world's people.

Against the background of the book's theme of promoting inclusive practice and growth in the context of the Fourth Industrial Revolution, this chapter will introduce the role of Unified Communication and Collaboration (UC&C) technologies in preparing enterprises for uncertain futures, and for societies that are changing at great speed in terms of their ability to drive job creation, economic growth and prosperity for millions in the future. It aims to unpack some of the issues around the 4IR, with reference to Science, Engineering, Technology (SET), productivity and innovation.

Enterprises all need to become more agile and find time to keep on mastering new technologies. Change management will have to be the new normal across all Information Technology (IT) departments. And now, more than ever before, fingers must be kept on the pulse of change by sharing knowledge with peers and colleagues. Exciting times lie ahead for the industry, and by working together, enterprises will be able to stay ahead of the changes and overcome challenges, to be more competitive globally.

Target Audience

The target audience for this chapter, as for the book as a whole, include general and human resources managers/directors, organizational design specialists, as well as IT professionals.

Having described the general perspective of this chapter, to end, and in line with some of the recommended topics for this book, the objectives of the chapter will now be specifically stated as to investigate:

- The challenges and opportunities associated with the impact of Industry 4.0 globally
- Changes needed to realize the potential of new technologies in manufacturing enterprises
- Challenges to making the impact of the technologies viable globally
- Using 4IR technologies to impact productivity and innovation
- Improving competitiveness and developing 4.0 technologies to enhance digital transformation.

BACKGROUND

This section of the chapter will provide broad definitions and discussions of the topic and incorporate the views of others (literature review) into the discussion to support, refute, or demonstrate the authors' position on the topic.

Industry 4.0 is considered to form part of the Fourth Industrial Revolution (Manu, 2015) and promises to impact productivity and innovation in industry and manufacturing services through the introduction of integrated data exchange and intelligent automation.

Digital disruption is profoundly impacting industry and society (The-Digital-Enlightment-Forum, 2016). Enterprises that get ahead of digital transformation stand to disrupt industry, reaching new markets and customers almost immediately. Entry into expanded digital markets and customers in many cases can be achieved at low cost and high profit margins (Brush, 2012). Productivity improvement can be introduced rapidly through combinatorial digital innovation. As the age of the Fourth Industrial Revolution emerges, digital disruption will be a catalyst in defining and iterative redefining of the modern enterprise.

Digitization is defined as a social transformation that is initiated by the mass and frequently rapid adoption of digital technologies. Modern society is increasingly recognizing the impact and influence that the digital era is having on people and society building on advancements in communications technologies (Katz & Koutroumpis, 2012). Attracting, managing and developing talent with the relevant skills to manage the impact of transformation and continuous innovation is a crucial challenge for every organization undergoing a digital transformation. The latter authors also added that in terms of measuring socio-economic digitization, a **paradigm** shift was required.

MAIN FOCUS OF THE CHAPTER

Building on the **paradigms** of the Internet and the Internet of Things (IoT), this chapter focuses on the impact of the process of digital transformation on industry and developing literature associated with digital communication within the enterprise. The chapter reviews literature surrounding the emergence of Industry 4.0, considered to be the Fourth Industrial Revolution, and unified communications and collaboration technologies, which provide a pathway for cyber-physical integration in a digital world.

In literature, Industry 4.0 is frequently described as the next phase in the digitization of manufacturing, building on technologies adjacent to, and stemming from, the Internet of Things. These technologies include advanced digital networks, data analytics, artificial intelligence, sensor technology, augmented reality systems and smart sensor technology. The combinatorial effect of digitization is resulting in an increasing number of innovative applications of technology within manufacturing. Industry 4.0 is progressing from what was the third revolution in manufacturing and automation, towards intelligent integrated systems. Industry 4.0 promises higher levels of integration of systems, people and machine technologies delivering benefits such as more intelligent proactive use of information, increased production uptime, real-time yield and production optimization.

Technologies that have a profound impact on industry and society are deemed to be those which blend seamlessly into the background of the associated environment, be it home, society or industry (Wieser, 1991). As dynamic workloads increase, cyber-physical integration is sought to integrate people as a 'thing' within the schema of Internet of Things systems; a method of seamless, real-time and multimodal integration and communication between things and people is required. Unified communications and collaboration technologies promise smooth and seamless integration of people with other people and systems through a portfolio of integrated communications and collaboration technologies (protocols, systems and infrastructure) via multiple mediums and a single interface or integrated technologies framework.

Industry 4.0

Like the **paradigm** of the Internet of Things, Industry 4.0 focuses on the effects of combinatorial innovation, enabled through recent advances in multiple technology areas, such as intelligent data analytics, artificial intelligence, Internet of Things sensors, contextual networks and the digitization of business processes and human interaction. Through what has been described as "Integrative Production Technology" (Brettel, Friederichsen, Keller, & Rosenberg, 2014, p. 37), IoT systems have the potential to create new data and information associated with the real-time status of the supply chain, production efficiency and production status. Advances in data management, "big data" systems (De-Mauro, Greco, & Grimaldi, 2014, p. 97) and intelligent automated data analytics are providing industry with improved understanding of production environments, through the intelligent leverage of the sea of new real-time data available via the IoT and digitally transformed systems.

Advances in computing and communications infrastructure and services are facilitating embedded and real-time integration of people and data, enabling cyber-physical integration and a high capacity to handle human-inclusive, real-time decision-making. Industry 4.0 also heralds the emergence of digital fabrication, extending the innovations in synthetic and made materials through digital three-dimensional (3D) printing technology (Almada-Lobo, 2016).

The combined effect of these technologies and integrated cyber-physical advances are resulting in the advent of "Smart Factories" (Shariat-Zadeh, Lundholm, Lindberg,

& Franzén-Sivard, 2016, p. 512), which are at the core of Industry 4.0. Industry 4.0 moves beyond the automation of manufacturing achieved through the integration of computers and machinery and into an age of intelligent integrated cyber-physical decision making and production.

Industry 4.0 is less about changing the core function of manufacturing and more about how things are done, responding to and integrating rapidly towards profound technological and social change.

From a societal perspective, Industry 4.0 compliments the **paradigm** of the Internet of Things and IoT sub-concepts, such as the contextual Internet of Things, the cognitive Internet of Things and smart environments.

The Fourth Industrial Revolution

As previously mentioned, and described in Bolton, Goosen and Kritzinger (2020b), prior to Industry 4.0, three preceding industrial revolutions are recognized, which each brought about significant changes in production, output and processes. The World Economic Forum positions the First Industrial Revolution as having brought about innovation in terms of mechanization and leveraging the steam engine and water power, while the Second Industrial Revolution was concerned with mass production, division of labor, assembly lines and electrification. The Third Revolution in industry witnessed increasing automation of production, characterized by the transformation of mechanical and analogue electronics to computers, digital electronics and integrated information and communication technologies within industry (Matthews, 2013).

The Fourth Industrial Revolution or Industry 4.0 differs from previous industrial revolutions in several ways. The combinatorial effect of technological innovation mainly characterizes these differences. Unlike previous revolutions, which focused mostly on technological advances in production, the fourth revolution introduces the integration of people, machinery and intelligent automated software systems, anticipating eliminating barriers between man and machine. Industry 4.0 builds on the advances of the previous three industrial revolutions, introducing innovation through the digitization and combination of existing processes and industrial technology. Industry 4.0 not only introduced cyber-physical systems, but also extended the cyber-physical characteristics of the Internet of Things and leveraged IoT technologies (Salkin, Oner, Unstundag, & Cevikcan, 2018), to increase the interoperability of systems and integration of people to the industrial world (Lee & Behrad Bagheri, 2015). Cyber-physical systems combine humans with the integrated systems within Smart Factories, communicating via IoT systems and Internet services. Industry 4.0 virtualizes the industrial landscape across the horizon of physical production and supply chain by linking IoT sensor data, people and plant information through real-time analytics and proactive simulation systems. Industry 4.0 also offers modularity in terms of service development, availability and leverage.

Industry 4.0 Drivers

Industry 4.0 and its associated technologies and strategies are relevant to all enterprises and the end-to-end supply chain, extending to IoT consumer services. The potential for productivity gains from Industry 4.0 is being applied across many enterprises today, including aviation, logistics, healthcare, manufacturing, oil and gas production and logistics. Within many of these enterprises (aviation, for example), increased productivity efficiency of even 1% in the form of fuel savings can have a tremendous impact on bottom line profits (Gilchrist, 2016). To attain these types of benefits and to profit and develop from market differentiation, enterprises must shift to adjust and adopt industrial aspects of the Internet of Things by embracing Industry 4.0 concepts and strategies.

Literature, such as Bartodziej (2017), suggested that global megatrends can significantly impact and drive structural changes within the manufacturing industry. For manufacturing, these megatrends include ageing, urbanization, individualism, sustainability, knowledge, finance, globalization and financial markets. These megatrends act as drivers of structural change across all areas of manufacturing through the influencing of developments in the technology of products, labor, resources, production and management processes (Westkämper, 2013). Industry 4.0 developments being introduced and integrated into manufacturing from the IoT **paradigm** are aligning in many use cases to address industry influencing megatrends, such as an ageing population, individualism, knowledge as an asset, globalization, urbanization, sustainability and global financial markets.

Boisot (1998, p. 3) described knowledge in the information age as assets that "are stocks of knowledge from which services are expected to flow for a period of time that may be hard to specify in advance". Knowledge assets have the potential, unlike physical assets, to last forever and can be extremely valuable from an economic standpoint, within industry, once identified, obtained and effectively leveraged.

Globalization and global supply chain and networks within manufacturing are facets of modern manufacturing (Westkämper, 2013). Estimates suggest that emerging markets will have shifted from approximately 30% of world Gross Domestic Product (GDP) in 1990 to 73% by 2050 (Errasti, 2013). Manufacturing operations are increasingly extending and relocating to these emerging markets and developing countries (Bi, Xu, & Wang, 2014). With the ensuing growth in competition within the global marketplace, diversified customer demand and new markets have driven a requirement for increased flexibility, customization, agility, networking, integration, green and socialization of manufacturing systems (Zhang & Tao, 2016). Industry

4.0 and IoT technologies are enabling a new **paradigm** in smart factories and flexible manufacturing that can be applied to the problems that arise in relation to the increasing complexity and dynamically changing requirements of global and distributed production (Radziwon, Bilberg, Bogers, & Madsen, 2014).

Informatization and the Outcome Economy

Paulin (2017, p. 40) suggested that the term 'informatization' can be used to describe "the ability to control concepts, systems, or things using information technology". Literature, such as Bartodziej (2017), suggested that informatization is the fourth evolution in technological generations and innovation associated with Industry 4.0. This fourth generation informatization acts a binding catalyst for the effective integration of cyber-physical systems within manufacturing, as well as the embedding of Internet of Things innovation and technologies into the fabric of manufacturing and industrial processes. The progression from electrified, mechanized and automated industrial and manufacturing systems to intelligent, smart factories with embedded intelligence and cyber-physical systems provides enterprises with significant opportunities to develop leading market and supplier strategies, as evidenced in developments within German manufacturing through Industry 4.0 adoption.

Industry 4.0 is changing the velocity, scale and diversity of information acquisition and the imperative to leverage information to enhance the intelligent capabilities within industrial, manufacturing and supply chain processes (Ackermann, 2015). According to the World Economic Forum, the shift to informatization and automated quantification capabilities through Industry 4.0 will contribute to driving transformation towards an outcome-based economy. Within the context of an outcome-based economy, Industry 4.0 facilitates a large-scale shift from selling products and services, to selling measurable outcomes (Porcaro, 2016).

Literature, such as Paganetto and Scandizzo (2016), suggested that this information-led transition, driven by Industry 4.0 and IoT technologies, represents a significant change that has the potential to redefine the base of competition and industry structures. The informatization of industry and manufacturing and integration of contextual real-time data and people within a cyber-physical ecosystem heralds a new industrial cycle, fueled by innovation. Digital technologies are combined with new skills and optimally integrated leverage of human capital.

Issues, Controversies, Problems

This subsection of the chapter will present the authors' perspective on issues, controversies, problems, etc., as they relate to the theme of promoting inclusive practice and growth in the 4IR, and arguments supporting the authors' position. It will also compare and contrast with what has been, or is currently being, done as it relates to the chapter's specific topic and the main theme of the book.

Issues, Controversies, Problems and Challenges Related to Industry 4.0 Adoption

Industry has had to deal with significant disruptions brought about as a result of previous revolutions and the new technologies and processes that these introduced. As established through a review of scholarly literature, Industry 4.0 will further influence and change business models, business process and the end-to-end spectrum of industry from supply chain through production. Because of this, many enterprises will experience challenges associated with the diversity of technologies and operational developments and new concepts and approaches introduced through Industry 4.0 (Schmidt, et al., 2015). One of the challenges related to adoption is increased risk of security and counterfeiting - this is discussed in Bolton, Goosen and Kritzinger (2020a). Other challenges related to adoption, existing in a number of areas, also include:

Data Analytics

Because of initiatives such as the IoT and Industry 4.0, global data is set to grow and increase fifty-fold by 2022 (Ackermann, 2015). The growth of data and the way it will be pervasively leveraged and shared between systems and partners across the digital landscape of Industry 4.0 creates new challenges for industry and manufacturing that extend beyond technical capability. How information is stored, shared and maintained is increasingly scrutinized at a governmental level to protect enterprises and people from misuse or careless distribution practices.

In a speech delivered by the European Data Commissioner, Vestager (2016) highlighted the importance of the non-technical aspects of data, stating that (t)he "future of big data is not just about technology. It's about things like data protection, consumer rights and competition. Things that give people confidence that big data won't harm them."

In her address, Vestager (2016) also focused on the importance of ensuring that laws and regulations progressed at a pace relative to technology and encouraged governments and regulatory bodies to adapt existing rules accordingly. Finally, Vestager (2016) suggested that if regulations and laws did not keep pace with technological developments, it would come at the price of diminished consumer and market protection.

Autonomous Systems

Internet of Things connected sensor and data strategies further increase the potential for the development of increasingly automated and autonomous systems within manufacturing and industry. The promise of increased efficiency, the potential of shortening time-to-market and enhancing the flexibility of manufacturing and supply chain systems fuels further automation.

Machine-to-Machine Communication

Machine-to-Machine (M2M) communication is a vital component of the value set upon which the IoT and Industry 4.0 are built. There are challenges and implications for industry and manufacturing as they develop and manage their strategies for machine-to-machine communication (Nourani, 2017). With an overwhelming number of proprietary systems existing within manufacturing and industrial environments, it is imperative that enterprises establish a concise and well-communicated strategy and architecture for machine-to-machine integration. The landscape of capability in machine-to-machine technology integration and systems has developed at a rapid pace. One of the results of this rapid innovation cycle is a lack of broadly accepted industry standards for M2M and industrial integration (Vollenweider, 2016).

Cyber-Physical Integration

Cyber-physical systems are rapidly emerging within industry, integrating physical and embedded systems with IT and the Internet. With the integration of physical systems and processes, including people, cyber-physical systems have the potential to bridge different technologies, domains and disciplines. The potential benefit of progression towards cyber-physical systems need to be balanced with plans of mitigation against potential challenges introduced through associated change. Ubiquitous computing is influencing widespread change within society; change that impacts the daily lives of individuals. These changes impact the work life and private lives of people in society (Song, Rawat, Jeschke, & Brecher, 2016).

Unified Communication and Collaboration Technologies

When Drucker (cited in Bressan, 2014, p. 32) first coined the term "knowledge worker", few could have conceived of its full importance and how prominently the concept would feature in the modern global economy. In 1959, the term was used to distinguish between the value of individuals who work with information and those who develop knowledge in the workplace (Bressan, 2014). The distinction between the two categories at that time lay in the opinion that the vast bulk of an enterprise's intellectual capital lay in paper-based systems managed and overseen by white-collar professionals.

With the expansion of the 21st-century global digital economy, technology is increasingly being applied to reduce the overhead of manufacturing and assembly through approaches such as High-Performance Work Systems (HPWS). Wealthy countries increasingly focus on the knowledge-based elements of design and engineering as a path to prosper (Ake, Clemons, Cubine, & Lilly, 2016). This shift is evident in developed economies, such as North America, where knowledge workers now outnumber other workers by a ratio of four to one.

Knowledge has become an essential resource within the global economy. In the developing digital economy, knowledge workers, as a collective within modern enterprises, own the means to production. Johnsen (2014) argued that knowledge is related to learning, collaboration and communication. Johnsen (2014) also suggested that the increasing value of knowledge as a resource within the economy increases the value of individual local experience.

Forces relating to globalization, such as market consolidation, virtualization, connected society and corporate social responsibility, are driving changes in the global workplace. Features, such as distributed workforces, increased mobility, distributed big data and external partner reliance, are now common in the global workplace and introduce new challenges for employers and employees alike (Tavani, 2011). Developing technologies in unified communications and collaboration technologies are increasingly leveraged within the global economy to mobilize and integrate knowledge workers and assets effectively.

UC&C technologies provide an integrated suite of presence-aware communication and collaboration capabilities. Involved technologies include an array of voice, video, email, chat and integrated communications-enabled business processes (Silic, Back, & Sammer, 2014). Silic et al. (2014) further suggested that capabilities offered through unique combinations of real-time communication processes and collaboration technologies present unprecedented value towards the goals of digitally transformed enterprises. Kim and Wang (2011) argued that UC&C technologies increase efficiency associated with communication within the enterprise by providing more direct methods of communication and collaboration between employees, partners, suppliers and clients.

Converging Communications

One of the key features delivered through a unified communications strategy and associated technical solutions is the convergence of multiple modes of communication. This convergence enables more than the convergence of technology: through new modes of access and the integration of multiple communication modes, new methods and approaches to communication are possible. To achieve this convergence and the associated benefits, enterprises must develop strategies and a framework facilitating legacy reduction and elimination in terms of e.g. Voice Over Internet Protocol (VOIP), video and conferencing infrastructure with unified communication feature and service components, frequently provided by different hardware and software providers (Tripathi, 2015).

The benefits associated with some of the standard features offered within the schema of a unified communications system have been previously reviewed in literature, including, for example, features such as Instant Messaging (Baskarada & Koronios, 2012), UC presence and group cohesion (Silic & Back, 2016), VOIP (Mathiyalakan, 2006), mobile device functionality (Ventola, 2014) and video conferencing (McConnell, Parker, Eberhardt, Koehler, & Lunderberg, 2013).

Further information related to UC&C functional architecture, as well as common protocols and infrastructure components, can be accessed in Bolton, Goosen and Kritzinger (2016).

Unified Communications Culture, Organization and Dynamics

Cultural differences are amongst the issues, controversies, problems and challenges encountered by distributed and global virtual teams. The first attributable definition of culture dates back to when the British anthropologist Tylor (1871, p. 1) described it as "that complex whole which includes knowledge, belief, art, morals, law, custom, and any other capabilities and habits acquired by man as a member of society". With the expansion of global virtual teams within large enterprises, it is likely that multiple different cultures will be brought together and required to engage in the virtual and distributed workplace. This amalgamation of different cultures can lead to the intersection of different communication styles, manners of conveying information and communicative social norms (Zhang, Min, & Wu, 2008). Culture influences the behavior of individuals and accordingly, consideration should be paid when planning changing work practices through the implementation of UC&C technologies, to avoid communication issues. Christiansen (2007) argued that in virtual teaming instances, such as those presented by offshore development, communication, if not taken seriously and poorly considered, has the potential to negate all benefits associated with greater access to talent, benefits attributed to lower cost resources and flexibility.

In the modern enterprise, the concept of collaboration has expanded and aligns to an increasingly sophisticated and broad meaning (Kryvinska, Auer, & Strauss, 2009). Today, enterprises must deal with communication requirements that span the entire value chain linking internal skills and resources with partners and customers. This convergence in communication reciprocally drives convergence in modes of communication leveraged by users, in what Kryvinska et al. (2009, p. 305) described as a "mash-up" of communication technologies and capabilities. Finally, Kryvinska et al. (2009) argued that such systems must accommodate regularly changing trading partners, multiple business processes, legacy reduction and elimination across multiple systems, communication across multiple internal and external organizational domains, multiple messaging formats and protocols.

Christiansen (2007) suggested that factors, such as differences in time zones, differences in culture, differences in language (accents, non-native speakers of primary business language), non-face-to-face communication (thin communication channels) and the leverage of different technology platforms across teams all add to the burden and stress of virtual teams. Cascio (2000) suggested that issues, controversies and problems in remote and teleworking environments closely aligned with limitations of physical and social interaction and face-to-face communication. These can result in misunderstandings and conflict between working groups and between workers and management.

In their study of virtual team behaviors, Dekker and Rutte (2007) identified eleven core characteristics/behaviors that differentiate effective or ineffective communication and behavior within virtual teams. These characteristics included clear and complete communication, use of appropriate media, planning and structuring the work process and meetings, predictable and reliable communication, involving all team members, participating in activities, pro-social activities, pro-social behavior, considering language, time zone, and cultural differences, tension control, superfluous communication, and non-task-related communication.

Zhang et al. (2008) suggested that communication is a primary component of the effectiveness of Global Virtual Teams (GVTs). In their study of communication management within GVTs, three categories of Critical Success Factors (CSFs) are proposed as influencers on the communication within virtual teams: these categories are communication technology, team learning and team leadership. Zhang et al. (2008) also outlined two primary communication styles engaged in virtual team communication, task communication and social communication, and suggested that these communication styles can be affected by team characteristics and CSFs.

Communication styles and critical success factors should be considered when addressing strategies to optimize effective communication between virtual teams. Christiansen (2007) suggested that the focus should be on synchronous communication to optimize virtual team communication, avoiding reliance on asynchronous communication technologies and approaches. Christiansen (2007) further argued that reliance on asynchronous forms of communication, such as e-mail, will increase the occurrences of misunderstandings between teams and slowdown in team delivery and outcomes.

Literature, such as Carte and Chidambaram (2004, p. 449), suggested that there are differing viewpoints about the value of face-to-face communication within distributed virtual teams. The latter authors further argued that where cultural diversity exists within a distributed virtual team, a reduction in the capabilities facilitated through traditional face-to-face communications, that is, "visual anonymity" and "immediate feedback", may be beneficial, especially in the early formation of teams and until relationships have been developed. Hrastinski (2008) suggested that synchronous communication, including face-to-face, enhances outcomes in situations with complex tasks or activities, providing support that is essential in task planning and execution.

Authors' Perspectives on Where the Exploration of These Issues Suggested Change

Literature reviewed in this chapter built on established research findings, introducing the concepts of Industry 4.0 (Brettel, et al., 2014) and unified communication and collaboration technologies. These two concepts from the **paradigm** of the Internet of Things align the concept of IoT to industrial applications and the cyber-physical integration of people with the Internet of Things, in the form of data acquisition, collaboration and communication.

Data access and dissemination information from the plethora of sensor-based connected devices will require an evolution in how information is not only searched, but also referenced and accessed. New communication **paradigms**, such as content-centric networking and information-centric networking are evolving (Aguayo-Torres, Gómez, & Poncela, 2015).

The potential application of the IoT to industrial and consumer use cases is expanding with the emergence of the cognitive Internet of Things as a new **paradigm** beyond connection (Wu, et al., 2014).

The Internet of Things is set to change both the business models and organizational structure of many commercial enterprises over the coming ten years. Krantz (2016) suggested that the change experienced, because of the Internet of Things, will exceed that of other business process change drivers, such as Six Sigma, agile development, lean manufacturing, business process re-engineering and computer telephony integration. Unlike other business and organization processes and efficiency drivers, the **paradigm** of the Internet of Things is not only associated with step improvements within the enterprise, but also represents the future commercial model for many enterprises, as they transition to the world of digital business (Kanniappan & Rajendrin, 2017). IoT not only introduces opportunities for efficiency, but also opens new markets and high margin business and service opportunities.

People are intrinsic to the value of the Internet of Things. One of the strengths espoused by the IoT **paradigm** is the significant impact that it can have on multiple aspects of the every-day life of people (Atzori, Iera, & Morabito, 2010).

The proliferation of connected mobile technologies, such as smartphones and tablets, further expand the potential access (Daurer, Molitor, Spann, & Manchanda, 2016) and utilization of data by businesses and consumers, providing a vehicle for product delivery and access to product information at any time from virtually any location. As a result of the global expansion of internet connectivity, machine-to-machine connectivity is emerging as a **paradigm** supporting communication for Internet of Things applications.

The third industrial revolution as described by scholars, such as Kuaban, Czekalski, Molua and Grochla (2019), introduced advances in digital and electronic technology that assisted in increasing automation, such as mainframe and personal computers. The Internet also evolved during this period. Following advancements reviewed in the literature, such as mobile communication and sensor technologies, and big data acquisition and management systems, the evolution of the Internet of Things is advancing a parallel industrial revolution described as Industry 4.0. Industry 4.0 advances these previously established concepts through the evolution of intelligent cyber-physical systems (Lee & Behrad Bagheri, 2015), integrating information and data acquired through IoT methods and technologies with physical industrial manufacturing systems and controls.

Industry 4.0 and CPS enhance opportunities for the implementation and exploitation of developing technologies, such as artificial intelligence, optimized by access to, and feeding data into, the data rich cognitive Internet of Things (discussed earlier). The combinatorial effect of these technological and cyber-physical advancements is driving a new **paradigm** in manufacturing, described as the "Smart Factory" (Shariat-Zadeh, et al., 2016, p. 512). Smart factories facilitate great capability to flexibly adapt manufacturing to changing requirements and complexity (Radziwon, et al., 2014). The ability to flex and adapt manufacturing processes holds potential to address challenges associated with digital disruption and enabling capability to rapidly respond and react to competitor disruption. Within the Industry 4.0 **paradigm**, specific network and information challenges are introduced to adopting companies, relating to security (Pereira, Barreto, & Amaral, 2017), data analytics (Ackermann, 2015), autonomous systems (Sharma, 2016), machine to machine communication (Nourani, 2017) and cyber-physical integration (Benias & Markopoulos, 2017).

A review of the literature also highlighted the emergence of concepts that align people with data and context (information) in the context of the Internet of Things. Scholars, such as Johnsen (2014), emphasized how people, their individual experiences and knowledge are increasingly valuable as resource within the modern economy. As a result of this shift in value, people in an industrial context are evolving into 'knowledge workers' (Bressan, 2014). The shift towards the value of people in an industrial context, extending to the knowledge and information that they hold as knowledge workers, creates new challenges for companies and for people in themselves (Tavani, 2011).

New strategies, processes and technologies are required in order to effectively manage the generation of knowledge capital as well as its sharing and re-use (Bhojaraju, 2005). To enable and support integration of people within the cyber-physical construct of the evolving cognitive Internet of Things, cyber-physical enabling technologies, such as UC&C technologies (Silic & Back, 2016), should be considered to increase the efficacy of digital integration with the knowledge management processes of knowledge acquisition, knowledge retrieval and knowledge reuse as described by Bhojaraju (2005).

SOLUTIONS AND RECOMMENDATIONS

This section of the chapter will discuss solutions and recommendations in dealing with the issues, controversies, or problems presented in the preceding section.

Solutions

Radziwon, et al. (2014) encouraged smart enterprises to work towards exploring adaptive and flexible manufacturing solutions.

Factors Identified from Survey

As solutions obtained from a research survey were based on suitable diversity in terms of participation, these suggested that UC&C technologies, deployed within the scope of the study via an Enhanced UC&C (E-UC&C) framework, can improve the communication process and outcomes of users in four key areas:

1. The digital enhancements and new capabilities delivered by the E-UC&C framework and tools increased enterprise efficiency with regard to communication in the execution of peer-to-peer and multi-user collaboration activities.
2. Users found that the intuitive central cockpit provided by the tool offered ease of use and adoption, allowing them to escalate communication through different modes of communication, leading to the establishment of new individual communication processes.

3. Findings indicated that the virtual persona and digitally transformed social presence established by end users positively impact productivity and team performance. UC&C digitally transformed technologies, established through the EUC&C framework, enhanced the ability of users to engage in communication activities, impacting their perceived levels of personal productivity.

4. Finally, the digitally transformed toolset enhanced the capability for users to participate in, host and drive highly collaborative meetings that they identify with impact on innovation.

Factors Impacting Productivity Identified from Interviews

Factors relating to productivity identified from the interview data in the study related to increased enterprise efficiency, convenience and speed, relationships and satisfaction.

Most users reported that the new toolset increased enterprise efficiency by helping to boost their participation in value generating innovation activities.

Users described the digital tools as increasing the convenience and speed of their communication processes through the UC&C client, finding access to all the features in one tool *convenient*. The convenience and speed of having one tool to access multiple channels for communication both within the office and remotely, when travelling or at home, is likely to be associated with end users' perception of productivity. The more convenient it is to do something and execute a task, the more productive users are when executing such a task.

Users also reported that digitally transformation established via UC&C technologies and systems helped to facilitate the building of new and more effective working relationships with colleagues and business partners. Relationship building was enhanced and enabled through the facilitation of virtual teams and peer engagement. Interview data suggested that digitally transformed communication using a UC&C software client provided the ability to flexibly escalate communication through different mediums of communication, facilitating the establishment of new relationships. The rich information sharing in a virtual workspace provided by UC&C also helped strengthen existing relationships.

Finally, interview data also indicated increased enterprise efficiency and user satisfaction relating to the digitally transformed communication experiences.

Factors Impacting Innovation Identified from Interviews

Factors relating to innovation identified from the interviews conducted in the study included changing work practices, collaboration, creativity and generating savings.

Users reported that the digitally transformed UC&C technologies led to changing work practices and transformed their ability to engage in collaboration. The digitally transformed UC&C experience increased the user's opportunity to engage in real-time collaboration on demand. Users further found that the multi-channel features facilitated richer virtual engagements, supporting creativity and engagement, even when users were remote from each other. Within creativity processes, the ability to engage in an ad-hoc collaboration, as needed, helped users capitalize when they had ideas, or needed problems and questions quickly addressed. Users' changing work practices thus reflected the capabilities of the UC&C technologies and digital transformed methods.

Evaluation of the interview data further suggested that enhanced communication delivered through the digital transformation of tools and technologies impacted inclusion and the engagement of users across the automotive enterprise, supporting increased collaboration. Users reported a positive experience aligned with leverage of the multi-channel communication features associated with unified communication and collaboration technologies.

Many users identified generating savings associated with leveraging the digitally transformed technologies within changing work practices, and this is likely due to users seeing the generation of innovation as an asset of the organization. Innovation leads to new products and/or product enhancement, and ultimately higher margins and revenue. If users can engage and drive more innovation through digitally transformed technologies, or increase enterprise efficiency in terms of innovation generation, the enterprise will benefit financially.

The factor related to <u>convenience and speed</u> (mentioned relating to productivity) within the UC&C toolset is likely to align with the changing work practices that users reported.

Factors Identified from Transformation and Adoption Metrics

Complementary statistical data collected through the duration of the research study and documented via an online reporting portal consisting of 130 individual reports and analysis of the quantitative system and transformation adoption metrics reports for UC&C supported a view of rapid and significant system ease of use and adoption in the form of installation and deployment to end users. These metrics were contrasted with actual usage metrics, such as call and message volume data, to support active functionality use of the new capability vs. functional deployment. Metric data presented supported observations from survey and interview processes that suggested the emergence of <u>changing work practices</u> (mentioned relating to innovation) and communication process among end-users, aligned to new features and the flexibility of a consolidated communication cockpit through UC&C. At a cyber-social level, suggestions of indicators of cultural change in communication among transformed end-users emerged. Finally, a summary of increased enterprise efficiency and generating savings, driven by technology deployment and subsequent ease of use and adoption in terms of functionality was presented and discussed, indicating financial benefits over a 16-month timeframe of more than $2 million (USD).

Using UC&C features, users reported ease of use and adoption in terms of engagement and collaboration (mentioned relating to innovation) with virtual teams. Users described the ability to engage in ad-hoc meetings with peers and virtual teams and obtaining answers to questions quickly.

UC&C technologies, which intuitively offers ease of use and adoption, combined with positive results from increased enterprise efficiency when desired versus restricted schedule were experienced, lead users to positively associate the technologies with supporting innovation and creativity (mentioned previously).

Survey and transformation and adoption metrics data indicated that the consolidated features of the UC&C software client, combined with the intuitive ease of use and adoption of the interface, resulted in many users reporting increased enterprise efficiency and establishing changing work practices (mentioned relating to innovation) with regard to communication.

A small number of users reported as having some difficulty in terms of ease of use and adoption or changing work practices (mentioned relating to innovation) to the UC&C tools; however, they still reported as identifying the tools as having the potential to impact their productivity. After being introduced to the digital tools and UC&C features, most users preferred to keep their new tools, leading to legacy reduction and elimination.

Within 60 days of use, 67% of users reported perceived increased enterprise efficiency in the execution of communication-related tasks.

Increased enterprise efficiency in terms of convenience and speed (mentioned relating to productivity) and creativity (mentioned relating to innovation) in terms of thoughts or tasks could also be achieved through the digitally transformed UC&C technologies. It is reasonable to assume that the increased enterprise efficiency due to the convenience and speed (mentioned relating to productivity) of engagement offered by the UC&C technologies was supported in terms of being able to maintain velocity and immediacy in collaboration and creativity (both mentioned relating to innovation), such as sharing and working through new ideas or rapidly developing plans and proof of concepts.

These observations contrast with legacy reduction and elimination of communication methods that required face-to-face communication to facilitate information exchange at any level beyond audio conference or basic slide sharing using external tools. Users also described positive attitudes relating to the ability to engage personally with peers and partners when working in remote locations. The new digitally transformed capabilities made it easier to include other parties in media-rich virtual meetings and facilitating their direct participation. Tracking of feature use across regions and room-to-room telepresence engagements supported the view of the increased cross-region and function engagement, inferring a high level of inclusion of people in virtual meetings outside of their local workplace locations.

Recommendations

In summary, the following solution factors were identified across the various data collection instruments used:

Factors Identified from Survey

1.   Increased enterprise efficiency
2.   Ease of use and adoption
3.   Impact on productivity
4.   Impact on innovation

Factors Impacting Productivity Identified from Interviews

1.   Increased enterprise efficiency
2.   Convenience and speed
3.   Relationships
4.   Satisfaction

Factors Impacting Innovation Identified from Interviews

1.   Changing work practices
2.   Collaboration
3.   Creativity
4.   Generating savings

Factors Identified from Transformation and Adoption Metrics

1.   Increased enterprise efficiency
2.   Ease of use and adoption
3.   Legacy reduction and elimination
4.   Indicators of cultural change in communication
5.   Generating savings

Increased enterprise efficiency was identified as one of the factors from the surveys, as well as productivity factor from the interviews and factor from the digital transformation and adoption metrics.

Ease of use and adoption was identified as one of the factors from the surveys, as well as factor from the digital transformation and adoption metrics.

Finally, generating savings was identified as one of the innovation factors from the interviews, as well factor from the digital transformation and adoption metrics.

In order to maximize the impact of unified communication and collaboration technologies on productivity and innovation in terms of promotion for the Fourth Industrial Revolution, it is therefore the recommendation of this chapter, which could result in positive change, that especially the latter three factors, but also all of those identified, be implemented.

FUTURE RESEARCH DIRECTIONS

This section of the chapter will discuss future and emerging trends and provide insight about the future of the book's theme from the perspective of the chapter focus. The viability of **paradigms**, models, implementation issues of proposed programs, etc., may be included in this section. If appropriate, future research opportunities within the domain of the topic will also be suggested.

Through Industry 4.0, business and supply chain can be further integrated into future smart cities, enabling the custom production and supply of critical products, on demand, through highly efficient automated systems and through a supply chain dynamically linked to a city's (societies') demands. By extending IoT innovation into the supply chain and production, Industry 4.0 offers new potential with regard to inefficient resource utilization and can minimize waste within the environment (Moreno & Charnley, 2016).

Future knowledge workers require skills to create and manipulate knowledge assets and data individually. It is also essential that they possess skills to facilitate collaboration and effective dissemination. The drive towards enhanced automation through IoT and Industry 4.0 will require increased development and investment in horizontal integration across the value chain (Sharma, 2016). Finally, Almada-Lobo (2016) provided further details around the Industry 4.0 revolution and the future of Manufacturing Execution Systems (MES).

CONCLUSION

This last section will provide discussion of the overall coverage of the chapter and concluding remarks. The chapter introduced developments in the conceptual Industry 4.0, a next-generation digitally integrated industrial platform as an extension of the Internet of Things (IoT) and the combinatorial effect of technologies, such as sensor data and Internet communication. The advent and development of a suite of digital technologies, commonly referred to as unified communication and collaboration technologies, were introduced through the lens of enhancing the cyber-physical integration of people with the IoT.

The background section presented the **paradigm** of Industry 4.0 as the next phase in the digitization of manufacturing. The suggestion by Brettel et al. (2014, p. 37) that IoT systems hold potential to achieve what they described as "Integrative Production" was discussed, enhancing opportunities for the creation of new real-time status, data and information. The concept of big data (De-Mauro, et al., 2014) emerged through the lens of real-time data intelligence strategies, together with the enhancement of production through IoT-enabled intelligent systems and data analytics.

The next section reviewed the emerging **paradigms** in modern enterprises, because of Industry 4.0. The drivers towards the transformation and adoption of Industry 4.0 were summarized and discussed. The **paradigm** of "Smart Factories" (Shariat-Zadeh, et al., 2016, p. 512) is emerging as a result of big data, intelligent systems, real-time integrated analytics and the cyber-physical integration of people through IoT-enabled industrial frameworks. Industry 4.0 grows the requirement for the increased integration of people, and the strategic importance and development introduction of cyber-physical systems also grows (Lee & Behrad Bagheri, 2015). The resulting integrated and IoT-enabled Industry 4.0 frameworks offer the flexibility to modularize (Thramboulidis, Vachtsevanou, & Solanos, 2018) and customize production systems and processes to the unique requirements of individual enterprises and their customers. Bartodziej (2017) highlighted that global megatrends, such as ageing, urbanization, individualism, sustainability, knowledge economy, globalization and financial markets, can influence and drive structural changes within the manufacturing industry.

Westkämper (2013) emphasized how these megatrends and drivers of structural change are influencing technological developments and new approaches to labor, resource management, production process and management, as evidenced through IoT-enabled Industry 4.0 integrated frameworks. Knowledge, inclusive of the subject matter expertise and experience held within the people associated with enterprise production, was valued through the lens of the knowledge economy. Perspectives on knowledge assets as "stocks" was discussed in the context of non-physical assets, from which new services are expected to develop and grow (Boisit, 1998, p. 3).

These concepts, combined with what Paulin (2017) described as the 'informatization' of industry, suggested a rising trend toward increased cyber-physical integration within industry as an adjunct to Industry 4.0, enabled by IoT technologies. Song et al. (2016) predicted that the resulting integration and changes will impact the work and private lives of people in society.

The following section presented concepts and developments associated with unified communication and collaboration technologies and tools. UC&C technologies entered the research narrative as a pathway for the digitization of human persona and the integration of people within the framework of the IoT. Although the knowledge worker as a concept significantly pre-dates the IoT via its conceptual introduction by Drucker in 1959 (Bressan, 2014), the concept of the knowledge worker was introduced, making its growing prominence within contemporary industry evident. The position of Johnsen (2014) on knowledge associated with learning, communication and collaboration was presented, focusing on suggestions related to the abstraction of local individual experience and economic release in the form of consumable knowledge. The converged nature of UC&C technologies was discussed (Silic & Back, 2016) and aligned to the suggestion by Kim and Wang (2011), who posited that UC&C technologies increased efficiency in communication within the enterprise through the provision of increased channels for direct communication by people across the enterprise. A scholarly review of literature on UC&C technologies was presented (Baskarada & Koronios, 2012; Mathiyalakan, 2006; McConnell, et al., 2013; Silic & Back, 2016; Ventola, 2014) and aligned with a functional description and overview of UC&C technical architecture (Mohammed, 2007; Reimer & Taing, 2009).

REFERENCES

Ackermann, M. (2015). *Reporting and Big Data. Big Data as one megatrend of industry 4.0 and the impacts on controlling*. GRIN Verlag.

Aguayo-Torres, M. C., Gómez, G., & Poncela, J. (2015). *Wired/Wireless Internet Communications: 13th International Conference, WWIC 2015, Malaga, Spain, May 25-27, Revised Selected Papers*. Malaga: Springer.

Ake, K., Clemons, J., Cubine, M., & Lilly, B. (2016). Information Technology for Manufacturing: Reducing Costs and Expanding Capabilities (Illustrated ed.). Boca Raton: CRC Press.

Almada-Lobo, F. (2016). The Industry 4.0 revolution and the future of Manufacturing Execution Systems (MES). *Journal of Innovation Management, 3*(4), 16–21. doi:10.24840/2183-0606_003.004_0003

Atzori, L., Iera, A., & Morabito, G. (2010). The Internet of Things: A survey. *Computer Networks, 54*(15), 2787–2805. doi:10.1016/j.comnet.2010.05.010

Bartodziej, C. J. (2017). *The Concept Industry 4.0: An Empirical Analysis of Technologies and Applications in Production Logistics*. Springer. doi:10.1007/978-3-658-16502-4

Baskarada, S., & Koronios, A. (2012). Exploring the Effects of Enterprise Instant Messaging Presence Information on Employee Attendance in a Distributed Workforce: An Ethnographic Study of a Large Professional Services Organization. *International Journal of e-Collaboration, 8*(3), 1–18. doi:10.4018/jec.2012070101

Benias, N., & Markopoulos, A. (2017). A review on the readiness level and cyber-security challenges in Industry 4.0. *South Eastern European Design Automation, Computer Engineering, Computer Networks and Social Media Conference (SEEDA-CECNSM)*, 1-5.

Bhojaraju, G. (2005). Knowledge Management: Why we need it for corporates. *Malaysian Journal of Library and Information Science, 10*(2), 37–50.

Bi, Z., Xu, L. D., & Wang, C. (2014). Internet of Things for enterprise systems of modern manufacturing. *IEEE Transactions on Industrial Informatics*, 1537–1546.

Boisit, M. (1998). *Knowledge Assets: Securing Competitive Advantage in the Information Economy*. OUP Oxford.

Bolton, A., Goosen, L., & Kritzinger, E. (2016). Enterprise Digitization Enablement Through Unified Communication and Collaboration. In *Proceedings of the Annual Conference of the South African Institute of Computer Scientists and Information Technologists*. Johannesburg: ACM. 10.1145/2987491.2987516

Bolton, A., Goosen, L., & Kritzinger, E. (2020b). Unified Communication Technologies at a Global Automotive Organization. In D. B. Khosrow-Pour (Ed.), *Encyclopedia of Organizational Knowledge, Administration, and Technologies*. IGI Global Hershey, PA, USA: . doi:10.4018/978-1-7998-3473-1

Bolton, T., Goosen, L., & Kritzinger, E. (2020a, March 8). Security Aspects of an Empirical Study into the Impact of Digital Transformation via Unified Communication and Collaboration Technologies on the Productivity and Innovation of a Global Automotive Enterprise. Communications in Computer and Information Science, 1166, 99-113. doi:10.1007/978-3-030-43276-8_8

Bressan, B. (2014). From Physics to Daily Life: Applications in Informatics, Energy, and Environment (Illustrated ed.). Hoboken: John Wiley & Sons.

Brettel, M., Friederichsen, N., Keller, M., & Rosenberg, M. (2014). How Virtualization, Decentralization and Network Building Change the Manufacturing Landscape: An Industry 4.0 Perspective. *World Academy of Science. Engineering and Technology International Journal of Information and Communication Engineering, 8*(1), 37–44.

Brush, K. (2012). *The Power of One: You're the Boss.* Scotts Valley: CreateSpace Independent Publishing Platform.

Carte, T., & Chidambaram, L. (2004). A Capabilities-Based Theory of Technology Deployment in Diverse Teams: Leapfrogging the Pitfalls of Diversity and Leveraging Its Potential with Collaborative Technology. *Journal of the Association for Information Systems, 5*(11-12), 448–471. doi:10.17705/1jais.00060

Cascio, W. (2000). Managing a virtual workplace. *The Academy of Management Executive, 14*(3), 81–90. doi:10.5465/ame.2000.4468068

Christiansen, H.-M. (2007). Meeting the Challenge of Communication in offshore software development. In B. Meyer, & M. Joseph (Eds.), *International Conference on Software Engineering Approaches for Offshore and Outsourced Development* (pp. 19-26). Berlin: Springer. 10.1007/978-3-540-75542-5_2

Daurer, S., Molitor, D., Spann, M., & Manchanda, P. (2016). *Consumer Search Behavior on the Mobile Internet: An Empirical Analysis.* Michigan Ross School of Business.

De-Mauro, A., Greco, M., & Grimaldi, M. (2014). What is big data? A consensual definition and a review of key research topics. *AIP Conference Proceedings, 1644*(1), 97–104.

Dekker, D., & Rutte, C. (2007). Effective Versus Ineffective Communication Behaviours in Virtual Teams. In *Proceedings of the 40th IEEE Hawaii International Conference on System Sciences* (p. 41). Waikoloa: IEEE.

Errasti, A. (2013). *Global Production Networks: Operations Design and Management* (2nd ed.). CRC Press.

Gilchrist, A. (2016). *Industry 4.0: The Industrial Internet of Things.* Apress. doi:10.1007/978-1-4842-2047-4

Hrastinski, S. (2008). The potential of synchronous communication to enhance participation in online discussions: A case study of two e-learning courses. *Information & Management, 45*(7), 499–506. doi:10.1016/j.im.2008.07.005

Johnsen, H. C. (2014). *The new natural resource: Knowledge development, society and economics.* Ashgate Publishing, Ltd.

Kanniappan, J., & Rajendrin, B. (2017). Privacy and the Internet of Things. In I. Lee (Ed.), *The Internet of Things in the Modern Business Environment* (pp. 94–106). IGI Global. doi:10.4018/978-1-5225-2104-4.ch005

Katz, R., & Koutroumpis, P. (2012, May 29). *Measuring Socio-Economic Digitization: A Paradigm Shift.* Retrieved October 24, 2016, from https://ssrn.com/abstract=2070035

Kim, K., & Wang, C. (2011). Enterprise VOIP in Fixed Mobile Converged Networks. In L. Weisi, D. Tao, J. Kacprzyk, Z. Li, E. Izquierdo, & H. Wang (Eds.), *Multimedia Analysis, Processing and Communications. Studies in Computational Intelligence* (Vol. 346, pp. 585–621). Springer. doi:10.1007/978-3-642-19551-8_22

Kranz, M. (2016). *Building the Internet of Things: Implement new Business Models, Disrupt Competitors, Transform Your Industry.* John Wiley & Sons.

Kryvinska, N., Auer, L., & Strauss, C. (2009). The Place and Value of SOA in Building 2.0-Generation Enterprise Unified vs. Ubiquitous Communication and Collaboration Platform. In *The Third IEEE International Conference on Mobile Ubiquitous Computing Systems, Services and Technologies (UBICOMM 2009).* 1, pp. 305-310. Sliema, Malta: IEEE. 10.1109/UBICOMM.2009.52

Kuaban, G. S., Czekalski, P., Molua, E. L., & Grochla, K. (2019, June). An Architectural Framework Proposal for IoT Driven Agriculture. In *International Conference on Computer Networks* (pp. 18-33). Cham: Springer. 10.1007/978-3-030-21952-9_2

Lanius, R., & McCurdy, H. (2008). *Robots in Space: Technology, Evolution, and Interplanetary Travel.* Baltimore: Johns Hopkins University Press.

Lee, J., & Behrad Bagheri, H.-A. K. (2015). A cyber-physical systems architecture for industry 4.0-based manufacturing systems. *Manufacturing Letters, 1*(3), 18-23.

Manu, A. (2015). *Value Creation and the Internet of Things.* Gower.

Mathiyalakan, S. (2006). VOIP Adoption: Issues & Concerns. *Communications of the IMMA, 6*(2), 19–24.

Matthews, J. (2013). *Encyclopedia of Environmental Change* (Vol. 1). Sage.

McConnell, T., Parker, J., Eberhardt, J., Koehler, M., & Lunderberg, M. (2013). Virtual professional learning communities: Teachers' perceptions of virtual versus face-to-face professional development. *Journal of Science Education and Technology, 22*(3), 267–277. doi:10.100710956-012-9391-y

Mohammed, A. (2007). Work together any place, any time. *Computer Weekly*, 38–40.

Moreno, M., & Charnley, F. (2016). Can Re-distributed Manufacturing and Digital Intelligence Enable a Regenerative Economy? An Integrative Literature Review. In R. Setchi, R. Howlett, Y. Liu, & P. Theobald (Eds.), *Sustainable Design and Manufacturing 2016* (pp. 563–577). Springer. doi:10.1007/978-3-319-32098-4_48

Nourani, C. F. (2017). *Ecosystems and Technology: Idea Generation and Content Model Processing: Innovation Management and Computing*. CRC Press.

Paganetto, L., & Scandizzo, P. (2016). Industrial Policy, Investment and Green Growth. In L. Paganetto (Ed.), *Stagnation Versus Growth in Europe: Capitalism in the 21st Century* (pp. 87–101). Springer.

Paulin, A. (2017). Data Traffic Forecast in Health 4.0. In C. Thuemmler & C. Bai (Eds.), *Health 4.0: How Virtualization and Big Data are Revolutionizing Healthcare* (pp. 39–52). Springer. doi:10.1007/978-3-319-47617-9_3

Pereira, T., Barreto, L., & Amaral, A. (2017). Network and information security challenges within Industry 4.0 paradigm. *Procedia Manufacturing*, *13*, 1253–1260. doi:10.1016/j.promfg.2017.09.047

Porcaro, G. (2016). Internet, Policy and Politics in the Era of the Industrial. In Porcaro, J. Klewes, D. Popp, & M. Rost-Hein (Eds.), Out-thinking Organizational Communications: The Impact of Digital Transformation (pp. 51-61). New York: Springer.

Radziwon, A., Bilberg, A., Bogers, M., & Madsen, E. (2014). The smart factory: Exploring adaptive and flexible manufacturing solutions. *Procedia Engineering*, *69*, 1184–1190. doi:10.1016/j.proeng.2014.03.108

Reimer, K., & Taing, S. (2009). Unified Communications. *Business & Information Systems Engineering*, *1*(4), 326–330. doi:10.100712599-009-0062-3

Salkin, C., Oner, M., Unstundag, A., & Cevikcan, E. (2018). A Conceptual Framework for Industry 4.0. In A. Ustundag & E. Cevikcan (Eds.), *Industry 4.0: Managing The Digital Transformation* (pp. 3–22). Springer. doi:10.1007/978-3-319-57870-5_1

Schmidt, R., Mohrin, M., Harting, R.-C., Reichstein, C., Neumaier, P., & Jozinovic, P. (2015). Industry 4.0 Potentials for Creating Smart Products: Empirical Research Results. In W. Abramowicz (Ed.), *Business Information Systems: 18th International Conference, BIS 2015, Poznań, Poland, June 24-26, 2015, Proceedings* (pp. 16-25). New York: Springer. 10.1007/978-3-319-19027-3_2

Schneider, F., & Friesinger, G. (2011). The digital reformulation of the relationship of mind and matter. In G. Friesingerl, J. Grenzfurthner, & T. Ballhausen (Eds.), *Mind and Matter: Comparative Approaches towards Complexity* (p. 20). Transaction Publishers. doi:10.14361/transcript.9783839418000.11

Shariat-Zadeh, N., Lundholm, T., Lindberg, L., & Franzén-Sivard, G. (2016). Integration of digital factory with smart factory based on Internet of Things. *26th CIRP Design Conference, 50*, 512-517.

Sharma, K. (2016). *Overview of Industrial Process Automation* (2nd ed.). Elsevier.

Silic, M., & Back, A. (2016). Factors driving unified communications and collaboration adoption and use in organizations. *Measuring Business Excellence, 20*(1), 21–40. doi:10.1108/MBE-05-2015-0026

Silic, M., Back, A., & Sammer, T. (2014). Employee Acceptance and Use of Unified Communications and Collaboration in a Cross Cultural Environment. *International Journal of e-Collaboration, 10*(2), 1–19. doi:10.4018/ijec.2014040101

Song, H., Rawat, D., Jeschke, S., & Brecher, C. (2016). *Cyber-physical Systems: Foundations, Principles and Applications*. Morgan Kaufmann.

Tavani, H. T. (2011). *Ethics and Technology: Controversies, Questions, and Strategies for Ethical Computing*. John Wiley & Son.

The-Digital-Enlightment-Forum. (2016). *Security for the Digital World Within an Ethical Framework*. IOS Press.

Thramboulidis, K., Vachtsevanou, D. C., & Solanos, A. (2018). *Cyber-Physical Microservices: An IoT-based Framework for Manufacturing Systems*. arXiv preprint arXiv:1801.10340

Tripathi, K. (2015). Optimizing Operational and Migration Cost in Cloud Paradigm (OOMCCP). In P. Sharma, P. Banerjee, J.-P. Dudeja, P. Singh, & R. K. Brajpuriya (Eds.), *Making Innovations Happen* (p. 89). Allied Publishers.

Tylor, E. B. (1871). Primitive Culture: Researches Into the Development of Mythology, Philosophy, Religion, Art, and Custom (Vol. 1). London: John Murray.

Ventola, L. (2014). Mobile devices and apps for health care professionals: Uses and benefits. *P&T, 39*(5), 356–364. PMID:24883008

Vestager, M. (2016). *Big Data and Competition - European Data Commisioner Speech to EDPS-BEUC Conference, 29 September 2016.* Brussels: European Commission. Retrieved Jan 10th, 2017, from https://ec.europa.eu/commission/2014-2019/vestager/announcements/big-data-and-competition_en

Vollenweider, M. (2016). *Mind+Machine: A Decision Model for Optimizing and Implementing Analytics.* John Wiley & Sons.

Westkämper, E. (2013). *Towards the Re-Industrialization of Europe: A Concept for Manufacturing for 2030.* Springer Science & Business Media.

Wieser, M. (1991). The computer for the 21st century. *Scientific American, 265*(3), 94–104. doi:10.1038cientificamerican0991-94 PMID:1675486

Wu, Q., Ding, G., Xu, Y., Feng, S., Du, Z., Wang, J., & Long, K. (2014). Cognitive internet of things: A new paradigm beyond connection. *IEEE Internet of Things Journal, 1*(2), 129–143. doi:10.1109/JIOT.2014.2311513

Zhang, Y., Min, Q., & Wu, L. (2008). GVTs Communication Management: A Conceptual Model. *IEEE Service Operations and Logistics and Informatics, 1,* 583–587.

Zhang, Y., & Tao, F. (2016). *Optimization of Manufacturing Systems Using the Internet of Things.* Elsevier.

KEY TERMS AND DEFINITIONS

Digital Transformation: Although digital transformation has existed in the lexicon of human thought for over fifty years and propelled humanity towards new horizons in terms of possibilities, the potential for digital transformation to enhance communication and collaboration in society and across enterprises is beginning to be realized.

Fourth Industrial Revolution: Industry 4.0 is considered to be the Fourth Industrial Revolution (4IR) and promises to impact productivity and innovation in enterprise services, as well as manufacturing, through the introduction of integrated data exchange and intelligent automation.

Global Automotive Enterprise: The context of a global automotive original equipment manufacturer, facing challenges as it digitally transforms its systems, services and work practices, is likely to be familiar to many large global enterprises.

Impact: One of the central issues addressed in this chapter is the relationship between the transformation of communication and collaboration through digital methods and technologies and the resulting impact within a global automotive enterprise on people's productivity and their innovation.

Innovation: Enterprises drive combinatorial innovation through technology convergence and standardization.

Productivity: Productivity improvement can be introduced rapidly through combinatorial digital transformation towards innovation.

Unified Communications and Collaboration Technologies: The term 'Unified Communications and Collaboration Technologies' represents a managed communications and collaboration system delivered via a converged platform of telecommunications and information technologies.

Chapter 3
Manufacturing Education for Society 5.0:
Reframing Engineering and Design

Jennifer Loy
ⓘ https://orcid.org/0000-0001-7153-0699
Deakin University, Australia

ABSTRACT

The last 20 years have brought significant developments to digital fabrication technology, known as additive manufacturing (3D printing), and it has finally started to shed its prototyping mantel in favor of an industrial one. Yet its innovations are in danger of being subsumed into existing commercial practices, as society arguably continues to underestimate its ability, in conjunction with data collection, analysis, and communication tools, to disrupt current systems and enable a more equitable distribution of manufacturing wealth, capability, and capacity. This chapter highlights the potential of emerging industrial technologies to support a shift towards a more human-centered, responsible society where social and environmental problems are addressed through systems that maximises cyberspace and physical space integration, through the reframing of higher education engineering curriculum and pedagogy for manufacturing in Society 5.0.

DOI: 10.4018/978-1-7998-4882-0.ch003

INTRODUCTION

In Japan, the political Cabinet's 'Society 5.0' initiative has sought to create the basis for a more sustainable society for human well-being and security in an increasingly digital era, through the use of socially conscious, ethical cyber-physical systems (Yato, 2019, p.1). Keidanren (the Japanese Business Federation) responded positively to this, with an intent to proactively deliver on the United Nations' Sustainable Development Goals intended to "end poverty, protect the planet, and ensure prosperity for all through the creation of Society 5.0" through collaborative ecosystem activities (Shiroishi, Uchiyama, & Suzuki, 2019, p.1). Shiroishi et al. (2019) described how the rise in computing power over the last twenty years has contributed to professed advances in business and society, yet the world is facing a growing economic disparity, global warming, the depletion of natural resources and an increased threat of terrorism. They argue that the situation is precarious, not least because of the rising complexity and uncertainty decision makers are having to face, with globalisation and the rapid development of complex digital technologies. ICT is perceived as essential to gain new knowledge in Japan, but the Society 5.0 initiative promotes its development alongside new value systems where there are greater connections between 'people and things' and also between the 'real and cyber'. This is seen as necessary to "effectively and efficiently resolve issues in society, create better lives for its people, and sustain healthy economic growth" (Shiroishi et al., 2019, p.1). However, Shiroshi et al. (2019) also point out that to do this, stakeholders at multiple levels will need to commit to a very different, shared vision of the future in order to realise the values of Society 5.0 for digitisation.

In most countries, the last few years have seen a shift in rhetoric in relation to automation, artificial intelligence and digital communication. Recent lessons, such as in the Cambridge Analytica / Facebook data harvesting example and its impact on politics, have given pause to the blinkered competitive development of digital technology innovations without thought to the unexpected consequences for societies that could arise. For manufacturing, correlations between the rise in greenhouse gas emissions and the accelerating effects of climate change (Morrison, 2019, p.2) continue. There is also an inequity in pay and conditions for workers around the world, not only seen in factory examples, but also in distribution centers, including Amazon (Sainato, 2019). In addition, there are risks to communities where there are dependencies on single employers or industries, highlighted by the bankruptcy of Detroit City following the loss of Ford Automotive (Leduff, 2014). These form part of the problematic impacts on the environment and communities highlighted recently by supply chain and life cycle assessment practices (e.g. Vezzoli, & Mansini 2008). Resource depletion, and the long-term damage to the environment and communities in some resource removal and resource production practices (e.g.

palm oil production displacing communities and mining destabilising land) are a concern. In addition, the pollution and waste generated through traditional twentieth century manufacturing practices, contribute to the conclusion that manufacturing should maximize opportunities provided by digitisation in order to substantially dematerialize product service systems. They should also focus on maximising the value of existing resources, and commit to the circular economy, supporting social, as well as environmental, sustainability.

Engineering and industrial design are the lead disciplines for the development of future practices in manufacturing. Mechanical engineering in particular is instrumental in feeding the development of technology and industrial practices that drive the expansion of manufacturing and the direction it takes in its adoption of digital technology. Robotics and electrical and electronics are also increasing their influence with the expansion of tracking technology in manufacturing in Industry 4.0 (Schwab, 2017). For the last decade, the direction for the adoption of digital technology has been a fairly relentless drive towards eliminating people out of production systems. As Cameron (2017, p.2) observes with regards to the rise in automation: "We're at the outset of a great debate. At one level, it's simple. It's about whether we need to worry that robots will take our jobs, or whether we don't."

Yet an awareness of the social and environmental problems that an unexamined, independent view of the adoption of digitalisation purely for narrow commercial benefits for shareholders, is beginning to emerge. This then leads to questions not only about the monitoring and legislation of manufacturing practices for environmental protection purposes, but also about social engineering, including urban planning, and the developing of sustainable product production systems for the benefit of society as a whole, rather than individual companies. For engineers, understanding these implications and contemporary aspirations for society 5.0 would involve updating their curriculums to look outside the usual domains of engineers. They need a broader view of the impact of their decision making, both individually and as a profession.

These developments underline the fact that technological design choices are in effect social choices with significant political ramifications and with distinct ethical valances....They make clear that in designing and developing technical objects and systems, we are doing more than merely creating new tools to be put at our disposal; we are affecting the social fabric, and indeed our own individual agency, in morally relevant ways. There is thus a growing discomfort on the part of some commentators, both journalists and academics, with the traditional understanding of engineering as a value-free domain of purely practical concerns. (Morrison, 2019, p.2)

Whilst this is a different concept for engineering education, there have been similar developments in the ontology of industrial and product design disciplines over the last forty years that could serve as a model for changing philosophy and practices. This would help inform the development of engineering education for a more sustainable, digital era. This chapter draws on the experiences in design and the development of ontology and ethics in response to changes to aspirations for society in the twenty-first century. It responds to the contemporary challenges being faced worldwide, to provide direction for new thinking on manufacturing education and planning for society 5.0.

BACKGROUND

Industry 4.0 began in German manufacturing, as a way of harnessing digital monitoring tools during production to maximize efficiencies and improve quality control. However, the rapid expansion in the capabilities and capacity of sensors, communication and data analysis tools, has led to its use beyond the factory, and out into distribution systems and the monitoring of products in use. This allows a company to better understand the lifecycle of its products, and gauge demand, maintenance needs and replacement requirements. Meanwhile, whilst subtractive manufacturing has been the mainstay of making for tools and products for traditional mass production over the last century, additive manufacturing is emerging as a key tool in the development of new, distributed production systems and agile products for a digital era. Yet digital fabrication is only part of a suite of digital tools that are rapidly changing the means by which products can be designed, made, distributed, used and recycled. Communication tools have had a major impact on interactions between business and their customers across industry sectors over the last twenty years, but it is the combination of evolving communication tools and advances in digital fabrication that have the potential to disrupt conventional patterns of production, distribution and consumption.

The benefits to society of a rethink of production and consumption in this digital era, include the opportunity to redesign for greater environmental and socio-cultural sustainability, as well as a more equitable economic sustainability across different communities. The challenges in a digital era are now less about the means as they are about the collective will and ability to redirect societal values and think long term, and for the benefit of humanity, rather than the profit of the few. Developments in digital technology have the potential to disrupt the control of making and distribution, and to enable a move towards dematerialisation for communities, aligned with current sustainability strategies (Ryan, 2004). It is possible step back from current practice to evaluate whether a reframing of product manufacture and resource consumption could be possible with developments in digital technology. However, there are significant barriers for the adoption of ambitious or radical digital production systems for social change that are embedded in current education curriculum and commercial practices. In addition, the rapid development of a range of digital technologies, including digital fabrication technologies, could, in itself, create confusion and mistrust in their adoption in a social development agenda. Society has an opportunity to take greater control of production and consumption in a digital era, through distributed manufacturing and digital communication tools, but equally existing structures and attitudes in society stand in the way of such a move. There is a need for change with the growing environmental imperative, and in response to current theories that support aspirations for a fairer society in the twenty-first century, such as Society 5.0. Strategies need to be developed in the education of a future workforce equipped to exploit the potential of digital manufacturing and digital monitoring and communication tools for a more equitable, sustainable society.

Technical Knowledge

For engineers and industrial / product designers at this time, digital manufacturing technologies, known as additive manufacturing (AM) or commonly as 3D printing (3DP), are creating two problems in the development of the profession. The first is that where there was a large body of documented knowledge on conventional manufacturing technology, built up incrementally since the industrial revolution, and passed on to students by experienced academics and practitioners, the emerging manufacturing technologies and their associated digital technologies, do not have a similar documented body of agreed knowledge. In addition, the knowledge that is there, does not build naturally on the established criteria laid out in the use of traditional manufacturing technology. There is a lack of existing industry expertize, in both academia and professional practice, and to add to the complications, the technologies are wide in scope. The second is that the myriad of additive manufacturing technologies (including extrusion based, resin based and powder based) developed over the last two decades not only arrive with their own constrains and opportunities, they also enable very different business operations (Diegel, Nordin, & Motte, 2019). Not only do engineers and designers have to understand the manufacturing techniques technically, in order to exploit their potential, they have to understand them from a business innovation perspective as disruptive technologies (Loy, 2015).

The last decade has seen significant developments in engineering additive manufacturing technology. Although research into the early technologies began thirty years ago, the last decade has seen them advances from essentially prototyping technologies to those suitable for end-use manufacturing. In particular, the additive manufacturing of metal parts has advanced considerably, with companies producing metal additive manufacturing machines aimed at production-scale output, mimicking traditional mass production, rather than research. New types of additive manufacturing have been invented, such as an extrusion-based metal system. In the meantime, companies have developed production-focused practices, for example in electron beam melting (EBM) additive manufacturing. As the range of technologies included in the term additive manufacturing has expanded, additive manufacturing research generally has shifted focus. From the invention of new technologies, research now tends to be focused on the adoption of the technologies in industry. As such, the last few years has seen an emphasis on research into quality control systems. These include the monitoring and adapting of behaviors within the actual build chamber itself. Melt-pool analysis in metal printing, for example, can be used to inform adjustments made to lasers during a 3D print, to ensure the best quality outcome. The topology optimization of parts and the development of new structures, particularly lattice structures have been studied, and composite 3D printing explored in more depth (Pei, Monzon, & Bernard, 2018). Essentially, the study of additive manufacturing in engineering research and education until now, has been focussed on developing new technologies, and replicating parts that are built using traditional manufacturing technologies, with the aim of matching the quality and reliability of the outputs.

However, the current research trend now, as highlighted at one of the major additive manufacturing industry events, FormNext, in 2019 (Le Merlus, 2019), is a shift from engineering developments to business ones to improve the integration of the technology in industry. In particular, as illustrated by the results of the work at GE Additive, the importance of the impact of additive manufacturing on supply chain operations in increasing the financial viability of the technology. Currently, however, there is little evidence of in-depth transition research in this field, where longitudinal and cross-sectional multi-layer research considers the perspective of all stakeholders. Currently the focus is on reducing costs, rather than the potential impacts of this on workers, the environment or future practices and workforce development. Whilst the majority of money spent in the industry remains on machinery and not product (Wohlers, 2019), arguably, the investments made in equipment suggest that there will be a growth in product manufacture using additive manufacturing the industry in the near future.

MANUFACTURING EDUCATION IN CONTEXT

Manufacturing has its roots in mechanical engineering, and is still serviced predominantly by mechanical engineering disciplines. In recent years, however, digital systems disciplines have contributed to developments in advanced manufacturing, and automation and the use of monitoring sensors have been integrated into practice. Social sciences have contributed to discussions on the impact of manufacturing systems, the division of labor, the control of the means of production, and the impact of sourcing on society and the environment. However, there is a lack of evidence of the integration of social sciences and engineering in developing manufacturing organisation and practices and a workforce for the future. In his book, Design Meets Disability (2009), Pullin laments the lacks of humanities representation in teams developing assistive technologies, highlighting that where fashion designers and product designers were included, there were significant differences in the usability of the outcome. Whilst engineers are not social scientists, they are not exempt from concerns beyond the functionality of their outputs. Accreditation for engineering programs in the US, for example, require that graduates demonstrate an ability to: "design a system, component, or process to meet desired needs within realistic constraints such as economic, environmental, social, political, ethical, health and safety" (ABET, 2015, p.1). This requires that engineers work outside the immediate mechanical requirements of the products and systems they are working on. Further, accreditation of programs also requires that engineers have a sound knowledge of contemporary issues and the "broad education necessary to understand the impact of engineering solutions in a global, economic, environmental, and societal context" (ABET, 2015, p.1).

Manufacturing in the twenty-first century can, and arguably should, fundamentally be changed for the benefit of society and the environment in a digitally connected world. Developments over the last ten years in additive manufacturing and associated digital technologies, such as data collection and analysis and communication, have created a role for the technology as a disruptor for the sector. The technology provides a potential to enable greater inclusivity and economic independence and broad benefits to society through the adoption of product service systems. The technology could support a commitment to distributed manufacturing, reversing the trends of industry since the industrial revolution, in response to global challenges. However, this would require new curriculum in manufacturing education to embed ethical and moral learning in engineering and product design study programs aligned to theoretical frameworks based on strategies such as Society 5.0. Learning to work with digital technologies in the twenty-first century for the benefit of society and new working paradigms requires new ways of learning, and new educational drivers, new priorities. In particular, it requires the breakdown of disciplinary silos. This does not negate the value of in-depth knowledge, but it does suggest the new forms of in-depth knowledge, beyond the accepted T-shaped profile, towards graduate that are socio-technically literate:

The goal of education for global leadership for social design may have to progress from the T-shaped skills profile (i.e., being specialized in one discipline and having the capability to collaborate with other disciplines) to the p-profile. Students for leadership in global designs must be qualified in a social and an engineering/natural science and literate and capable to know, relate, and govern different disciplines, cultures, or systems which have to be included in the sustainable transitioning of cultural and socio-technological systems. (Scholz, Yarime, & Shiroyama, 2018, p.1)

The challenges as ever in this situation is creating those lead educators that will build the transdisciplinary, sociotechnical knowledge foundations that can be built on. However, the adoption of a more fluid, lifelong learning approach in place of conventional educational practices could help create a new generation of flexible learners. This issue is one of old power versus new power. As discussed by Heimans and Timms (2018), this is the clash of old hierarchical systems and ideas, and new ones. Gore (2013) states the changes for society this century will not be in degrees of difference, but in kind, meaning that the changes currently being experienced in society from the rise of digital capabilities, will not create incremental change, but disruptive change. Similarly, Seldon and Abidoye (2018), in their book on the potential infantilization of humanity through artificial intelligence, questions the ability of humanity to comprehend the extent of current changes brought about by digital technology, and to respond appropriately for the benefit of society. Planning for alternative futures in a digital era should be based on the potential benefits to individuals and to societies. Understanding the potential benefits and problems in an unknown future is arguably more difficult at this time than at any other time in history because of the maturing of the paradigm shifting digital technology developed over the last decades, and the impact that change can make in a digitally connected world. Becker (2012, p.30) highlights strategies in the design discipline's approach: "Recent pairings of ethics and sustainability are evident in the formulation of designer-focused and populated groups such as The Designer's Accord[1] or The Living Principles[2], with its broader mission of 'creative action for collective good'."

Engineering Ethics Education

There is little disagreement that many disciplines are witnessing an 'ethical' turn. The raised awareness of environmental degradation and climate change, inequalities in wealth distribution and persisting conflict around the world have caused individuals who are practitioners in different disciplines to question their ethical obligations, not merely to those close to them, but to global 'Others' whom they cannot fully define. (Loo, 2012, p.10)

In utopian visions of society, such as described by (Bregman, 2017), it is possible to propose societies operated for the good of humanity as a whole, the protection of the environment, and built on an equitable economic model. In the present, it is more difficult. However, an important step in considering changing an existing paradigm in manufacturing is ensuring that ethical and moral education are integral to engineering and design disciplines, and that this is embedded in manufacturing education. Hess and Fore (2018, p.583) observed that "Promoting the ethical formulation of engineering students through the cultivation of their discipline-specific knowledge, sensitivity, imagination and reasoning skills has become a goal for many engineering education programs throughout the United States."

Since early in the twentieth century, the engineering profession has developed its own requirements for ethical practice from its practitioners (Morrison, 2019). This requirement was heightened after the first world war in response to concerns over the development of engineering outcomes that could be detrimental to humanity.

It was in the years following World War II that "engineering ethics" began to emerge as a distinct field of research and teaching in US colleges and universities...the first formal trans-disciplinary engineering ethics code was drawn up in the United States in 1947 by the Engineer's Council for Professional Development (ECPD), which called on engineers to "interest [themselves] in public welfare." (Morrison, 2019, p.5)

In the 1980s, disasters such as the ill-fated Apollo Challenger, where a rubber O-ring seal on the rocket booster failed, releasing gas, damaging the fuel tank (Wall, 2016) were the topics used in ethical education. The dilemmas presented to the students reflected an individualistic understanding of ethical decision-making and a very pragmatic approach to professional responsibilities with a focus on public safety (Conlan, & Zandvoort, 2011). As Morrison (2019, p.5) concluded, the intent was to ensure the student was cognisant of their "rights of conscientious refusal and professional dissent from management" in the judgement of acceptable risk. In the Apollo example, communication skills and concern over communication protocols in place were cited as preventing the problems identified by engineers being communicated effectively to the launch team. The problem with these crisis-based examples was that it tended to present a dilemma both reductive and decontextualized. The focus was on teaching professional codes of conduct, and that the whistle-blower role could be used to alert external authorities to unsafe practices.

Over the last decade, research on ethics teaching in engineering suggested that this educational approach was insufficient. There has been growing interest in expanding the ethical responsibilities and understanding of graduates to a broader evaluation of the context in which they are working, and the impact of engineering as a profession. Aligned with criteria set by engineering educational standards organisations, such as ABET, researchers now recommend updated learning activities in engineering education ensuring a broader understanding of ethics is taught, using deeper learning strategies. Seldon and Abodoye (2018), in their book *The Fourth*

Education Revolution, argue for a revision of educational intent in response to the potential impact of digital technology on society, particularly in relation to artificial intelligence. This has been driven by sustainability studies, where the impact of individual engineering companies on both the environment and communities, can no longer be considered independently, but as a contributor to a larger system. This has led to the introduction of sustainability studies in engineering programs, however, the integration of social sciences within these courses is limited where engineers are the academics. The focus will naturally tend to be on the impact of material sourcing, and the pollutants and waste expelled during manufacturing, and the reclamation and disposal of parts, liquids and materials. Recently, this has been called into question, as the larger ethical questions arising from sustaining current manufacturing practices for society, the political and sociocultural impacts of engineering operations and the collective impact of operations on the environment globally are being reassessed through the lens of twenty-first century values. Walling (2015) highlights a rise in scholarly interest in ethics in science and engineering and Colby and Sullivan (2008) and Morrison (2019), emphasize broader issues as integral to engineering education. Mirroring developments in Science and Technology Studies (STS) theory, engineering ethics research is emerging as the study of how engineering practice and education should be situated in social contexts. According to Zelenko and Felton (2012, p.3): "The practice of ethics as a mode of being shaped by socially determined attitudes and beliefs is positioned beyond any single disciplinary perspective". As Walling (2015, p.1637) states, "Engineering ethics education needs to extend beyond the narrow range of human action associated with the technical work of the engineer and explore ways to draw on broader lifeworld experience to enrich professional practice and identity."

Yet, whilst universities state that they favor this approach, a study of 18 undergraduate programs in the US (Colby, & Sullivan 2008) found that whilst faculty had clear learning outcomes relating to the professional code of ethics, learning outcomes for those relating to the wider context of aspirations for contemporary society in the twenty-first century, or relating to the digital revolution were not defined. In contrast, over the last forty years industrial and product design disciplines have faced considerable changes in their terms of reference. The scope and content of design education has changed considerably, and much of the change it has faced can relate to the current experiences that engineering as a discipline are currently facing. Zelenko and Felton (2012, p.3) explain that design has undergone "a reconceptualization triggered by debates about its potential to instigate meaningful social, cultural and environmental change."

Product design for manufacturing developed into a distinct discipline in response to the need for manufacturers to have a new form of practitioner who could identify trends, work with both function and aesthetics and translate a design into its component parts, detailed suitable for manufacturing in a factory setting (e.g. Forty, 1986). The designers focussed narrowly on the product itself, with commercial drivers and responsibility to the employer paramount. In the 1990s a movement that highlighted the sustainability issues caused by the way products were designed, manufactured, distributed, used and disposed of, began to make an impact on educational practice. Students were taught life cycle analysis for the sourcing of product materials, and the manufacture and recycling of components. In the early 2000s, conventional product design was usurped by a shift towards a design thinking approach, which favored design as a business strategy (Brown, 2009). This rapidly expanded over the next ten years, until it was subsumed into business teaching. Traditional product design began to lean towards engineering, at a time when engineering had started to look towards design to add an element of creativity into engineering education for greater innovation in engineering practice. Yet, design research overall shifted further towards the role of the designer for the benefit of society and the environment, with an educational overview taught to students that emphasized the emerging role of designers as shaping the future environment for the benefit of humanity and the environment. This was taught as an extension of philosophy and ethics, responding to current sustainability imperatives for both the environment and society. Designer maker John Makepeace (Myerson, & Makepeace, 1995) described good design as the embodiment of the knowledge, values and aspirations of society at a particular point in time. Based on the content of design exhibitions, such as The Future is here at the V&A, the need for designers to understand the cross-disciplinary, current context, contemporary knowledge and think about the needs and aspirations of society is essential for critical success. According to Zelenko and Felton (2012, p.3), "Taking a cross-disciplinary approach to ethics requires a recognition of the plurality of opinions, practices and socio-cultural perspectives and the opportunity to open established value systems to questioning and renegotiation."

These ambitions are aligned with the ABET list of criteria for accreditation (2015), with research into engineering for the twenty-first century underlining the ethical responsibilities of engineers to society at large. Learning from the pathway of design over last twenty years, there is an argument that where there is a drive to greater inclusivity, and social and environmental responsibility, engineering as a discipline needs to educate its students in looking beyond the functionality of the product itself, and their ethical responsibilities, towards the environmental impact of its manufacturing. The discipline needs to look towards a broader humanities approach to consider the ethical consequences of the operations and behaviors enforced by the systems they are create. The profession needs to rethink the consequences of innovation enabled by emerging digital technologies for society and the environment, beyond the individual product or outcomes for a company or even industry sector. Pinker (2018, p.414) argues "Much of what we call wisdom consists of balancing the conflicting desires within ourselves, and much of what we call morality and politics consists in balancing the conflicting desires among people." Learning from the experiences of design, engineering in a digital age cannot be divorced from its consequences. This suggests that a considerable drive in the disciplines needs to be in incorporating designers and social scientists into teams, and programs need to expand their ethical and moral education to include their integration.

Disruptive

National policies, regional strategies, and long accepted economic theories are now irrelevant to the new realities of our new hyper-connected, tightly integrated, highly interactive, and technologically revolutionized economy.... the global economy is being transformed by changes far greater in speed and scale than any in human history." (Gore, 2013, p.4).

Al Gore (2013) describes the changes brought about by the digital revolution as paradigm shifts that require new ways of thinking. An example of new thinking about making in society can be seen in the Fab Lab initiative launched by Neil Gershenfeld, Director of the MIT Center for Bits and Atoms. The facilities provide access to advanced digital making technologies to the general public (Gershenfeld, 2005). The more than 120 Fab Labs of different sizes, with different project outcomes, and demonstrate different ways of organizing. Fab Labs provide access to electronics, CNC routering, computerized embroidery machines, laser cutting equipment, and 3D printing technology (additive manufacturing), but with the addition that they are networked to share information, education and ideas, based on an open source strategy. These facilities have been set up in very different communities, from the university-based facility in Wellington, New Zealand to the independent one in Manchester, UK, to facilities in Barcelona and Afghanistan. The most significant technology introduced to the maker society was 3D printing.

According to Anderson (2012), 3D printing provided the missing link between digital communication and communities and physical making. He argued that it unified the virtual and the physical environments, changing the relationship that people had with making, and each other and therefore the world around them. Anderson saw 3D printing as the precursor for a digital revolution in independent manufacturing that would change the way the physical world was constructed. He predicted a democratization in making that would revolutionize how products were viewed, constructed and recycled. Aldersey-Williams' (2011) vision was more profound, arguing that 3D printing and associated digital technologies would allow for a welcome return to the distributed manufacturing model that characterized production before the industrial revolution. He predicted a re-ruralisation as people chose to become independent of the machinery of the industrialization and able to provide for themselves, working in a community-based market model, rather than a factory-based one.

Yet, nearly a decade later, the reality of 3D printing as a radical tool for democratization is not being realized. Back in 2014, 3D printing was clearly having a significant impact on the maker society. It burgeoned as a digital making tool that allowed for makers to create parts for products previously not possible without a batch production model and considerable investment in tooling. Since then, however, the initial hype of 3D printing has slowed, as the realities and limitations of working with the technology as an individual maker have become apparent to the making public. This is in part because at the height of the hype about 3D printing, there was confusion about what the technology was capable of, and predictions frequently based on misunderstandings about the many different types of technology included in the umbrella term additive manufacturing. For example, it is possible to manufacture very sophisticated, end-use metal parts using 3D printing, such as the turbo prop engine produced in 2018 by GE Additive (Kellner, 2019), but this requires the use of high-end machinery and a high level of skill and expertize in working with the technology. The cost of the machines used are in the millions of US dollars, and even the cost of filling the machines with metal powder is in the tens of thousands. This is not an option for the independent maker. In describing 3D printing in the context of the democratization of making at the height of the public hype on the topic, the difference between the cost and capabilities of a desktop fused deposition, filament printer, and a laser-based powder printer were rarely clarified.

Lipson and Kurman (2013) predicted an alternative future business model that was based on Cloud manufacturing. Rather than conventional mass production, Cloud manufacturing relied on "small-scale, decentralized nodes of production" connected online, with off-line models of production in a new, combined cyber physical system. In this approach, producers would connect with their customers online to 3D print products on demand, rather than in anticipation, with online service bureaus provide additional services to makers with limited making capabilities on site. This approach is increasingly seen as more realistic in developing a semi-autonomous distributed manufacturing system. As part of this, independent makers, or makers with a number of printers, could contribute to a team of makers together for a large project. Clusters of 3D printers have been described as a 'build farm'. This term has its roots in information technology, but has more recently been applied to networked 3D printers creating components for a large-scale product (Redwood, Schoffer, Garret, & Debicki, 2017). Advantages of this approach include the lack of capital investment required, the ability to create products as they are requested, rather than for stored inventory, and the ability to modify designs in response to customer feedback. Yet the impact on businesses as a whole is minor. Whilst Anderson's

(2013) vision still has good foundations, the last decade has proved it is not going to be the radical, society changing technology predicted, without alternative drivers and considerable legislative assistance.

CHALLENGES

Academic Intransigence

Teaching students to understand and reflect on their own decisions leads to better moral cognition. To achieve this, instructors who teach ethics need to understand themselves and their own meta-moral cognitive abilities....before teaching ethics to students, instructors of ethics should engage in self-reflection. Instructors ignorant of their own strengths and weaknesses in taking moral decisions cannot teach their students to reflect on their own moral judgment. (Cheruvalath, 2019, p.593)

There is a perception by existing faculty that professional ethics is sufficient for the education of students in this field, and in fact any straying into moral debate could violate the personal lives of students (Cheruvalath, 2019). There is therefore the issue of ensuring the ongoing professional education of academics to help them to lead learning activities on the integration of digital technology and its impact on society. Their own education is unlikely to include exploring the technology from a social science perspective and therefore impact their ability to reimagine manufacturing for a social context "...the focus on cognitive learning may not promote, and may even impair, our efforts to foster moral sensitivity" (Walling, 2015, p 1637). Yet with social scientists having insufficient expert knowledge of the range and complexities of digital manufacturing technologies, any debate introduced in that sphere will inevitably focus only on broader implications. As a result, there are unlikely to be learning activities specific to the ethical and moral development of manufacturing in a digital era that questions whether current practice is appropriate for the changing needs of society and the environment in the twenty-first century, or whether there are more appropriate models for a sustainable, equitable future. One challenge to this is the control of learning as it responds to existing manufacturing practices. For example, where research and industry needs are overtly linked by funding rules, it could mean that research would remain aligned to current industry needs and generating profits for shareholders of a particular company or consortium, rather than improving society for the wider population long-term.

Ultimately, we ought to formulate an enquiry that works to dislodge designers from our comfort zones and unpack the ramifications of embedding ourselves simultaneously and sequentially in groups that not only replicate, but actually magnify, unexamined assumptions that we are 'right' and that we know in some intuitive way what constitutes 'right action.' (Becker, 2012, p.21)

Utopian studies have provided the basis for the proposal of a universal income, enabled by automation (Bregman, 2017). However, as the hype over automation and artificial intelligence begins to wane in favor of a more realistic view of machine learning, it is perhaps time for the potential of digitally connected, additive manufacturing to be revisited for the development of a more independent, distributed production system. If the expansion of open source file sharing was formalized and extended, then potentially it could be possible for a wider variety of parts to be manufactured locally. Whilst the cost of metal machines is currently out of the reach of communities, the cost of end-use polymer printing machines is rapidly reducing, particularly since the advent of multi-jet fusion technology for end-use polymer parts. It is therefore a realistic proposition that within five years, this technology will be affordable in a next level Fab Lab-type of operation.

Controlling the means of production is central to economic freedom. A connected, digital infrastructure has political as well as economic implications. Since Anderson, Lipson and Kurman's publications early in the last decade, there has been a significant growth in the use of online service providers for independent trade (e.g. Shapeways[3], iMaterialise[4]), but as yet, no clear evidence of a growth in the democratization of making through the adoption of digital fabrication technology. In particular, Aldersey-Williams' (2011) predictions of consigning mass production of the twentieth century to history have, as yet, failed to materialize. As major challenges face societies across the globe, such as population distribution, inclusivity and sustainability, additive manufacturing and its associated digital technologies, could provide the opportunity for a rethink of the fundamental organization of production systems. It could be possible to re-imagine manufacturing, disrupting current systems to provide more human-centered, equitable access to the means of production. Pinker (2018, p.410) states, "It is humanism that identifies what we should try to achieve with our knowledge. It provides the ought that supplements the is. It distinguishes progress from mere mastery."

Population distribution is becoming a significant issue. The pollution in cities such as Delhi is a serious health issue, for example, and in Australia, whilst immigration policy has attempted to revive the falling populations of rural areas, the metropolitan areas continue to grow at their expense. One of the key reasons is the availability of jobs. Imagine, though, a future where re-ruralisation occurred in a country such as Australia. This may have been prompted by a lack of services or infrastructure in the cities sufficient for the rise in population, or it may be political, such as an increase in terrorist attacks in metropolitan centers. It may be due to air pollution, as in Melbourne in 2020 after the fires, or it may be because of a lack of power and water in the cities, promoting more people to move off grid (already the case in many areas of Queensland in Australia). For whatever reason, if there was a wholesale need to dematerialize the economy, and rethink the supply and recycling of products in a more localized, circular fashion, additive manufacturing would be at its core. If consumers were educated to a different set of expectations on the availability of products, and the means of production, it could also be possible to rethink the organisation of the economy. Interestingly, the current situation in Detroit, striving to recover from the closure of the car industry there, is modelling a widespread entrepreneurial model of income generation and community collaboration (Arnaud, 2017). Alternative narratives for the future of manufacturing in Society 5.0 need to be constructed.

The emphasis on 'counter-narrative' is important as it suggests that it is somehow different from the main narrative, either that which is explicitly and collectively agreed upon by society as being 'mainstream' or being implicit in accepted behaviour (the underlying paradigm). The implication is that design activism voices other possibilities than those that already exist with a view to eliciting societal change and transformation. (Fuad-Luke, 2009, p.27)

SOLUTIONS AND RECOMMENDATIONS

Rethinking Educational Models

In manufacturing, mass production across an integrated trade network across the world still dominates the business model. Economies depend on the flow of goods, and factories still work on a traditional assembly line production system, albeit increasingly automated. There is little evidence across the world of a revolution in making allowing for new ways of working at any scale. Yet there has been a documented rise in entrepreneurship. As digital platforms, such as Uber and You Tube, have fostered a shift towards zero-hour contracts, the interest in independent income generation has risen. Where it was previously not possible for an independent worker to reach enough customers to establish a critical mass suitable for generating sufficient revenue to live, online communication platforms are now making that possible (Atkinson, 2011). Early business models bring with them their own problems for society, such as the risks of exploitation associated with zero-hour contracts, and a potential lack of quality control. These issues aside, however, there is a rise in the entrepreneurial mindset in 2020 suggesting the potential to introduce viable distributed manufacturing operations.

To build the potential for the democratization of manufacturing into a more widespread, realistic proposition, the barriers to adoption need to be considered, as well as strategies for overcoming those barriers. However, underlying these concerns, there first needs to be an argument in favor of the benefits of distributed manufacturing practices for society. Ryan (2004, p. 30), listed what he termed 'strategic sustainability principles'. These were:

- *"Valuing prevention*
- *Preserving and restoring 'natural capital'*
- *Life-cycle thinking (closing system cycles)*
- *Increasing 'eco-efficiency' by 'factor x'*
- *Decarbonising and dematerialising the economy*
- *Focusing on design – of products and product-service".*

As additive manufacturing, with print on demand, value added products, moves into viable end-use production for distributed manufacturing, there is theoretically the mechanisms for a more inclusive, equitable means of production enabled by the digital technology ecosystem it in central to. Aldersey-Williams (2011) was arguably correct in this thinking about 3D printing and tits reversal of the industrial revolution, but it will take a radical rethink of priorities in the twenty-first century for this to happen. As discussed at DAVOS[5], in 2020, climate change mitigation will reprioritize economies, and in doing so, it could allow for a rethinking of the organisation of labor, a redistribution of populations, and potentially a greater equality and inclusivity in controlling the means of production.

..design and designers are implicated in the generation and materialisation of much of what can loosely be considered the artificial or constructed environment. From nano-machines to giant skyscrapers, including the crossover realms of human technology and 'natural' biology, design as a mode of thinking and practice has been instrumental in modifying the nature of inter-human and environmental relations. More specifically, design has chartered new human relations to the non-human, non-sentient, non-living and technologically mediated realm of objects and constructed environments. (Loo, 2012, p.10)

The challenges to reframing manufacturing and business practice in this fast-paced, changing environment, is that this is not an incremental change but a paradigm shift that actively contradicts the established practices of conventional mass production. Engineers need to recognize their role in reimaging the environment and disrupting manufacturing practice. Engineering academics need to the education to make this possible.

FUTURE RESEARCH

Radical Change

According to Martin Charter, Director of the Center for Sustainable Design, UK, the term Circular Economy (CE), describes a new world where "product life extension through repair, refurbishment and remanufacturing is the prevailing social and economic model" (Charter, 2018, intro). He describes the intent of product circularity as the maximization of the material and product value, and the value of the components in economic systems to the highest level over the longest time. He also emphasizes the importance of maximizing these values for social systems, describing the approach as providing "new business opportunities, radical business models, disruptive innovation, social change and new consumer attitudes." (Charter, 2018, intro.)

There is the need for a paradigm shift in manufacturing, and the education of a future workforce based on a more realistic, long term view of society and the environment, responding to the opportunities provided by digital technology and the rise of digital economies (Greenfield, 2017). Education of a future workforce needs to respond to contemporary knowledge and aspirations for society, as distinct from those of the last century. The current educational constructs need to be subverted by transition interventions, based on an action research methodology to challenge embedded ideas and practice. In engineering, this could be based on the recent developments in ontology in product design, that shift the focus from product, to product service system to values and ethics for an inclusive, equitable society.

The traditional roles of design, designer and designed object are thus refined through new understandings of the relationship between the material and immaterial aspects of design, where the design product and process are understood as embodiments of ideas, values and beliefs. This notion brings to the fore central questions around social responsibility, sustainability and consideration for the life of the object beyond the design studio. (Zelenko, & Felton 2012, p.3)

Without a commitment to infrastructure supporting distributed manufacturing, additive manufacturing will not change the current paradigm. Policy needs to support this shift, and legislation formulated to enforce it. This is similar to the legislation driving changes in business practice in Europe and the US with regards to waste and pollution. An example of this is Extended Producer Responsibility legislation, that requires companies in certain industries (such as the automotive industry in Europe) to be responsible for the end of life of their products. This involves the reclamation of materials and absorbing the cost of the disposal of any waste. Given appropriate supporting legislation, additive manufacturing could be integral to developing the circular economy. An example of the change in thinking additive manufacturing supports relates to spare parts. Companies are required to store spare parts for several years even after a product is no longer available. However, additive manufacturing and digital modelling and storage allows for a significant change in practice, reducing landfill and potentially transport miles as files can be sent to destinations for distributed manufacture, rather than the actual product:

Warehouses that hold unsold and unused inventory consume electricity for heating, cooling and lighting. Replacing physical inventory with digital inventory would green the supply chain. Physical inventory not only needs to be transported, it also takes up a lot of shelf space while it waits. In contrast, a digital inventory – or design files for a 3D printed machine part – is cheap and easy to store and transport. 3D printing technologies could help clean up the manufacturing process if their unique capabilities are put to use. (Lipson, & Kurman, 2013, p 206)

CONCLUSION

A Society Worth Living

Since the turn of the century, digital technologies have matured and converged to provide a cyber-physical system allowing products to be designed virtually, by designers and stakeholders, and 3D printed for real world applications. 3D printing is no longer limited to prototyping, but is now a viable, quality-controlled technology for end-use, functional products. That said, it is a range of technologies that have very different capabilities, and very different opportunities and constraints. As a result, there has been some confusion about the technology that led initially to an overhype of its capabilities in the democratisation of making, and a subsequent narrowing of interest in the applications it can be used for. Essentially it is the domain of aerospace, automotive and medical research, much as it was twenty years ago. Architecture and the Fashion industry demonstrate the research potential of the technology, though rarely its commercial application, but individual companies in other areas, such as dentistry, jewellery and the stop motion animation industry, have shown how it can radically change commercial practice.

For manufacturing to significantly respond to the aims of society 5.0, there needs to be a radical change in thinking, that is cultural and organisational as much as technical. Within existing companies corporate culture based on traditional hierarchical systems of power, and gatekeepers of knowledge will make it difficult to evolve practice. As Klein (2017, p.154) said CEOs "may believe that they want insights and innovations but are most receptive to new ideas that fit with existing practices and maintain predictability". However, as the length of time a company exists in reducing and pressures from sustainability (environmental, societal and economic) are rising, it is possible that a more distributed system of manufacturing and control of the means of production could emerge as an alternative model based on collective responsibility. As people have been treated essentially like machine parts in factories since assembly line production was introduced (with notable exceptions), there has been an acceptance of factory work as inevitable to maintain a standard of living, Yet with the digital revolution, surely it is time for society to revisit its conventions to see if the digital economy can create new ways of working, new ways of being that support an inclusive, sustainable, more equitable society. Time to provide education for future generations that focusses on its value, not only for society as a whole but for the life experiences of individuals on a daily basis. It may be utopian, but society has to decide if it wants to be increasingly dependent on centralized mechanisation, or re-organize the means of production and working practices around quality of life, rather than subjected to it.

Cyber-physical systems, as the basis for manufacturing in the twenty-first century, support the possibility of paradigm shifts that could benefit society as a whole, and individuals currently excluded or disadvantaged in the current system. Critically evaluating manufacturing practices and the development of systems and products in engineering and design from a societal and environmental point of view was lacking at the turn of the century/ However, there has been a recent rise in interest on broadening ethics education to include the development of personal values and moral decision making based on contemporary knowledge and values, and the complexities that brings. Currently, the potential of digital manufacturing and product service systems thinking to respond to the intent of society 5.0 are in danger of being subsumed into existing commercial practices, as society arguably continues to underestimate its ability to disrupt current systems and enable a more equitable distribution of manufacturing wealth, capability and capacity. This chapter provides an argument for exploiting the potential of emerging industrial technologies to support the development of a more human centered society where social and environmental problems are acknowledged and addressed. For this to happen, society needs to learn to think responsibly, collectively and imaginatively. Manufacturing education needs to change. Manufacturing futures for Society 5.0 need to be built on learning experiences that inculcate personal reflection, collective and personal responsibility and an understanding of ethics beyond professional codes of conduct and are led by the social sciences and engineering together.

REFERENCES

ABET. (2015). *Criteria for accrediting engineering programs.* Engineering Technology Accreditation Commission. Retrieved from https://www.abet.org/wp-content/uploads/2015/04/criteria-eac-2010-2011.pdf

AdditiveG. E. (2018). Retrieved from https://www.ge.com/additive/blog/new-manufacturing-milestone-30000-additive-fuel-nozzles

Aldersey-Williams, H. (2011). *The new tin ear: Manufacturing, materials and the rise of the user-maker. RSA Design Projects.* RSA.

Anderson, C. (2012). *Makers: The next industrial revolution.* Crown Business.

Arnaud, M. (2017). *Detroit: The dream is now: The design, art, and resurgence of an American city.* Abram Books.

Atkinson, P. (2011). Orchestral manoeuvres in design. In Open Design Now. Amsterdam: BIS.

Becker, L. (2012). Design, ethics and group myopia. In E. Felton, O. Zelenko, & S. Vaughan (Eds.), *Design and ethics: Reflections on practice.* Routledge.

Bregman, R. (2017). *Utopia for realists.* Bloomsbury.

Brown, T. (2009). *Change by design: How design thinking transforms organisations and inspires innovation.* Harper Business.

Cameron, N. (2017). *Will robots take your job?* Polity.

Charter, M. (2018). Introduction. In M. Charter (Ed.), *Designing for a circular economy.* Routledge. doi:10.4324/9781315113067-1

Cheruvalath, R. (2019). Does studying 'ethics' improve engineering students' meta-moral cognitive skills? *Science and Engineering Ethics, 25,* 583–596. doi:10.100711948-017-0009-x

Colby, A., & Sullivan, W. (2008). Ethics teaching in undergraduate engineering education. *Journal of Engineering Education, 97*(3), 327–338. Advance online publication. doi:10.1002/j.2168-9830.2008.tb00982.x

Conlan, E. & Zandvoort, H. (2011). Broadening ethics teaching in engineering: Beyond the individualistic approach. *Science Engineering Ethics, 17,* 217-232. doi 10.100%11948-010-9305-?

Diegel, O., Nordin, A., & Motte, D. (2019). *A practical guide for design for additive manufacturing.* Springer. doi:10.1007/978-981-13-8281-9

Fuad-Luke, A. (2009). *Design activism: Beautiful strangeness for a sustainable world*. Earthscan.

Gershenfeld, N. (2005). *Fab: The coming revolution on your desktop – from personal computing to personal fabrication*. Basic Books.

Gore, A. (2013). *The future: Six drivers for global change*. WH Allen.

Greenfield, A. (2017). *Radical technologies: The design of everyday life*. Verso.

Heimans, J., & Timms, H. (2018). *New power: How power works in our hyperconnected world – and how to make it work for you*. Macmillan.

Hess, J., & Fore, G. (2018). A systematic literature review of US engineering ethics interventions. *Science and Engineering Ethics, 24*, 551–583. doi:10.100711948-017-9910-6 PMID:28401510

Kellner, T. (2019). Mad props: Why GEs new catalyst turboprop engine is turning heads. *GE Additive Reports*. Retrieved from https://www.ge.com/reports/mad-props-ges-new-catalyst-turboprop-engine-turning-heads/

Klein, G. (2017). *Seeing what others don't: The remarkable ways we gain insights*. Nicholas Brealey Publishing.

Le Merlus, L. (2019, December 16). Formnext 2019: A lot of new players, but where is the business value? *3D Print.com*. Retrieved from https://3dprint.com/261368/formnext-2019-a-lot-of-new-players-but-where-is-the-business-value/

Leduff, C. (2014). *Detroit: An American autopsy*. Penguin.

Lipson, H., & Kurman, M. (2013). *Fabricated: The new world of 3D printing, the promise and peril of a machine that can make (almost) anything*. John Wiley and Sons.

Loo, S. (2012). Design-ing ethics. In E. Felton, O. Zelenko, & S. Vaughan (Eds.), *Design and ethics: Reflections on practice* (pp. 10–19). Routledge.

Loy, J. (2015). The future for design education: Preparing the design workforce for additive manufacturing. *International Journal of Rapid Manufacturing, 5*(2), 199–212. doi:10.1504/IJRAPIDM.2015.073577

Morrison, L. (2019). Situating moral agency: How postphenomenology can benefit engineering ethics. *Science and Engineering Ethics*. Advance online publication. doi:10.100711948-019-00163-7 PMID:31792776

Myerson, J., & Makepeace, J. (1995). *Makepeace: Spirit of adventure in craft and design*. Conran Octopus.

Pei, E., Monzon, M., & Bernard, A. (Eds.). (2018). *Additive manufacturing – developments in training and education*. Springer.

Pinker, S. (2018). *Enlightenment now: The case for reason, science, humanism and progress*. Penguin.

Pullin, G. (2009). *Design meets disability*. MIT Press.

Redwood, B., Schoffer, F. Garret, B. & Debicki, T. (2017). *The 3D printing handbook: Technologies, design and applications*. Amsterdam: 3D Hubs B.V.

Ryan, C. (2004). *Digital eco-sense: Sustainability and ICT – a new terrain for innovation*. Melbourne: Lab 3000.

Sainato, M. (2019). Revealed: Amazon touts high wages while ignoring issues in its warehouses. *The Guardian*. Retrieved from https://www.theguardian.com/technology/2019/aug/06/amazon-workers-minimum-wage-injuries-working-conditions

Scholz, R., Yarime, M., & Shiroyama, H. (2018). Global leadership for social design: Theoretical and educational perspectives. *Sustainability Science*, *13*(2), 447–464. doi:10.100711625-017-0454-0

Schwab, K. (2017). *The fourth industrial revolution*. Currency.

Seldon, A., & Abidoye, O. (2018). *The fourth education revolution: will artificial intelligence liberate or infantilise humanity?* The University of Buckingham Press.

Shiroishi, Y., Uchiyama, K., & Suzuki, N. (2019). Society 5.0: For human security and well-being, Cyber-physical systems. Hitachi Research and Development Group.

Vezzoli, C., & Manzini, E. (2008). *Design for environmental sustainability*. Springer.

Wall, M. (2016). Challenger disaster 30 years ago shocked the world, changed NASA. *Space.com*. Retrieved from https://www.space.com/31760-space-shuttle-challenger-disaster-30-years.html

Walling, O. (2015). Beyond ethical frameworks: Using moral experimentation in the engineering ethics classroom. *Science and Engineering Ethics*, *21*(6), 1637–1656. doi:10.100711948-014-9614-0 PMID:25431220

Wohlers. (2019). *Wohlers report: 3D printing and additive manufacturing, State of the Industry*. Wohlers. https://wohlersassociates.com/2019report.htm

Yato, S. (2019). Japan pushing ahead with Society 5.0 to overcome chronic social challenges. *UNESCO*. https://en.unesco.org/news/japan-pushing-ahead-society-50-overcome-chronic-social-challenges

Zelenko, O., & Felton, E. (2012). Framing design and ethics. In E. Felton, O. Zelenko, & S. Vaughan (Eds.), *Design and ethics: Reflections on practice*. Routledge.

ADDITIONAL READING

Bitonti, F. (2019). *3D printing design: Additive manufacturing and the materials revolution*. Bloomsbury.

Gibson, I., Rosen, D., & Stucker, B. (2014). *Additive manufacturing technologies: 3D printing, rapid prototyping, and direct digital manufacturing*. Springer.

Milewski, J. (2017). *Additive manufacturing of metals: From fundamental technology to rocket nozzles, medical implants and custom jewelry*. Springer. doi:10.1007/978-3-319-58205-4

KEY TERMS AND DEFINITIONS

Additive Manufacturing: Also known as 3D printing, refers to a range of making technologies that build an object without the need for moulds or other tooling, based on information provided by a 3D computer model.

Distributed Manufacturing: Decentralized manufacturing.

Gig Economy: Zero-hour contract work.

Society 5.0: Sustainable society to support human well-being and security through the use of socially conscious, ethical cyber-physical systems.

ENDNOTES

[1] Designers' accord: www.designersaccord.org
[2] Living Principles: www.livingprinciples.org
[3] Shapeways: https://www.shapeways.com
[4] iMaterialise: https://i.materialise.com/en
[5] DAVOS: https://www.weforum.org/events/world-economic-forum-annual-meeting-2020

Chapter 4

New Challenges for Education in the Forthcoming Era of the Fourth Industrial Revolution

Michael Voskoglou
Technological Educational Institute of Western Greece, Greece

ABSTRACT

The rapid industrial and technological development of the last years has transformed the human society to its current form of knowledge and globalization. As a result, the formal education is nowadays faced with the big challenge of preparing students for a new way of life in the forthcoming fourth industrial revolution. This new revolution could be characterized as the era of the internet of things and energy and of the cyber-physical systems. The present chapter focuses on the role that computers and artificial intelligence could play in future education and the risks hiding behind this perspective. It is concluded that it is rather impossible that computers and the other "clever" machines of artificial intelligence will reach to the point of replacing teachers for educating students in future, because all these devices have been created and programmed by humans and therefore it is logical to accept that they will never succeed to reach the quality of human reasoning. However, it is certain that the role of the teacher will be dramatically changed in the future classrooms.

DOI: 10.4018/978-1-7998-4882-0.ch004

INTRODUCTION

The rapid industrial and technological development of the last 100-150 years caused radical changes to our lives and behaviours, transforming the traditional and mainly agrarian human society of the last centuries to a modern society of knowledge and globalisation. Machines especially designed for massive industrial production, computers, robots and various other "clever" mechanisms and methods of *Artificial Intelligence (AI)* have already replaced humans in an increasing number of routine jobs. This continuous development of new technologies could create many new, yet unforeseen/unpredicted jobs in the future. As a result, formal education, from elementary school to university/tertiary, is faced with the great challenge of preparing students for a new way of life in a rather uncertain future of the forthcoming era of a new, but not yet explicitly known, industrial revolution, as the outcomes have not yet been fully determined.

The objective of the present work is to express some thoughts about this challenge and the difficulties connected to it. In no case, however, can this chapter be considered as an attempt to fully analyse the topic mentioned above, because such an effort requires hundreds of pages, as most of the subjects related to education need to be integrated. The attention/focus here is turned mainly to the role computers and AI could play in future education and the risks associated with perspective/development.

The rest of this chapter is organised as follows: In the Background Section a connection is made between the past industrial revolutions and the forthcoming new one, which could be characterised as the era of the *Internet of Things and Energy (IoT & E)* and the *Cyber-Physical Systems (CPS)*. The Main Focus of the chapter examines the role of computers and *Computational Thinking (CT)* in modern education and the recent developments and perspectives of introducing methods and mechanisms of AI to education. Future directions of research and final conclusions follow, and the chapter closes with a list of references and additional readings, as well as a summary of the key terms and definitions contained therein.

BACKGROUND

The Industrial Revolutions and the Forthcoming Era of the Internet of Things and Energy

A revolution is defined in general as a rapid and massive series of changes that lead to a radical transformation of human society. It could be a social, political, economic, industrial or other kind of revolution, but involves changes in/to the core of society.

The *First Industrial Revolution (1IR)*, which began in the UK's textile factories at the end of the 18th Century and spread throughout the world, involved the gradual replacement of manual labor by mechanical production, where machines were used mainly as power sources. The parallel development in the transportation sector led to the establishment of big industries and companies on a national and later on an international level, for which new scientific functional and management methods had to be developed (Voskoglou, 2016).

Various names and definitions have been proposed for the several industrial revolutions that took place since then. According to the World Economic Forum (WEF), the first industrial revolution, characterized by mechanization, on the basis of steam and water power, was followed by a second one, which started in the middle of the 19th Century. The *Second Industrial Revolution (2IR)* used the power of electricity for the mass production of large quantities of standardized goods in assembly lines. However, some social thinkers believe that the 2IR, which ended by the middle of the 20th Century, must be regarded as an inseparable part of the 1IR (Rifkin, 2011).

Regarding the *Third Industrial Revolution (3IR),* according to Rifkin's (2011) view the 2IR, is also known as the *era of automation*. This revolution, which began in the 1940's, was mainly characterized by the development of electronics, automated production and the gradual replacement of the human hand by computers as means of control (Voskoglou, 2016).

In conclusion, the combined effects of the last three industrial revolutions have replaced manpower and animals with machines, making mass production of goods possible and leading human society to its current digital era. However, there were undesirable effects as well, such as the negative environmental impact, caused mainly by the unlimited use of coal and petrol and nuclear energy accidents. The economies of many countries are in danger of collapse, the people of the poor countries are suffering with no recovery in sight. Facing the prospect of a new collapse of the global economy, we desperately need a new economic plan that could lead us into a better future.

The idea of a forthcoming new industrial revolution has surfaced at the beginning of the 21st Century (Anton et al.., 2011). New York Times bestselling author Jeremy Rifkin, a famous social thinker of our time, introduced the term 3IR for this new revolution. In two books published in 2011 and 2014 (Rifkin, 2011, 2014) he describes how Internet technology, renewable energy and 3D-printing are merging to form this powerful revolution. The new technology will, for instance, facilitate the distribution of electrical energy or allow smart home and household devices to communicate via the internet. Consequently, a new advanced IoT & E will be created, providing energy at the right time and place, and goods and services anytime at any place.

The term *Fourth Industrial Revolution (4IR)* has an almost identical meaning as Rifkin's 3IR. It was first introduced by Professor Klaus Schwab, Founder and Executive Chairman of the WEF, in an article published in "Foreign Affairs" (Schwab, 2015). In a recent book (Schwab, 2016) Prof. Schwab argues that we are already at the beginning of the 4IR. The 4IR is about the emergence of CPS which will be controlled through the Internet by computer programs. Examples of CPS are autonomous automobiles and control systems, distance medicine, robots, etc. The world now has the potential to improve the efficiency of services and organisations impressively/greatly and even find ways to regenerate the natural environment from some of the damages caused by previous IR's.

However, Schwab (2016) also expresses serious concerns about the great potential risks associated with 4IR in his book. He stresses that our current political, business, educational and social structures need to be fundamentally changed in order to smoothly absorb the resulting 4IR shifts and maximize profits in order to create a better future for our society. This was the theme of the 2016 WEF annual meeting in Davos, titled "Mastering the 4IR". It should be noted that Germany's industrial plan promoted the term *Industry 4.0 only* for the subset of the 4IR in industry. Furthermore, at the 2019 WEF annual meeting, Japan promoted another round of developments called *Society 5.0.*

MAIN FOCUS OF THE CHAPTER

Computers in Modern Education

It is hard to deny that in our modern society of knowledge and information computers are a valuable tool for teaching and learning. The wealth of information in the hands of the students, the animation of figures and representations provided by educational software can serve to increase the students' imagination and problem solving skills. The rich variety of data and resources will help teachers keep their students engaged in the classroom. These are just some of the benefits obtained by using computers in education.

In recent years, an innovative teaching method known as *Flipped* or *Reverse Learning (FL)* has been promoted using computers. FL, which has its roots in the work of Lage, Piatt and Tegla (2000), is a mixed process involving both online and face-to-face teaching. It requires turning around the daily didactic processes which we are accustomed to. In fact, the student's acquisition of new knowledge happens outside the classroom by using digital platforms and technological tools that specialists or teachers have developed. Aaron Sams and Jonathan Bergmann (2012) were able to develop online audiovisual teaching materials, thereby enabling students to study regardless of factors such as place and time. On the other hand, what was traditionally undertaken as homework is done in class with the supervision of the teacher in order to favour the productivity of learning and the autonomy of the students and allow more time for practicing, problem solving and deepening of content (Lee et al., 2017).

The ideas of *social constructivism* for learning are used in the development of the FL teaching model. The theory of *constructivism* for learning, proposed by Piaget and formally introduced by von Clasersfeld during the 1970's, involves two principles: Firstly, that knowledge is actively built up by the learner, and not passively received from the environment, and secondly the importance of the *"coming to know"*, which is understood to be a process of adaptation and is constantly changed by the learner's experience of the world (Taber, 2011). On the other hand, according to Vygotsky's theory of *social development* (Crawford, 1996), learning takes place within some socio-cultural setting. Shared meanings are formed through negotiation in the learning environment, leading to the development of common knowledge. Social constructivism is a synthesis of the ideas of the two learning approaches above (McKinley, 2015).

Some years ago, it was believed that teaching required human-to-human contact, but today's technology allows us to do much of this virtually, using computers, videos, etc. Consequently, *distance learning* will become an inseparable part of our lives in future. The *Communities of Practice (CoP's)* are groups of people, be they experts or practitioners sharing a craft or profession. They interact regularly, which allows them the opportunity to develop themselves personally and professionally (Wegner, 1998). By using the Web, *virtual CoP's* appear to be as a very promising tool for Education, especially for developing countries, where people, due to budgetary constraints, do not have many opportunities to travel abroad to participate in conferences, seminars, educational exchanges, etc. Students and teachers from different countries can form such CoP's for learning particular subjects, while education teachers and researchers can promote teaching and the research on teaching (Voskoglou, 2019a).

However, there are also reports in literature that speak against the use of computers in classrooms. For example, a study published by the Massachusetts Institute of Technology found that students who were prohibited from using laptops or digital devices in lectures and seminars did better in their exams than those who were allowed to use computers and access the Internet (see https://seii.mit.edu/research/study/the-impact-of-computer-usage-on-academic-performance-evidence-from-a-randomized-trial-at-the-united-states-military-academy/). Tom Bennet, who led a UK government-commissioned review on smartphone used in classrooms, noted that even the brightest students appeared to be distracted by the presence of digital devices (see http://www.theguardian.com/education/2015/sep/13/mobile-phone-impact-school-lessons-scrunity). In contrast, a study published by the London

School of Economics found that banning mobile phones in classrooms improves the outcomes of low-achieving students, but has no significant impact on high-achievers (see http://www.theguardian.com/education/2015/may/15/mobile-phone-bans-improve-school-exam-results-research-shows).

In general, computers should not be viewed as tools that can perform miracles by solving any kind of problems, but rather as machines performing operations in high speed, therefore enabling users to dedicate their time to quality reasoning and ideas (Einhorn, 2012). Since a computer is created and programmed by humans, the old credo "garbage in, garbage out" is still valid. Nevertheless, through programming it is possible to enter information and get output results almost at the speed of light. On the other hand, the practice of students having to do all kinds of calculations is likely to continue, or else people will gradually loose the sense of numbers and symbols, the sense of space and time, and they will become unable to create new knowledge and technology (Voskoglou & Buckley, 2012).

Computational Thinking in Problem Solving

Problem-solving (PS) is a very important component of the human cognition and has been affecting our lives for ages (Voskoglou, 2011, 2016). The ability to solve composite non-routine problems requires *critical thinking (CrT)*, which is a higher mindset that combines analysis, synthesis and evaluation. It also leads to other skills such as inferring, estimating, predicting, generalising and creative thinking. (Halpern, 2003)

However, the rapid development of technology in recent decades has led to new complex technological problems. The solution of which requires the combination of CrT with a different way of thinking called *computational thinking (CT)*. The term CT was first introduced by S. Papert, who is widely known as the "father' of the Logo software. However, it was brought to the forefront of the computer society by Jeannette Wing (2006), who describes it as "involving solving problems, designing systems and understanding human behaviour based on principles of computer science". CT includes the analysis and organisation of data, the automation of problem-solving and applications involving abstract, logical, algorithmic, constructive thinking and modelling thinking that synthesizes all previous mindsets in order to find solutions for problems (Liu and Wang, 2010).

CT does however suggest that problems do not necessarily have to be solved exactly the same way as a computer solves them. Voskoglou and Buckley (2012) viewed the problem as an obstacle/challenge needing a solution. They presented two alternative approaches to clarify the relationship between CrT and CT during the PS process (Giannakopoulos, 2012). The first approach is a 3-D model that could be used to conceptualize the PS process of complex technological problems. This model is graphically illustrated in Figure 1.

Figure 1. The 3-D PS model

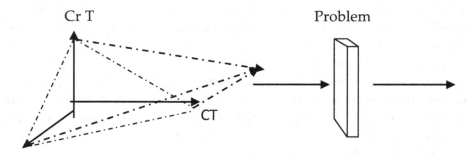

In this model, the three components of CrT, CT and existing knowledge act simultaneously on the problem at hand. The model is based on the hypothesis that, if there is sufficient background knowledge, the new (necessary) knowledge is triggered with the help of CrT; then CT is applied and the problem is solved.

In the case of simpler problems, the 3-D model could be transformed to the linear form of Figure 2. In this case, the existing knowledge is extracted and critically analyzed, as soon as awareness of the problem is reached. The problem solver then delves into his/her knowledge base and uses/applies the knowledge to solve the problem by thinking in a computer-like manner.

Figure 2. The linear PS model

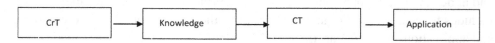

Recent studies address the necessity of becoming trained in CT *before* learning **computer programming** (Kazimoglu et al., 2011). The best way to learn CT explicitly/thoroughly is through programming. In fact, programming employs all the components of CT and provides a framework not only for computer science, but for all sciences. In thinking like a computer scientist, students become aware of processes that need to be analysed within an algorithmic framework. Thus, CT forms a new way of thinking that has the potential to bring about positive changes in society.

Applications of Artificial Intelligence to Education

AI is a branch of Computer Science focusing on the creation of intelligent machines which mimic human reasoning and behavior. The term AI was first coined by John McCarthy (1927-2011) in 1956, when he held the first academic conference in Dartmouth College, USA, on the subject (Moor, 2006). The commemorative plaque of the 50th anniversary of the conference placed in Dartmouth Hall in 2006 is shown in Figure 3. However, the effort to understand whether machines can truly think began much earlier, even before Alan Turing's abstract "learning machine" invention in 1936. It proved the capability to simulate the logic of any computer's

Figure 3. The Dartmouth Hall Commemorative Plaque

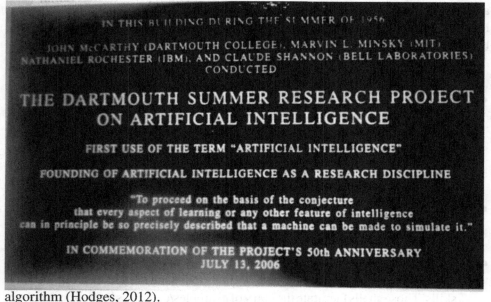

algorithm (Hodges, 2012).

AI has its roots in mathematics, engineering, technology and science. Synthesizing ideas from all of these areas has created a new situation, which is just beginning to bring enormous changes and benefits for human society. This section discusses recent advances and perspectives in the introduction of AI methods and mechanisms in education (Holmes et al., 2019). Among them, *Machine Learning (ML)*, *Smart*

Learning Systems (SLS), Case-Based Reasoning (CBR) Systems in computers, *Social Robots* and *Fuzzy Systems* serve as examples.

The term "ML" comes from the idea that an algorithm learns from a training dataset. ML encompasses *supervised learning*, in which both input and desired output data can be considered teachers and are classified to provide a learning basis for future data processing, In *unsupervised learning*, only the input data is given and the algorithms can work freely to learn more about the data. As a simple example of the former case, we consider the sequences of positive integers 1, 2, 3, 4, 5, 6, 7, … as input and 1, 4, 8, 16, 25, 35, 49, …. as output, which indicates the raising to the second power. Applications of supervised learning are typically broken down into two categories, *classification,* where the output value is a linguistic expression (e.g. true or false); and *regression*, where the output is a real value (e.g. price or weight). If some of the input data is labelled with output information, we speak about *semi-supervised learning* (Das et al., 2015).

Using the Internet, researchers have recently utilized ML techniques to develop a new generation of web-based SLS for various educational tasks. A SLS is a knowledge-based software used for learning, which acts as an intelligent tutor in real teaching and training situations. Such systems have the ability of reasoning and of providing inferences/interactions/interfaces and recommendations by using heuristic, interactive and symbolic processing and by producing results from the big data analytics (Salem & Parucheva, 2018, Salem, 2019).

The successive phases for developing a SLS are:

- *Construction of the knowledge base,* involving collection, acquisition and representation of the required knowledge. The success of the task presupposes the choice appropriate in each case, amongst the many existing, technique (e.g. lists, trees, also semantic networks, frames, production rules, cases, ontologies, etc.) that fit better to the knowledge domain for a solution to the problem.
- *Selection of suitable reasoning and inference methodology,* e.g. commonsense, model-based, qualitative, causal, geometric, probabilistic or fuzzy reasoning, etc.
- *Selection of intelligent authoring shells*, which allow the course instructor to easily enter the knowledge domain without requiring computer programming skills. Those shells facilitate the entry of examples/exercises including problem statements, solution steps and explanations and the integration of suitably developed multimedia course wear by the specialists. The examples may be in the form of scenarios or simulations. In addition to the course knowledge, the instructor has the possibility to specify the pedagogical instruction, i.e. the best way to teach a particular student, and to choose how to assess actions and

determine student mastery. The most common authoring shells are DIAG, RIDES-VIVIDS, XAIDA, REDEEM, EON, INTELLIGENT TUTOR, D3 TRAINER, CALAT, INTERBOOK, and PERSUADE (Salem & Nikitaeva, 2019).

In conclusion, the efficiency of a SLS is based on the selection of the appropriate knowledge representation technique and reasoning methodology and the choice of suitable authoring shells. Therefore, from a technical point of view, a SLS is complex to build and difficult to maintain. Two of the most popular methodologies used for constructing the knowledge-base of a SLS are *Ontological Engineering* and CBR.

The term "ontology" has its roots to philosophy and metaphysics, and refers to the nature of being. The ontologies used in computer science are knowledge-based intelligent systems designed to share knowledge among computers or among computers and people. Those types of ontologies include a relatively small number of concepts and their main objective is to facilitate reasoning. In intelligent educational systems, ontologies are used in the search for learning materials and pedagogical resources on the internet or as a chain, playing the role of a "vocabulary" among heterogeneous educational systems (*multi-agent systems*) that have been programmed to communicate with each other (Tankelevcience & Damasevicius, 2009, Cakula & Salem, 2011).

CBR is the process of solving problems based on the solutions of similar, previously solved problems. For example, a physician who heals a patient based on therapy previously used on patients with similar symptoms, or a lawyer who predicts a particular outcome in a trial based on legal precedents, are using the CBR methodology. The use of computers enables the CBR systems to preserve a continuously growing *"library"* of previously solved problems, referred to as *past cases*. Each time, the suitable previously solved problem can be retrieved for the corresponding new problem. CBR is often used where experts find it difficult to articulate their thinking processes when solving problems. This is because acquiring knowledge in a classical knowledge-based system would be extremely difficult in such cases, and would likely produce incomplete or inaccurate results. When using CBR, the need for knowledge acquisition can be reduced to characterizing cases as an information source.

CBR, as an intelligent-systems' method, enables information managers to increase efficiency and reduce costs by substantially automating processes. However, the CBR approach, apart from commercial and business purposes, has got a lot of attention over the last decades in *education* as a new approach to PS and learning (Voskoglou, 2008).

In fact, the CBR methodology organizes knowledge with reference to previous problems. Each case typically contains a description of the problem plus a solution and/or the outcomes. The knowledge and reasoning process used to solve the problem are not recorded, but they are implicit in the solution. This structure/process treats the knowledge in a lesson-oriented manner and facilitates the automatic generation of tests and exercises.

CBR's coupling to learning occurs as a natural by-product of PS. When a problem is successfully solved, the experience is retained in order to solve similar problems in future. When an attempt to solve a problem fails, the reason for the failure is identified and remembered in order to avoid the same mistake in future. This process is termed as *failure-driven learning*. Thus CBR is a cyclic and integrated process of solving a problem, learning from the experience and solving a new problem.

Effective learning in CBR, sometimes referred to as *case-based learning*, requires a well worked out set of methods in order to extract relevant knowledge from the experience, integrate a case into an existing knowledge structure and index the case for later matching with similar cases. In addition, to the knowledge represented by cases, most CBR systems also use general domain knowledge. Representation and use of this domain knowledge includes the integration of the CBR method in other methods, for instance, rule-based systems or in-depth-models such as casual reasoning/commonsense. The overall architecture of the CBR system must determine the interactions and the control regime/relationship between the CBR method and the other components.

The driving force behind the CBR methods comes largely from the ML community and is regarded as a sub-area of ML. In fact, the term CBR not only refers to a particular reasoning method, but also to an ML paradigm, which enables sustainable learning by updating the case base after a problem has been solved. CBR first appeared in commercial systems in the early 1990's and since then has been used to create numerous applications in a wide range of domains including diagnosis, help-desk applications, assessment, decision support, design, etc. Organisations as diverse as IBM, VISA International, Volkswagen, British Airways, NASA and many others have already made use of CBR.

Despite the fact that the CBR methodology has been proved to be effective in most cases, critics of CBR argue that it is an approach which accepts anecdotal evidence as its main operating principle. But, without statistically relevant data there is no guarantee that the generalisation is correct. There is, however, recent work which develops CBR within a statistical framework and formalises case-based inference as a specific type of probabilistic inference. Thus, it becomes possible to produce case-based predictions equipped with a certain level of confidence.

CBR has been formulated for computers and people as a four step process involving the following actions:

- **R₁**: *Retrieve* from the system's library a suitable past case.
- **R₂**: *Reuse* this case for the solution of the given problem.
- **R₃**: *Revise* the solution of the retrieved case for solving the new problem.
- **R₄**: *Retain* the revised solution for possible use with similar problems in future.

Through the revision, the solution is tested for success. If successful, the revised solution is directly saved in the CBR library, otherwise it is revised and evaluated again. If the final result is a failure, the system tries to compare it to previous similar failures (transfer from R₃ back to R₁) and uses the information in order to understand the present failure, which is finally saved in the library. A graphical representation of the above process is shown in Figure 4 (Voskoglou, 2017a).

Figure 4. Graphical representation of the CBR process

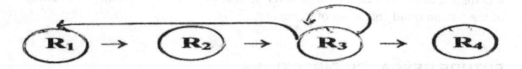

More details about the history, development and applications of CBR can be found in Voskoglou & Salem (2014) and in the references provided in this paper corresponding/referencing to earlier studies on CBR, in Leake (2015), etc.

A social robot is an AI machine that has been designed to interact with humans or other robots. Social robots may understand speech and facial expressions, and are used at home, in customer service, in education, etc.(Taipale et al., 2015). Cynthia Breazel was one of the first to develop such robots in MIT (Breazel, 2002). Examples of applications in education are the robot *Tico* that has been designed to improve children's motivation in the classroom. The robot *Bandit,* has been developed to teach social behaviour to autistic children, etc.

The theory of *Fuzzy Sets (FS),* introduced by Zadeh (1965) and its further stage, *fuzzy logic*, which is an infinite-valued logic that generalises the traditional bi-valued logic constitute to further developments of AI. Fuzzy mathematics today has found many important applications for almost all sectors of human activity (Klir & Folger, 1988; Chapter 6, Voskoglou, 2017b, Chapters 4-8, etc.). Courses on fuzzy mathematics and fuzzy logic have already appeared in the curricula of several university departments (Voskoglou, 2019b) and it is expected to expand rapidly in the near future. Since Zadeh introduced the concept of FS and in order to more effectively combat the uncertainty caused by the inaccuracy that characterises many situations in science, technology and our daily life, various generalisations of FS have been proposed (type-2 FS, interval-valued FS, intuitionistic FS, hesitant FS, Pythagorean FS, complex FS, neutrosophic sets, etc.), as well as several alternative theories (grey systems, rough sets, soft sets, etc.); for more details see Voskoglou (2019c).

AI's impressive advances in education have led a number of professionals and social thinkers to believe that teachers will be replaced by "clever" teaching education machines in future. They argue "when cars were invented, horses became obsolete", parallelising the two situations. However, many others believe that this will never happen. Learning information is indeed valuable for the students, but the most important thing is to learn how to argue logically and creatively. The latter seems to be impossible with only the help of the computers and other "clever" AI devices, since all those devices have been created and programmed by humans. Consequently, although many of those devices impressively exceed the speed of the human brain, it is logical to accept that they will never be able to achieve the quality of thinking of the human mind and sense of humanity.

FUTURE RESEARCH DIRECTIONS

This chapter focused mainly on the role of computers and AI in future education and the risks that lie behind this perspective. Although it has been concluded that it is rather unlikely that computers and other "clever" AI devices will replace teachers to educate students in future, it is certain that the role of the teacher will change dramatically in future classrooms. An interesting direction for future research is therefore required to examine the role of the new teacher. This requires changes or even a complete replacement of traditional teaching methods as well as the proper use of the new technological tools, both in and out of the classroom; as well as- familiarisation with the ideas and techniques of distance learning, etc. Obviously, this kind of research is closely related to the changes that the upcoming 4IR will bring about in society at large, and the effects which are not yet known exactly. Consequently, preparing our society at large and our students, in particular, to smoothly accommodate these changes is another important direction/impulse for future research.

CONCLUSION

The discussion in this chapter leads to the following conclusions:

- The upcoming, but not yet explicitly defined, new industrial revolution (the fourth according to Schwab, or the third according to other social thinkers) could be characterized as the era of IoT & E and the CPS. It has the potential to change our lives by bringing humanity to a better future, provided our society is ready to accept the dramatic changes that will follow.
- Formal Education today faces the major challenge of preparing students for a new way of life (and thinking) in the upcoming 4IR era, with rather uncertain future prospects.
- In this work, the important role that computers and AI could play in future education and the risks that lie behind this perspective were discussed. However, it is rather an illusion to believe that computers and other "clever" AI machines will replace the teachers for student education in the future, since all these machines were created and programmed by humans and therefore, although many of them impressively outperform people in speed, it is unlikely that they will ever be able to argue like humans do.
- Examining the changing role of teachers in future classrooms and the ways to prepare society to smoothly accommodate the dramatic changes in our lives the forthcoming 4IR will bring about are two important areas of future research.

ACKNOWLEDGMENT

The author wishes to thank the anonymous reviewers of the chapter for their valuable comments and suggestions that helped to improve its content and style.

REFERENCES

Anton, P. S., Silberglith, R., & Schveeder, J. (2011). *The Global Technology Revolution Bio/Nano/Materials Trends and their Synergies with Information Technology*. RAND.

Bergmann, J., & Sams, A. (2012). *Flip Your Classroom: Reach every student in every class every day* (1st ed.). ISTE.

Breazeal, C. (2002). *Designing Sociable Robots*. MIT Pres.

Cakula, S., & Salem, A. B. M. (2011), Analogy-Based Collaborative Model for e-Learning. *Proceedings of the Annual International Conference on Virtual and Augmented Reality in Education*, 98-105.

Crawford, K. (1996). Vygotskian approaches in human development in the information era. *Educational Studies in Mathematics*, *31*(1-2), 43–62. doi:10.1007/BF00143926Das, S., Day, A., Pal, A., & Roy, N. (2015). Applications of Artificial Intelligence in Machine Learning. *International Journal of Computers and Applications*, *115*(9).

Einhorn, S. (2012). *Micro-Worlds, Computational Thinking, and 21ˢᵗ Century Learning*. White Paper, Logo Computer Systems Inc.

Giannakopoulos, A. (2012). *Problem solving in academic performance: A study into critical thinking and mathematics content as contributors to successful application of knowledge and subsequent academic performance* (Ph.D. Thesis). University of Johannesburg, South Africa.

Halpern, D. (2003). *Thought and knowledge: An introduction to critical thinking* (4th ed.). Earlbaum.

Hodges, A. (2012). *Alan Turing: The Enigma (The Centenary Edition)*. Princeton University Press. doi:10.1515/9781400844975

Holmes, W., Bialik, M., & Fadel, C. (2019). *Artificial Intelligence in Education - Promises and Implications for Teaching and Learning*. Center of Curriculum Redesign.

Kazimoglu, C., Kiernan, M., Bacon, L., & MacKinnon, L. (2011). Understanding Computational Thinking Before Programming: Developing Guidelines for the Design of Games to Learn Introductory Programming Through Game-Play. *International Journal of Game-Based Learning*, *1*(3), 30–52. doi:10.4018/ijgbl.2011070103

Klir, G. J., & Folger, T. A. (1988). *Fuzzy Sets, Uncertainty and Information*. Prentice-Hall.

Lage, M. G., Platt, G. J., & Tregla, M. (2000). Inverting the classroom: A gateway to create an inclusive learning environment. *The Journal of Economic Education*, *31*(1), 30–43. doi:10.1080/00220480009596759

Leake, D. (2015). Problem Solving and Reasoning: Case-Based. In J. D. Wright (Ed.), *International Encyclopedia of the Social and Behavioral Sciences* (2nd ed., pp. 56–60). Elsevier. doi:10.1016/B978-0-08-097086-8.43075-8

Lee, J., Lim, C., & Kim, H. (2017). Development of an instructional design model for flipped learning in higher education. *Educational Technology Research and Development, 65*(2), 427–453. doi:10.100711423-016-9502-1

Liu, J., & Wang, L. (2010). Computational Thinking in Discrete Mathematics. *IEEE 2*nd *International Workshop on Education Technology and Computer Science*, 413-416.

McKinley, J. (2015). Critical argument and writer identity: Social constructivism as a theoretical framework for EFL academic writing. *Critical Inquiry in Language Studies, 12*(3), 184–207. doi:10.1080/15427587.2015.1060558

Moor, J. (2006). The Dartmouth College Artificial Intelligence Conference: The Next Fifty years. *AI Magazine, 27*(4), 87–91.

Rifkin, J. (2011). *The Third Industrial Revolution: How Lateral Power is Transforming Energy, the Economy and the World.* Palgrave - McMillan.

Rifkin, J. (2014). *The Zero Marginal Cost Society: The Internet of Things, the Collaborative Commons and the Eclipse of Capitalism.* St. Martins Press.

Salem, A.-B. M. (2019). Computational Intelligence in Smart Education and Learning. In *Proceedings of the International Conference on Information and Communication Technology in Business and Education*, (pp. 30-40). University of Economics.

Salem, A.-B. M., & Nikitaeva, N. (2019), Knowledge Engineering Paradigms for Smart Education and Smart Learning Systems. *Proceedings of the 42nd International Convention of the MIPRO Croatian Society*, 1823-1826. 10.23919/MIPRO.2019.8756685

Salem, A.-B.M., & Parusheva, S. (2018), Exploiting the Knowledge Engineering Paradigms for Designing Smart Learning Systems. *Eastern-European Journal of Enterprise Technologies, 2*(92), 38-44.

Schwab, K. (2015). *The Fourth Industrial Revolution.* Retrieved from https://www.weform.org/ press/2015/fourth-industrial-revolution

Schwab, K. (2016). *The Fourth Industrial Revolution.* Crown Publishing Group.

Taber, K. S. (2011). Constructivism as educational theory: Contingency in learning, and optimally guided instruction. In J. Hassaskhah (Ed.), *Educational Theory.* Nova Science Publishers.

Taipale, S., Vincent, J., Sapio, B., Lugano, G., & Fortunati, L. (2015). Introduction: Situating the Human in Social Robots. In *Social Robots from a Human Perspective* (pp. 1–17). Springer. doi:10.1007/978-3-319-15672-9_1

Tankelevcience, L., & Damasevicius, F. (2009). Characteristics for Domain Ontologies for Web Based Learning and their Applications for Quality Evaluation. *Informatics in Education*, *8*(1), 131–152.

Voskoglou, M. Gr. & Buckley, S. (2012). Problem Solving and Computers in a Learning Environment. *Egyptian Computer Science Journal*, *36*(4), 28–46.

Voskoglou, M. Gr. & Salem, A-B. M. (2014). Analogy-Based and Case-Based Reasoning: Two Sides of the Same Coin. *International Journal of Applications of Fuzzy Sets and Artificial Intelligence*, *4*, 5–51.

Voskoglou, M. Gr. (2017b). Finite Markov Chain and Fuzzy Logic Assessment Models: Emerging Research and Opportunities. Createspace Independent Publishing Platform (Amazon).

Voskoglou, M. G. (2008). Case-Based Reasoning: A Recent Theory for Problem-Solving and Learning in Computers and People. *Communications in Computer and Information Science*, *19*, 314–319. doi:10.1007/978-3-540-87783-7_40

Voskoglou, M. G. (2011). Problem Solving from Polya to Nowadays: A Review and Future Perspectives. In R. V. Nata (Ed.), *Progress in Education* (Vol. 22). Nova Science Publishers.

Voskoglou, M. G. (2016). Problem solving in the forthcoming era of the third industrial revolution. *International Journal of Psychological Research*, *10*(4), 361–380.

Voskoglou, M. G. (2017a). An Absorbing Markov Chain Model for Case-Based Reasoning. *International Journal of Computers*, *2*, 99–105.

Voskoglou, M. G. (2019a). Communities of practice for teaching and learning mathematics. *American Journal of Educational Research*, *7*(6), 186–191. doi:10.12691/education-7-6-2

Voskoglou, M. G. (2019b). An Application of the "5 E's" Instructional Treatment for Teaching the Concept of Fuzzy Set. *Sumerianz Journal of Education. Linguistics and Literature*, *2*(9), 73–76.

Voskoglou, M. G. (2019c). Generalizations of Fuzzy Sets and Relative Theories. In M. Voskoglou (Ed.), *An Essential Guide to Fuzzy Systems* (pp. 345–353). Nova Science Publishers.

Wenger, E. (1998). *Communities of Practice: Learning, Meaning, and Identity.* Cambridge University Press, UK. doi:10.1017/CBO9780511803932

Wing, J. M. (2006). Computational thinking. *Communications of the ACM, 49*(3), 33–35. doi:10.1145/1118178.1118215

Zadeh, L. A. (1965). Fuzzy Sets. *Information and Control, 8*(3), 338–353. doi:10.1016/S0019-9958(65)90241-X

ADDITIONAL READING

Denning, P. J. (2009). Beyond computational thinking. *Communications of the ACM, 52*(6), 28–30. doi:10.1145/1516046.1516054

Green, A. J. K., & Gillhooly, K. (2005). Problem solving. In N. Braisby & A. Gelatly (Eds.), *Cognitive Psychology*. Oxford University Press.

Lu, J. J., & Fletcher, G. H. L. (2009), Thinking about computational thinking, *Proceedings of the ACM Special Interest Group on Computer Science Education*, March 3-7, 260-264.

McSherry, D., & Stretch, Ch. (2011), Learning More for Experience in Case-Based Reasoning, *Proceedings of ICCR 2011, Lecture Notes in Computer Science*, Vol. 6880, pp. 151-165, Springer. 10.1007/978-3-642-23291-6_13

Qualls, J. A., & Sherrell, L. B. (2010). Why computational thinking should be integrated into the curriculum. *Journal of Computing Sciences in Colleges, 25*, 66–71.

Salem, A.-B.M., & Voskoglou, M.Gr. (2013). Applications of the CBR Methodology to Medicine. *Egyptian Computer Science Journal, 37*(7), 68–77.

Williams, R. L. (2005). Targeting critical thinking within teacher education: The potential impact on Society. *Teacher Educator, 40*(3), 163–187. doi:10.1080/08878730509555359

Yadav, A., Zhou, N., Mayfield, C., Hambrusch, S., & Korb, J. T. (2011), Introducing Computational Thinking in Education Courses, *Proceedings of the 42nd ACM Technical Symposium on Computer Science Education*, 465-470.

KEY TERMS AND DEFINITIONS

Artificial Intelligence (AI): AI is a branch of Computer Science that focuses on the creation of intelligent machines which mimic human reasoning and behavior.

Case-Based Reasoning (CBR): CBR is the process of solving problems based on previously solved similar problems (past cases). The use of computers enables a CBR system to build a continuously increasing "library" of past cases and to retrieve them for solving new problems.

Computational Thinking (CT): The term CT, coined by Jeannette Wing in 2006, describes solving problems, designing systems and understanding human behaviour based on the principles of computer science. CT includes analysing and organising data, automated problem solving and using it to solve similar problems. Nowadays, CT has become necessary to solve complex technological problems. If sufficient background knowledge is available and the necessary new knowledge is acquired through critical thinking, CT may help to solve the problem. CT is actually a hybrid of several other modes of thinking, like abstract, logical, algorithmic, constructive and modelling thinking, which summarises all previous modes for solving the corresponding problem.

Cyber-Physical Systems (CPS): Systems controlled through the Internet by computer programs, such as autonomous automobiles, autonomous control systems, distance medicine and robots.

Flipped Learning (FL): FL is a mixed process that involves both online and face-to-face teaching and requires turning around the didactic processes to which we are accustomed. The students acquire new knowledge outside the classroom through the use of digital platforms and technological tools. On the other hand, the homework is done in the classroom under the supervision of a teacher in order to promote the adequacy of learning and student autonomy and increase the time spent to practicing, problem solving and deepening of content.

Industrial Revolutions (IRs): A revolution is generally defined as a rapid and massive series of changes that lead to a radical transformation of human society. The first IR (1IR) began at the end of the 18th century and was characterized by the replacement of manual labour based on steam and water power. The second IR (2IR) began in the mid-19th century, used the power of electricity and was characterized by the mass production of goods. The third IR (3IR) started during the 1940's and is characterized as the era of automation, in which computers replaced humans as means of control. The upcoming fourth IR (4IR), although not yet explicitly known, could be described as the era of the Internet of Things and Energy and Cyber Physical Systems. Some social thinkers consider the 1IR and 2IR as the 1IR, which makes the upcoming 4IR to be considered as the 3IR.

Internet of Energy (IoE): This refers to the upgrading and automating of electricity infrastructures for energy producers and distributors. The IoE allows energy production and distribution to function more efficiently and cleanly with less waste. It is connected to the IoT. Large energy consumers, such as heaters, washing machines and boilers could be switched on when there is sufficient energy in the grid.

Internet of Things and Energy (IoT): This is a system of interrelated mechanical and digital devices that interact via the internet without requiring human-to-human or human-to-computer interaction (https://en.wikipedia.org/wiki/Internet_of_things). Products which use IoT technology are typically in the field of "smart home" like lighting, heating, security systems, cameras, appliances. Amazon's Alexa is another example of the IoT, providing services such as music, mail orders or switching smart home devices on and off in response to spoken commands.

Social Robots: Social robots are AI devices to interact with humans and other robots. They may understand speech and facial expressions, and are used at home, and in customer service, education, etc. Examples of educational applications include the Tico robot, which was developed to improve children's motivation in the classroom, and the Bandit robot, which was developed to teach social behaviour to autistic children, etc.

Chapter 5
Promoting the Growth of Fourth Industrial Revolution Information Communication Technology Students:
The Implications for Open and Distance E-Learning

Dalize van Heerden
https://orcid.org/0000-0002-7539-8995
University of South Africa, South Africa

Leila Goosen
https://orcid.org/0000-0003-4948-2699
University of South Africa, South Africa

ABSTRACT

The purpose of this chapter is providing readers with an overview of the content promoting the growth of the Fourth Industrial Revolution (4IR) and the implications for information and communication technology (ICT) open distance e-learning (ODeL) students. Preparing students for the 4IR presents important and complicated opportunities towards changing higher education. Education should be about content design and delivery for teaching, learning, and assessment, with the profile of ODeL ICT students at the core. This chapter reports on issues, controversies,

DOI: 10.4018/978-1-7998-4882-0.ch005

and problems arising from the 4IR. The mixed-method research approach adopted involved collecting and analyzing quantitative and qualitative data obtained from first-year courses at a Southern Africa institution. The emerging picture cautions concerning students' real biographic information and digital literacy in a developing world context. The conclusion summarizes the content and informs instructors to examine their perceptions of student profiles regarding teaching, learning, and assessment in preparation for the 4IR.

INTRODUCTION

The Fourth Industrial Revolution (4IR) feels like the ghost in the machine. It is coming or may already be here. It seems to be all around. However, there is no common understanding of what 4IR means. There are many names and definitions for the 4IR. 4IR is the naming convention used, as it is a widely communicated definition (World Economic Forum (WEF) Asian Development Bank (ADB), 2017). The latter positions the First Industrial Revolution to be that of water and steam power towards mechanization, while the Second Industrial Revolution was based on mass production, the division of labor, assembly lines, and electricity. According to Rouse (2017), the Third Industrial Revolution, which is also called the digital revolution, is seen as involving the development of computers, electronics, Information Technology (IT) and automated production "since the middle of the 20th century."

The 4IR is about the emergence and penetration of "the current and developing environment in which" very advanced, highly disruptive Unified Communication and Collaboration (UC&C) technologies and IT trends (Bolton, Goosen, & Kritzinger, 2016), "such as the Internet of Things (IoT)," Virtual Reality (VR), networks, Artificial Intelligence "(AI), robotics, blockchain and 3D printing, that are transforming" (WEF ADB, 2017, p. 4) "spheres of life never before imagined, from" Cyber-Physical Systems (CPS) to enterprise digitization enabled by embedding technology within our larger societies, cultural community lives, and even in the home and the human body (Bozzoli, 2019).

Preparing students for the Fourth Industrial Revolution is of paramount importance and could be complicated and dialectical, with numerous opportunities towards changing higher education. All education systems should be designed for teaching, learning and assessing the knowledge of students; the core of any educational system should thus always be the student. With the student being the core of the educational system, the profile of Open and Distance e-Learning (ODeL) Information and Communication Technology (ICT) student determine the design and delivery of content. Like the book, this chapter will therefore concentrate on the role of formal education in preparing students for uncertain futures, and for societies that are changing at great speed in terms of its ability to drive job creation, economic growth and the prosperity for millions in the future.

The purpose of this chapter is to provide readers with an overview of the content exploring aspects regarding promoting the growth of the 4IR for ICT students, together with the implications for ODeL. It aims to unpack some of the issues around 4IR, with reference to the context of the College of Science, Engineering and Technology (CSET) and innovation.

Universities need to become more agile and find time to not only keep on mastering new technologies, but, in fact, use Information Communication Technologies (ICTs) to facilitate teaching and learning (Libbrecht & Goosen, 2016). Change management will have to be the new normal across all Information and Communication Technology departments. And now, more than ever before, fingers should be kept on the pulse of change – sharing knowledge with peers and colleagues. Exciting times lie ahead for the industry, and by working together, universities will be able stay ahead of these changes, and overcome challenges to be more competitive globally.

The qualifications applicable to this study are the Diploma in Information Technology, Bachelor of Science in Computing and the Bachelor of Science in Informatics. These qualifications are offered by the University of South Africa (UNISA), which is the largest Open and Distance e-Learning institution in Africa and the longest standing dedicated distance education university in the world. The main objectives of these qualifications are to provide students with the abilities to demonstrate an understanding of the underlying concepts and principles of computing, together with choosing the 'best' and most applicable and applying these in programming languages in the workplace (Goosen, 2008). The students should also show a high level of cognitive and other generic skills, including problem solving, as well as those related to written and spoken communication.

As can be derived from the objectives of the qualifications and the use of the blended teaching and learning approach, some inroads have already been made towards preparing students for the 4IR. The main focus of the chapter will therefore be to report on openness and connectedness in ODeL, technologies for the 4IR and how these will be associated with the impact of Industry 4.0 on higher education globally, and quality assurance of ODeL institutions and programs, with specific emphasis on the profile of ODeL ICT students towards the 4IR.

What are the *issues, controversies and problems* related to realizing the rich potential of 4IR technologies in education? This chapter therefore also reports on *issues, controversies and problems* related to the profile of ODeL ICT students towards needs arising from the 4IR. The irony is that standing on the brink of a brave new 4IR world, life could potentially be made better for all the world's people.

The chapter will also explore aspects related to the implications of the Fourth Industrial Revolution for Open and Distance e-Learning and Information and Communication Technology students.

This chapter reports on concepts, opportunities and challenges that are related to the profile of the ODeL ICT student towards the needs arising from the Fourth Industrial Revolution. Data was obtained from two first year ICT modules presented at an open, distance and e-learning institution in Southern Africa. Although a mixed-method research approach was adopted, which involved the collection and analysis of both quantitative and qualitative data, only quantitative results will be presented in this chapter.

The emerging picture paints a cautionary tale, particularly concerning the lived reality of students' biographic information and digital literacy in a developing world context. In this regard, the chapter informs instructors to examine their perceptions of student profiles in light of teaching, learning and assessment in preparation for the Fourth Industrial Revolution.

Target Audience

The target audience for this chapter, as for the book as a whole, includes educators, general and human resources managers/directors, organizational and learning design specialists, as well as IT and e-learning professionals.

Having described the general perspective of the chapter, to end, and in line with some of the recommended topics for this book, the objectives of the chapter will now be specifically stated as covering:

- The *issues, controversies and problems,* as well as numerous opportunities towards changing higher education, associated with the impact of Industry 4.0 globally
- Changes needed to realize the potential of new technologies in industry
- Skills training relevant to Industry 4.0
- Using 4IR technologies to increase efficiency
- Eliminate poverty and reduce inequality while advancing the economy and increasing competitiveness.

BACKGROUND

This section of the chapter will provide broad definitions and discussions related to the chapter's specific topic of promoting the growth of 4IR ICT students, and the implications for ODeL and incorporate the views of others (literature review) into the discussion to support, refute, or demonstrate the authors' position on the topic.

According to Akbar, Rashid and Embong (2018, p. 192), in the previous decade, Internet of Things technologies were motivating nations to move towards digital transformation. This transformation was part of the "Fourth Industrial Revolution (Industry 4.0)" and the latter authors considered a technology-based learning system in the context of Internet of Things education.

Safiullin, Krasnyuk and Kapelyuk (2019, p. 1) defined the term 'Smart city' "as a concept and model of new urbanization based on" the Fourth Industrial Revolution and the application of the "new generation technologies of Industry 4.0 (Internet of things, cloud computing, cyber-physical systems, big data and other technologies)".

The purpose of the paper by Shahroom and Hussin (2018) was discussing what was happening to education systems in the era of the Fourth Industrial Revolution, by investigating links between the Industrial Revolution 4.0 and education. D'Souza and Mudin (2018, p. 1) more specifically looked at the role of universities in these contexts, where it will indeed "be a revolution that may" involve changing towards new ways in which "human beings think, live and work".

The study by Botha and Coetzee (2016, p. 242) investigated the relationship between students' "self-directedness (as measured by the Adult Learner Self-Directedness Scale) and" the influence of "biographical factors such as age, race, and gender of adult" students enrolled in a South African ODeL environment, whereas Goosen and Van Heerden (2019b) delved into student support for Information and Communication Technology modules in ODeL environments towards self-directed learning.

"Academic institutions such as the University of South Africa" are using ICT "in order to conduct their daily primary operations, which are teaching and learning." With UNISA being "the only distance learning university in South Africa", Mkhize, Mtsweni and Buthelezi (2016, p. 295) implemented a diffusion of innovations approach towards the evaluation of learning management system usage at this ODeL institution.

"As technology advances, using gadgets like smart phones, iPads, tablets and other mobile devices is becoming popular among people today as the rise in technology is overwhelming. Recently", the use of mobile technologies have started "playing an increasingly significant role in" promoting Education 4.0 for higher education (Karim, Abu, Adnan, & Suhandoko, 2018, p. 34) – although such development is in line with the theme of the book, of promoting inclusive growth in the Fourth Industrial Revolution, it is especially so with the topic of this chapter, of promoting the growth of 4IR ICT students, and the implications for ODeL in such a context.

"Given the rapid rise of mobile-only users", Correa, Pavez and Contreras (2018, p. 1) investigated whether the digital inclusion process could be achieved through (mobile) "smartphones. By using Chile as a case study, a country that has strongly promoted mobile connections to address internet access gaps", the latter authors compared mobile-only and computer users' internet access, skills and use.

In a discussion, Haldane (2019, p. 2) indicated that "the societal side-effects of the Fourth Industrial Revolution may be even greater than its predecessors. The focus of" most previous studies had "been on the effects of new technologies on private companies. There has also been some analysis, though far less, on how the Fourth Industrial Revolution might reshape the public sector. There has been little, if any, consideration of how this technological wave will break over the" so-called 'Third Sector' - charities, community groups, and social enterprises.

Considering the frictions and tensions around Africa's socio-cultural and economic development in the dawn of the Fourth Industrial Revolution (Tondi, 2019, p. 239), "and the existence of some of tendencies and actions that are not in" favor "of the continent's advancement, the main aim of" the article by the latter author was arguing for deliberate attention to the significance of Indigenous Knowledge Systems (IKS) in this regard.

Levin (2018, p. 34) explored how building people-centered "and people-driven approaches to governance and development have been shaped by reactions to corporate capture of the state as well as the discourses of good governance and new public management and the influence" these "have had on public" service and administration culture in Africa for youth empowerment and development.

In the context of the Association of Southeast Asian Nations (ASEAN), the WEF ADB (2017) asked what the Fourth Industrial Revolution means for regional economic integration?

"While the 4IR has the potential to impact on all industries and all nations, regardless of their location or state of development, many of the discussions of the 4IR and its impact are focused on advanced economies" (Ayentimi & Burgess, 2019, p. 641). The latter authors therefore asked whether the Fourth Industrial Revolution is relevant to Sub-Saharan Africa, and what "the prospects and constraints of the 4IR" were in such a context.

The Fourth "Industrial Revolution provides a window of opportunity for the developing world and in particular, Sub-Saharan Africa to catch-up in terms of social and economic development by enhancing growth through technological advances" (Gross, 2019, p. 1). The latter author therefore queried whether technological leapfrogging can be used as a strategy to enhance such economic growth?

The objective of the paper by Letaba, Pretorius and Pretorius (2018, p. 171) was scrutinizing and deriving innovation profiles "in developing countries, such as South Africa, from" the perspective of technology road mapping practitioners. The specific research questions addressed included "the main priorities for innovation in" such a context.

"As the world population ages and older adults comprise a growing proportion of current and potential Internet users, understanding the state of Internet use among older adults as well as the ways their use has evolved may clarify how best to support" their digital media use (Hunsaker & Hargittai, 2018, p. 3937) – the latter authors therefore provided an applicable review.

Looking at digital inequality among older adults, from internet access to internet skills, Hargittai, Piper and Morris (2018, p. 1) indicated that although much research examined "the factors that affect technology adoption and use, less is known about how older adults as a group differ in their ability to use the Internet. The theory of digital inequality suggests that even once people have gone online, differences among them will persist in important ways such as their online skills". The latter authors therefore analyzed "survey data about older American adults' Internet skills to examine whether skills differ in this group and if they do, what explains differential online abilities." Hargittai, et al. (2018) found that there was considerable variation in Internet know-how and this related "to both socioeconomic status and autonomy of use. The results suggest that attempts to achieve a knowledgeable older adult population regarding Internet use must take into account these users' socioeconomic background and available access points".

Caruso (2018, p. 379) enquired whether digital innovation and the Fourth Industrial Revolution represented epochal social changes, since ICTs "have come to comprehensively represent images and expectations of the future. Hopes of ongoing progress, economic growth, skill upgrading and possibly also" democratization "are attached to new ICTs", but also fears of totalitarian control and alienation.

"Industrial engineering is concerned with the design, improvement, and installation of integrated systems of people, material, information, equipment, and energy. Industrial engineering science and knowledge play a very important role in" development, and Sutopo (2019, p. 1) therefore looked into the roles of industrial engineering education for promoting innovations and technology commercialization in the digital era.

"Computer programming has been gradually emphasized in recent computer literacy education and regarded as a requirement for all ... students in some countries. To understand ... students' perceptions about their own learning", Tsai, Wang and Hsu (2019, p. 1345) developed the computer programming self-efficacy scale for computer literacy education.

According to Goosen and Van Heerden (2013b, p. 159), lecturers seem to prefer constructivist learning as a pedagogy for driving "the teaching taking place in" their modules. "Collaborative-constructivist online learning also appears to be "well aligned with Ukraine's post-revolutionary aspirations for" globalized and transformed higher education. The study by Blayone, et al. (2018, p. 279) surveyed the digital competencies of university students and professors in Ukraine, in terms of technology, pedagogy and education, for fully online collaborative learning.

Finally, Goosen and Van Heerden (2013a), (2013b) and (2018) looked at tools and tips, as well as how the project-based learning and assessment of students in higher education were influencing the pass rates of an ICT module in an ODeL context at such an institution.

MAIN FOCUS OF THE CHAPTER

Issues, Controversies, Problems

This section of the chapter will present the authors' perspective on issues, controversies, problems, etc., as these relate to the theme of promoting inclusive growth in the 4IR, and arguments supporting the authors' position. It will further compare and contrast with what has been, or is currently being, done as it relates to the chapter's specific topic of promoting the growth of 4IR ICT students, and the implications for ODeL in this context, and the main theme of the book.

Although concerns "about student attrition and failure is not a new phenomenon", Higher Education Institutions "(HEIs) have struggled to significantly reduce the" so-called 'revolving door syndrome' (Slade & Prinsloo, 2015, p. 1). ODeL HEIs are particularly susceptible and the latter authors therefore attempted to stem the flow by improving retention for such students.

Using fourteen focus group interviews, Cross, Frazier, Kim and Cross (2018, p. 111) provided a comparison of the perceptions of barriers to academic success among "high-ability students from high- (n= 36) and low-income (n= 45)" family groups, which they were asked to describe. "Three themes were identified through the qualitative analysis", which, in line with the last objective set for this chapter, can be implemented towards not only exposing, but ultimately eliminating poverty of a different kind, and reducing inequality, while advancing the economy and increasing competitiveness.

Challenges and Questions

The "Industrial Revolution 4.0 has dawned with a new challenge wherein" Information Technology, the "internet and cyber-physical systems are" increasingly becoming a priority across the globe (D'Souza & Mudin, 2018, p. 1).

Driverless cars with AI "and automated supermarkets run by collaborative robots (cobots) working without human supervision have sparked off new debates" around whether what is happening is, actually, the 4IR (Özdemir & Hekim, 2018,

p. 65). There are numerous frameworks available, ranging from this merely being an extension of the Third Industrial Revolution, to it being the birth of Industry/ Society 5.0.

According to Dogo, Salami, Aigbavboa and Nkonyana (2019, p. 107), the advancement and convergence of the Internet of Things, "mobile devices technology, big data and cloud computing with its various technological implementations are finally enabling the vision of Smart Cities and Industry 4.0." In light of the Fourth Industrial Revolution, Nick and Pongrácz (2016) presented, as possible answer to some of the challenges these cities are facing, a concept to be introduced for creating Industry 4.0 'ready' urban environments and build Smart Cities. In their paper, Lom, Pribyl and Svitek (2016, p. 1) similarly proposed "the conjunction of the Smart City Initiative and the concept of Industry 4.0" as a part of smart cities.

On the way from Industry 4.0 to Industry 5.0, from digital manufacturing to digital societies (Skobelev & Borovik, 2017), suddenly, AI and machine learning are mainstream, the 'amplification' of everything is becoming a reality, and 5G and even 6G are on the horizon. With new technologies having the potential to revolutionize manufacturing industries, everyone is putting in an effort towards making sense of Big Data with artificial intelligence and Next-Generation technology policies, by asking questions like "what will be the impacts of extreme automation, turbocharged by the Internet of Things" (Özdemir & Hekim, 2018, p. 65)?

Although several challenges are obstacles to the kind of digital transformation envisioned by the 4IR, one of which "is talent in this field" (Akbar, et al., 2018, p. 192), Shahroom and Hussin (2018, p. 314) are of the opinion that information "management is the most challenging issue faced by any" organization in developing countries.

In terms of the future of **jobs,** employment, skills and workforce strategy, the "Fourth Industrial Revolution is interacting with other socio-economic and demographic factors to create a perfect storm of business model change in all industries, resulting in major disruptions to" labor "markets. New categories of **jobs** will emerge," (World Economic Forum, 2016). Artificial intelligence and robotics are already partly or wholly displacing many routine **jobs,** and while technology may create many as yet unimagined **jobs,** teachers and professors are in the position of having to educate for the unknown. How can teaching, lecturing, nurturing, mentoring, and the curation and transmission of knowledge be reimagined? How can students be prepared to thrive when confronted with the unexpected? How can plans be made for yet unknown disruptive change?

Lamprini and Bröchler (2018, p. 2) probed how collaborative innovation and technology in an educational ecosystem could meet the challenges raised by the Fourth Industrial Revolution. Nowadays, ICT students are confronted by the 4IR, featuring "a great range of new and advanced technologies that influences all the domains of economies and industries". In light of the issues, controversies, problems and challenges already mentioned in this chapter, the primary research "question that this revolution raises" and that will be addressed by this chapter is: How "it can lead to a future that", although uncertain, has education, which had been repurposed to respond effectively to promote the growth of 4IR ICT students and what are the implications of the latter for ODeL?

The secondary research questions would then be to determine:

- How can the growth of 4IR ICT students be promoted?
- What are the implications of the latter for Open and Distance e-Learning?

METHODOLOGY

In order to address the objectives set for this study, student profiles were evaluated, to determine the impact of the 4IR for Open Distance e-Learning Information and Communication Technology students, based on their demographic details, computer literacy and technology usage. The research focused on students who were registered for the Diploma in Information Technology, the Bachelor of Science in Computing and the Bachelor of Science in Informatics.

The researchers conducted a survey. The survey approach was chosen, because of the nature and objectives of the study (Creswell, 2014). This approach provides the opportunity to use questionnaires or interviews as the instrument of data collection (De Vaus, 2014). The advantages stated by Olivier (2009), which included the ease of distribution over a wide geographic area, as well as the reduction in cost and bias incurred when using interviews (Fink, 2016), lead the researchers to use a questionnaire. The first section of the questionnaire consisted of the respondent profile and the second of the respondent's access to, and usage of, technology.

Students were contacted via Short Message System (SMS) and requested to participate in the survey. Four SMSs were sent to 3,896 students registered in the second semester of 2019.

SOLUTIONS AND RECOMMENDATIONS

This section of the chapter will discuss solutions and recommendations in dealing with the issues, controversies and/or problems presented in the preceding sections.

Solutions

Data towards solutions were obtained from two first-year ICT modules presented at an ODeL institution in Southern Africa. A mixed-method research approach was adopted (Creswell, 2014), with a research design in social research involving the collection and analysis of both quantitative and qualitative data; only quantitative results, however, are presented in this chapter.

A total of 422 respondents from first year programming modules answered the survey voluntarily, for a response rate of 11%.

The respondents consisted of 135 (32%) female and 287 (68%) male students (see Figure 1).

Figure 1. Student sample gender distribution

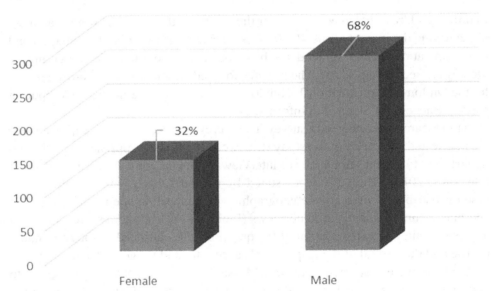

Only 125 (30%) of these students indicated English as their home language, with various other South(ern) African and European languages for the remainder (see Figure 2).

Similar to the university profile of all students, the ages of students doing these modules show that 52 (12%) of them were between the ages of 19 and 21, 178 (42%) were between the ages of 22 and 30, 150 (36%) were between the ages of 31 and 40, with the remaining 42 (10%) older than 41 (see Figure 3).

Figure 2. Student sample home languages

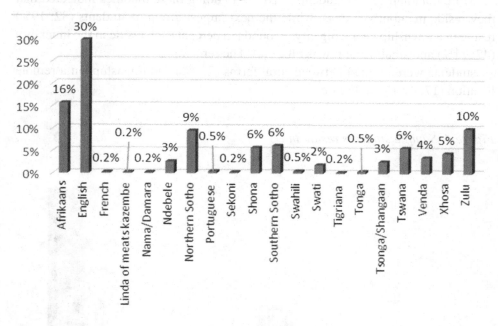

Figure 3. Sample students' age distribution

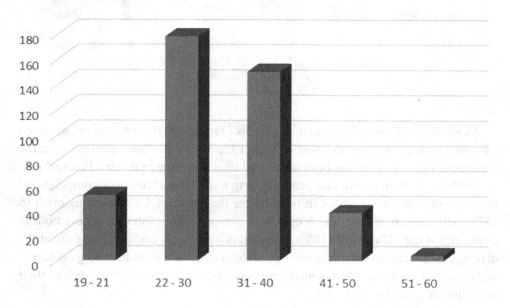

More than half on the students (228; 54%) doing these modules indicated that they reside in suburban areas, while the next largest group of students (82; 19%) reside in a township near a big city. Around ten percent each reside in the inner city (47; 11%) and small rural towns (40; 9%). The remaining

students were divided between rural farms (7; 2%) and townships in a remote location (17; 4%) - see Figure 4.

Figure 4. Sample students reside in ...

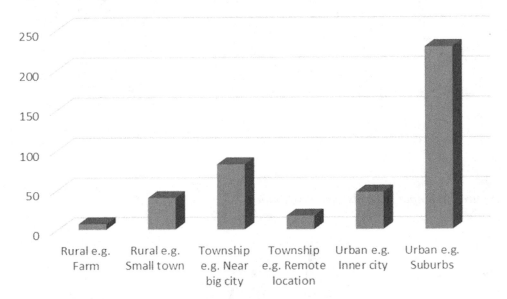

More than half on these students (245; 58%) indicated that they were employed on a full-time basis, while almost a third (132; 31%) were unemployed, with the remainder (45; 11%) having been employed on a part time basis (see Figure 5).

Students studying computer programming must have access to a computer and the internet in order to successfully complete the modules. Of these students, 156 (37%) indicated that they had access to a computer with internet access both at home and at the office, 120 (19%) indicated at home only and 22 (5%) only at the office. UNISA regional centers assisted sixteen (4%) of the students to gain access and eleven (3%) of the students made use of public computer facilities, such as their local library or an internet café.

Figure 5. Sample students' employment status

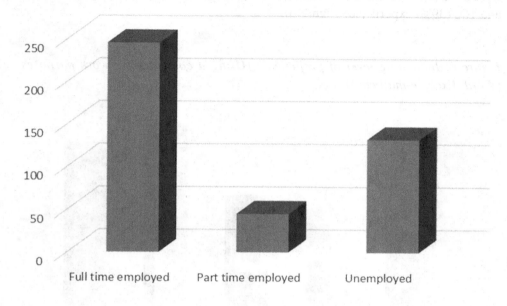

Computer Literacy

Fifty-two (12% of the) students indicated a fundamental awareness (basic knowledge) when using a computer for relaxation (gaming, social media etc.), thirty (7%) were novices with limited experience, 81 (19%) were at an intermediate level (practical application), a third (138; 33%) advanced (applied theory) and 121 (29%) considered themselves to be experts (recognized authority) - see Table 1.

Table 1. Sample students' level of proficiency when using a computer for relaxation

	Number	Percent
Fundamental Awareness (basic knowledge)	52	12%
Novice (limited experience)	30	7%
Intermediate (practical application)	81	19%
Advanced (applied theory)	138	33%
Expert (recognized authority)	121	29%

When using a computer for work purposes (Word, Excel, e-mail, etc.), the number of students with a fundamental awareness was forty (9%), 21 (5%) indicated they were novices (had limited experience), 51 (12%) intermediate, 144 (34%) advanced and 166 (39%) experts (see Figure 6).

Figure 6. Indicating level of proficiency [Using a computer for work purposes (Word, Excel, e-mail etc.)]

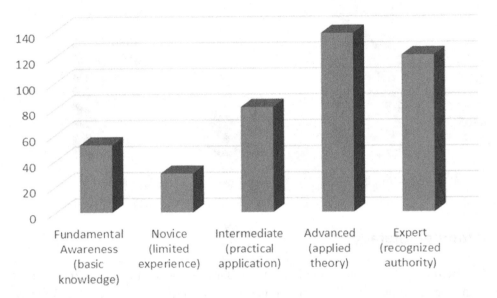

Computer usage for study purposes, for example Google or using their institutional Learning Management System (LMS) for ICT education in the cyber world (Goosen & Naidoo, 2014), showed that

41 (10%) of the students had a fundamental awareness, 11 (3%) were novices, 33 (8%) were at an intermediate level, 161 (38%) considered themselves to be advanced users and 176 (42%) as expert users (see Figure 7).

The respondents to the questionnaire were all studying first year programming modules and indicated that 54 (13%) had a fundamental awareness of programming (writing code, rendering code, find errors, etc.), 45 (11%) were novices at programming, 98 (23%) were at an intermediate level, 136 (32%) were advanced and 89 (21%) considered themselves to be experts at programming (see Figure 8).

As Information and Communication Technology and engineering students' computer literacy also includes the installation of software, the respondents indicated that 44 (10%) had a fundamental awareness, 25 (6%) were novices, 50 (12%) were

Figure 7. Proficiency [Using a computer for studying (finding information, accessing myUNISA, etc.)]

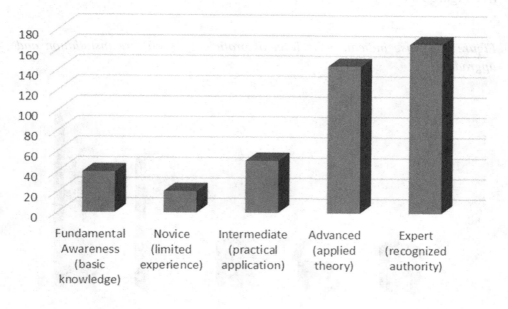

Figure 8. [Using a computer for programming (writing code, rendering code, find errors, etc.)]

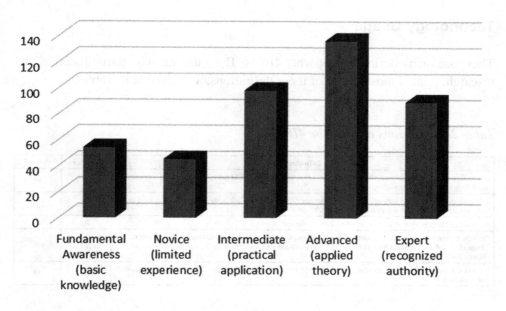

intermediate, 132 (31%) were advanced and 171 (41%) were experts in this regard (see Figure 9).

Figure 9. Please indicate your level of proficiency [Software installation and upgrading]

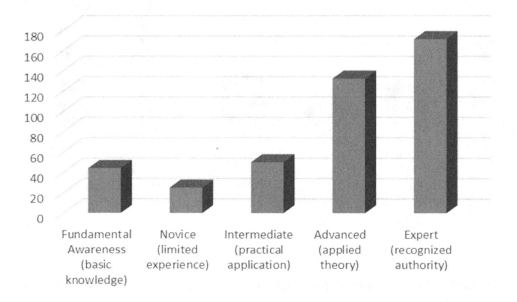

Technology Usage

There are many definitions of what 4IR is. The students, who participated in this research, related most to two of these definitions, as indicated in Table 2.

Table 2. Definitions of what the 4IR is

Definitions	Number	Percent
It describes a world where individuals move between digital domains and offline reality with the use of connected technology to enable and manage their lives	33	8%
It "entails the penetration of very advanced technology and IT into spheres of life never before imagined, from the body and the home, to work and cultural and social life" (Bozzoli, 2019).	78	18%
It is a deeper integration of technology into societies and the human body	26	6%
"It is the current and developing environment in which disruptive technologies and trends such as the Internet of Things (IoT), robotics, virtual reality (VR) and artificial intelligence (AI) are changing the way we live and work" (Rouse, 2017).	267	63%
It refers to a systemic transformation that impacts on civil society, governance structures, human identity, economics and manufacturing	18	4%

Discussion of the Implications for Open and Distance e-Learning

The gender distribution for this particular sample is very similar to what had previously been reported for similar samples in these modules (see Table 3). As there are no gender related issues in the teaching and learning of these modules, it is not necessary to make any adjustments to the presentation or development of the modules and their learning materials. It is, however, very important to provide extra motivation and support to the female students, due to the national and international shortage of females in the Science, Engineering and Technology fields.

Table 3. Student gender distributions in other publications for similar samples

	Male
Van Heerden and Goosen (2012)	71%
Goosen and Van Heerden (2013b)	70%

As the subject field of Information and Communication Technology is predominantly English, the modules are presented in English only. The online study material is, however, written in a fairly informal and direct manner to assist with ease of understanding.

Mature students, who are able to take responsibility for their studies and have the stability and discipline to make a success of it, should undertake studying through ODeL. The fact that the largest percentage of students doing these modules were younger than 30 is somewhat concerning. Experience has shown that younger students are still starting their careers, getting married, starting families and enjoying being young, thus causing them to not have the drive or discipline to succeed in ODeL. In an attempt to keep these students motivated and on schedule with their studies, regular communication is sent to them via e-mail and SMS messages.

With the ongoing debate surrounding access to technology, the statistics with regard to the distribution of where students reside were kept in mind when the modules were developed.

While designing these modules, facts related to students' employment status had to be taken into consideration, as employed students generally have less time to spend on their studies, compared to those who are not employed. For this reason, the number of assessments used in an open distance e-learning environment to promote self-directed learning (Van Heerden & Goosen, 2019) in the modules were increased in an attempt to motivate students to continuously work on their studies.

Recommendations

In summarizing the content of the chapter, the recommendation is made that teachers and professors should examine their perceptions of student profiles in light of teaching, learning and assessment in preparation for the 4IR.

Since Van Heerden and Goosen (2012, p. 146) indicated that empirical research was "needed in order to compile pedagogical evidence about the use of vodcasts in" educational contexts, the authors of this chapter recommend that vodcasts be used to teach programming, especially in ODeL environments.

It is further recommended that teachers and professors use e-learning management system technologies for taking the teaching and learning of programming in an ODeL environment beyond the current horizon, as well as to address online and open distance education context *issues, controversies and problems* (Goosen & Van Heerden, 2016). Along with Goosen and Van Heerden (2019a), the authors of this chapter also recommend that research-based opportunities for first-year programming students should be promoted by providing them with relevant and quality ICT education.

Curriculum

Similar to previous publications (Goosen & Van Heerden, 2013a, p. 1432), the authors of this chapter recommend that students be encouraged towards interacting through the LMS, as this "not only enhances the learning experience, but also enforces the importance of the **curriculum** they are studying for" these modules and qualifications.

"In terms of the set of guiding criteria offered" to students (Goosen & Van Heerden, 2013a, p. 1434), the authors of this chapter recommend that "project-based learning projects should be focused on" questions, which lead students towards encountering "concepts that are central to the curriculum", as well as problems, which "occur in the real world and" which people care about.

"To ensure that project-based learning and assessment are applied successfully" and "in order to be valid" (Goosen & Van Heerden, 2013a, p. 1435), the authors of this chapter recommend that these should be aligned with the curricula of the modules being taught. For these modules, the prescribed books being used not only suit the curricula, but also use and promote project-based learning. Hence, the curricula for these particular modules are suited to project-based learning.

To ensure that Project-Based Learning (PBL) was implemented authentically, the authors of this chapter recommend that the **curricula**, instruction and assessment of applicable modules "were redesigned to include PBL, as opposed to simply adding project-based assessment into" existing modules (Goosen & Van Heerden, 2013b, p. 158).

According to Goosen and Van Heerden (2019a, p. 217), student-centeredness is multi-dimensional, relating to module design and implementation, the selection of a "relevant **curriculum** suited to the likely" module needs, the organization of module materials and the delivery of such modules. In order to comply with current knowledge about e-learning and assessment, the authors of this chapter recommend that e-learning be steered towards achieving the "sustainable motivation and engagement of" students.

Pedagogy

Along with Chun (2010), the authors of this chapter recommend that teaching should be performed in such a way that pedagogical and assessment practices are linked.

As "improved interactivity has been one of the key drivers in pedagogical shifts in teaching and learning methods", in line with Van Heerden and Goosen (2012, p. 149), the authors of this chapter recommend that lecturers use their LMS for welcoming students and integrating pedagogical applications into their modules.

According to Goosen and Van Heerden (2013b, p. 159), "finding authentic methods of assessment in Higher Education, especially in the case of" ODeL, "is a question of good pedagogy." As lecturers, who present programming modules like the ones discussed in this chapter through ODeL, the authors recommend that "theoretical guidelines or instructional principles" be found, which could assist "students in developing and applying the required skills".

Goosen and Van Heerden (2015, p. 116) presented an introduction "on aspects relating to what the pedagogy underlying" these modules was, and how the modules were "adapted for a blended e-learning approach." In light of the former, the authors of this chapter warned that every teacher "adopting technology as part of their teaching strategy" would be "confronted with the question of whether the technology they use enhances their pedagogy". It is therefore recommended that they consider that incorporating "technology into teaching for the mere purpose of using technology, without considering the pedagogical implications, will cause a lot more harm than good."

In line with Goosen and Van Heerden (2015), the authors of this chapter recommend that teachers at higher education institutions incorporate blogging into their pedagogy, in terms of helping their students to understand introductory programming concepts.

"In an attempt to address the high drop-out" rates in modules, such as those discussed in this chapter, as lecturers responsible for such modules, the authors recommend that "a number of educational technologies", which can "include Additional Resources, Announcements, Blogs, Discussion Forums, Learning Units, Meetings, Schedule and Self-Assessments", be selected (Goosen & Van Heerden, 2017, p. 82). The latter can be used to enhance the effects of a social constructivist pedagogy on such modules (Chetty & Barlow-Jones, 2012) and "to incorporate the different learning strategies of" at-risk students completing a computer programming module at a post-secondary institution "in an attempt to ultimately improve the performance outcomes and motivate students to make use of the" LMS.

FUTURE RESEARCH DIRECTIONS

This section of the chapter will discuss future and emerging trends and provide insight about the future of the book's theme of promoting inclusive growth in the 4IR, from the perspective of the chapter's specific topic of promoting the growth of 4IR ICT students, and the implications for ODeL. The viability of a paradigm, model, implementation issues of proposed programs, etc., may be included in this section. Future research opportunities within the domain of the topic will also be suggested.

In a book on adaptation, resistance and access to instructional technologies towards assessing future and emerging trends in education, Reid (2011) recommended that the momentum of technology in the classroom be retained. In terms of understanding such technology adoption, Straub (2009) looked at some of the related theory and future directions for informal learning, while Evans (2019) presented findings and future directions from ten years of learning design at the Open University.

Referring to the movie 'Back to the Future', Lochlainn, Mhichíl, Beirne and Brown (2019) explained that feedback and reflection were key elements in MOOC re-design.

Blayone, et al. (2018, p. 292) indicated that their future "research might develop a short version of the instrument" that these authors had been using "aimed at the specific context of use to increase data-collection efficiency and obviate the need for data reduction."

As Slade and Prinsloo (2015, p. 1) warned that words like 'crisis' "have become endemic to discourses on the current and future states of higher education", in the context of digital learning theory, Ehlers (2019) suggested that the viability of **future** skills and higher education, as well as 'future skill readiness' should be included.

"The way people work, the skills they need to thrive in their **jobs** and the trajectories of their careers are rapidly evolving" (World Economic Forum, 2017, p. 01). These changes - driven by technological innovation, demographics, shifting business models and nature of work - "are significantly altering the skills required by the" labor "market. Continuous learning lies at the heart of thriving in the context of" accelerating workforce reskilling for the fourth industrial revolution. Social, economic and political systems are "placing pressure on leaders and policy-makers to" shape an agenda for the **future** of education, gender and work (WEF ADB, 2017, p. 4).

In terms of predictive modelling, Slade and Prinsloo (2015, p. 5) indicated that work had "been underway for some time on a set of predictive models which have the potential to identify a range of possible future outcomes at individual student or module level. .... When applied to current students, the model" provided "predictions of the likelihood of each student reaching a series of future milestones. This model" used "demographic and previous study history data and" had potential use for Student Support Teams (SSTs) "wanting to employ a more rigorous approach to identifying students at potential future risk of" for example, non-completion.

The approach described by Slade and Prinsloo (2015, p. 6) had "been piloted on a number of" first level modules and seemed "to provide a reliable indication of students at risk of" for example, non-submission "of future work and thus of" non-completion for providing such student support for Information and Communication Technology modules in open distance environments towards self-directed learning (Goosen & Van Heerden, 2019b).

CONCLUSION

This last chapter conclusion section will provide discussion of the overall coverage of the chapter, summarizing the content, as well as concluding remarks.

The purpose of this chapter was introduced as providing readers with an overview of content promoting the growth of Fourth Industrial Revolution Information and Communication Technology students and the implications for Open and Distance e-Learning. Preparing students for the 4IR presents important and complicated opportunities towards changing higher education, which should be about content design and delivery for teaching, learning and assessment, with the profile of ODeL ICT students at the core.

The background section of the chapter provided broad definitions and discussions of the chapter's specific topic of promoting the growth of 4IR ICT students, and the implications for ODeL and incorporated the views of others (literature review) into the discussion to support, refute, or demonstrate the authors' position on the topic.

The main focus of the chapter presented the authors' perspective on *issues, controversies and problems* arising from the 4IR, as these relate to the theme of promoting inclusive growth in the 4IR, and arguments supporting the authors' position. It further compared and contrasted with what has been, or is currently being, done as it relates to the chapter's specific topic of promoting the growth of 4IR ICT students, and the implications for ODeL and the main theme of the book.

In terms of the methodology used, although the mixed-method research approach adopted involved collecting and analyzing both quantitative and qualitative data, obtained from first-year modules at a Southern African institution, only quantitative results were presented in this chapter.

The next section of the chapter discussed solutions and recommendations in dealing with the issues, controversies and/or problems presented in preceding sections, based on students' demographic details, *computer literacy* and *technology usage*.

The emerging picture cautions concerning students' real biographic information and digital literacy in a developing world context.

Finally, the future research directions section of the chapter discussed future and emerging trends and provided insight about the future of the book's theme of promoting inclusive growth in the 4IR, from the perspective of the chapter's specific topic of promoting the growth of 4IR ICT students, and the implications for ODeL. The viability of a paradigm, model, implementation issues of proposed programs, etc., were also included in this section. Future research opportunities within the domain of the topic were also suggested.

In summary, recommendations were made that teachers and professors should examine their perceptions of student profiles in light of teaching, learning and assessment in preparation for the 4IR.

REFERENCES

Akbar, M. A., Rashid, M. M., & Embong, A. H. (2018). Technology Based Learning System in Internet of Things (IoT) Education. In *7th International Conference on Computer and Communication Engineering (ICCCE)* (pp. 192-197). Kuala Lumpur, Malaysia: IEEE. 10.1109/ICCCE.2018.8539334

Ayentimi, D. T., & Burgess, J. (2019). Is the fourth industrial revolution relevant to sub-Sahara Africa? *Technology Analysis and Strategic Management, 31*(6), 641–652. doi:10.1080/09537325.2018.1542129

Blayone, T. J., Mykhailenko, O., van Oostveen, R., Grebeshkov, O., Hrebeshkova, O., & Vostryakov, O. (2018). Surveying digital competencies of university students and professors in Ukraine for fully online collaborative learning. *Technology, Pedagogy and Education, 27*(3), 279–296. doi:10.1080/1475939X.2017.1391871

Bolton, A., Goosen, L., & Kritzinger, E. (2016). Enterprise Digitization Enablement Through Unified Communication and Collaboration. *Proceedings of the Annual Conference of the South African Institute of Computer Scientists and Information Technologists*. Johannesburg: ACM.10.1145/2987491.2987516

Botha, J.-A., & Coetzee, M. (2016, June). The influence of biographical factors on adult learner self-directedness in an open distance learning environment. *The International Review of Research in Open and Distributed Learning*, *17*(4), 242–263. doi:10.19173/irrodl.v17i4.2345

Bozzoli, B. (2019). *The ANC vs the Fourth Industrial Revolution - OPINION | Politicsweb*. Retrieved Sept 25, 2019, from https://www.politicsweb.co.za/opinion/the-anc-vs-the-fourth-industrial-revolution

Caruso, L. (2018). Digital innovation and the fourth industrial revolution: Epochal social changes? *AI & Society*, *33*(3), 379–392. doi:10.100700146-017-0736-1

Chetty, J., & Barlow-Jones, G. (2012, June 26). The Effects of a Social Constructivist Pedagogy on At-Risk Students Completing a Computer Programming Course at a Post-secondary Institution. In *Proceedings of World Conference on Educational Multimedia, Hypermedia and Telecommunications* (pp. 1914 - 1919). Denver: Association for the Advancement of Computing in Education.

Chun, M. (2010). Taking Teaching to (Performance) Task: Linking Pedagogical and Assessment Practices. *Change: The Magazine of Higher Learning*, *42*(2), 22–29. doi:10.1080/00091381003590795

Correa, T., Pavez, I., & Contreras, J. (2018). Digital inclusion through mobile phones?: A comparison between mobile-only and computer users in internet access, skills and use. *Information Communication and Society*, 1–18. doi:10.1080/1369118X.2018.1555270

Creswell, J. W. (2014). *Research Design: Qualitative, quantitative and mixed methods approaches*. SAGE Publications, Inc.

Cross, J. R., Frazier, A. D., Kim, M., & Cross, T. L. (2018). A comparison of perceptions of barriers to academic success among high-ability students from high- and low-income groups: Exposing poverty of a different kind. *Gifted Child Quarterly*, *62*(1), 111–129. doi:10.1177/0016986217738050

D'Souza, U. J., & Mudin, D. K. (2018, January). Industrial Revolution 4.0: Role of Universities. *Borneo Journal of Medical Sciences*, *12*(1), 1–2.

De Vaus, D. (2014). *Surveys in social research* (M. Bulmer, Ed.; 6th ed.). Routledge.

Dogo, E. M., Salami, A. F., Aigbavboa, C. O., & Nkonyana, T. (2019). Taking cloud computing to the extreme edge: A review of mist computing for smart cities and industry 4.0 in Africa. In *Edge Computing* (pp. 107–132). Springer. doi:10.1007/978-3-319-99061-3_7

Ehlers, U.-D. (2019). Future Skills and Higher Education "Future Skill Readiness". In *European Distance and E-Learning Network (EDEN) Annual Conference Proceedings* (pp. 85-96). Bruges, Belgium: EDEN.

Evans, G. (2019). 10 Years of Learning Design at The Open University: Evolution, Findings and Future Direction. In *European Distance and E-Learning Network (EDEN) Annual Conference Proceedings* (pp. 341-346). Bruges, Belgium: EDEN.

Fink, A. (2016). *How to conduct surveys: A step-by-step guide* (6th ed.). SAGE.

Goosen, L., & Naidoo, L. (2014). Computer Lecturers Using Their Institutional LMS for ICT Education in the Cyber World. In C. Burger, & K. Naudé (Ed.), *Proceedings of the 43rd Conference of the Southern African Computer Lecturers' Association (SACLA)* (pp. 99-108). Port Elizabeth: Nelson Mandela Metropolitan University.

Goosen, L., & Van Heerden, D. (2013a). Project-based learning and assessment of an IT module in an ODL context. *South African Journal of Higher Education, 27*(6), 1430–1443.

Goosen, L., & Van Heerden, D. (2013b). Project-Based Assessment Influencing Pass Rates of an ICT Module at an ODL Institution. In E. Ivala (Ed.), *Proceedings of the 8th International Conference on e-Learning* (pp. 157-164). Cape Town: Academic Conferences and Publishing.

Goosen, L., & Van Heerden, D. (2015). e-Learning Management System Technologies for Teaching Programming at a Distance. In C. Watson (Ed.), *Proceedings of the 10th International Conference on e-Learning (ICEL)* (pp. 116 - 126). Nassua: Academic Conferences and Publishing International. Retrieved from https://scholar.google.co.za/scholar?oi=bibs&cluster=16255326938393691479&btnI=1&hl=en

Goosen, L., & Van Heerden, D. (2016). e-Learning Environment Tools to Address Online and Open Distance Education Context Challenges. In R. M. Idrus, & N. Zainuddin (Ed.), *Proceedings of the 11th International Conference on e-Learning (ICEL)* (pp. 275 - 284). Kuala Lumpur, Malaysia: Academic Conferences and Publishing International.

Goosen, L., & Van Heerden, D. (2017). Beyond the Horizon of Learning Programming with Educational Technologies. In U. I. Ogbonnaya, & S. Simelane-Mnisi (Ed.), *Proceedings of the South Africa International Conference on Educational Technologies* (pp. 78 - 90). Pretoria: African Academic Research Forum.

Goosen, L., & Van Heerden, D. (2018). Assessment of Students in Higher Education – Information and Communication Technology Tools and Tips. *Progressio, 40*(1). doi:10.25159/0256-8853/4706

Goosen, L., & Van Heerden, D. (2019a). Promoting Research-Based Opportunities for First Year Programming Learners: Relevant and Quality Information Technology Education. In N. Govender, R. Mudaly, T. Mthethwa, & A. Singh-Pillay (Ed.), *Proceedings of the 27th Conference of the Southern African Association for Research in Mathematics, Science and Technology Education (SAARMSTE)* (pp. 215 - 228). Durban: University of KwaZulu-Natal.

Goosen, L., & Van Heerden, D. (2019b). Student Support for Information and Communication Technology Modules in Open Distance Environments: Towards Self-Directed Learning. In M. M. Van Wyk (Ed.), *Student Support Toward Self-Directed Learning in Open and Distributed Environments* (pp. 26–58). IGI Global Hershey, PA, USA . doi:10.4018/978-1-5225-9316-4.ch002

Gross, A.-K. (2019, May). *Sub-Saharan Africa and the 4th Industrial Revolution: Technological Leapfrogging as a Strategy to enhance Economic Growth?* (Master's Thesis). Lund University.

Haldane, A. G. (2019, May 22). *The Third Sector and the Fourth Industrial Revolution.* Retrieved from Pro Bono Economics Annual Lecture: https://www.probonoeconomics.com/sites/default/files/files/Andy%20Haldane%20-%20Pro%20Bono%20Economics%20Annual%20Lecture%20%282019%29_0.pdf

Hargittai, E., Piper, A. M., & Morris, M. R. (2018). From internet access to internet skills: Digital inequality among older adults. *Universal Access in the Information Society*, 1–10.

Hunsaker, A., & Hargittai, E. (2018). A review of Internet use among older adults. *New Media & Society, 20*(10), 3937–3954. doi:10.1177/1461444818787348

Karim, R. A., Abu, A. G., Adnan, A. H., & Suhandoko, A. D. (2018). The Use of Mobile Technology in Promoting Education 4.0 for Higher Education. *Advanced Journal of Technical and Vocational Education, 2*(3), 34–39.

Lamprini, K., & Bröchler, R. (2018). How collaborative innovation and technology in educational ecosystem can meet the challenges raised by the 4th industrial revolution. *World Technopolis Review, 7*(1), 2–14.

Letaba, T. P., Pretorius, M. W., & Pretorius, L. (2018). Innovation profile from the perspective of technology roadmapping practitioners in South Africa. *South African Journal of Industrial Engineering, 29*(4), 171–183. doi:10.7166/29-4-1919

Levin, R. (2018). Building a people-centred, people-driven public service and administration culture in Africa for youth empowerment and development. *Africa Journal of Public Sector Development and Governance, 1*(1), 34–45.

Libbrecht, P., & Goosen, L. (2016). Using ICTs to Facilitate Multilingual Mathematics Teaching and Learning. In R. Barwell, P. Clarkson, A. Halai, M. Kazima, J. Moschkovich, N. Planas, & M. Villavicencio Ubillús (Eds.), *Mathematics Education and Language Diversity* (pp. 217–235). Springer. doi:10.1007/978-3-319-14511-2_12

Lochlainn, C. M., Mhichíl, M. N., Beirne, E., & Brown, M. (2019). Back to the Future, the Learner Strikes back: Feedback and Reflection as key Elements in MOOC re-design. In *European Distance and E-Learning Network (EDEN) Annual Conference Proceedings* (pp. 365-372). Bruges, Belgium: EDEN.

Lom, M., Pribyl, O., & Svitek, M. (2016, May). Industry 4.0 as a part of smart cities. In *Smart Cities Symposium Prague (SCSP)* (pp. 1-6). Prague: IEEE. 10.1109/SCSP.2016.7501015

Mkhize, P., Mtsweni, E. S., & Buthelezi, P. (2016, April). Diffusion of innovations approach to the evaluation of learning management system usage in an open distance learning institution. *The International Review of Research in Open and Distributed Learning, 17*(3), 295–312. doi:10.19173/irrodl.v17i3.2191

Nick, G. A., & Pongrácz, F. (2016). Hungarian Smart Cities Strategies Towards Industry 4.0. *Industry 4.0, 1*(2), 122-127.

Olivier, M. (2009). *Information Technology research: A practical guide for Computer Science and Informatics* (3rd ed.). Van Schaik.

Özdemir, V., & Hekim, N. (2018). Birth of industry 5.0: Making sense of big data with artificial intelligence, "the internet of things" and next-generation technology policy. *OMICS: A Journal of Integrative Biology, 22*(1), 65–76. doi:10.1089/omi.2017.0194 PMID:29293405

Reid, S. (2011). The Momentum of the Technology of the Classroom. In *Adaptation, Resistance and Access to Instructional Technologies: Assessing Future Trends In Education* (pp. 316–331). IGI Global. doi:10.4018/978-1-61692-854-4.ch018

Rouse, M. (2017). *What is fourth industrial revolution?* Retrieved Sept 25, 2019, from https://whatis.techtarget.com/definition/fourth-industrial-revolution

Safiullin, A., Krasnyuk, L., & Kapelyuk, Z. (2019, March). Integration of industry 4.0 technologies for "smart cities" development. *IOP Conference Series. Materials Science and Engineering*, 497(1), 012089. doi:10.1088/1757-899X/497/1/012089

Shahroom, A., & Hussin, N. (2018). Industrial revolution 4.0 and education. *International Journal of Academic Research in Business and Social Sciences*, 8(9), 314–319. doi:10.6007/IJARBSS/v8-i9/4593

Skobelev, P. O., & Borovik, S. Y. (2017). On the way from Industry 4.0 to Industry 5.0: from digital manufacturing to digital society. *Industry 4.0, 2*(6), 307-311.

Slade, S., & Prinsloo, P. (2015). Stemming the flow: Improving retention for distance learning students. In *European Distance and E-Learning Network (EDEN) Annual Conference Proceedings*. Barcelona: EDEN. Retrieved from http://www.eden-online.org/system/files/Book%20of%20Abstracts EDEN%202015%20Annual%20 Conference Barcelona.pdf

Straub, E. T. (2009). Understanding technology adoption: Theory and future directions for informal learning. *Review of Educational Research*, 79(2), 625–649. doi:10.3102/0034654308325896

Sutopo, W. (2019, April). The Roles of Industrial Engineering Education for Promoting Innovations and Technology Commercialization in the Digital Era. *IOP Conference Series. Materials Science and Engineering*, 495(1), 012001. doi:10.1088/1757-899X/495/1/012001

Tondi, P. (2019, March). The significance of Indigenous Knowledge Systems (IKS) for Africa's socio-cultural and economic development in the dawn of the Fourth Industrial Revolution (4IR). *Journal of Gender, Information and Development in Africa (JGIDA), 8*(Special Issue 1), 239-245.

Tsai, M.-J., Wang, C.-Y., & Hsu, P.-F. (2019). Developing the computer programming self-efficacy scale for computer literacy education. *Journal of Educational Computing Research*, 56(8), 1345–1360. doi:10.1177/0735633117746747

Van Heerden, D., & Goosen, L. (2012). Using Vodcasts to Teach Programming in an ODL Environment. *Progressio*, 34(3), 144–160.

Van Heerden, D., & Goosen, L. (2019). Assessments Used in an Open Distance e-Learning Environment to Promote Self-Directed Learning. In R. Ørngreen, M. Buhl, & B. Meyer (Ed.), *Proceedings of the 18th European Conference on e-Learning (ECEL 2019)* (pp. 593 - 602). Copenhagen: Academic Conferences and Publishing International Limited. doi:10.34190/EEL.19.003

World Economic Forum. (2016, January). The future of jobs: Employment, skills and workforce strategy for the fourth industrial revolution. In *Global Challenge Insight Report*. Geneva: World Economic Forum. Retrieved from https://www.voced.edu.au/content/ngv:71706

World Economic Forum (WEF) Asian Development Bank (ADB). (2017). *ASEAN 4.0: what does the Fourth Industrial Revolution mean for regional economic integration?* Geneva: World Economic Forum.

World Economic Forum. (2017). *Accelerating Workforce Reskilling for the Fourth Industrial Revolution: An agenda for Leaders to Shape the Future of Education, Gender and Work.* Geneva: World Economic Forum. Retrieved from https://www.voced.edu.au/content/ngv:77198

KEY TERMS AND DEFINITIONS

E-Learning: Learning that takes place via the internet, using a variety of devices to access the web.

Fourth Industrial Revolution (4IR)Family-Centricity: The Fourth Industrial Revolution (4IR) is about the emergence and penetration of very advanced disruptive Unified Communication and Collaboration (UC&C) technologies and Information Technology (IT) trends, such as Virtual Reality (VR), networks, Artificial Intelligence (AI) and robotics, which bringing changes, from Cyber-Physical Systems (CPS) involving new ways in which we work in terms of enterprise digitization enabled through embedding technology within our larger societies, cultural community lives, to even in the home and the human body.

Information and Communications Technology (ICT): Any device used for creating and/or capturing, storing, processing, managing, as well as any dissemination/transmission/transfer and/or display of data and information by using digital means.

Institution: The ODeL institution has state-of-the-art technology and technologically literate staff to assist facilitators with the design, development and production of quality ODeL material, as well as to provide technical support.

Open and Distance E-Learning (ODeL): In ODeL, technology is used for teaching and e-learning, student support and communication.

Students: Are the center, around which Open and Distance e-Learning environments pivot, which means that certain requirements need to be met to ensure they are able to succeed.

Sub-Saharan Africa (SSA): Those African countries located towards the south of the Sahara Desert.

Chapter 6
Impact of ICTs for Sustainable Development of Youth Employability

Abiodun Alao
University of Johannesburg, South Africa

Roelien Brink
University of Johannesburg, South Africa

ABSTRACT

The Fourth Industrial Revolution (41R) era requires industries to adopt the use of technology and specialised study accomplished with digital knowledge. This has contributed to the high rate of unemployment and job loss of people, especially the youths without digital knowledge. The objective of this study is to understand how ICTs can be used for the sustainable development of youth employability. The youths are among the low-income populations that require access to information on industry requirement for improved employability and the provision of digital skills training will allow them to have the knowledge to use ICTs to access information on the relevant job skills needed in the labour market. The sustainable livelihood theory was used to guide the study. Recommendations for the study will allow the government, ICT policymakers, and stakeholders to use ICTs for the sustainable development of youths and improve employability.

DOI: 10.4018/978-1-7998-4882-0.ch006

INTRODUCTION

The rate of unemployment is escalating in the third world. In countries such as South Africa, unemployment has risen over the years, from 21.5% to almost 28.0% (Statistics SA, 2018), and it still continues to be on the rise. Unemployment refers to when persons above a specified age (usually above 15) are not in paid employment or self-employment and are currently available for work (OECD, 2003). The Quarterly Labour Force Survey of 2018 (Statistics SA, 2018) claims 6.2 million South Africans are now unemployed, and 4.3 million have been unemployed for a year or longer. There was a steep decline in employment (down by 237, 000) and an increase in unemployment (up by 62, 000) between the first quarter of 2019 and the fourth quarter of 2018; this led to a decline in the labour force participation rate, which was at 59.3% at the time of this study (Statistics SA, 2019).

The South African unemployment rate in the 1st quarter of 2019 increased by 0.5 percentage points, to 27.6% (Statistics SA, 2019). Moreover, youths are significantly affected by the high unemployment rate (Marumo & Sebolaaneng, 2019). The rate of youth unemployment in South Africa has increased to 58.2% in the third quarter of 2019, from 56.4% in the first quarter of 2018. Remarkably, the South African youth unemployment rate averaged 52.65% in 2013, increased to 58.2% in 2019, and reached a record low of 48.80% in the fourth quarter of 2014 (Table 1 presents the rate of youth unemployment).

To tackle unemployment and boost economies, most developing countries are propagating the Fourth Industrial Revolution (4IR), and the adoption of technology in the industries is a necessity (Bloem, Van Doorn, Duivestein, Excoffier, Maas & Van Ommeren, 2014). Countries like South Africa are in need of digital skills as forerunners of the 4IR era to boost their economy (Fernández-Sanz, Gómez-Pérez & Castillo-Martínez, 2017; Bloem et al., 2014; Attwood, Diga, Braathen & May, 2013). The country has therefore compelled social partners, research institutions and higher education institutions to adopt the use of information communication and technologies (ICTs) as a possible approach to job creation (Calitz, Poisat & Cullen, 2017).

In order to adopt digital skills, the use of ICT has become crucially important in many countries and have been used as a possible intervention to tackle unemployment (Michael & Samson, 2014). ICTs are those technologies that interlink information technology devices, such as computers and internet connection, with communication technologies like telephones and their telecommunication networks. Michael and Samson (2014) explored the impact of ICTs on the youths and its vocational opportunities in Nigeria. The scholars claim that the unemployment rate has been on the increase globally and has become an epidemic that affects the socio-economic buoyancy of any country (Van Broekhuizen & Van Der Berg, 2016). They claim the high rate of youth unemployment over the years has been used by political aspirants to canvass citizens for political agenda and support in elections, and over time the issue of unemployment has not been adequately addressed (Van Broekhuizen & Van Der Berg, 2016). Hence, the use of ICTs for information gathering and skills development can contribute to overcoming the unemployment epidemic. This indicates that the advent of ICT to access information on industry requirements for improved employability is needed (Michael & Samson, 2014). Ghosh (2011:1) defined ICTs as "A range of electronic technologies which when converged in new configurations are flexible, adaptable, enabling and capable of transforming organisations and redefining social relations". Moreover, while international organisations such as the United Nations Commission on Science and Technology for Development (UNCSTD) claim the costs of using ICTs to build national information infrastructures that contribute towards innovative knowledge societies are high, the cost of not doing so are likely to be much higher if not implemented in countries (Balouza, 2019; Kamel, 2010).

The use of ICTs to disseminate information on skills development can assist the youth to vigorously reflect on their professional desires or drive to build their career capabilities to avoid being excluded from the labour market and add value in the workplace (Kirlidog, van der Vyver, Zeeman & Coetzee, 2018; Mckenzie, Coldwell-Neilson & Palmer, 2017; Hamilton, Carbone, Gonsalvez, & Jollands, 2015). ICTs are often associated only with the most sophisticated and expensive computer-based technologies (Sadiq & Mohammed, 2015); hence, many people underestimate their capacity to contribute to development goals. However, the 4IR has introduced more advanced technological innovations that promote the use of robotics, AI and other technical devices which are expected to enhance development (Bloem et al., 2014). Technological advances are also dramatically influencing people's lives in a way that have been channelled not only for industrial use but also for human purposes. These include the full range of electronic technologies and techniques that are used to manage information and knowledge (Michael & Samson, 2014).

There have been studies that show the impact of ICTs from other countries. Manalo, Pasiona, Bautista, Villaflor, Corpuz & Biag-Manalo (2019) examined the use of ICTs, digital divide and the effectiveness of these interventions on young people. In their study, the Rice Crop Manager (RCM) was used as an ICT-enabled nutrient management application to explore the intersections between community development and youth development with 30 farmers' children in high school, from the provinces of Pangasinan, Isabela, Camarines Sur, Iloilo, Bukidnon, and Davao del Norte from November 2016 to October 2017 in the Philippines. The project organised a group of farmers' children who were RCM infomediaries (information mediators) to interact with the research team (the authors) and the RCM-SMS platform to use the ICT-enabled nutrient management application as a communication tool to send text messages regarding fertiliser recommendations to other farmers.

The researchers conducted three rounds of interviews with the students concerning the messages and calls that they received and what they did with the information. The result showed that farmers' children could achieve infomediary roles quite effectively, as they are academically excellent and involved in farmwork, thereby performing at their best. Manalo et al's. (2019) the research looked into channelling young people in agricultural development. The study used the Community Youth Development (CYD) Theory to understand the community and the youth development intersections, and some identified outcomes that may overlap and may not be very easy to observe. However, the identified outcomes may be revisited for clarity and to make them more all-encompassing.

Research conducted by Saad and Majid (2014) presents the findings of a survey of 299 Malaysian employers from diverse types of agencies and organisations that employed engineering and ICT graduates. The objective of the survey was to explore employers' perceptions of the five most important employability skills that graduates can adopt for them to be considered for employment in the labour market. A 13-item scale of engineering employability skills was employed from the Engineering Accreditation Council's (EAC) manual and the Malaysian Future of Engineering Education Report of 2007. This was utilised as the instrument to examine the perceptions of employees. The findings of the study revealed that problem-solving, tool handling competency, presentation skills and teamwork skills were highly valued among employers as important skills for students. Students were required to be competent in their use of ICT techniques, skills and modern tools in their area of expertise, and have the drive to acquire and apply knowledge in these areas. The findings derived from the study were useful to improve Malaysian universities' understanding of the employability skills perceived as important in the industry. This research allowed institutions to improve on equipping their graduates with the expected ICT skills that met industry requirements.

BACKGROUND

Over the years, there has been the human development and capabilities approach and the sustainable development goals (SDGs), otherwise known as the "Global Goals", as a universal call to action to end poverty, protect the planet and ensure that all people enjoy peace and prosperity (Sachs, 2015). Other credible approaches/goals point to empowerment and participation as an essential aspect in tackling obstacles relating to poverty and development (Pandey & Zheng, 2019). These goals include the provision of improved health facilities, employment opportunities, education, skills development, economic growth, improved quality of life and other necessities vital to human life.

However, the world has transformed into a new development period due to the introduction of the 4IR era that thrives on the adoption of new technology innovation in the industrial sectors and most aspects of human activity to boost countries' economies (Bloem et al., 2014). This new revolution is considered as the era of the internet of things and energy, and of the cyber-physical systems (Bloem et al., 2014). The term 'revolution' means a swift and immense succession of changes that lead to a fundamental change of humanity. This includes social, political, economic, industrial or any other type of revolution that requires a change in human society.

The First Industrial Revolution (1IR) started in the 18th century with textile factories in Great Britain. This was a transition to new manufacturing processes in Europe and the United States, in the year 1760 to 1840. It spread globally, involving ongoing replacement with hand-by-machine production, where machines were mainly used as a power source. The industrial revolution was defined as changes in manufacturing and transportation that began with fewer things being made by hand and instead made using machines in larger-scale factories. The development of transportation led to the nationwide establishment of industries and companies to an international level that evolved the development of new scientific methods of function and management (Voskoglou, 2016).

The 1IR was considered as the mechanisation of steam and water power, which was followed by the Second Industrial Revolution (2IR) that started in the middle of the 19th century into the early 20th century. The 2IR, also known as the Technological Revolution, was a phase of rapid standardisation and industrialisation. In the same period, new technological systems were introduced; most significantly, electrical power, and the mass production of large quantities of standardised goods in assembly lines, such as telephones. The 2IR occurred due to natural resources, abundant labour supply, strong government policy, new sources of power, railroads and American inventors and invention. The social thinkers' scholars considered the 2IR as a joined-at-the-hip part of the 1IR (Rifkin, 2011, 2014).

The Third Industrial Revolution (3IR) started in the 1940s, mainly considered as the era of the development of electronics, automated production and the gradual replacement of human hands by computers as means of control (Voskoglou, 2016). Hence, the three revolutions have substituted the power of human hands and animals by machines, allowing the mass production of goods and directing human society to its existing digital era. However, there were non-lucrative magnitudes as well, as the negative environmental impact of the high industrialisation, mainly caused by the unlimited use of coal and petrol, and as a result of nuclear energy accidents. Presently, the price of energy and food is increasing, unemployment is high, the economies of many countries are in danger of breakdown, most countries are in distress, and the repossession is not evident (Oye, Inuwa & Shakil, 2011) The view in terms of the breakdown of the global economy is that humankind is greatly seeking a new economic plan for a prosperous future. This led to the new industrial revolution at the beginning of the 21st century (Anton, Silberglith & Schveeder, 2011) the 3IR introduced the digitalisation of technology and led to the 4IR.

The chapter focuses on the impact of digital skills for the sustainable development of youths' employability. The 4IR era propagates the use of machines and robotics intended for massive industrial production, computers, robots and various 'ingenious' types of machinery and systems of artificial intelligence (AI) that have substituted humans with machines for routine jobs. There are debates that the 4IR will promote the creation of new jobs for future needs to sustain the new era of technological development. However, this may contribute to the loss of jobs (Bloem et al., 2014). For instance, it is envisaged that the 4IR may create fewer job opportunities for the youth due to their limited digital skills. The issue of unemployment is thus becoming alarming, and globally youths are among the most affected (Stukalina, 2018; Michael & Samson, 2014; Oye et al., 2011), as the dawn of new technology innovation contributes to an inevitable change in industry operations (Bloem et al., 2014).

The 3IR and the 4IR are interrelated, as the 3IR promoted digital skills such as ICTs. These included the full range of electronic technologies and techniques that are used to manage the information which youths can use to improve their knowledge of computerisation (Calitz et al., 2014). The 4IR thus plays the role of computers and of computational thinking (CT) and mechanisms of AI. The essence of both revolutions is to boost the industry and economy of any country (Bloem et al., 2014). The aim of introducing new innovations is thus to contribute to development; however, the focus of transforming societies, industries and economies are not enough to grasp the development opportunities (eTransform Africa, 2012; World Bank, 2012; Ponelis & Holmner, 2015); especially when the adoption of new technological innovation is encouraged in all aspects of human activity. As human capital strengthens the socio-economic development of any country, the adaptability of the 4IR would improve the unemployability gap that exists globally (Calitz et al., 2014).

MAIN FOCUS OF THE CHAPTER

Scope of the Study

The 4IR has led industries to create jobs that require technology and higher levels of education, while only a few available jobs include manual labour or routine tasks (Bloem et al., 2014). This has affected the youth who are currently facing a lack of unemployment due to the lack of skills development in the area of advanced technology, as required in the labour market (Bloem et al., 2014). Therefore, access to advanced technological innovation will allow the youth to share their knowledge, concerns, best practices and experiences, gain a greater understanding of their current situation, solve issues that were previously beyond their capability, and enhance their livelihood (Heeks, 2010).

The youth are perceived as the future leaders of any country, and identifying the factors that contribute to their unemployment is essential (Eynon & Geniets, 2016). The study recommends access to digital skills to provide knowledge of computerisation among youths to improve the employment gap that exists in today's world (Stukalina, 2018; Michael & Samson, 2014; Hart & Barratt, 2009). The study proposes the essence of digital skills as the beginning of the knowledge of computerisation and information that prepare youths to access industrial requirements for employability.

The Objective of the Study

The objective of this study is to understand how digital skills can be used for the sustainable development of youths' employability. The development of digital skills among youths can be challenging (Vinichenko, Makushkin, Melnichuk, Frolova & Kurbakova 2016), but to improve youths' employment there is a need for the development of digital skills, such as ICT skills (Hamilton et al., 2015). This study, therefore, examines how ICT skills can be used for the sustainable development of youths' employability. As computers and CT and mechanisms of AI are of importance in the 4IR, the implementation of digital skills training among youths can enforce their knowledge of computerisation required in the labour market.

Statement of Problem

The research problem of the study shows that the youth lack access to information on industry requirements for improved employability and livelihood. Many youths lack adequate digital knowledge which is the main contributor to the dearth of computer skills and knowledge. The concept of building and enhancing their knowledge and closing the information gap through the use of ICTs is necessary. This is a significant problem because of the lack of access to information through ICTs can be a factor that contributes to the lack of digital skills (Eynon & Geniets, 2016). In this study, we refer to the lack of digital skills as a contributing factor that hinders the youth from gaining employment. This obstructs access to information to the necessary industry requirements for employment (Zelenika & Pearce, 2013).

In order to examine the use of ICTs for the sustainable development of youth employability, the study considers the following research question as a guide: How can ICTs impact youths' sustainable development for employment? To address this question, the Sustainable Livelihood (SL) theory was used as a theoretical framework to guide the study. The framework was considered suitable for the study due to individuals drawing on certain assets or capitals in pursuit of their livelihood strategies, mediated by context. Policies, regulations and institutions, as well as the ICT systems, influence people's livelihood strategies to overcome poverty (Waema & Miroro, 2014).

The chapter offers a critical synthesis and background that supports scholarly reviews on the impact of ICTs on the sustainable development of youths' employability (Oyelana & Thakhathi, 2015). The chapter explains the importance of ICTs which is a recipient of the third industrial revolution as an information catalyst for improved employability and access to information for industry requirement for employability. This section explains how the 3IR digitalisation drive has driven the 4IR as an ICT-based convergence.

ICTs Promoting SDG Goals

The penetration of ICTs increased across the African continent in the late 2000s and early 2010s, which facilitated development and made a significant contribution to the economic growth and social development of the communities (Attwood et al., 2013). However, the focus shifted to the uptake and impact of ICTs in transforming societies and economies since enhancing information flow alone is not enough to grasp development opportunities (eTransform Africa, 2012; World Bank, 2012).

Many African countries are aspiring to become information societies, and ultimately knowledge societies, allowing them to participate as equal partners in the global information-based economy (Gorova, 2019). It has similarly led African countries to initiate ICT development projects that address the lack of digital skills and other communication networks (Ponelis & Holmner, 2015; Kayisire & Wei, 2016). This has allowed the world to transform into a new development period due to the digital technology, physical technology, and biological technology which has undergone unprecedented development in their own fields; at the same time, their applications are converging greatly (Li, Hou & Wu, 2017).

This technological drive has motivated the 4IR as ICT-based convergence industries contain various fields such as driverless cars, lighter and tougher materials, robotics, 3D printing, biotechnology and other technological innovations. Industries have become the forefront of this development which is a silent revolution that allows ICTs, such as the internet, sensors and embedded systems as new opportunities that open up new combinations of mental, physical and mechanical work.

According to Bloem et al., (2014), the latest phase of what we call "Pervasive Computing" is currently underlying the far-reaching integration of information technology (IT) and operational technology (OT). This integration knows many forms, produces a profit by reducing costs as a consequence of predictive maintenance, and is greater in speed and intelligence thanks to machine-to-machine communication and improved human-machine interaction (HMI) (Bloem et al., 2014). There is a need for multi-stakeholder engagement and cooperation to consider the existing barriers that affect ICT adoption in their industrial sectors and among the citizens of the respective countries. Joint action by policymakers, multilateral organisations and the ICT sector has been required to connect the billions of currently unconnected individuals and deliver a range of life-enhancing and life-changing services at the required speed, scale, and complexity of transformation needed to achieve the SDGs by 2030 (Sachs, Schmidt-Traub, Mazzucato, Messner, Nakicenovic & Rockström, 2019). This is because ICTs can promote youth productivity and boost economic buoyancy (Sadiq & Mohammed, 2015).

The positive impact of ICTs in sectors such as the telecommunications industry has been promoting, advancing and measuring the SDGs in terms of collaborating on accelerated data revolution for sustainable development to ensure that tools and applications are developed with vulnerable communities and individuals in mind so that no one is left behind (Eşkinat, 2016; Caiado, Leal Filho, Quelhas, de Mattos Nascimento & Ávila, 2018). Also, the industries' commitment to work together in partnership will be a game-changer in leveraging the socio-economic impact of mobile technologies on individuals, businesses and governments around the world (Sachs et al., 2019).

SDG Goals Support ICTs for Development

In past years "sustainable development" has become a development slogan embraced by non-governmental and governmental organisations as the new paradigm of development (Lele, 1991). Organisations like the United Nations Development Program (UNDP, 2001:2) have also embraced ICTs has a development tool. Chitla (2012:32) says "ICTs are basically information handling tools, a varied set of goods, applications and services that are used to produce, store, and process, distribute and exchange information for the development of any country". The 2030 Agenda for Sustainable Development identifies that the introduction of ICTs and global interconnectedness will have great potential to accelerate human progress to bridge the digital divide and develop knowledge societies and scientific and technological innovation (UN General Assembly, 2015).

SDG goals can be implemented with the provision of ICT infrastructures such as Goal 9 – universal and affordable access to ICTs – and Goal 17 – partnerships and means of implementation that is an important aspect that the government of any country can use to provide ICTs for the empowerment of youths (UN General Assembly, 2015). The gap in the literature shows that ICT-based empowering solutions for SDGs' achievement indicate that access to technologies has grown at a fast pace, yet the impressive gains are still hampered by existing gaps in ICT access between and within countries, between urban and rural settings, and among young people of different genders (UN General Assembly, 2015). The study, therefore, reviews digital skills for the sustainable development of youths' employability in the following sub-section.

Critical Review of Digital Skills and 4ir for Sustainable Development of Youth Employability

Prior research has been conducted by various scholars that buttresses the challenges of access to ICTs to attain digital skills. Eynon and Geniets (2016) analysed 20 participants using in-depth interviews to investigate the reasons youths find digital skills challenging and problematic. Their study showed that the poor access to technology, limited support networks and current socio-economic situations prevent the youth from gaining the experience needed to support the development of digital skills. The study further explained how the lack of experience and inadequate skills limit youths' perception of computerisation. It was argued that individuals' experiences of ICTs are shaped by the social structure to which they belong, and intervention measures should be adopted to address the digital inequalities that exist among the young generation by making sure that young people are not allowed to learn digital skills by themselves.

Other studies found that digital skills have become significant in our everyday life as it becomes essential in today's world in terms of educational needs, social needs, commercial needs and, above all else, security needs (Sadiq & Mohammed, 2015). ICTs are known to be essential in all aspect of human capacity building, and youths are generally employed to manage digital centres in developing countries (Alao, 2019). These centres are mostly occupied by young people but are primarily used to gain technical knowledge of computer maintenance, repairs and architectural design, seek employment, socialise and propagate political views (Sadiq & Mohammed, 2015; Alao, 2019). This study supports the major role that digital skills play in the developing world and its contribution to human capacity building and job creation.

Significance of Digital Skills for Youth Development

ICT for development connects people to accurate and up to date information and equips people with new skills (David & Surmaya, 2005). The institutional proponents of ICTs for development, for example, UNDP and the World Bank, suggest that easily accessible and abundant supply of information foster knowledge formation that can induce economic empowerment (World Bank, 2008b). Therefore, ICTs can boost the socio-economic growth of the youth of any country if properly used (Koutroumpis, 2009).

Studies show that technology can be explained as a contributing factor to a growing digital divide as ICTs enhance inequalities and lead to potential social exclusion (Talbot & Bizzell, 2016; Oyelana & Thakhathi, 2015). However, other scholars claim the implementation of ICTs offer access to technology which provides economic opportunities, informs people and allows them to use technologies that are available in the domains in which they function (Merkel, Heinze, Hilbert & Naegele, 2019); especially when countries are propagating the 4IR era and encourage the use of technological devices, robotics, computers and systems of AI to boost their economies and all aspects of industrial sectors (Helbing, 2019).

Having basic digital literacy not only qualifies people, namely youths, for jobs in conventional sectors, but also opens doors for them to participate in rapidly growing markets such as business process outsourcing, crowdsourcing, and microwork (Göll & Zwiers, 2019). People with more advanced digital skills can take advantage of an even wider range of opportunities brought about by the growth of the 'application economy', mobile phones and National ICT, and broadband strategies should reflect these dynamics to the youths to realise the full potential of the digital revolution (Helbing, 2019). Hence, ongoing ITU research suggests that at present, around 43% of national strategies reference the youth (Ma, Vachon & Cheng, 2019; Göll & Zwiers, 2019).

It is argued that the implementation of digital centres that offer free digital skill programmes in disadvantaged communities can be used to tackle the lack of access to technology for information access and enhance their self-development (Gorova, 2019; Willard & Halder, 2003). The centres can be used to motivate youth participation in computer skills training programmes. These could focus on computerisation and dissemination of the necessary industrial skills to prepare them for employability (Hallberg, Kulecho, Kulecho & Okoth, 2011); youths are presumed to lack knowledge of how to access information using ICTs, affecting their ability to enhance their skills development. This is due to some contextual factors such as lack of ICT infrastructure, resources, education, computer skills, socio-economic factors, religious, traditional and cultural beliefs that contribute towards identity formulations, roles and responsibilities, and personal aspirations (Hilbert, 2011). It is therefore assumed that these contributing factors are related to the high rate of youth unemployment.

The Sustainable Livelihood Analysis

The theoretical framework proposed for this research is derived from the approaches and literature concerned with sustainable livelihood in whose development of the Department for International Development (DFID) has played a significant part in recent years (DFID, 2005). The framework emerged from a more complex system perspective on how people can use the resources available to them to sustain their livelihoods. It also explains how development interventions can hinder available resources and the way people interact with them (Parkinson & Ramirez, 2007).

Furthermore, the framework explains that individuals draw on certain assets or capitals in pursuit of their livelihood strategies, mediated by contexts such as policies, regulations, institutions and the ICT systems, which influence people's livelihood strategies (Messer & Townley, 2003). This theory explains that people need information about livelihood options and opportunities, such as using ICTs for individual development to learn to combine their assets and secure their own livelihoods. Strategies are often diverse and flexible, reinforcing the need for up to date information on which to base choices (DFID, 2005).

According to the theory, livelihood is sustainable when it allows people to cope and recover from shocks and stresses (such as natural disasters and economic or social upheavals) and improve their well-being without sabotaging the natural environment or resource base (DFID, 2005). The SL framework is mostly used by development agencies for planning and assessing development interventions (Parkinson & Ramirez, 2007). Hence, a sustainable livelihoods analysis is concerned with the range of assets that individuals, households and communities access and use in order to sustain themselves (Morse & McNamara, 2013). Its starting point is the 'Vulnerability Context' within which individuals and households live.

People's lives, particularly those of the disadvantaged (youths), are strongly affected by three groups of factors which make them (and their assets) vulnerable and are beyond their control. These are (1) trends (such as population change, national and international economic trends and technological change); (2) shocks (such as natural disasters, epidemics, civil conflict and economic crises); (3) and seasonality (variations in prices, costs, production, food supply and, economic opportunity) (Morse & McNamara, 2013). Together or individually, these factors can drastically affect (though not necessarily reduce) people's assets and options (Morse & McNamara, 2013). Within this 'Vulnerability Context', people access and use a variety of assets to achieve positive livelihoods outcomes. And while information, knowledge and communication are not explicitly acknowledged in livelihood frameworks, they are crucial to people's ability to develop appropriate and sustainable livelihood strategies. The sustainable livelihood approach organises these assets into five categories:

- **Human capital:** These are skills, knowledge and the ability to work/produce (the knowledge base and information resources available to individuals).
- **Social capital:** This refers to the networks, participation in social, productive groups and mutually beneficial relationships.
- **Natural capital:** This includes natural resources.

- **Physical capital:** This includes buildings, infrastructure (including power and water), productive tools, etc.
- **Financial capital:** This is the funds available for investment, production and consumption, including income generation and financial savings from other activities required to achieve certain ends.

Molema and Quan-Baffour (2019) claim that ICTs have an impact on livelihood assets through ICT training workshops which can be a possible intervention for the sustainable development of youths' improved employability. Table 1 presents the assets and their impact on youth sustainable development for employability.

Table 1. Assets and impacts on youths' sustainable development (DFID, 2005)

ASSETS	IMPACT
Human Capital	The youths should have improved access to ICT digital centres such as public access points to access information on education, training and educational tools in a wide range of formats. The potential to transfer digital content to remote locations easily in the form of text, images, video and radio, combined with the vast storage capacity of PCs, CDs and DVDs, reduce many of the costs associated with barriers to broad-based information access. The impact of increased information flow on human capital development will depend equally on the effective translation of material into different languages and appropriate formats for the intended users and their local cultural context.
Natural Capital	People should have improved access to organisations that deal with different aspects of natural resource management, administrative and legal information. There should be enhanced communication channels with applicable authorities like the government. People should be allowed to share their personal experiences in the community and communities should be allowed to share information that can be used to compare strategies and develop local solutions to problems and conflict situations in their communities.
Financial Capital	There should be the support and strengthening of local financial institutions, including micro-credit organisations to improve the information provided on services and available facilities such as loans and savings schemes to assist youths who are entrepreneurs to support their businesses.
Social Capital	The youth should have improved 'networking' both at the community level and with people of authority, existing networks and potentially among a much wider community. The ability to build new social networks at a regional and national level can help young people to air their concerns with unemployment, bring benefits to existing networks and institutions at a local level. A reduction in the cost and time taken to travel to pursue social networking goals can also have a positive impact on youths and their family members. Social networks can provide increased opportunities for employment both locally and away (potentially increasing rural-urban migration).
Physical Capital	In terms of the youth using digital centres to access markets and market information. They will have improved choices of the sale of goods on local markets that will allow enhanced information on prices, comparative supply and demand for products. In the longer-term, new markets, techniques and processes for production, processing and marketing of product can be explored.

Factors Contributing to Youth Unemployment

Prior research found that graduate careers held in the year 2015 in developed countries such as Australia have shown that youths lack basic computer skills and knowledge of the appropriate skill set required in the work environment (Ohei, Brink & Abiodun, 2019). This was due to young people not having appropriate computer skills which can equip them for the job market (Mckenzie et al., 2017). Scholars like Mutula and Van Brakel (2007) claim there are serious global shortages of highly skilled professionals and hands-on employees essential for advancing the ever-changing digital economy; both in the developed and developing nations. The youth need to be skilled and matured in their capacity to make appropriate decisions in their choice of career before advancing into the job market (Mckenzie et al., 2017).

Scholars such as Duncombe (2014) state that in the livelihood arena, there is a lack of understanding of the interrelationship of the use of ICTs as a technological artefact, socio-economic development processes, and the assessment of the outcomes that arise from their use. Also, 41R encourages the use of technological devices such as smartphones and computers for economic improvement (Li, Hou, & Wu, 2017). However, it has been realised that only a limited number of South African youths use ICT tools to research information on how to enhance their employability status. Moreover, few young people can afford to own ICT tools such as personal computers, iPads and smartphones, and the ones who have access, use it for socialising and private use. This situation has become a challenge and has worsened the unemployment rate of young people in most countries. Other reasons that can contribute to the lack of ICT access include the following:

- **Lack of wages and productivity:** This is usually caused by the high rates of under-employment and decline in inflation and inflationary expectations causing economic recessions which affect industries from employing additional manpower (Sabiar, 2015). Minimum wage increases restructure the gross domestic product from lower-skilled industries but rather diversifies towards the direction of the higher-skilled industries that are mostly ineffective in assisting the underprivileged during both peaks and troughs in the business cycle (Sabiar, 2015).
- **Unfavourable exchange rate:** An exchange rate is the worth of a country's currency as opposed to the currency of another country (Avdjiev, Bruno, Koch & Shin, 2019). The worth of exchange rates is a significant aspect in this global economy and countries with unfavourable exchange rate can skew investment returns and collapse exchange ideas (Avdjiev et al., 2019). While a country with a favourable currency rate and a strong domestic currency have good imports due to "cheaper" international goods, while an economy

with weak foreign currency will be more into exports, due to "cheaper" goods produced domestically for countries overseas (Avdjiev et al., 2019). This affects the economy and led to high rate youth unemployment which in turn may affect the financial independence of the youths to own or access technology.

- **Lack of resources:** The lack of resources such as technology exchange and innovation education and skills development regulatory barriers can contribute to the lack of access to ICTs (Amesheva, Clark & Payne, 2019). Youths with entrepreneurs' business ideas will find it difficult to finance small business, while other youths seeking employment will struggle to access the necessary resources needed to access information on the industrial requirement for employability.

- **Political instability:** This is caused when the government of a country collapses due to conflicts or rampant competition between various political parties (Hendrix & Kang, 2019). This violent nature diminishes the productive, as well as the transactional capacities of the economy which in turn affects the industries and decreases employability of the country (Hendrix & Kang, 2019).

Factors Contributing to Lack of ICT Access in Youths

The factors that contribute to a lack of access for youths are a visible reflection of the adaptability of ICT use to youths. The youth have challenges getting educated and learning basic computer skills that can be used to enhance their livelihood. They also face barriers that hinder them from becoming educated or computer literate; these barriers include limited time to obtain basic education due to sociocultural factors. Other factors include poverty, lack of ICT infrastructure, resources, computer skills that are confronted with software and hardware applications that contribute to the lack of digital skills that are required in the labour market (Pande & van der Weide, 2012).

At times, youths lack the motivation to use ICTs such as computers to enhance their personal development goals (Waema & Miroro, 2014). Using ICTs constructively should be addressed as some youths use their access to computers for social media networking and other sites that do not contribute to their self-development. Conversely, others are still struggling to learn to use ICTs for their personal development due to a lack of experience and familiarity with technology (Hallberg et al., 2011).

Many youths value the use of ICTs, even though some are unlikely to have the opportunity to learn for themselves or accept help due to their inability to identify the opportunities they can derive from its use (Oyelana & Thakhathi, 2015). This is based on individual-level self-development, lack of skills development, lack of technology access and ownership, household and many other aspects of social, political, cultural and economic life. Individuals also frequently lack the self-confidence to use computers among other skilled computer users. These factors are a visible reflection of their adaptability to use ICTs, and contribute to shaping and influencing how the youths relate to the use of ICTs (Waema & Miroro, 2014). Further discussions on the theoretical framework used to guide the study are highlighted in the following section.

Theoretical Framework: Sustainable Livelihood Theory

The SL Theory was used to support the study (DFID, 2005).

Advantages of Sustainable Livelihood (SL) Theory

The theory explains livelihood as being sustainable when it can be sustained and recovered from hindrances to livelihood (Morse & McNamara, 2013). Moreover, it is said to possess improved capabilities and assets both now and in the future, without undermining the natural resource base (Rakodi, 2014). Hence, the aim of the study was to use digitization to tackle unemployment. ICTs and 4IR are interrelated in terms of both being technological innovations that expected to influence industrial development, human enhancement and economic buoyancy of countries.

The SL Theory was used for the study due to its usefulness in conducting development work and its relevance to poverty alleviation as a multidimensional concept from the perspective of young people's lack of ICT access to information on industry requirements for employability and improved livelihood (DFID, 2005).

The theory buttresses the empowerment of people and the significance of understanding peoples' personal abilities in the human capital factor (Morse & McNamara, 2013). The theory is centred on people and development, and it offers a multidimensional conceptualisation of poverty (Morse & McNamara, 2013). The theory allows people to have a voice in tackling inequality and it possesses a holistic approach to development, considering economic, social, subjective factors, as well as natural, physical and financial capital as practical realities that need to be addressed for poverty reduction to occur in people's lives (Morse & McNamara, 2013).

The theory further assists vulnerable poor people to have the capability and resilience to deal with external shocks that might affect their livelihood (DFID, 2005). The SL approach is useful for identifying unanticipated impacts as the framework reflects how development projects can affect the types of decisions people make, given the risks they face and the assets they are able to access, thus putting impact assessment in a more comprehensive context (Parkinson & Ramirez, 2006).

Finally, the theory allows for the development of community projects that empower people and enhance their personal development. The establishment of public access points or centres, such as telecentres and digital centres, can provide ICT access to the youth in disadvantaged communities (Attwood, 2014). Digital centres are sometimes government-sponsored but they are not available in most disadvantaged communities in South Africa. There are digital centres in some provinces such as the Western Cape of South Africa (Alao, Lwoga & Chigona 2017), but there is a need to disseminate these centres to other provinces in the country.

Disadvantages of Sustainable Livelihood (SL) Theory

SL approaches are limited in their ability to identify how livelihoods link together at the national or global level, and in identifying sector-wide or economy-wide solutions to poverty (DFID, 2005). The theory has been operationalised with the assistance of donors for several years, but its explicit use for rural development has declined over time (Rakodi, 2014). The approaches and principles of the SL Theory have not been favoured, but the core principles have become part of much conventional development thinking and continue to be influential (Rakodi, 2014).

According to Small (2007), the aim of the SL Theory is mainly focused on poverty which is a multidimensional phenomenon that cannot simply be reduced to economic deprivation. Other dimensions include technology dimensions, human dimensions and institutional dimensions. The dimensional terms are defined as follows:

- Technology dimension refers to the use of infrastructures such as ICTs to develop and transform people's lives and work within a city in a relevant way. This dimension includes the concept of the digital city, virtual city, information city, wired city, ubiquitous city and intelligent city.
- Human dimension refers to people's education, learning and knowledge that are the key drivers for the smart city. These dimensions are the concepts of learning city and knowledge city.
- Institutional dimension refers to the government and policy. The cooperation between stakeholders and institutional governments are important in designing and implementing smart city projects. This dimension entails the concept of smart community, sustainable city and green city.

The SL approach transforms the structures and processes that have the capacity to change livelihoods or employment opportunities in a way that provides better opportunities to the deprived (DFID, 2005). However, the progression is complex because of the informal structures of social supremacy and power in societies.

The implementation of digital centres in communities can allow young people to access the relevant industry information needed for employability. However, most communities lack public access centres such as telecentres and digital centres that are government-sponsored. The lack of ICT development initiatives in disadvantaged communities affect people's ability to empower themselves and influence young people's access ICT resources for employment opportunities (Ledwith, 2020; Scanlon, Jenkinson, Leahy, Powell, & Byrne 2019).

Small (2007) further claims that the SL Theory has challenges in logical capacity and information requirements to allocate manpower to work in community projects as the approach assumes. This is mainly due to the lack of constructive use of the SL approach based on insufficient analytical capacity or understanding of poverty and livelihood issues that affect people, since all people-centred rhetoric of SLA people is strangely invisible (Mosse, 1994).

Implementation of Sustainable Livelihood Theory

The SL Theory has a considerable impact on policies and strategies of development agencies and can be used as a development intervention (DFID, 2005). The SL approach can be applied by the government and stakeholders to design livelihoods that can be of benefit in tackling unemployment among the youth. The SL Theory can be implemented as follows:

- **People-centred:** The SL Theory is people-centred and using ICTs as an intervention tool to provide access to information on the industry requirements for employment is essential. This can be achieved through the provision of digital knowledge using computer training skills programmes and workshops as a delivery measure on the required industry skills. This measure can assist in reducing unemployment and poverty if external support from the government focuses on what matters to the youth by implementing strategies that focus on ways to overcome the challenges that contribute to their lack of livelihood.
- **Responsive and participatory:** The youth must be key actors working with external bodies to identify and address livelihood priorities. The government, ICT policymakers and stakeholders need processes that will allow them to listen and respond to the needs of the youth.
- **Multi-level:** In order for poverty reduction to take place among unemployed youths, the government needs to develop policies that will allow an effective enabling environment such as digital training centres. These will promote the facilitation of digital skills programmes that will allow young people to build on their own strength and empower them with digital literacy.

- **Conducted in partnership**: Government should collaborate with the public and private sectors to implement ICT development initiatives that focus on youth empowerment.
- **Sustainable**: The dimensions of sustainability consist of economic, social, environmental and institutional aspects. All these dimensions need to be balanced evenly for sustainability to be achieved.
- **Dynamic commitment**: External support, such as the government and all stakeholders, need to recognise the essence and nature of livelihood strategies, respond flexibly to changes in the personal circumstances that hinder the access of ICTs among young people and develop longer-term commitments.

METHODOLOGY

This research used a conceptual analysis as a principal qualitative research technique (Cronin, Ryan & Coughlan, 2008). The conceptual analysis was realised using similar studies that present ICTs' impact on youths. The literature review supports the main critical research question: How can digital skills impact the sustainable development of youth employability?

For an in-depth critical analysis and identification of themes to be achieved, existing literature was consulted on the impact of digital skills on youths' sustainable development. It was realised that from the literature analysis, concepts were not in contradiction with each other and they disclosed some shared features that were partially overlapping (Cronin et al., 2008).

Some scholars used digital skills as a suitable tool for youth sustainability development which justifies the suitability of ICTs among the youths. Table 2 presents the studies that focus on the impact of ICTs on youths' sustainable development.

The study conducted data collection using a qualitative method distributing questionnaire survey through email invites accompanied with a consent letter to participants e.g. Youths that are active users of ICTs were targeted to participate in the study. The respondents of the study were males and females between the ages of 18 and 35 living in Johannesburg, Gauteng province in South Africa. A sample size of 200 youths was used for the pilot study and 100 participant's responded to the questionnaire.

RECOMMENDATION

The study recommends ICTs as a possible intervention for the sustainable development of youths. Critical questions are presented on how ICT policymakers

Table 2. Studies on the impact of ICTs on youths' sustainable development

Concept	Description	Reference
Youth Digital Culture	The youths grew up in the era of the digital revolution which engendered the development of digital culture, characterised by an unprecedented exposure to technology in adolescent years.	Loh, R. S. M., & Lim, S. S. (2019).
Telecentre for youth empowerment	The use of telecentres to influence the economic empowerment of youths in disadvantaged communities in South Africa. The study further investigates the factors that affect ICT use.	Booi, S. L., Chigona, W., Maliwichi, P., & Kunene, K. (2019).
ICTs on Knowledge management	The impact of ICT on knowledge management among the staff of Hamedan Organization of Sports and Youth (Bakhshalipour et al., 2019). This study surveys the effect of the use of ICT skills with empowerment indicators on staff in the Ministry of Sports and Youth of Islamic Republic Iran.	Bakhshalipour, V., Sareshkeh, S. K., & Azizi, B. (2019).
ICTs for employability	ICT for youth employability by improving their access to productive employment and their ability to cope with their social environment through creativity and innovation experience.	Semutenga, E., Aquarius, I., & Sengendo, L. (2019).
ICTs and graduate challenges for employability	The study examines ICT graduates and challenges of employability. The study was used to enhance employment opportunities in South Africa.	Ohei, K. N., Brink, R., & Abiodun, A. (2019).
ICTs and student employability skills	The study explores employers' perceptions of the five most important employability skills required from graduates for them to be considered as employable in the job market. This article presents findings of a survey of 299 Malaysian employers from diverse types of agencies and organisations, which employ engineering and ICT graduates.	Saad, M. S. M., & Majid, I. A. (2014).
ICT supports employability	IPTS launched a research project on how ICT can support employability in the context of its policy support activities for the implementation of the Europe 2020 strategy, and the Digital Agenda for Europe.	Green, A., de Hoyos, M., Barnes, S. A., Owen, D., Baldauf, B., & Behle, H. (2013).

and all stakeholders can use ICTs for skills development to contribute to the socio-economic development of youths' unemployment. ICTs are valuable tools that provide information on how to improve the employability of youths and enhance the economic standards of young people. The study further recommends that government, ICT policymakers, and all ICT stakeholders adopt the use of ICTs for skills development through computer skills training programmes and workshops. The research recommends that governments use ICTs to bridge the digital literacy of young people and enhance access to ICT tools in disadvantaged communities. The study contributes to knowledge and the academic environment in the ICT4D research area that relates to human science research, policy-relevant and social-scientific projects for public-sector users, and science and technology to address poverty.

Issues, Controversies, Problems

The World Economic Forum claims the main causes of youth unemployment include a lack of quality education and relevance to the needs of the labour market. A lack of ICTs to access information on industry requirement for employability is another deterring factor (Oye et al., 2011). Thus, the contributing factors to access are mostly structural and conceptual. The lack of ICT access is a visible reflection of the hindrance to the adoption of ICT use to seek information for individual needs. The factors that youths encounter include a lack of education, socio-economic, religious, traditional and cultural beliefs that contribute to their identity formulations, roles and responsibilities, and personal aspirations (Hilbert, 2011). Other barriers include the lack of ICT infrastructure, resources, computer skills, such as software and hardware applications, and these usually contribute to the lack of digital skills in the employment market.

More Issues, Controversies, Problems

South Africa's youth have challenges in getting educated and learning basic computer skills that can empower them. The youth living in disadvantaged areas are not marketable to the labour market due to their lack of ICT skills, and they have more barriers that hinder them from becoming educated than their urban peers. This is because of the lack of livelihood, adequate time to attend school to obtain a basic education, and societal norms that afford them little urgency in gaining an education; such as peer groups that contribute to the lack of focus, poverty and other contributing factors (Pande & van der Weide, 2012). The youth from disadvantaged areas can benefit from using ICTs if they are motivated to use computers to enhance their personal developmental goals (Waema & Miroro, 2014) because most young people use ICTs to socialise on social media networks and other sites that do not contribute to their self-development. Others are still struggling to learn to use ICTs for their personal development due to a lack of experience and familiarity with technology (Hallberg et al., 2011).

Numbered Lists

1. **Key Term (KT):**
   a. Fourth Industrial Revolution
      i. Technology
      ii. Digital Literacy
   b. ICT Access
2. Sustainable Development

   Bulleted Lists

- **Key Term (KT):**

  ○ Youths.
    § Employability

  Block Quotes

"ICTs can be realized as being part of a process that leads to development as ICT tools can be used as an information tool which young people can use to derive vital information and obtain the necessary needed for their self-development" (Mazibuko, Hart, Mogale, Mohlakoana & Aliber 2008:5).

SOLUTIONS AND RECOMMENDATIONS

Prior studies show that technology can be explained as contributing to a growing digital divide as ICTs enhance inequalities and lead to potential social exclusion (Talbot & Bizzell, 2016). However, the significance of ICTs for development connects people to accurate and up to date information and equips them with new skills (David & Surmaya, 2005). The youth have the potential to transform the economy of any country that invests their resources in improving their digital skills (Bakhshalipour, Sareshkeh & Azizi, 2019). Institutional proponents of ICTs for development, for example, the UNDP and the World Bank, suggest that an easily accessible and abundant supply of information fosters knowledge formation that can induce economic empowerment (World Bank, 2008b). Therefore, ICTs can boost the socio-economic growth of the youth of any country if properly used (Koutroumpis, 2009).

Thus, the implementation of ICTs creates access to technology which provides economic opportunities, informs people and allows them to use technologies available in the domains in which they function (Michael & Samson, 2014). It is argued that ICTs can be used to tackle the lack of youth access to technology. The youth should be enabled to access information to enhance their self-development and economic standards through their participation in computer skills training programmes offered at government-sponsored digital centres (Hallberg et al., 2011; Attwood et al., 2013). These digital centres can provide solutions for the lack of ICT access because they present users with free digital training and issue professional certificates – such as the International Computer Driving Licence (ICDL) – to users in various computer modules. These include the basic and advanced computer training, e-learner entry-level accredited computer certificate and informal computer training at the ICDL Accredited Test Centres (ATC). The certificates are accredited and accepted at industry entry levels.

FUTURE RESEARCH DIRECTIONS

The study recommends future research on the use of ICTs for professionalism in all economic sectors for an improved economic buoyancy. Such studies should investigate how technology can bridge the unemployment gap that exists among the youth in other developing countries. Further investigation of the implementation of the 4IR and its significance for the country should also be considered.

The recommendation for probable future research includes how the 4IR era can be of benefit to all citizens of a developing country, especially when the implementation of advanced technology has been adopted in the industry. Finally, it should be asked how the adaptability of ICTs can improve the employability gap among the youths of developing countries.

CONCLUSION

This study defined ICTs and discussed how technology could be applied successively for the sustainable development of youths for certain development to be realised and new capabilities to be established and sustained. The use of ICTs can deliver information and knowledge which is the key to providing potential networks and easy engagement that may enhance youth development. The findings of the study present input and indicators to policymakers on the use of ICTs for the sustainable development of the youth. This research makes a significant and valuable scholarly contribution to existing knowledge in the academic environment. The concluding findings of the study reflect the benefits of employing ICTs to access information that could be used for the sustainable development of youth employability. Using ICTs to source information on skills development could potentially enhance youths' employability, although the study implied that the specific usage patterns and perceptions of ICTs led to factors that contributed to the lack of computer skills by the youths. It was realised that socio-economic barriers, lack of digital skills and other factors hinder youths' access to information on how to improve the digital skills required for the job market.

ACKNOWLEDGMENT

We would like to acknowledge the University of Johannesburg for providing the resources used for the write-up of this chapter.

REFERENCES

Alao, A. (2019). *How telecentres contribute to women empowerment in rural communities: Case of Western Cape, South Africa* (Doctoral dissertation). Faculty of Commerce.

Alao, A., Lwoga, T. E., & Chigona, W. (2017, May). Telecentres use in rural communities and women empowerment: Case of Western Cape. In *International Conference on Social Implications of Computers in Developing Countries* (pp. 119-134). Springer. 10.1007/978-3-319-59111-7_11

Amesheva, I., Clark, A., & Payne, J. (2019). Financing for Youth Entrepreneurship in Sustainable Development. *Sustainable Development Goals: Harnessing Business to Achieve the SDGs through Finance, Technology, and Law Reform*, 253-273.

Anton, P. S., Silberglith, R., & Schveeder, J. (2011). *The Global Technology Revolution Bio/Nano/Materials Trends and Their Synergies with Information Technology*. RAND.

Attwood, H., Diga, K., Braathen, E., & May, J. (2013). Telecentre functionality in South Africa: Re-enabling the community ICT access environment. *The Journal of Community Informatics*, *9*(4).

Attwood, H. E. (2014). *Researching QoL change from ICT training, access and use at South African telecentres: empowerment through participatory research* (Doctoral dissertation).

Avdjiev, S., Bruno, V., Koch, C., & Shin, H. S. (2019). The dollar exchange rate as a global risk factor: Evidence from investment. *IMF Economic Review, 67*(1), 151–173. doi:10.105741308-019-00074-4

Bakhshalipour, V., Sareshkeh, S. K., & Azizi, B. (2019). The effect of the use of information and communication technology skills with empowerment indicators on staff in the Ministry of Sports and Youth of Islamic Republic of Iran (Case Study in Youth and Sports General Directorate of Guilan Province). *Arquivos de Ciências do Esporte, 6*(3). Advance online publication. doi:10.17648/aces.v6n3.2938

Balouza, M. (2019). The Impact of Information and Communication Technologies on the Human Development in the Gulf Cooperation Council Countries: An Empirical Study. *Management Studies and Economic Systems, 4*(2), 79–113.

Bloem, J., Van Doorn, M., Duivestein, S., Excoffier, D., Maas, R., & Van Ommeren, E. (2014). The fourth industrial revolution. *Things Tighten, 8.*

Booi, S. L., Chigona, W., Maliwichi, P., & Kunene, K. (2019, May). The Influence of Telecentres on the Economic Empowerment of the Youth in Disadvantaged Communities of South Africa. In *International Conference on Social Implications of Computers in Developing Countries* (pp. 152-167). Springer. 10.1007/978-3-030-18400-1_13

Caiado, R. G. G., Leal Filho, W., Quelhas, O. L. G., de Mattos Nascimento, D. L., & Ávila, L. V. (2018). A literature-based review on potentials and constraints in the implementation of the sustainable development goals. *Journal of Cleaner Production, 198*, 1276–1288. doi:10.1016/j.jclepro.2018.07.102

Calitz, A. P., Greyling, J. H., & Cullen, M. D. (2014). *South African industry ICT graduate skills requirements.* Southern African Computer Lecturers' *Association.*

Calitz, A. P., Poisat, P., & Cullen, M. (2017). The future African workplace: The use of collaborative robots in manufacturing. *SA Journal of Human Resource Management, 15*(1), 1–11. doi:10.4102ajhrm.v15i0.901

Chitla, A. (2012). Impact of Information and Communication Technology on Rural India. *IOSR Journal of Computer Engineering.*

Cronin, P., Ryan, F., & Coughlan, M. (2008). Undertaking a literature review: A step-by-step approach. *British Journal of Nursing (Mark Allen Publishing), 17*(1), 38–43. doi:10.12968/bjon.2008.17.1.28059 PMID:18399395

David, J., & Surmaya, T. (2005). A Best Process Approach for Using ICTs in Development. Intermediate Technology Development Group. The Schumacher Centre for Technology and Development. *IRFD World Forum on Information Society – Tunis 2005.*

DFID. (2005). *The economic impact of telecommunication on rural livelihood and poverty reduction.* Available: www.livelihoods.org

Duncombe, R. A. (2014). Understanding the impact of mobile phones on livelihoods in developing countries. *Development Policy Review, 32*(5), 567–588. doi:10.1111/dpr.12073

Eşkinat, R. (2016). The Importance of Digital Technologies for Sustainable Development. *Inclusive and Sustainable Development and the Role of Social and Solidarity Economy, 106.*

eTransform Africa. (2012). *The transformational use of information and communication technologies in Africa.* The World Bank and the African Development Bank, with the support of the African Union.

Eynon, R., & Geniets, A. (2016). The digital skills paradox: How do digitally excluded youth develop skills to use the internet? *Learning, Media and Technology, 41*(3), 463–479. doi:10.1080/17439884.2014.1002845

Fernández-Sanz, L., Gómez-Pérez, J., & Castillo-Martínez, A. (2017). e-Skills Match: A framework for mapping and integrating the main skills, knowledge and competence standards and models for ICT occupations. *Computer Standards & Interfaces, 51*, 30–42. doi:10.1016/j.csi.2016.11.004

Ghosh, A. (2011). Initiatives in ICT for Rural Development: An Indian Perspective. Global Media Journal: Indian Edition, 2(2).

Göll, E., & Zwiers, J. (2019). Technological Trends in the MENA Region: The Cases of Digitalization and Information and Communications Technology (ICT). *MENARA*, 206.

Green, A., de Hoyos, M., Barnes, S. A., Owen, D., Baldauf, B., & Behle, H. (2013). *Literature Review on Employability, Inclusion and ICT, Part 1: The Concept of employability, with a specific focus on young people, older workers and migrants* (No. JRC75518). Joint Research Centre (Seville site).

Hallberg, D., Kulecho, M., Kulecho, A., & Okoth, L. (2011). Case studies of Kenyan digital villages with a focus on women and girls. *Journal of Language, Technology & Entrepreneurship in Africa*, *3*(1), 255–273.

Hamilton, M., Carbone, A., Gonsalvez, C., & Jollands, M. (2015, January). Breakfast with ICT Employers: What do they want to see in our graduates? *Proceedings of the 17th Australasian Computing Education Conference (ACE 2015)*, *27*(1), 30.

Heeks, R. (2010). Do information and communication technologies (ICTs) contribute to development? *Journal of International Development*, *22*(5), 625–640. doi:10.1002/jid.1716

Helbing, D. (2019). Societal, economic, ethical and legal challenges of the digital revolution: From big data to deep learning, artificial intelligence, and manipulative technologies. In *Towards Digital Enlightenment* (pp. 47–72). Springer. doi:10.1007/978-3-319-90869-4_6

Hendrix, C. S., & Kang, S. (2019). *19-10 Keeping Up with the Future: Upgrading Forecasts of Political Instability and Geopolitical Risk*. Academic Press.

Hilbert, M. (2011, November). Digital gender divide or technologically empowered women in developing countries? A typical case of lies, damned lies, and statistics. *Women's Studies International Forum*, *34*(6), 479–489. doi:10.1016/j.wsif.2011.07.001

Kamel, S. (2010, October). The evolution of the ICT sector in Egypt–Partnership4Development. In *International Business Information Management Association (IBIMA) Conference on Innovation and Knowledge Management in Twin Track Economies: Challenges and Opportunities*. International Business Information Management Association (IBIMA).

Kayisire, D., & Wei, J. (2016). ICT adoption and usage in Africa: Towards an efficiency assessment. *Information Technology for Development*, *22*(4), 630–653. doi:10.1080/02681102.2015.1081862

Kirlidog, M., van der Vyver, C., Zeeman, M., & Coetzee, W. (2018). Unfulfilled need: Reasons for insufficient ICT skills in South Africa. *Information Development*, *34*(1), 5–19. doi:10.1177/0266666916671984

Koutroumpis, P. (2009). The economic impact of broadband on growth: A simultaneous approach. *Telecommunications Policy*, *33*(9), 471–485. doi:10.1016/j.telpol.2009.07.004

Ledwith, M. (2020). *Community development: A critical approach*. Policy Press.

Lele, S. M. (1991). Sustainable development: A critical review. *World Development, 19*(6), 607–621. doi:10.1016/0305-750X(91)90197-P

Li, G., Hou, Y., & Wu, A. (2017). Fourth Industrial Revolution: Technological drivers, impacts and coping methods. *Chinese Geographical Science, 27*(4), 626–637. doi:10.100711769-017-0890-x

Loh, R. S. M., & Lim, S. S. (2019). *Youth Digital Culture*. The International Encyclopedia of Media Literacy. doi:10.1002/9781118978238.ieml0245

Ma, J. K. H., Vachon, T. E., & Cheng, S. (2019). National income, political freedom, and investments in R&D and education: A comparative analysis of the second digital divide among 15-year-old students. *Social Indicators Research, 144*(1), 133–166. doi:10.100711205-018-2030-0

Manalo, J. A. IV, Pasiona, S. P., Bautista, A. M. F., Villaflor, J. D., Corpuz, D. C. P., & Biag-Manalo, H. H. M. (2019). Exploring youth engagement in agricultural development: The case of farmers' children in the Philippines as rice crop manager infomediaries. *Journal of Agricultural Education and Extension, 25*(4), 1–17. doi:10.1080/1389224X.2019.1629969

Marumo, P. O., & Sebolaaneng, M. E. (2019). Assessing the state of youth unemployment in South Africa: A discussion and examination of the structural problems responsible for unsustainable youth development in South Africa. *Gender & Behaviour, 17*(3), 13477–13485.

Mazibuko, S., Hart, T., Mogale, M., Mohlakoana, N., & Aliber, M. (2008). Baseline information on technology-oriented initiatives in rural areas to promote economic development. Academic Press.

Mckenzie, S., Coldwell-Neilson, J., & Palmer, S. (2017). Career aspirations and skills expectations of undergraduate IT students: are they realistic? In *HERDSA 2017: Research and development in higher education: curriculum transformation: Proceedings of the 40th HERDSA Annual International Conference* (pp. 229-240). Higher Education Research and Development Society of Australasia.

Merkel, S., Heinze, R. G., Hilbert, J., & Naegele, G. (2019). Technology for all. In The Future of Ageing in Europe (pp. 217-253). Palgrave Macmillan. doi:10.1007/978-981-13-1417-9_8

Messer, N., & Townsley, P. (2003). *Local institutions and livelihoods: guidelines for analysis*. Food & Agriculture Org.

Michael, O. I., & Samson, A. J. (2014). The impact of information and communication technology on youth and its vocational opportunities in Nigeria. *Journal of Good Governance and Sustainable Development in Africa, 2*(1).

Molema, T. M., & Quan-Baffour, K. P. (2019). Participation in the Acet Programmes in Mashashane-Maraba Area of Limpopo Province: Gender Discriminatory? *Rethinking Teaching and learning in the 21st Century, 355.*

Morse, S., & McNamara, N. (2013). *Sustainable livelihood approach: A critique of theory and practice.* Springer Science & Business Media. doi:10.1007/978-94-007-6268-8

Mutula, S. M., & Van Brakel, P. (2007). ICT skills readiness for the emerging global digital economy among small businesses in developing countries. *Library Hi Tech, 25*(2), 231–245. doi:10.1108/07378830710754992

Ohei, K. N., Brink, R., & Abiodun, A. (2019). Information and Communication Technology (ICT) graduates and challenges of employability: A conceptual framework for enhancing employment opportunities in South Africa. *Gender & Behaviour, 17*(3), 13500–13521.

Oye, N. D., Inuwa, I., & Shakil, A. M. (2011). Role of information communication technology (ICT): Implications on unemployment and Nigerian GDP. *Journal of International Academic Research, 11*(1), 9–17.

Pande, R., & van der Weide, T. P. (2012). *Globalization, technology diffusion and gender disparity: Social impacts of ICTs.* Information Science Reference. doi:10.4018/978-1-4666-0020-1

Pandey, P., & Zheng, Y. (2019, May). Unpacking Empowerment in ICT4D Research. In *International Conference on Social Implications of Computers in Developing Countries* (pp. 83-94). Springer.

Parkinson, S., & Ramirez, R. (2007). Using a Sustainable Livelihoods Approach to Assessing the Impact of ICTs in Development. *The Journal of Community Informatics, 2*(3). http://jat.gws.uky.edu/index.php/ciej/article/view/310

Ponelis, S. R., & Holmner, M. A. (2015). ICT in Africa: Enabling a better life for all. *Information Technology for Development, 21*(1), 1–11. doi:10.1080/0268110 2.2014.985521

Rakodi, C. (2014). A livelihoods approach–conceptual issues and definitions. In *Urban livelihoods* (pp. 26–45). Routledge.

Rifkin, J. (2011). *The Third Industrial Revolution: How Lateral Power is Transforming Energy, the Economy and the World*. Palgrave - McMillan.

Rifkin, J. (2014). *The Zero Marginal Cost Society: The Internet of Things, the Collaborative Commons and the Eclipse of Capitalism*. St. Martins Press.

Saad, M. S. M., & Majid, I. A. (2014). Employers' perceptions of important employability skills required from Malaysian engineering and information and communication technology (ICT) graduates. *Global Journal of Engineering Education*, *16*(3), 110–115.

Sabia, J. J. (2015). Do minimum wages stimulate productivity and growth? *IZA World of Labor*, (221).

Sachs, J. D. (2015). *The age of sustainable development*. Columbia University Press. doi:10.7312ach17314

Sachs, J. D., Schmidt-Traub, G., Mazzucato, M., Messner, D., Nakicenovic, N., & Rockström, J. (2019). Six Transformations to achieve the Sustainable Development Goals. *Nature Sustainability*, *2*(9), 805–814. doi:10.103841893-019-0352-9

Sadiq, A. M., & Mohammed, M. (2015). The role of information and communication technology (ICT) in providing job opportunities for youth in the developing world. *Journal of Emerging Trends in Engineering and Applied Sciences*, *6*(7), 174–179.

Scanlon, M., Jenkinson, H., Leahy, P., Powell, F., & Byrne, O. (2019). 'How are we going to do it?'An exploration of the barriers to access to higher education amongst young people from disadvantaged communities. *Irish Educational Studies*, *38*(3), 343–357. doi:10.1080/03323315.2019.1611467

Semutenga, E., Aquarius, I., & Ssengendo, L. (2019). *ICT for Youth Employability*. Academic Press.

Small, L. A. (2007). The sustainable rural livelihoods approach: A critical review. *Canadian Journal of Development Studies*. *Canadian Journal of Development Studies*, *28*(1), 27–38. doi:10.1080/02255189.2007.9669186

Statistics SA. (2018). *Youth unemployment still high in Q1: 2018*. Statistics South Africa.

Statistics SA. (2019). *Statistical release P0211: Mid-year population estimates 2019*. Statistics South Africa. Available: http://www.statssa.gov.za/publications/P0211/P02111stQuarter2019

Talbot, P., & Bizzell, B. (2016). Teaching, Technology, and Transformation. In *Educational Leaders without Borders* (pp. 83–104). Springer. doi:10.1007/978-3-319-12358-5_4

UN General Assembly. (2015). *Sustainable development goals. SDGs, transforming our world: The 2030.* Author.

United Nations Development Programme (Kenya). (2001). *Kenya Human Development Report.* United Nations Development Programme.

Vinichenko, M. V., Makushkin, S. A., Melnichuk, A. V., Frolova, E. V., & Kurbakova, S. N. (2016). Student employment during college studies and after career start. *International Review of Management and Marketing, 6*(5S).

Voskoglou, M. G. (2016). Problem-solving in the forthcoming era of the third industrial revolution. *International Journal of Psychological Research, 10*(4), 361–380.

Waema, T. M., & Miroro, O. O. (2014). Access and use of ICT and its contribution to poverty reduction in Kenya. ICT pathways to poverty reduction: Empirical evidence from East and Southern Africa, 102-131. doi:10.3362/9781780448152.005

World Bank. (2008b). *Understanding Poverty report.* Available: http://web.worldbank.org/wbsite/external/topics/extpoverty0contentmdk:20153855~menupk:373757~page:148956~pipk:216618~thesitepk:336992,00.Html

World Bank. (2012). *Information, Communication Technologies, and infoDev (Program) (2012) Information and Communications for Development 2012: Maximizing Mobile.* World Bank Publications.

Zelenika, I., & Pearce, J. M. (2013). The Internet and other ICTs as tools and catalysts for sustainable development: Innovation for 21st century. *Information Development, 29*(3), 217–232. doi:10.1177/0266666912465742

ADDITIONAL READING

Eşkinat, R. (2016). The Importance of Digital Technologies for Sustainable Development. Inclusive and Sustainable Development and the Role of Social and Solidarity Economy, 106.

Gorova, S. (2019). *Identity of informational society: problems of realisation.* Litres. doi:10.29013/SVGorova.IISPR.208.2019

Hart, T., & Barratt, P. (2009), the employment of graduates within small and medium-sized firms in England. People, Place and Policy. Available from: http://www.extra.shu.ac.uk/ppp-online/the-employment-of-graduates-within-small-and-medium-sized-firms-in-england/. Assessed: November 2019.

Kamel, S. (2010). *E-Strategies for Technological Diffusion and Adoption: National ICT Approaches for socioeconomic development.* IGI. doi:10.4018/978-1-60566-388-3

Mutula, S. M., & Van Brakel, P. (2007). ICT skills readiness for the emerging global digital economy among small businesses in developing countries: A case study of Botswana. *Library Hi Tech, 25*(2), 231–245. doi:10.1108/07378830710754992

Oyelana, A. A., & Thakhathi, D. R. (2015). The Impact of Effective Utilization of Information and Communication Technology (ICT) in Enhancing and Improving Employees Performance in the Local Government Organizations in South Africa. *Journal of Communication, 6*(2), 248–253. doi:10.1080/0976691X.2015.11884869

Stukalina, Y. (2018). Career Management in a Technical University as an Essential Factor Influencing Its Competitiveness. In I. Kabashkin, I. Yatskiv, & O. Prentkovskis (Eds.), *Reliability and Statistics in Transportation and Communication. RelStat 2017. Lecture Notes in Networks and Systems* (Vol. 36). Springer. doi:10.1007/978-3-319-74454-4_61

Van Broekhuizen, H. and Van Der Berg, S. (2016). How high is graduate unemployment in South Africa? A much-needed update.

Willard, T., & Halder, M. (2003). The Information Society and Sustainable Development. International Institute for Sustainable Development (IISD), Winnipeg, Canada http://www. iisd.org/PUBLICATIONS/pub. aspx.

KEY TERMS AND DEFINITIONS

Digital Centre: Refers to as the public access points places where people are allowed to access ICT technologies, the internet as well as other ICT oriented services.

Employability: This refers to a person's ability to gain, maintain employment and obtain new employment when necessary. The term, employability means when a person is capable of attaining a job. For example, employability involves having a set of skills, knowledge, understanding and personal attributes.

Fourth Industrial Revolution (41R): Is referred to as Industry 4.0, which describes the age of intelligence that involves the use of technologies like artificial intelligence, augmented reality, 3D printing and cloud computing.

ICTs: Information Communication and Technologies.

Sustainable Development: The sustainable development goal refers to the need to meet the desires of people today, without compromising their future needs. This means people cannot continue to use the current resources but are expected to consider reserving the resources for future needs and for future generations. Stabilising and reducing carbon emissions is key to living within environmental limits.

Telecentres: Telecentres serve as a public centre that consists of computers that are connected to the internet, with a variety of technologies such as telephones, radio, fax, copiers, scanners, laminations and printers in communities where domestic ownership of such equipment is not affordable.

Youths: This refers to a group of young people who may be regarded as young adults. For example, a youth is a person that is from the age of 18 and above.

Chapter 7
Education 4.0:
Future of Learning With Disruptive Technologies

Sana Moid

ⓘ https://orcid.org/0000-0003-4768-6508

Amity University, India

ABSTRACT

Education 4.0 is an education model aligned with future trends in order to develop and enhance individualized education that will eventually go on to define the manner in which youngsters of the future will work and live. Since youth are the main asset of any nation, education becomes the most powerful tool for social transformation. India's demographic structure is changing; while the world grows older, the Indian population is becoming younger, and by 2025, about two-third of Indians will be in its workforce. A few issues addressed in this study are to identify the drivers of Education 4.0, to identify and understand the role of disruptive technologies, to study the transition from Education 1.0 to Education 4.0 and its relevant impact on the higher education system.

INTRODUCTION

Global connectivity, smart machines, and new media are some drivers reshaping how we think about work, what constitutes work, and how we learn and acquire the skills to work in the future. The concept of a "100 year life" becoming the norm, and the majority of that spent studying and working, means that learning will be more important, and different, for next generations. Most people will have at least

DOI: 10.4018/978-1-7998-4882-0.ch007

6 different careers that will require fundamental reeducating, whilst the relentless speed of innovation will constantly require new skills and knowledge to keep pace, let alone an edge (Fisk, 2017).The basic purpose of education and training is to empower an individual to lead a successful life and contribute best to himself, family, society, nation and humanity.

Since youth are the main asset of any nation, education becomes the most powerful tool for social transformation. India's demographic structure is transforming, while the world grows older, the Indian population is becoming younger and by 2025 about two-third Indians will be in its workforce (Fisk, 2017). A constantly growing older world offers a huge opportunity for talented and competent young generation as this older population will retire making way for youths to come in the mainstream. To reap full advantage of this transition, the youth need to be prepared by higher quality education thus making them most productive. Therefore, the system needs transformation completely.

The current system of education comes from the Prussian system which was designed to create good employees and obedient soldiers, who blindly follow orders and always need to be instructed. This system was not designed to teach students to follow orders and not to think.(Schrager 2018)

A few pertinent questions are:

(i)   Whether India's higher education is "relevant to the era"?
(ii)   Why should a student pay for education, when he is unable to earn his livelihood after getting his 'Degree'?
(iii) Why should a student attend classes, when more updated knowledge is available to him via outside resources?

The World Economic Forum @ Davos-2016 announced the Fourth Industrial Revolution, and predicted 'major shift about the future of jobs'. Disruptive technologies, driven by Industry 4.0 have been adding more fire to the already volatile, uncertain, complex & ambiguous world and effecting our lives, our relationships, and what future of jobs.

The technological breakthrough is rapidly moving the frontiers between the work task performed by humans and those performed by machines. We are in transition, the learner is at the epicentre of a futuristic learning ecosystem. It is expected that "Education 4.0" is likely to require paradigm shift in

- Demand-led instead of supply-led education which means that education should be as per what students want and their requirements rather than following a set established pattern.

- Competency-based instead of knowledge-based which requires that education should be such that matches the competence of students and should be customized as per that.
- Incorporate disruptive technologies &skill-sets which requires focus of education to be skill based rather than a normal standardized pattern.
- Lifelong learning instead of front-loaded learning which means that topics taught should be such that students are able to apply it practically and it stays with them throughout rather than just confining the knowledge acquired in their brains only.
- Emphasis on EQ than IQ alone so that the youth is emotionally stable and sensitive enough to empathize rather than just running in a rat race.
- Focus on purposefulness, mindfulness leading to overall Happiness & Wellbeing leading to creation of a positive world.

The present chapter aims to:

To identify the drivers of Education 4.0
To identify and understand the role of disruptive technologies
To study the transition from Education 1.0 to Education 4.0 and its relevant impact
    on Higher Education System
To offer suggestions for implementation.

CHANGES IN EDUCATION ECOSYSTEM OVER TIME

Education 1.0: In ancient ages education was not accessible to all as it was confined to few privileged ones and was mostly influenced under religious purview involving informal methods of teaching. During the Renaissance age and post Industrial Revolution, transformation took place in the field of education focusing more on development of people with emphasis on providing them with basic learning and skills. When state was given the prime responsibility of the state, society witnessed a rapid increase in enrollments across all ages and sections. Ancient education became popular with the dawn of informal education in India, China, Israel, Rome and Greece and was primarily focused on imparting it only to elite classes and educating boys. In the Middle Ages, education transformed as with the dominance of religion in Western Europe and India, along with attention on scientific research in Rome.

Concept of education in Ancient and Middle Age include close connect between teacher and students, absence of standardized curriculum, taking religious leaders as teachers and limited scale of education

In Education 2.0, with the overture of printing presses and establishment of universities, teaching process evolved and there developed a notion in higher education (HE) emphasising both academics and research developed. Universities such as Yale, Harvard, Columbia University and Princeton University were established in US during this duration. Various new age scholars developed practical learning for preparing students in managing their affairs (social, economic, and political)efficiently rather than just emphasizing on religious dimensions. With the introduction of the printing press, knowledge dissemination was no longer dependent on just one person and was possible to be delivered to the masses through printed books. The evolution of educational institutes being centers of discussion and incorporation of science and experimentation further helped with social, philosophical and scientific innovations. Major traits were: Education to the masses, the concept of one-to-many came into existence, Introduction of physical books as a mode for disseminating knowledge, The "process" of education delivery evolved overtime — to impart teaching to masses around a university system with fixed structures — and also introduced in a culture of research.

In the present millennium, technology has touched almost every aspect of life, and **Education 3.0** was no different exception. Technology provided a platform that has greatly stretched access to education and changed the ways of learning. The transition from Education 2.0 to 3.0 that took place as a result of movement from Industry 2.0 (1870) to Industry 3.0(1969),it took around a couple of decades and the period saw a significant increase in enrolments because of increased accessibility of higher education (Sharma,2019). The traditional set up of a lecture hall has been transformed by integration of updated tools and technologies in teaching helping students to learn virtually and deliver desired information to them effectively and properly. In Education 3.0, there has been a huge increase in global demand for education, the role of an educator has altered from that of an instructor to a facilitator, and technology has become ubiquitous for content delivery in various online and distance learning programs. Major traits are: Technology driving the use of interactive boards, thus replacing chalkboards and white boards, Increase in use of personal devices in colleges, better administrative structures through LMS (Learning Management System), improved learning through better collaborations, transition toward platform-enabled learning drove exponential growth in the education technology (edtech) market, but the core learning methods have remained untouched.

While education delivery evolved over the ages — through Education 1.0 to Education 3.0 — the main process of teaching has remained almost same. A teacher-instructed classroom has always been the mode through which knowledge is disseminated. Content is prepared in a fixed curriculum structure, delivered at one point of time to the learner cohort and standardized in terms of the content and its delivery. The table mentioned below talks about this transition in the basic structure from Education 1.0 to Education 3.0.

Table 1. Characteristics of Education 1.0- Education 3.0

	Faculty	Curriculum and pedagogy	Research	Partnerships	Infrastructure	Funding	Governance/ Leadership
Education 1.0	Prests and religious figures. No qualification requirements	Unstructured and undocumented. Person to person	Limited to debate on religion and social aspects	Limited to the co religionists and segregated by kingdom boundaries	Bordering to religious areas, in gurukul, church or mosque with strong connects with the society	Supported by religious donations and support from monarchies	Social monitoring through the court of the kings. Informal hierarchy among faculty on the basis on religious seniority
Education 2.0	Full time career teachers. Rigid educational qualification requirements	Structured and rigid in class teaching. One to many mass teaching systems existed with a fixed curriculum	Strong research systems in scientific and social sciences	Limited to the country or region	Evolution of university campus- large physical spaces with lecture halls, residential and recreational areas	Evolution of fee based funding and government support for public institutions	Advent of country level regulators. Defining the institute governance systems and rigid ladder
Education 3.0	Full time career teachers. Rigid educational qualification requirements	Rigid curriculum but some flexibility through online modes of learning	Transition toward collaborative research using technology	Growth in partnerships due to enhancements in telecommunications	Some investments in technology, infrastructure in addition to the physical based infrastructure	Funding pattern is fee based	Move towards accreditation in addition to firm regulations

Source: Author's compilation

The pace at which evolution today is taking place can be now measured in years and not centuries. Today, we are again in a transition phase where learner will be at the center of the future ecosystem in Education 4.0. Education 4.0 empowers learners in structuring their learning ways. It is characterized by personalization of learning experience, where the learner has complete freedom to paint his own canvas, to be the architect of his or her own future and has the unrestricted notion for aspiring, approaching and achieving personal goals by choice.

Introducing Education 4.0

Higher Education has been evolving constantly as a response of internal and external forces. Evolution today is taking place at a speed where changes are measured in years and not in centuries. Privilege to few is now an open accessible platform for all. In Education 4.0, learning gets connected to the learner, focused on the learner, illustrated by learner and led by the learner. It is the learner who is in the epicenter of responsibility for defining various dimension of his education path. Education 4.0

is personalization of the learning process, where learner has complete flexibility to devise their own learning path and has complete freedom to aspire for, approach and achieve personal goals by choice. The aim of Education 4.0 is around "experiential learning" by individual – the instructional theory and foundations are delivered across technology-enabled platforms – and a composite integration with the Industry and society provide a complete platform for learning from the peers, social interactions and real-world issues.

Key Stakeholders

Learner: Needs greater flexibility and freedom and look out for alternatives that are affordable and can be customized as per their individual aspirations and requirements.

University: which is the prime education provider at the forefront of knowledge creation and dissemination with a sustainable business model

Industry: They are on hunt for for industry-ready personal who possess problem-solving skills, creativity and analytical thinking capabilities; also view the Higher Education ecosystem for collaborative research opportunities and solution development

Society: Expects the ecosystem in creating individuals with better emotional quotient (EQ) and who are empathetic and work toward solving challenges of the community together.

University in the Era of Education 4.0

This movement from one platform to the other has been uneven and how easily and timely universities can adjust to this transformation and continue to evolve will only decide what lies in store for them. Consequently, in this changing paradigm, it is important for universities to focus on enriching student experience and aligning their individual needs across the student life cycle.

Technological advancement has enclosed the student and access and affordability of the content have never been more crucial. The student-centric shift has challenged the present models of enrolment, teaching and learning processes, assessment and credential systems and also the image of the university being the main knowledge provider. At this juncture, universities have critical choices to think about to decide: embrace new opportunities and succeed or make the wrong choice and perish. After all, making the wrong choice is not an option at all. The following section explores how the current university model might need to evolve in order to keep pace with the changing paradigm and advent of Education 4.0 in the near future.

Inimitable Student Experience

Student experience refers to their overall experience of university life and specially focuses on meeting individual expectations right across the student life cycle. The larger and more diverse student population in the present time has a wide range of expectations, which largely comes under the ambit of the university.

Student experience is a function of not only teaching and learning but also other aspects that creates remarkable impact on core teaching and learning that should be taking place in the university. As universities are not the only knowledge providers, they will need to invest in providing a different experience and complete flexibility at every stage to appeal the prospective students.

Flexible Program Structures

The present educational ecosystem is involving a concentrated learning model with focus on fixed duration for the courses. However, with technological advancements there are chances of providing increased flexibility across the learner's life cycle through blended learning as well.

Programs should focus on enrolling learners for a lifetime with an in built flexibility to come back to attend more courses over duration of, say, 10 or 20 years as per their own convenience, making it self paced. In essence, courses should be designed in such a way that universities get students enrolled perpetually.

Peer Reviewed Learning Platforms

Peer-to-peer learning improves the learning experience of students by helping them gain insights from the experiences of others. Direct and continuous interaction with peers promotes active learning and students are more comfortable in opening up and interacting with their peers. Universities should be in a position to make imaginative use of this omnipresent knowledge among peers so as to enrich the learning and also reduce the cost of content and knowledge creation.

Lifelong Learning

The learner presently has lifelong learning requirements, which can only be met by having various entry and exit points throughout the working life of the learner. The university system will have to evolve to cater to these changing needs and allow the student in coming back to the education ecosystem to re skill and up skill themselves throughout their lives. Therefore, admission/enrollment should be for a lifetime and not just for just a fixed time duration.

Blended Learning

Blended learning has resulted from the increasing availability of eLearning and the continuing importance of in person interaction throughout the learning process of student. It offers flexibility, reduce down the cost of delivery and at the same time allows universities in engaging with a wider audience spread across multiple space and time. What is required on the part of Universities is to develop programs that is blended learning mode in a differentiated online and offline ratios in catering to different categories of students

Role of Disruptive Technologies

Disruptive technologies are those that disrupt the set established practices, often starting with small number of users and eventually growing over time to the extent that they displace a previously dominant, incumbent technology. Christensen and Raynor (2003) subsequently changed the term "disruptive technology" to "disruptive innovation", with the justification that disruption is not an intrinsic feature of the technology, but, instead, emerges through practice. 'Even when computers were introduced in the classroom, they were used in enhancing the existing instructional approaches, rather than to supplement them. Lectures, for example, were amplified with computer graphics, but the lecture itself existed in its fundamental form. While Christensen predicted in 2008's Disrupting Class great disruptions in the segment of online learning, the reality so far is that greater adoption of online learning has continued as expected but not very disruptive: price points for education continue to rise ahead of inflation and while online education continues to grow it is largely seen as reflecting traditional models rather than disruption.

What elements of usage can disrupt traditional practices? Faculty lectures, for example, whether podcasts or streaming video, are still single-way, passive instructional models. Cleborne Maddux and D. Lamont Johnson (2005) call these Type I uses of technology, which automates or replicates an existing practice. Type II uses technology allowing students and teachers to do things that was not possible before. Their approach provides another method in conceiving disruption: one technology maintains existing relationships among faculty and students and content, while another changes these relationships in fundamental ways.

Terry Anderson (2004) pointed towards the importance of placing the student at the center of the learning experience. That means greater emphasis is on student-generated content, students' use of collaboration and sharing tools like Web 2.0 applications, and modular tutoring.

In light of digital revolution, disruption causes a change that may seem particularly unwelcome to those forced to uproot their traditional ways of doing things. But it doesn't emerge from nowhere. Disruption is driven by convergence of forces: from the capabilities of new technologies, to the changing demands of customers, or rapidly evolving practices of competitors. When it comes to students, there are some significant innovations disrupting the way their higher education experience is being delivered as discussed below:

Mobile Learning: The epoch of mobile learning as encouraged by the devices like Smartphone and tablet is about a decade old now, where students and teachers are dependent on their mobile devices for learning experience. As mobile devices become more effective and affordable, and as ownership reaches ubiquity in different countries, the options for engaging learning experiences are becoming limitless and boundless. The augmented usage of augmented reality (AR), virtual reality (VR), and mixed reality (MR) has enabled the entire process of mobile learning to be more active and collaborative. Mobile learning has evolved from an option of supplementing course content with stand-alone applications of occupying a strategic consideration for access to the course and delivery. The flexibility, convenience, and sometimes the requirement of using a mobile device in accessing learning content have become drivers in higher education. As per 2018 study in the United States, 79% of students access online courses using a mobile device, and the most popular feature is accessing course readings. This is further supported by increasing and improving mobile-friendliness of learning management systems (LMS) apps and Moodle.

The following links provide examples of mobile learning in use that have direct implications for higher education.

The GLOBE Zika Education and Project Prevention

Global Learning and Observation for benefiting the Environment (GLOBE) is an inventiveness for Zika-affected countries through crowd sourcing data on mosquitoes in a global mapping project

Gamified Learning Using Kahoot

This University of Memphis project uses an interactive gaming tool accessible from mobile devices to provide instant feedback and class data for keeping students motivated

CloudClassRoom

National Taiwan Normal University developed the CloudClassRoom (CCR) mobile platform for transforming smartphone devices to a powerful interactive tools for classroom learning. CCR enables students in responding to instructors' prompts, and answers are automatically consolidated and analyzed, providing the teacher with a rough image of student learning progress in time.

Analytics Technologies

Analytics technologies are primary element for student success initiatives through institutions and a motivating force behind the collaborative, targeted strategic planning and improved decision-making for higher education leaders. Analytics capabilities that comprises of dynamic, connected, predictive, and personalized systems and data. Whether data are primarily used for business gain or for advancing global human thriving, the increase of data-driven human society has brought with it enhanced interest and investment in data- and analytics-based competencies, as well as in technologies and systems for helping facilitate and improve our complex practices of collecting, analyzing, and interpreting data. Institutions of higher education are also affected from the data-analysis interests and investments. At the base of institutional data are students with varieties of needs that differs for each along the path toward certificate or degree completion.

The following links provide examples of analytics technologies in use that have direct implications for higher education.

Crowdsourced Adaptive Platform for Recommendation of Learning Activities

University of Queensland's Student Strategy focuses on the development and dissemination of a crowdsourced adaptive platform called RiPPLE that recommends personalized learning resources for students.

Jefferson Competency Assessment Tool

The Jefferson Competency Assessment Tool (JeffCAT) is a dashboard product developed in collaboration with industry for monitoring student performance, and for providing a holistic view of performance to students, faculty, and administration.

Student Relationship Engagement System

The University of Sydney's Student Relationship Engagement System (SRES) is a complete platform that gives instructors complete control of the data life cycle from a single web application, from capturing the right data to curating relevant sources, then analyzing and acting on the data.

Mixed Reality

At the intersection of the online and offline worlds is an emerging and dynamic environment like mixed reality (MR), where digital and physical objects coexist together. This hybrid space is integrating digital technologies into the physical world thus creating virtual simulations of physical spaces, blurring the difference between worlds. Virtual reality puts the user in a simulation, for example the experience of flying or being on Mars. Augmented reality layers information over physical spaces and objects, such as labels and other supplementary data over museum displays. Mixed reality (MR) is an umbrella term for a variety of technologies.

MR technologies are well suited for experiential education. Through simulations and 360° video, VR can enable users to visit places they might otherwise not be able to access, like art museums, archaeology sites, a refugee camp, or Mount Everest, as well as places that are entirely inaccessible. By dramatically expanding the variety of tasks and activities with which a learner can gain experience, MR technology enables experiential learning where it may not have previously been possible. Reflection and self-assessment are also critical aspects of experiential learning but are not necessarily enabled by MR technology.

The following links provide examples of mixed reality in use that have direct implications for higher education.

*Virtual Immersive Teaching and Learning (VITaL):*The Virtual Immersive Teaching and Learning (VITaL) initiative at San Diego State University provides a variety of virtual reality, augmented reality, and mixed reality immersive tools to be used across the pedagogical spectrum.

Parsons Fashion Study Collection in Virtual Reality: The XReality Center at The New School and the School of Fashion at Parsons School of Design partnered for creating an immersive learning experience.

Virtual Field Trip to Iceland: It is a scientific collaboration between New Zealand and Iceland, for providing University of Canterbury students connections through geological landscape, hazard management, and geothermal power.

Artificial Intelligence

Artificial intelligence (AI) involves computer systems for achieving tasks and activities that have mostly historically relied on human cognition. Advances in computer science are creation way for development of intelligent machines that facilitate approximate human reasoning more than ever before. Using big data, AI applies foundations of algorithmic machine learning for predicting issues that allow for task completion like human beings and decision-making. From the excitement of over self-driving cars to raising concerns about their safety and having discussions about the social justice aspects AI can bring and the challenges it provides, 2018 was a big news year, and 2019 is no different.

As per a 2017 report from the MIT Sloan Management Review found that 85% of industry leaders think AI will prvide their industries a competitive advantage, but approximately only about 20% have done anything to prepare for this eventuality. While skepticism remains regarding to AI's application in educational contexts, and like fears abound that human instructors will be replaced with artificial intelligence apps or bots, these stories paint a picture of the need for students to have more and better opportunities to work with AI and gain experience in its use.

What remains a constant concern for everyone in the field of education "how to increase student engagement in learning?" Engagement is not something which is new but a high-visibility conundrum. The *Chronicle of Higher Education* recently profiled Georgia State University's use of the AI tool AdmitHub as a successful option of connecting with prospective and incoming students, addressing issues about enrollment, financial aid, and many more. Engagement is also basic for student success and support initiatives.

The following links provide examples of artificial intelligence in use that have direct implications for higher education.

Student Data Science & Machine Learning Platform: UCSD IT Services built a data science/machine learning cluster for undergraduate and graduate students using low-cost GPUs, allowing students unparalleled access to extremely high-speed computation.

*IU Boost:*IU Boost is a machine learning–driven model and a smartphone app whose primary function is to deliver a simple nudge: a push notification when a student hasn't submitted an assignment that has an approaching deadline.

*Edulai:*It has been designed for university students and teachers for monitoring and measuring the development of skills including critical thinking, effective communication skills, collaboration, leadership, problem resolution, and inter culturalism

Blockchain: This technology works as as a decentralized digital ledger and is currently used primarily for supporting the cryptocurrencies. The technology involves usage of a distributed data structure where the records in ledger are replicated in various locations. Blockchain removes the role of a central authority over the ledger, creating a secure model whose integrity is mainly built on trust of all participants. Meanwhile, colleges and universities are finding out options in which the technology could be used for areas like transcripts, smart contracts, and identity management. Advocates argue that blockchain has the potential of fundamentally transforming a wide range of industries that depend upon on intermediaries—like banks enabling a broad ecosystem solution instead, one that features decentralized verification and storage. In higher education, the legacy of blockchain might be what the technology inspired rather than the broad adoption of blockchain technology itself.

Most of the current thinking about blockchain in higher education would be issues of transcripts and records of achievement. Blockchain could extend that model thus creating a permanent, detailed record of formal and informal learning allowing individual users in controlling what is included in their learning record and by whom information can be accessed. A blockchain-based transcript could include information about courses and degrees, certifications, badges and other required microcredentials, co-curricular activities, internships and employment and other important credentials. This will be of great help as Such record could easily follow students from one institution to another, serving as verifiable evidence of learning and enabling simpler transfer of credits across different institutions.

As education increasingly becomes a lifelong activity, that involves not only formal academic settings but workplace training, courses from professional associations, workshops, online learning and numerous other formal and informal models, blockchain could be of great help that could provide means for individual students in maintaining an accurate and perfect record of their knowledge and skills.

Below mentioned are some of the examples of blockchain in use that have direct implications for higher education.

*FlexchainEdu:*FlexchainEdu uses a blockchain-based system that has the capability of transforming the way higher education organizes, stores, and validates student data, as well as provide credentials that are student-owned and universally respected by an evolving employment marketplace.

Woolf: Building a Borderless University: Woolf is a two-sided marketplace—a regulated network for accredited teaching between students and teachers. It will allow students anywhere in the world to study with academics anywhere in the world for accredited degrees irrespective of their geographical locations.

EdRec: Next Gen by Design: This is a collaboration between different bodies including BrightHive, Concentric Sky, and DXtera Institute. The Annex document outlines their winning proposal for a student-centered future powered by sovereign records that will open a combination of microcredentials, competency frameworks, and learning pathways to propel students towards their desired careers.

Virtual Assistants

In the 1987 Knowledge Navigator and 1988 Future Shock videos, Apple envisioned a future where users of different ages and abilities can naturally interface with a device screen by speaking commands, asking questions or using gestures for learning, working, and remain connected to others in the virtual environment. AI-augmented machine learning has spectacularly increased the accuracy of both automatic speech recognition (ASR) and related language processing and the underpinnings of virtual assistants like Siri, Alexa, Bixby, or Google Assistant. Virtual assistants are commonly available on most smartphones, tablets, and computers, and a complete new range of independent passive listening smart speakers like the Amazon Alexa and Google Assistant speakers have rapidly become popular amongst home affordances.

Chatbots that provide students with 24-hour support like the AgentBot developed for Siglo 21 University in Argentina were adapted from a customer service solution for providing academic student support. Amazon Echo Dots are being piloted at several US universities to provide students with information ranging from academic advisory services to help with financial aid.

The below mentioned links provide examples of virtual assistants in use that have direct implications for higher education.

Alexa@SLU: It was basically developed for Saint Louis University EchoDot pilot delivers answers to over 130 campus-specific questions and aims at getting students answers to common querries enabling them to focus on their time on deeper engagement with their studies.

Voice-Activated Apps for University of Colorado Denver and Anschutz: VoxScholar apps foster academic success by focusing on academic performance or evidence-based teaching advice. VoxScholar apps are available for students and faculty at the University of Colorado Denver and the Anschutz Medical Campus. Both can get just-in-time tips for study skills, faculty development, and a custom lab tutor through Google Assistant. The apps can respond intelligently for coach learners and faculty in meeting their learning goals.

*LibChat @ VicUni:*Victoria University Library introduced a live chat service (LibChat) for providing an alternative information service in an online world. The library chat service helps students for developing the skills and capabilities which required in succeeding in blended learning environments and provides staff with strong digital information skills, analytical proficiency, and computer literacy.

Making Higher Educational Institutions Ecosystems Future Ready

Indian and Global Universities need to recalibrate their strategies for Higher Education to remain germane. The pillars of HE foundation are Faculty, Curriculum and Pedagogy, Research, Partnership and Infrastructure.(Meiers. & Marion 2017)

For curriculum and Pedagogy, it is recommended

- to design curriculum which is in sync with real world, learning methods delivered as student experience and in class learning while the conceptual program delivery is through blended education.

- Develop flexible learning programs with various entry and exit points for better movement.
- Invest in technology-driven flexible curriculum feedback and redesigning the model for real time learning validation and course correction apposite to individual learner
- Recognize out-of-class learning done through options like online certifications, work experience and experiential learning at entry points.
- Integrating life skills into the curriculum by proper integration of real world stakeholders like industry, society and entrepreneur networks.

For Research, following suggestions are made:

- Develop collaborative models involving experts of different platforms from academia and industry for research and innovation.
- Develop multi-disciplinary and applied research capabilities through adjunct and industry exposure .
- Promoting universities as local community-focused centers of research with in built linkages with local industry and society in the region
- Offer in-site joint research opportunity for small and medium enterprises with limited research infrastructure

For Faculty, it is required that:

- Invest more and with a focused in faculty training that is towards developing facilitator mindset and pedagogy
- Develop and implement continuous professional development (CPD) programs for supporting the development of digital literacy skills among academicians and staff
- Create a group of champion academicians from different department who are well versed with technology and leading the way in the development of digital skills or new innovative teaching techniques utilizing technology
- Train faculty for adopting technology as a source of teaching design and delivery, including refresher training in trends like flip classroom, synchronous video lecture, chat rooms, LMS learning etc.
- Develop learning analytics solutions and facilitate faculty for using them for curriculum development and updating

Partnerships or collaborations are required on the following grounds:

- Partner with industry and local society across all aspects of the education value chain for curriculum development, faculty, infrastructure, research, study experience and placements
- Develop curriculum, teaching, MOOC and faculty partnerships with global universities to develop offerings for liberal curriculum programs and promoting digital learning.
- Invest in professional development platforms that encourages and promotes partnerships with individuals and alumni who could act as mentors and facilitators for industry-academia linkages

For improving infrastructure, it is suggested to:

- Prepare a strategy where technology drives not just the student lifecycle but also the complete functioning of the university
- Develop off campus learning centers for providing global exposure to learners and partnership development for academic enrichment by various MOUs.
- Invest in a modern, high-performance network, including campus backbone, improved wireless connectivity and a managed network service for departments and colleges or in other words making technology that is glitch free.
- Make information and systems as open and accessible in a way that makes it possible for the data can be consumed in innovative ways

In case of Governance and Leadership, it is suggested to:

- Work with regulating bodies for creating policy interventions involving flexible programs, online through blended programs etc.
- Build social media leaders in every department of university for establishing an interwoven communication network in influencing conversations, expand their social power and build trust.
- Develop a digital media strategy for attracting different stakeholders throughout their lifecycles and for promoting the university leadership

For *revision of funding pattern,* it is required to:

- Develop a technology driven university strategy by building low cost models of outreach, delivery, and acquisition of student, industry engagement and alumni connect

- Create proper models for delivery by monetizing innovative technology assets
- Explore usage of freemium domains for knowledge assets and programs of the university
- Look for research-based funding from funding bodies like local society and industry for developing solutions that solve local issues and challenges

Within scientific and technical education, we will need to educate and reeducate students in developing and shaping the use of today's most rapidly emerging technologies. One innovative initiative exploring new sequencing of higher education is the Stanford2025 project, which envisions several mechanisms whereby students can extend their education over longer timeframes (Penprase 2018). One model is the "open loop university" where students can experience six years of higher education over their entire adult careers allowing them in blending their learning with life experience and provide value to the campus by returning as expert practitioners over several intervals—enabling students to refresh their skills while interacting with the campus community. Another model known as the axis flip prioritizes skill development and competency training over content and disciplinary topics, requiring new methods of assessment and a degree known as a skill-print that students would constantly renew and extend through their careers.

CONCLUSION

The first three industrial revolutions provided proofs for the profound shifts in society, the economy and education which resulted in a proliferation of curricular innovation and establishment of new educational institutions. As in the previous three industrial revolutions, the most profound effects of the 4IR on the society will not be realized for many decades. Unlike previous industrial revolutions, however, the 4IR features the effect of several compounding exponential technologies which all share the capacity for rapid increment in scale and reduction of cost. This rapid advances in technologies demanding a more proactive response from the educational sector than the more gradual societal evolution and subsequent response from educational institutions in earlier industrial revolutions.

The impacts of the emerging 4IR technology in economic and environmental terms alone will require a drastic rethinking of the curriculum within higher education for enabling students to comprehend the individual technologies in detail as well as to thoughtfully analyze and predict the evolution of networked systems of technology, the environment and sociopolitical systems.

The 4IR STEM curriculum will need to focus on emerging technologies—robotics, AI, IoT, nanomaterials, genomics and biotech—for providing a workforce not only capable of developing new applications and products, but also capable of interpreting the effects of these technologies on society and using their training to provide sustainable and ethical uses of science and technology. More than any particular content area, curriculum needs to help students in developing the capacity for ethical reasoning, for awareness of societal and human impacts and to be able to comprehend the impacts of 4IR technologies on people, so they are trained to not only increase our material prosperity but also to improve our social and cultural fabric. While earlier industrial revolutions have prioritized some of the raw materials needed to fuel their factories or cities—placing a premium on capital based in physical resources such as land, water power, coal, oil and wood—the 4IR will place a premium on intellectual capital and in capacity for collective thought. Students who are able to learn in residential environments with diverse colleagues and develop solutions together in teams will be well trained for the types of tasks that will be asked of them in the 4IR. Our colleges and universities owe it to these students and our future for developing more interactive forms of pedagogy at all levels and for embracing a curriculum that lays emphasis from multiple disciplinary and cultural perspectives over static swathes of disciplinary "content."

REFERENCES

Anderson, T. (2008). *Disruptive, Online Education to Go Main Stream*. Virtual Canuck blog entry.

Anderson, T., & Wark, N. (2004). Why Do Teachers Get to Learn the Most?: A Case Study of a Course Based on Student Creation of Learning Objects. *E-Journal of Instructional Science and Technology*.

Christensen, C. M., & Raynor, M. E. (2003). *The Innovator's Solution: Creating and Sustaining Successful Growth*. Harvard University Press.

EDUCAUSE. (2019). *Horizon Report Preview*. Retrieved from https://er.educause.edu/articles/2010/3/the-role-of-disruptive-technology-in-the-future-of-higher-education

Maddux, C. D., & Lamont Johnson, D. (2005). Type II Applications of Technology in Education. *Computers in the Schools*, 22(1 & 2), 1–5. doi:10.1300/J025v22n01_01

Meiers, M. (2017). *Teacher Professional Learning, Teaching Practice and Student Learning Outcomes: Important Issues*. . doi:10.1007/1-4020-4773-8_27

MIT Sloan Management Review. (n.d.). Retrieved from https://sloanreview.mit.edu/projects/reshaping-business-with-artificial-intelligence/

Penprase, B. E. (2018). The Fourth Industrial Revolution and Higher Education. In N. Gleason (Ed.), *Higher Education in the Era of the Fourth Industrial Revolution.* doi:10.1007/978-981-13-0194-0_9

Sharma, P. (2019). Digital Revolution of Education 4.0. *International Journal of Engineering and Advanced Technology*, 9(2).

Stanford 2025. (n.d.). *Learning and Living at Stanford – An Exploration of Undergraduate Experiences in the Future.* http://www.stanford2025.com/

The Chronicle of Higher Education (n.d.). Retrieved from https://www.chronicle.com/article/How-AI-Is-Infiltrating-Every/243022'

ADDITIONAL READING

Aziz Hussin, A. (2018). Education 4.0 Made Simple: Ideas For Teaching. *International Journal of Education and Literacy Studies.*, 6(3), 92. doi:10.7575/aiac.ijels.v.6n.3p.92

Diwan, P. (2017). Is Education 4.0 an imperative for success of 4th Industrial Revolution? Accessed from https://medium.com/@pdiwan/is-education-4-0-an-imperative-for-success-of-4th-industrial-revolution-50c31451e8a4

Flavin, M. (2017), *Disruptive Technology Enhanced Learning,* Palgrave Macmillan, London. https://www.businesswire.com/news/home/20170515006621/en/VR-Education-Market---Trends-Forecasts-Technavio

Haseeb, M., Hussain, H. I., Ślusarczyk, B., & Jermsittiparsert, K. (2019). Industry 4.0: A solution with regards to technology challenges of sustainable business performance. *Social Sciences*, 8(5), 154. doi:10.3390ocsci8050154

Puncreobutr, V. (2016). Education 4.0: New Challenge of Learning., *St. Theresa. Journal of the Humanities and Social Sciences*, 2, 92–97.

KEY TERMS AND DEFINITIONS

Analytics Technologies: Technology for discovery, interpretation, and communication of identifiable or sensible patterns in data.

Artificial Intelligence: Intelligence demonstrated by machines through simulating the ability to think like humans and mimic their actions of reasoning, logic through past experience in a controlled manner, also known as machine intelligence.

Block Chain: Digital pieces of information stored in a public database, also referred to as distributed ledger technology.

Disruptive Technologies: Any improved version of the existing technology or a completely new technology that disrupts the already established one.

Education 1.0: Education frame where students were consumers of information and assessment was typically exam based.

Education 2.0: Transition frame where education focused on teaching and research.

Education 3.0: An approach towards education that integrates technology with learning for creating a virtual learning environment.

Education 4.0: A school of thought with focus on imparting skills to make students industry ready.

Mixed Reality: A platform which merges real and virtual world thus creating a learning platform that involves amalgamation of physical and digital objects.

Mobile Learning: A flexible approach of learning where students can access learning material through mobile devices

Virtual Assistants: An independent service provider rendering services to clients from remote locations.

Chapter 8
Industry 4.0:
A Practical Approach

Sandeep Mathur
Amity Insitute of Information Technology, Amity University, Noida, India

Samaira Mendiratta
iD https://orcid.org/0000-0001-5810-4230
Amity Insitute of Information Technology, Amity University, Noida, India

ABSTRACT

Industry 4.0 is a key activity as of late presented by the German government. The objective of the activity is a change of mechanical fabricating through digitization and misuse of possibilities of new advancements. An Industry 4.0 generation framework is in this way adaptable and empowers individualized and modified items. The point of this chapter is to introduce and encourage a comprehension of Industry 4.0 ideas, its drivers, empowering influences, objectives, impediments. Building squares are depicted and a keen industrial facility idea is displayed. An architecture model and job of institutionalization in the future execution of Industry 4.0 idea are addressed. Also, sure contextual investigations of organizations, for example, Bosche and Siemens case studies, have been mentioned. These case studies emphasize on practical implementation of Industry 4.0 and future challenges to deal with successful adoption of Industry 4.0. The current status of Industry 4.0 availability in the German organizations is introduced and remarked.

DOI: 10.4018/978-1-7998-4882-0.ch008

INTRODUCTION

Industry 4.0 insinuates another phase in the Industrial Revolution that spotlights energetically on interconnectivity, robotization, AI (Artificial Intelligence), and consistent data. Industry 4.0, moreover suggested as IoT (Industrial Internet of Things) with splendid electronic development, AI, and gigantic data to make a logically and widely inclusive better-related condition for associations that accentuate and accumulating on the board. While every association and affiliation working today is phenomenal, they all face a run of the test that is a necessity for connectedness and access to consistent bits of learning transversely over methodology, accessories, things, and people. Industry 4.0 is not just about placing assets into new advancements and instruments to improve creating viability. Rather it is connected to modifying how your entire business works and creates (Industry 4.0 and the Industrial Internet of Things, n.d.).

Figure 1. Glimpse of Industry 4.0 Applications (Industrial | Industry 4.0 | TI.com, 2020)

Evolution of Enterprise 1.0 To 4.0

Since the 1800s there are square measures for distinct industrial revolutions that this world either has skilled or continues to expertise these days. The main mechanical upheaval occurred between the late 1700s and mid-1800s. During this timeframe, fabricating advanced from concentrating on difficult work performed by individuals and helped by the workforce to a more streamlined type of work performed by individuals using water and steam-fuelled motors and different sorts of machine instruments. In the early bit of the twentieth century, the world entered a second current change with the introduction of steel and the use of intensity in assembling plants. This steel makes augmentation profitability and helped to make modern office equipment continuously adaptable. Beginning in the late 1950s, a third modern upheaval gradually started to develop, as makers started fusing electronics and in the long run PC innovation into their manufacturing plants. During this period, makers started encountering a move that put less accentuation on simple and mechanical innovation and more on computerized innovation and robotization programming. In the previous couple of decades, fourth modern unrest has risen, known as Industry 4.0. It partners physical substances with electronics and considers better-organized exertion and access across divisions, accessories, dealers, items, and people. Industry 4.0 takes the emphasis on cutting edge advancement from progressing a long time to an incomprehensible level with the help of interconnectivity through the IoT, access to persistent data, and the introduction of computerized physical structures. Industry 4.0 empowers business visionaries to even more probable control and see each piece of their action and empowers them to utilize minute data to help productivity, improve methods, and drive advancement. Figure 1 depicts the evolutionary growth of Industry 1.0 to 4.0.

(Zhou et al., 2015) While the principal reference to Industry 4.0 would not happen until 2011, the German Federal Ministry of Education and research started to investigate the different patterns that were occurring. They needed to distinguish things in abnormal state innovation that could improve the world and lift innovation. This would permit those who looking for future work in the modern part to have a disentangled work understanding while at the same time enabling us to accomplish more in a small amount of the time. By 2012, the Germans had amassed several studies and that they applied these statistics to preserve the primary advent regarding the matter. As a first-rate thing of this creation, they took the savvy manufacturing line setting and started to grandstand a portion of the capability. This enabled capability clients and industry specialists to increase a more profound comprehension of what all changed into potential. Presently machines should nearly assume and reply to authentic circumstances a good way to help viability and assist to make the enterprise more remarkable than every other time in current reminiscence. The German authorities changed with the effects and that they began to raise financing to the examination inside the expectations. It would propel their kingdom and help them to turn into a pacesetter all through the Industrial Revolution. When the examination was resolved and there was an understanding that the web was undeniably more dominant than initially accepted, the joining of data and the hand-off over the web encouraged impel the web of things, which was at that point increased noteworthy, unmistakable quality in different nations. Subsidizing was not at another high through Germany's assembling industry and the innovation of the procedure was hardening. It was right now that the Platform of Industry 4.0 was presented. Be that as it may, it was yet far from where we discover Industry 4.0 today. In 2014, organizations outside of Germany started to step in. There were more virtualization and contribution from neighbouring nations, so successful work arrangements could be made. Decentralization turned into a key part of the procedure and guaranteeing that advanced assembling would at last profit by the most newest preparing. This is where the web of things turned out to be flawlessly lined up with the modern upset and a sweet amicable association was framed. Further advancement happened as new things showed up gratitude to the innovative work that has occurred during the fourth modern upset. This incorporates propelled medicinal innovation, successful cost sparing mechanics for generation plants. This is an energizing time in our reality to be alive and witness the unfathomable changes that are occurring.

NEED FOR INDUSTRY 4.0

Facilitates Current Difficulties for Producers

According to the authors in (November 2016, n.d.) in a universe of increasing marketplace unpredictability, shorter object life cycles, better item multifaceted nature, and worldwide stockpile chains, businesses are looking to turn out to be increasingly adaptable and receptive to enterprise patterns. The Industry 4.0 imaginative and prescient offers proposals on how groups can facilitate those difficulties: The digitalization of the complete item lifecycle will permit corporations to utilize facts from the introduction, administration, and net-based total lifestyles a good way to spark off faster item improvements. Brilliant things will bring extra grounded incorporation of the very best floor and save ground and hence more knowledge and adaptableness to advent. With those improvements, companies can respond quickly to request changes and actualize new preparations less difficult or even re-plan advent loads faster.

Prompts an Advancement Economy

Advanced chains will not just improve productivity yet additionally accelerate developments as new plans of action can be executed a lot quicker. Here are two models of how Industry 4.0 accelerates developments:

a.   Makers can create new business by sharing hardware or selling limits and they do not require commercial centres.

b.   Because of sensors and availability, items will be enhanced by administrations, for example, prescient upkeep or even changed into administrations. A motor maker probably will not sell motors any longer later however give them as an administration to clients.

Puts the Client in the Point of Convergence Everything Considered

The present customers demand only made things and organizations ("Made-for-Me"). Adroit things matter and machines will have interaction creators to get down to component gauge one and produce revamp matters without greater value. Digitalization will incite an extra trustworthy brazenly assisting to initiate a snappier shape manner.

Places Individuals Into the Point of Convergence of Creation

As machines are becoming the possibility to be more and more notable, the work in progress traces might be advanced and acculturated. Fundamental guide responsibilities will disappear. Versatility will be a key accomplishment factor. Workers will be consigned where help is required. This will put higher demands similarly as supervising flightiness, basic reasoning, and self-affiliation, yet also grant the work capacity to end up being logically versatile. Fixed developments consistently will be enhanced by one of a kind and self-dealt with degree evaluation that thinks about agents' tendencies. This will improve the work of affection equality everything considered and license shorter response time to a changed solicitation condition.

Empowers Maintainable Success

The vintage models of industrialization run out: Economies and with-it social orders step by step understand the risks of globalization, paintings misfortunes, and asset deficiencies. Creating an advantage and acknowledging improvement want to be placed into an all the greater long-haul element of view, for example with the aid of coming across techniques to comply with boundaries on energy, property, condition, and social and financial results. Industry 4.0 can discover solutions for one's problems. In the event that it is smart and innovative, era can decrease power utilization, help companies to help their commercial enterprise with present and new plans of movement and make use of recent advances to create anywhere within the route of the arena (even at mind-boggling value regions) near the business enterprise sectors and on the affability of the worker's.

ARCHITECTURE OF INDUSTRY 4.0

Various mechanical and collecting attempts have started Industry 4.0 (I4.0) exercises to construct skill, improve operational execution, and additional pay from the pile of new automated things and organizations now available. These exercises have conveyed some accomplishments anyway the advancement to the Industry 4.0 vision of smart, deliberately related, and free age lines, plants, and supply-chains are still at the hidden stages. It is critical for these undertakings to keep progressing on their experience as it will be difficult to compensate for wasting time with the settled in automated delivering pioneers at later arranges. To enable development towards 4.0 they ought to manufacture essential endeavours application, data and figuring plans which can progress with the new vision of the electronic endeavor. Figure 2 represents the architecture of industry 4.0. A portion of the key components/activities for building up primary design.

Amassing Execution/Operations System

There is a view that the MES structures need monotonous utilization, their benefits are firm, hard to assess, and not required in the IoT world. MES systems or some flavor (in kind of IoT applications for express helpfulness) are required as a foundation for high operational execution, thing conspicuousness, consistent detectable quality into shop-floor assignments, and the contextualization of shop-floor data being assembled for assessment for further operational upgrades. The endeavours ought to pick an MES structure which is fit to their industry and collecting system type have been estimated, passes on the huge out of the box value with the fundamental course of action, extendable, can scale over the similar past with individual assembling plants and has a thing manual for reliably benefit by IoT progressions. The MES should be interfaced with ERP systems subject to the ISA-95 measures and with PLC/DCS distributed systems on shop-floor using OPC-Unified Architecture.

Thing Engineering and Innovation

Customers today foresee splendid related things, modified to their present needs at acceptable costs, which are in like manner fit for improving with their creating necessities. The standard PLM structures used by associations by and by a need to create as stages for thing progression. They need to consolidate additional capacities, for instance, model-based systems structuring and blend of model-based re-enactments with the certifiable IoT data from sent things/plant assets. This is required for structure mechanized twin capacity and better fuse with shop-floor and supply chains for getting things information over the propelled string. The gathering adventures need to pick or update their PLM/PDM (Product Lifecycle Management/ Product Data Management) structures as per these examples.

Data and Application Blend

A coarse-grained business blend layer can be completed which can serve as the prerequisites of any applications or organizations given by the aims. The applications should be employed to help Service Oriented Architecture based interfaces. Event-driven illuminating build using disperse/purchase in instruments should be realized for business procedure work forms. An authorized data model for normal business objects could be established on the industry express reference model. It should be used inside the endeavour and accessories/suppliers with the objective that data translation is constrained.

Circled Analytics and Decision

The creation system for most of the collecting ventures will have chronicled databases and data conveyance places for assessment of shop-floor and Enterprise IT data. This developed assessment establishment should then be gotten together with new data sources (for instance - IoT, electronic interpersonal interaction, atmosphere) using data lakes on Cloud system for gigantic data assessment and AI, to achieve adventure wide procedure overhauls. This will be despite the persistent watching and control required at plant contraptions/gear (Edge) and at PLC/SCADA systems which can moreover fill in as IoT Gateways for sending shop-floor data to Cloud-based colossal data examination establishments. The bits of learning from assessment structure for endorsed strategy changes would then have the option to be continued back using the method work process/API frameworks for achieving the perfect outcomes.

CHARACTERISTICS OF INDUSTRY 4.0

Vertical Networking

Progressed to-physical methodology engage makers to rapidly respond to various changes that come as an outcome of moving solicitations, stock levels or astounding equipment issues. Sharp mechanical offices are incredibly related substances, with

Figure 2. Architecture of Industry 4.0 (Zezulka et al., 2016)

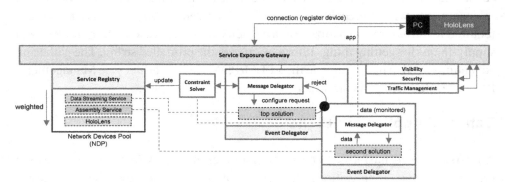

different structures having the alternative to speak with one another and adjust their presentation.

Level Joining Through Another Period Of Overall Worth Chain Frameworks

The physical-electronic physical (PDP) circles engage a progressively raised measure of straightforwardness. Associations can discover and respond to issues snappier. Such affiliation wide frameworks can record information from all the undertakings including intralogistics and warehousing to prototyping and creation, to elevating and arrangements to downstream benefits. Each piece of every method is logged and can be reviewed and separated at whatever point.

Through-Planning Over The Entire Worth Chain

All the things improvement and amassing activities are consolidated and encouraged with the thing life cycles. New agreeable energies ascend between thing progression and age structures.

Accelerating Through Exponential Headways

(Gilchrist, 2016) suggested the guideline reason for Industry 4.0 is to make an unyieldingly self-administering and particularly educated condition. It relies upon developments, for instance, AI, significant learning, moved mechanical self-rule and present-day IoT to further animate adequacy.

CHALLENGES OF MANUFACTURING IN INDUSTRY 4.0 ADOPTION

Driving affiliation with progression is outrageous. By and by, 6 out of 10 makers surrender that the execution limits are strong to such a degree, that they made sense of how to achieve simply compelled headway with their industry 4.0 exercises during the earlier years. Among the top referred to be challenging are:

- Nonappearance of united activity that makes cross-unit coordination inconvenient inside the association.
- Data ownership concerns when picking outcast vendors for encouraging and operationalizing association data.
- Nonattendance of valor to dispatch the extraordinary digitalization plan.
- Nonappearance of in-house capacity to support the headway and course of action of Industry 4.0 exercises.
- Issues with planning data from various sources to engage early on accessibility.
- Nonattendance of finding out about progressions, traders, and IT re-appropriating associates that could help execute the middle movement

While there is no "one-fits-everything" approach to manage reviving an Industry 4.0 program, there are a couple of things every association can do to decrease determination impediments. The underlying advance is to doubtlessly evaluate the ROI (Return on Investment) assorted propelled courses of action must make for the business (Mohamed, 2018).

BENEFITS

The upsides of Industry 4.0 consolidate improved effectiveness and capability, better versatility and expertise, and extended profitability. Industry 4.0 improves the customer experience. With Industry 4.0, the ROI openings are basic because of the favourable circumstances the advances offer. This consolidates progressions that improve automation, machine-to-machine correspondence, manufacturing oversite, and essential administration (Benefits of Industry 4.0 - SL Controls, 2018).

Improved Productivity

In fundamental terms, Industry 4.0 developments engage you to achieve more with less. In a way of speaking, you may convey more and speedier whilst dispersing your blessings more value-efficiently and capably. Your age lines will furthermore enjoy much less near domestic time due to progressed gadget checking and automated/ semi-motorized important initiative. Believe it or now not, general OEE (Overall Equipment Effectiveness) will enhance as your office moves towards transforming into an Industry 4.0 Smart Factory.

Efficiency Improved

Various domain names of your age line will turn out to be a continuously powerful result of Industry 4.0-associated developments. A little bit of those efficiencies is referenced above sections and much less time in addition to the ability to make more elements and cause them to faster. Various examples of improved capability be a part of quicker bunch changeovers, modified music and pursue strategies, and automated itemizing. NPIs (New Product Introductions) moreover become regularly successful as cooperates essential authority and this is only a hint of something large.

Extended Knowledge Sharing and Collaborative Working

Ordinary accumulating flora paintings in storage facilities. Offices are storage facilities as are individual machines inner a workplace. This consequences in inappropriate collaboration or information sharing. Industry four.0 tendencies license your age traces, business methods, and places of work to bestow paying little regard to zone, time region, degree, or some other element. This engages, as an example, statistics found out via a sensor on a machine in one plant to be spread for the duration of your affiliation. Best of all, it is feasible to do this consequently, as an example machine-to-machine and shape to-machine, without a human mediation. Figuratively speak me, facts from one sensor can in a moment make a development over numerous creation strains determined anyplace on the earth.

Versatility and Agility

The advantages of Industry 4.0 also join redesigned versatility and ability. For example, it is miles more trustworthy to scale age up or down in a Smart Factory. It is likewise greater straightforward to familiarize new matters with the age line in addition as making open entryways for unplanned accumulating runs, excessive-blend amassing, and this is best the begin.

Makes Compliance Easier

Consenting to rules in organizations like pharmaceutical and helpful contraption amassing should not be a manual system. Or maybe, Industry 4.0 advances make it viable to modernize consistence including track and pursue, high-quality appraisals, serialization, data logging, and anything is viable from that point.

Better Customer Experience

Industry 4.0 similarly acquaints probabilities with improve the employer you offer to clients and redecorate the patron revel in. For example, with modernized song and pursue limits, you can fast clear up problems. Moreover, you will have less issues with issue availability, aspect high-quality will enhance, and you may provide clients progressively.

Diminishes Costs

Transforming right into a Smart Factory does not happen without a thinking beforehand, and it might not appear completely (Discover industry 4.0 in manufacturing with HARTING, n.d.). To reap it, you need to make contributions, so there are candid costs. In any case, the cost of gathering at your workplaces will essentially fall since Industry 4.0 headways, for instance computerization, structures joining, data the board, and that is just a glimpse of something larger. Basic drivers for those faded charges include:

- Better utilization of advantages
- Snappier amassing
- Less device and age line person time
- Less exceptional issues with matters
- Less resource, cloth, and factor waste
- Lower all matters considered working charges
- Makes Innovation Opportunities

Industry 4.0 headways give you gradually unmistakable information of the gathering approach, supply chains, dissemination chains, business execution, and even the belongings you manufacture. This makes opportunities to development, paying little heed to whether this is converting an enterprise method, growing any other element, streamlining a generation arrange, enhancing OEE, and anything is viable from that factor (The Practical Application of Industry 4.0, 2015).

Higher Revenues

A tremendous range of the above centres can attain higher wages for your age office. For example, with the aid of mechanizing your age line and finishing different Industry

4.0 headways, you may comprise some other circulate with immaterial staffing expenses to meet an uptick out of good fortune or compete for another knowledge.

Extended Profitability

You will obtain this Industry 4.0 preferred position thru enormous quantities of the concentrations above becoming a member of higher wages with lessened prices. Moreover, Industry 4.0 headways engage you to make better fine, higher edge, or conceivably steadily creative things. For instance, Industry 4.0 trends make it possible to offer customers changed matters whilst up 'til now using tremendous scale fabricating methodologies to make the ones things.

Getting a Return on Investment

Industry 4.0 headways are converting accumulating over the sector. The upsides of Industry four.0 and capacity level of gainfulness are what is extraordinarily critical, be that as it may. To stay forceful and set up your age lines for the future, a chance to consider the accompanying period of your Industry 4.0 experience is as of now.

PRACTICAL ASPECT OF INDUSTRY 4.0

Industrie 4.0, 2019) claims that with industry terms being bandied about like the Internet of Things (IoT) and Industry 4.0, it may not generally be anything but difficult to understand what they truly mean for assembling. With an end goal to demonstrate its clients the viable use of Industry 4.0, Bosch Rexroth and wholesaler Morrell Group set up together a demonstrate this week at Morrell's offices in Auburn Hills, Mich., to not just clarify the items and abilities that affect these advances, yet additionally, allow them to see everything very close. With a subject of "Shrewd Factory Is Now," Rexroth and Morrell needed to have the option to exhibit the substances of what IoT abilities truly mean in an assembling situation that is how the converging of data innovation (IT) and activity innovation (OT) can profit generation. "I think we know since both of those gatherings advantage when they cooperate well, and that is the thing that the Smart Factory is," said Scott Hibbard, VP of innovation production line robotization for Bosch Rexroth Americas, during a press review the day preceding the Automation Open House. The Smart Factory is certainly not another idea, he included, "yet the meaning of Smart Factory is changing, and evolving rapidly. (Industry 4.0 - the Nine Technologies Transforming Industrial Production, n.d.)" The Smart Factory ought to be shrewd from multiple points of view, Hibbard noted. It should utilize all assets; it ought to be earth shrewd, and not simply to meet codes or guidelines; quality ought to be guaranteed forthright instead of upheld later through restorative activity; it ought to be prescient, giving ceaseless improvement; and it needs to convey data progressively. Bosch Rexroth was perceived not long ago with honor for its Industry 4.0 mechanical production system that coordinates human, machine and, item to financially fabricate tweaked items. Exhibiting the idea at Morrell's offices, Bosch demonstrated the simplicity of making altered items—memory sticks or spotlights in an assortment of hues, for this situation—on a solitary machine. The different stations on the machine work independently, speaking with one another to do the assembling activity (September 3 et al., n.d.).

Bosch matches its movement rationale framework Indra Motion MLC with the business rules the executive's parts of Bosch Software Innovations' IoT Suite to consolidate machine occasions and IT procedures utilizing principles and administrations. The client can make models for the required guidelines utilizing instinctive realistic instruments and after that port the models to the controller. The principles keep running nearby the PLC program legitimately on the controller. At that point, machine information can be dissected during creation to produce choices, for example, programmed material stock or machine advancement. The framework is profoundly adaptable, giving the client a chance to change existing guidelines whenever they make a model for new principles and move these onto the controller notwithstanding during activity. This empowers singular acclimations to be made powerfully, without making machine program changes. A vital aspect for making this all work is the Open Core Engineering (OCE) capacity that the MLCs have (Pinheiro et al., 2018). OCE bolsters an expansive scope of conventions and programming dialects to make it simpler for controls and drives to cross over any barrier between PLC-based computerization and the IT world. As a major aspect of a lot bigger activity inside the organization, "Rexroth has created libraries to help various information situations," Hibbard stated, making reference to the poor software engineering graduate who starts his new position in assembling just to be advised he needs to program in a language he hasn't scholarly. "Why not let the person who's gone to class to figure out how to control information program it in the language he's found out it in?" he inquired. An as of late reported organization with National Instruments (NI) utilizes the Open Core Interface in a LabView programming condition without composing PLC code. "Indeed, even movement can be led straightforwardly from that point," Hibbard included. "What Open Core Engineering offers, it opens up the assembling scene to a totally different arrangement of developers," Hibbard said during a board talk. With OCE instruments, he included, "kids are turning engine shafts in minutes. Presently little organizations can do it as well. I'm not catching this' meaning for what's to come?" Seeking the future for clients of all shapes and sizes, Bosch Rexroth and Morrell Group are attempting to cut past the promotion encompassing IoT, Industry 4.0, Smart Factory, what have you. "Everyone's found out about something other than what's expected. A great deal of those terms all gets blended into one small mixing pot," said Mark Majewski, VP of computerization and guard deals for Morrell. "Our main responsibility is to instruct the individuals about what's accessible today and what may be accessible later on, and more where it's valuable." Simply gathering information is not helpful. "Ten years prior, everyone needed increasingly more diagnostics," Majewski said. "Actually, what did they ever do with it? We were giving them this data, and they did not have the foggiest idea of how to manage it. How would you take this data and have the option to accomplish something helpful with it?" Bosch is attempting to drive clients from planned upkeep checks, Hibbard said. "Unquestionably, you would prefer not to hold up until something breaks. Our piece of that is to build up that information," he said. "Twenty to 30 years back in this town, individuals were stating we have to gather all the data of the machine. From that point forward, we will make sense of how to break down it. Someplace along the line, individuals lost attachment and changed the channels. We took that equivalent thought and moved it down into the gadgets."

FUTURE HEADWAYS THAT WILL DRIVE INDUSTRY 4.0

(Industry 4.0: Optimize Operations & Shape Future Innovation | PTC, 2019) Machines that self-ruling, recognize when they need additional parts. Age systems that run their own special quality control during movement, decreasing evaluation costs. Robots that self-governing can see and move fragments. Circumstances like these bit by bit are transforming into a reality in the present-day age. They are built up on future progressions like man-made mental aptitude (AI) and edge figuring. These offer immense open entryways for the discrete and technique undertakings since they open new game plans and proficiency potential. This makes them basic to ensure mechanical associations' force in the domain of tomorrow (Industry 4.0 - the Nine Technologies Transforming Industrial Production, n.d.).

Data as the Foundation for New Propels

(Future technologies will drive Industry 4.0, n.d.) suggested that the advances of things to come will be built upon the openness of data. Besides, those data are getting the opportunity to be open in riches, on account of the mechanized difference in the industry. Mechanized game plans like Siemens' Digital Enterprise portfolio are starting at now reflecting every movement in current age from a thing's arrangement, to its creation, to its use in a virtual structure, with what is known as a propelled twin. These methods are giving indications of progress and better interlinked to one another cautiously, to yield expansive data pools. Future advancements directly make it possible to separate and manhandle these data pools in totally new ways. The instance of AI indisputably demonstrates what that infers. AI is not especially new. Siemens, for example, presented neural frameworks in steel forms as far back as the 1990s. Regardless, the advancement has increased colossal ground starting now and into the foreseeable future. Preparing power has extended numerous events over. Computations have ended up being incredibly improved. Hardware underway line passageways perform better. Moreover, the data move has revived colossally. That infers the rising volume of available data that can be accumulated and separated faster and more comprehensively than already, and data assessment has ended up being significantly progressively in the present days. In view of that, we need stages like MindSphere, Siemens' open, and cloud-based working system for the IoT.

Getting Ready Industry for Future Progressions

On a phase along these lines, customers can achieve more than gather and view data as they can similarly dismember them using AI counts, and make their age frames progressively successful on that premise. For example, AI counts at Siemens' Amberg plant use data from handling machines to tell when the machines' axles are touching base at the piece of the deal lives and ought to be replaced. That makes light of unscheduled individual time, saving costs of around €10,000 per machine each year (Industry 4.0, n.d.). Likewise, AI need not run exclusively on IoT organizes in the cloud. By higher-powered PCs and higher-execution gear, it can continue in like manner work in the mechanical office hall itself – which means legitimately on the machine. This development is known as edge enrolling. It is a bit of scope for skilful applications that can continue running close with the short move ways and continuously getting ready data. Edge enlisting is starting at now at work at Siemens' Amberg plant, in quality control for circuit sheets, for example. Man-caused insight computations can tell from creation data which circuit sheets might be harmed that has cut appraisal costs by about 30%. PC based knowledge is also opening new potential results for self-decision dealing with systems. To take just one model, it used to be essential to contribute in the dull endeavor of getting ready robots with known articles, portraying each advancement, and programming it in cautious detail. Be that as it may, AI enables dealing with systems to see even cloud articles, and to figure the best holding concentrations for them. This limit finds its application in totally robotized successive development frameworks for complex things like cars, lines that must be as versatile as could sensibly be normal. To do that, robots ought to in like manner have the choice to discover and move different parts. These future progressions are starting now into a reality. In any case, they have the unmistakably progressively conspicuous potential for making age dynamically strong, progressively gainful, logically accomplished. That is the most ideal approach to fulfill the requirement for dynamically modified things in little sums, directly down to bundle size one and what is more, to do it quickly, with high gauge, and at a charming expense.

Future Accomplishment Takes Various On-Screen Characters Coordinating

In these kinds of circumstances, future developments reliably call for new routes in inventive work. They should be realized successfully when associations everything being equivalent and in all endeavours coordinate, on an equal parity. The key here is to merge modernized and mechanical inclination. Express portions have built up significant learning of their mechanical applications over decades, and that perception is critical in applying propelled courses of action and man-made cognizance, edge figuring, and independent managing systems in present-day conditions. Furthermore, this many-sided subject requires the capacities of a contrasting extent of performers from business, science, and government.

Government Must Offer Improvement To Investigate, System, It Security, And Guidance

It is necessary to have the benefit of regulatory impetus from the government. In this, four following perspectives are especially critical:

- What is required is an organic framework where progressions can create – through assistance for application-related research and theories. That is the primary way for future developments and can quickly be changed into usable things.
- A region-wide IT establishment and fast web access are fundamental essentials. Industry 4.0 needs, more transmission limit, yet likewise speedy move times, got together with most prominent availability. That is key to the destiny of the industry. By what means should a little or medium-sized association, for example, gain induction to the propelled future if its zone does not have tasteful access to the web? This is the spot government needs to act.
- IT security is major to the achievement of Industry 4.0. Digitalization and cybersecurity need to go inseparable. That is the reason, Siemens and different accessories manufacturers developed what is known as a Charter of Trust for cybersecurity. The fact of the matter is to develop general least

standards for cybersecurity that are the front line. At present, the Charter of Trust is maintained by 16 associations and affiliations.

- All degrees of preparation must be reoriented to the new propeller upgrades. Broadened aptitudes in IT, programming, programming, correspondences advancement, IT security, and data assessment will be key for future mechanical applications. That is not something that can be obtained medium-term. We need to convey the present and tomorrow's laborers close by us on along these lines to what is to come. This is the principle way we will have the alternative to abuse the huge open entryways that these future advances bring to the table.

Future Progressions Must Fulfil A Social Reason

Amidst this (Future technologies will drive Industry 4.0, n.d.), advances ought to never be considered complete in separation. They must add to associations' monetary accomplishment. Be that as it may, they ought to similarly fulfill a social reason, by contributing towards improving people's lives. Finally, people ought to reliably be the point of convergence of thought. New developments like man-made cognizance and edge handling can commit people's work less error slanted and make more space for imaginative assignments. However, notwithstanding a consistently voiced estimation, they will not replace people. On the other hand, perhaps, these are basically progressing that will enable us to stay powerful, in the Business – to-Business zone, and along these lines sustain our business zones.

CONCLUSION

In various sections of this chapter, we mentioned the evaluation and architecture of Industry 4.0 standers. We have discussed the benefits and challenges in implementing industry 4.0 in all possible domains. In the 2020 Industry era, the power of Information technology and Artificial Intelligence discipline plays a vital role in accepting and adopting Industry 4.0 procedures. Working algorithms of Computerization Modelling and robotics will help in automation of Industry 4.0 standards. In future research work, we will explore further in these research areas for applying and accepting Industry 4.0 standards in all possible areas including the E-commerce domain.

REFERENCES

A Short History of the Fourth Industrial Revolution. (n.d.). *IoT World Today*. Retrieved May 15, 2020, from https://iotworldtoday.com/2016/11/02/short-history-fourth-industrial-revolution/

Benefits of Industry 4.0 - SL Controls. (2018). *SL Controls*. https://slcontrols.com/benefits-of-industry-4-0/

Discover industry 4.0 in manufacturing with HARTING. (n.d.). Retrieved May 15, 2020, from http://harting.com/IT/en-gb/topics/industry-40

Future technologies will drive Industry 4.0. (n.d.). *World Economic Forum*. Retrieved May 15, 2020, from https://www.weforum.org/agenda/2019/01/future-technologies-will-drive-industry-4-0/

Germany. (2019). *GTAI - Industrie 4.0 – What is it? Gtai.De*. https://www.gtai.de/GTAI/Navigation/EN/Invest/Industries/Industrie-4-0/Industrie-4-0/industrie-4-0-what-is-it.html

Gilchrist, A. (2016). Introducing Industry 4.0. In Industry 4.0. Apress.

Industrial I Industry 4.0 I TI.com. (2020). http://www.ti.com/applications/industrial/industry-4-0.html

Industries 4.0. (2019). *Fraunhofer-Gesellschaft*. https://www.fraunhofer.de/en/research/fields-of-research/production-supply-of-services/industry-4-0.html

Industry 4.0 I Advantages Engineering Execs Can't Ignore. (n.d.). Retrieved May 15, 2020, from https://www.autodesk.com/industry/manufacturing/resources/engineering-leadership/industry4-0-efficiency-gains-cant-ignore

Industry 4.0 and the Industrial Internet of Things. (n.d.). *Atos*. Retrieved May 15, 2020, from https://atos.net/en/solutions/industry-4-0-the-industrial-internet-of-things

Industry 4.0. (n.d.). *Roland Berger*. Retrieved May 15, 2020, from https://www.rolandberger.com/en/Insights/Global-Topics/Industry-4.0/

Industry 4.0: Optimize Operations & Shape Future Innovation I PTC. (2019). https://www.ptc.com/en/solutions/digital-manufacturing/industry-4-0

Industry 4.0 - the Nine Technologies Transforming Industrial Production. (n.d.). Retrieved May 15, 2020, from https://www.bcg.com/en-in/capabilities/operations/embracing-industry-4.0-rediscovering-growth.aspx

Mohamed, M. (2018). Challenges and benefits of Industry 4.0: An overview. *International Journal of Supply and Operations Management*, 5(3), 256–265.

Oleksandr Shkabura. (2019). *The Main Benefits and Challenges of Industry 4.0 Adoption in Manufacturing*. https://www.infopulse.com/blog/the-main-benefits-and-challenges-of-industry-4-0-adoption-in-manufacturing/

Pinheiro, P., Santos, R., & Barbosa, R. (2018). Industry 4.0 Multi-agent System Based Knowledge Representation Through Blockchain. In *International Symposium on Ambient Intelligence* (pp. 331-337). Springer.

The Practical Application of Industry 4.0. (2015). *Automation World*. https://www.automationworld.com/article/technologies/motion-control-systems/practical-application-industry-40

Top 5 things to know about Industry 4.0. (n.d.). *TechRepublic*. Retrieved May 15, 2020, from https://www.techrepublic.com/article/top-5-things-to-know-about-industry-4-0/

Xu, L. D., Xu, E. L., & Li, L. (2018). Industry 4.0: State of the art and future trends. *International Journal of Production Research*, 56(8), 2941–2962. doi:10.1080/00207543.2018.1444806

Zezulka, F., Marcon, P., Vesely, I., & Sajdl, O. (2016). Industry 4.0–An Introduction in the phenomenon. *IFAC-PapersOnLine*, 49(25), 8–12. doi:10.1016/j.ifacol.2016.12.002

Zhou, K., Liu, T., & Zhou, L. (2015). Industry 4.0: Towards future industrial opportunities and challenges. In *2015 12th International conference on fuzzy systems and knowledge discovery (FSKD)* (pp. 2147-2152). IEEE.

Chapter 9
Emerging Opportunities for Entrepreneurs in the Renewable Energy Segment

Kesavan Dhanapal
Hindustan College of Arts and Science, Chennai, India

ABSTRACT

Considering the breathtaking changes in global business models, all entities foresee to develop new markets and products for survival in the economy. Increasing pollution levels at major cities around the globe, changing climatic conditions, and global warming makes a cloud bubbling thought of making safer and environmentally friendly products. This agenda leads to generate ideas that may create innovative products or practices may bring a competitive advantage for the new establishments. We all know that energy production constitutes to majority of the pollution in the environment. In order to tackle this situation, fostering entrepreneurs can think of ideas that are relating to renewable energy generation. Recently the rise of electric vehicles market seems to be a playground for new technology breakthroughs. This segment has huge potential for the next two decades. New entrepreneurs can take advantage of the renewable energy in making new business prospects.

INTRODUCTION

Considering the breathtaking changes in global business models, all entities fore see to develop new markets and products for survival in the economy. Increasing pollution levels at major cities around the globe, changing climatic conditions, and global warming makes a cloud bubbling thought of making safer and environment

DOI: 10.4018/978-1-7998-4882-0.ch009

friendly products. This agenda leads to generate ideas that may create innovative products or practices may bring a competitive advantage for the new establishments. We all know that, energy production constitutes to majority of the pollution in the environment. In order to tackle this situation, fostering entrepreneurs can think of ideas that are relating to renewable energy generation. Recently the rise of electric vehicles market seems to be a playground for new technology breakthroughs. This segment has the huge potential for the next two decades. New entrepreneurs can take advantage of the renewable energy in making new business prospects.

INDUSTRIAL REVOLUTION AND ENVIRONMENTAL IMPACTS

The well renowned Industrial Revolution started during the late 18th and 19th centuries and was an era of significant economic development covered by the introduction of power-driven machineries. The Industrial Revolution originated in Britain and then later it spread to other countries. During the Industrial Revolution, several power-driven machines were invented; this eventually replaced the traditional hand tools used in production. This included the cotton gin, a machine used to remove cotton fibres and their seeds. The cotton gin, along with few inventions in spinning and weaving, paved the way for mass production of cloth possible and gave a huge propel to the textile industry.

This period also led to a huge increase in the use of coal. Coal was replaced with wood and other fuel sources because it was available in abundant, efficient and it was comparatively involved less work to mine than cutting wood. Coal was also used in making iron parts and components, which was highly used in the production of machines and tools, as well as the construction of bridges and ships. The Industrial Revolution also saw the invention of the steam engine, which was an engine that consumed steam to generate kinetic energy. Steam engines were used for transportation and to generate power for factories.

Ever since the orientation of industrial revolution with no doubt it has contributed enormously for the development and growth of nations as well as their economies. While tasting the prosperity, what about the cost that was borne for tasting this prosperity? **Yes it has taken a lot from the human environment.**

After 1930 there was a steady increase in the population of all the countries in the world. In order to address the needs of the growing population, many industries were established in a drastic manner. This included too much consumption of the non-renewable energy sources like the coal and fossil fuel for power generation and transportation. This usage is has taken us to a position of facing global catastrophe

- Global warming

- Changing climatic patterns
- Increased frequency of drought
- Melting ice caps
- Green house emission

OBJECTIVES

- To address the need for alternate power source
- To evaluate the feasibility of Renewable resources
- To analyse the factors to be considered in Renewable energy
- To suggest possible implications for renewable energy

THE TIME TO RETHINK

Since the cost that was spared for these many developments and advancements has not only questioned our survival but all also shows a bitter truth of extinction. In order to come out this chaotic box, prominent entrepreneurs should concentrate on renewable energy business to promote sustainable growth. This re thinking can open the doors of profit making accompanied with zero environmental accountability and zero carbon foot print. So many countries has already started to invest and promote new business ventures to take up renewable energy linked ideas for power generation, transportation and technology.

RENEWABLE ENERGY

Renewable energy utilises energy sources that are not depleted over time. For example, solar power from the sun is renewable as we won't deplete all the sunlight from the sun. On the other hand of non-renewable energy sources include fossil fuels like coal and oil. Once we consume or burn these resources, they are depleted forever and are non-recurring in nature. Thus renewable energy is a key to open the door of sustainable development among the nations. There is a possibility that renewable energy could be a leading business venture among several fostering entrepreneurs.

RENEWABLE ENERGY AND ENVIRONMENT

Much of the world depends on non-renewable energy to comfort their homes, power their electronic devices, and to power their cars. Once these energy resources are depleted, they will be gone forever. Developing possible technologies that can efficiently use renewable energy sources is the vital element to us and also for our future generations.

Many renewable energy sources are also considered as friendly for the environment as burning coal and fossil fuels. Considerably renewable energy resources produce less pollution which will help us to protect the environment and provide us with cleaner air and water.

Sustainable development is an inclusive growth strategy that satisfies the needs of the present without compromising the wants of future generations to meet their own needs. This is the definition propounded by the renowned world commission on environment and development in its report. Economist have also stated a definition of sustainable development as being an economic cycle in which the quantity and quality of our reserves of natural resources like forests and the integrity of biogeochemical routines like climate are sustained and passed on to the future generations by sacrificing our present needs.

The comparison of the earth from past decade to this decade, there is a notable change of the Planet, the climatic conditions, the condition of water bodies, existence of several species, forests, glaciers, rain etc. All these changes are mandated by the humans who were in the perspective of earning money, building large industries, hazardous machine works, and commercialising nature and the key resources of the nature.

Almost many renewable energy sources produce little to no global warming emission. Even when including total process cycle emission of clean energy i.e., the emission from each stage of technologies that include manufacturing, installation, operation, decommissioning, the global warming emissions associated with renewable energy are comparatively minimal to that of the conventional coal and fossil fuel avenues. The exact type and intensity of environmental impacts differs depending on method of technology used, the geographic location, and other considerable factors. By understanding the present and potential environmental issues linked with each renewable energy source, the nations can take steps to effectively avoid or minimize global impacts as they become a larger component of energy supplies. So with minimal environmental effects business thinkers can shift their focus towards renewable energy segment.

CONSIDERING RENEWABLE ENERGY AS A POTENTIAL BUSINESS OPPORTUNITY

Investing in renewable energy segment is comparatively cheaper than that of coal mining and fossil fuel excavation and process. Any business potential of profit

Table.1 Renewable Energy Generation Sources (Source: Renewable energy world)

Solar	This form of energy depends on the nuclear fusion power from the core of the Sun. This form of energy can be collected and converted in a few different ways. This is the most widely used method of renewable energy generation.
Wind power	The movement of the atmosphere is driven by differences of various temperatures at the Earth's surface due to varying temperatures of the Earth's surface when lit by sunlight. With the help of those winds these blades generate electricity.
Hydroelectric	This form uses the gravitational potential of elevated water that was lifted from the oceans by sunlight. The turbines are rotated by the water movement and electricity is generated.
Geo thermal	Energy left over from the original accretion of the planet and augmented by heat from radioactive decay seeps out slowly everywhere, every day from the earth's core. Turbines are rotated with the help of those geo forces and electricity is generated. It is also a cost effective and long term benefitting method of energy generation.
Bio mass	Energy in this form is very commonly used throughout the world. Unfortunately the most popular is the burning of trees for cooking and warmth. City waste, ethanol powered fuel, domestic bio gas tanks are used to generate energy.
Hydrogen and fuel cells	These are also not strictly renewable energy resources but are very abundant in availability and are very low in pollution when utilized.
Hybrid	Combination of two or more renewable energy source for more reliability. Hybrid is also termed as mixed source of energy generation
Tidal	Small rotating turbines are used at tidy waters where waves are raising to the tune of 5 meters and above, electricity is generated using those small turbines by the movement of the waves. This requires huge investment.

making and zero accountability is a Pandora's Box of surprises for the investors. Entrepreneurs may consider this sector as an eye opener for the next industrial revolution.

Governments Promoting Renewable Energy

Many countries are shifting their energy generation from the conventional coal and fossil fuel towards renewable energy. And several countries eyes on developing full power generation through renewables in the next decade. The time is too short for them to shift from an hundred year tradition to a newer technology. But the need has pushed them to think for their future generation's well-being. Countries like Iceland, Sweden, Costa Rica, are completely relying on renewable energy for power generation. They are also encouraging new investments in this sector.

More developing nations are implementing the potential policies needed for the widespread penetration of renewable energy technologies and markets, which have

Table 2. Countries generating electricity with renewable energy (Source: IRENA 2018)

Name of the country	% of energy generated with renewables	Quantum of energy in GWh	Source of energy generation
China	25.5	1622585	Renewable hydropower, onshore wind mills, solar, solid biomass, offshore wind mills, bio gas
United states of America	16.4	637076	Onshore wind mills, renewable hydropower, solar, mixed plants, solid biomass, geothermal
Brazil	80.4	475579	Hydro power, solid biomass, onshore wind mills
Canada	61	445681	Renewable hydropower, onshore, solid biomass
India	18	261790	Renewable hydropower, onshore wind mills, solar, solid biomass

traditionally been dominated by countries like Japan, North America and Europe. The exceptions include countries like Brazil, which has constructed the world's leading biofuels industry, China, India, which are leaders in promoting decentralized renewable methods such as small hydro, small wind, biogas, and solar water heating. However, certain specific policies like feed-in tariff are implemented. Besides, with the dream policy like Kyoto Protocol, the program called the Clean Development Mechanism that permits industrialized nations to invest in projects that considerably reduce carbon and greenhouse gas emissions in developing countries as an alternative to huge expensive emission reductions in their own nations.

Globally, national and subnational governments are playing a vital role in establishing policies and formulating targets in support of renewable energy. Support policies in developed countries have been escalating capacity for several years, but recently there has been a considerable increase in the interest of developing countries in renewable energy. For almost a decade, China stands to be the leading developer of renewable power and heat worldwide, and other emerging and developing countries are increasing their capacities and transforming their energy sectors, benefiting from the efficiency and reducing cost of renewables and from technological improvements. Subnational governments are also playing a vital role, with many positively inclined policies and targets that are more ambitious than those of their respective governments and emerging as global leaders in the renewable energy transition. (Ellaban, Omar 2014)

According to IRENA at least 150 countries had fixed targets relating to the share of energy from renewables in power generation; at least 47 countries had renewables targets in domestic purpose for heating and cooling; and at least 42 countries had renewables targets for transport.

Investment Banks Promoting Renewable Energy Sector

Figure 1. Various renewable energy products

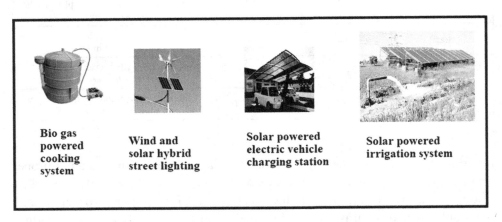

Bio gas powered cooking system

Wind and solar hybrid street lighting

Solar powered electric vehicle charging station

Solar powered irrigation system

Annually new investments into clean energy segment have doubled since 2006, with an average of 60 per cent growth recorded so far. Countries are moving drastically in to this sector. Leading investment banks are advising and promoting investors to consider about renewables segment. The global giant Citi Bank had stated during 2017 March that the era of Renewables is beginning. A more optimistic outlook for the European Union results from larger planned renewables auction volumes and faster penetrated solar PV growth in member states to achieve renewable energy targets. In the United States, wind and solar PV manufacturers are rushing to complete assignments before federal tax incentives end, while corporate power purchase agreements (PPAs) and state-level policies also evenly contribute to growth of the renewables.

Distributed solar PV systems for domestic purpose, commercial buildings and industrial facilities are ready to take off, bringing considerable changes in power systems. A rapid growth in the ability of consumers to generate their own electricity needs opens up new opportunities and challenges for electricity providers, government and policy makers around the world. (Armaroli, Nicola 2016)

Faster Deployment Avenue

Renewable energy sources are considerably faster deployment avenues than the conventional coal and fossil fuel mode of energy generation. The total time taken for deploying a renewable energy generation facility is comparatively less than the conventional medium. A wind mill can be installed within a time period of 3 days in developed countries due to the availability of technology.

Japan has installed 11 GW of solar energy within 2 years from 2015-2017. In terms of electricity quantum, that equals more than two nuclear reactors (constructing a fully equipped nuclear plant typically takes a decade). On the other hand, Japan has approved 72 GW of renewable energy generation projects, most of which are solar. This is almost equal to about 16 nuclear reactors, or about 20 coal powered power plant units. China installed as much new wind power as the rest of the world combined during 2017-18. This is more than that of the solar panels US installed in the past decade. With an ambitious target of four years, China aims to double its wind power capacity and triple its solar capacity. So considering the faster deployment parameter, renewables are far ahead of non-renewable segment.

Declining Cost of Raw Materials

According to the IRENA reports on cost of raw materials of renewables, the price of onshore wind electricity has reduced to the tune of 18% since 2009, with turbine costs declining nearly 30% since 2008, making it as the cheapest sources of new electricity generation in a wide and growing range of markets. In countries with large geographical space like Australia, Brazil, Mexico, South Africa, Turkey, India and U.S., the cost of electricity generation from onshore wind power is on par with, or lower than, fossil fuels.

Entrepreneurs can consider this as the most influential factor for taking up ventures in renewables sector. The primitive obstacle for all entrepreneurs is the cost of sourcing raw materials. With constant reduction in the prices of raw materials, new business thinkers can make use of the opportunity to make timely entry in the market. Calculating the long term profitability, renewables are much cheaper in case of maintenance and repair related issues. On the other hand renewables pose a significant investment avenue in terms of less depreciation value compared to that of the conventional modes of electricity generation. (OECD 2017)

Financial and Tax Incentives (4)

Financial and fiscal incentives are offered to improve access to capital, lower financing costs, reducing the burden of high initial outlay or the production expenses of large-scale renewable energy projects, and address specific incentives linked with energy-efficient technologies. Tax related incentives are offered in the form of reductions in direct sales, energy, value-added or other taxes or in the form of outlay tax credits, production tax credits or accelerated depreciation. Rebate in sales, energy, value-added or other taxes reduce the cost of renewable energy component for the equipment/generator and improve their affordability and profitability. These are the most notable policy instruments globally as they can be confined to projects and installations of all volume, and in areas that are out of the grid. Tax reductions had been implemented in 100 countries by 2017 and they have been the primitive instrument of choice in some countries in Southeast Asia and sub-Saharan Africa like Myanmar, Cameroon, Guinea, Liberia, Gambia, Madagascar, Niger and Togo. In other countries where they exist, they have been implemented alongside other promotions. In some countries where decrease in sales, energy, value-added or other taxes have comforted deployment, policy amendments were strongly resisted for fear they would lead to higher electricity cost or escalate a threat to the industry. (Mariana Mazzucato 2017)

Promoting Envipreneurs (Environment Friendly Entrepreneurs)

There is a new bottom line for the enterprise. Besides including financial success, companies are increasingly taking account of environmental and social performance as well. Entrepreneurs with a keen business sense and a desire to make the world a better place will reap the rewards in the future. In response to environmental and regulatory pressures, technology is progressing forward. To keep notified of opportunities and to identify potential markets, entrepreneurs should consider the following suggestions:

- Closely monitoring trends in organizations and models, this can create or close markets overnight. Governments do often change regulations for a variety of reasons, including lobbying and systematic propagations.
- Knowing about the various international environmental agreements. The market opportunities created from these agreements will be massive and cut across many regions and industrial sectors. Technologies invented to comply with the agreements will focus on eco-friendly, pollution prevention, and sustainability.
- Monitor advancements in technological parameter, such as those relating to electronics and photovoltaic. Technical developments, and decreasing costs, can make new activities, products or services oriented market possible.
- Watch for economic and social trends that are propelling the development of sustainable technologies. These include higher cost for resources and a

    move by governments away from regulation towards economic monetary instruments and performance standards.

- When we're using sustainability goals and benchmarks in business process, it's important that we don't just think about one or two components of the business — we need to look at the system as a whole.

Renewable Energy Compliments Green Marketing

Green marketing and green supply chain have been gaining the attention of both academics and business entities in the recent decade. However, no overall framework has been developed on building green industrial brands and corporate brands. The question of sustainable/green supply chains can be accompanied with green industrial marketing in establishing greener organizations and brands is still unclear. On the other hand, little is known on the components of new green industrial product development or how organizations adopt those products in profit making and capturing the market.

Table 3. Notable thinkers (Source: Virgin eco-friendly)

UNILEVER	Three quarters of non-hazardous waste does not go to landfills and the share of its agricultural suppliers that use sustainable products and practices has tripled
IKEA	Sourcing 50 per cent of its wood from sustainable foresters and 100 per cent of its cotton from farms that meet the Better Cotton standards
IBM	Smart buildings that reduce resource demand, green procurement, water resource management

    Green marketing is a type of marketing strategy that envisages on an organization's commitment towards the environment by promoting its sustainability efforts. Developing the successful green marketing strategy can lead to huge impact on getting investors, maintaining loyal consumer relationships, hiring and retaining employees, and gaining a competitive advantage. Green marketing may also refer to the manufacturing and marketing of goods based on their pro-environmental elements. Products or service may be environmentally friendly in itself, in addition to being produced using renewable energy means. This may include avoiding toxic materials in the production process, the use of recycled materials in the product, products made from renewable materials.

Industries adopting renewable energy generation for production tend to reduce the carbon foot print. They may also avoid unwanted tax and expenses relating to environmental damage, as it was enacted by several countries for making the corporates to reduce the carbon foot print, "**The polluters has to pay**". Entrepreneurs can consider this factor and concentrate on renewable energy for powering their office and industries. As it is said earlier renewable energy brings down their operating expenses in the long run. (URBAN GRID 2019)

Entrepreneurs can also think of products that are substitutable for conventional single use plastic bags, straw, nylon ropes, packing materials, aluminium foil, and plastic containers. The horizons of replacing the polluting items are huge bags of opportunities which most of the countries are looking forward to implement and reduce the damage caused to the environment. It can be rightly said that "**Protect the environment while you earn**". So entrepreneurs can adopt green marketing with the help of renewable energy sources. They should see the two sided coin of the business namely, making green products as well as making it with renewables.

The rising air pollution concern has again captured the attention of the government and ecologist together to promote the use of non-conventional energy resources. Since clean energy has been used for most of the economic and industrial activities, from generating electricity to heat water, it has created fresh and significant business opportunities for green energy entrepreneurs.

Starting and managing a renewable energy business can provide a magnificent opportunity to participate in this growing sector, while providing a better solution to reduce the dependence on depleting reserves of natural resources. In order to produce green energy easily and promptly accessible to people, the domain requires fostering entrepreneurs who with their innovative ideas, prompt action and willingness to take risks, can reap significant profits from the production and sale of energy to all possible sectors. Though there are many entrepreneurial opportunities in the energy sector, the biggest challenge is to make them economically viable. Large scale opportunities using wind energy, solar or biomass require huge global investments in promoting hi-tech solutions and developing new business models.

However, new entrants in this sector looking for profits are enthusiastic to make use of the governments' initiative to provide a funding and financing for new startups and offering incentives to propel entrepreneurship and employment creation around the world. There are several scopes at all stages of the transformation in the supply chain of renewable energy. With the increasing growth of solar water heating in urban areas, now solar uninterrupted powering units and solar street lighting are of high need. Moreover, making of small scale level wind energy and hybrid plant is also taking steady space in developing countries.

Future sustainable energy industry requires educated and enthusiastic entrepreneurs to succeed in this sector. If those entrepreneurs have decided to start their own renewable energy business, should look around for identical businesses in the other parts of the world, offering a similar product or service, before devising their own plan. Benchmarking fundamentals should be adopted by those enterprises for developing potential business plan. This method of planning will assist them to thrive in the long range perspective. Always analysing initial outlay, cost and revenue projections for establishing business projects will result in better performance.

TARGET INDUSTRIES FOR RENEWABLE ENERGY

Agriculture =

The primary activity of majority of the population around the globe is Farming. Agriculture contributes huge employment as well as to the GDP. Renewable energy can be used in developing new products and practices that can bring down the cost of farming. (Renewable Energy and Agriculture: A Natural Fit. 2008; Chel 2011)

For instance **Solar powered weed cutters, brush cutters, cultivators, sprayers, water pumps** can substantially bring down the consumption of gasoline by the farmers for day to day activities. This eventually reduces their farming expenditure and leads to increased income. Targeting a huge sector with potential products and practices will yield stronger customer base as well as market base for the entrepreneurs. (UCS 2008)

Targeting agriculture oriented countries with innovative renewable energy products can open up a door for long term profit making and market retention. Some companies manufacturing farming equipment has already started to think about renewable energy products in farming practices. Simple, affordable and necessary products for farmers can capture huge markets around the globe. This includes green house cultivation machineries, cooling systems, aquaculture, poultry farming, prawn farming, fish farming, cattle rearing, and irrigation system.

Transport Sector

The use of renewable energy in transport segment offers various benefits, such as enhanced energy security, reduced carbon emissions and up scaling opportunities for sustainable economic growth and jobs. Renewable energy solutions for transport vary from liquid biofuels, bio methane, renewable electricity, and renewable electricity-derived hydrogen, to ammonia and synthetic fuels. Many governments around the world have formulated policies for adopting renewable energy in transportation segment in the following grounds. (Running on Renewables, 2018; How transporation, n.d.; Armayoli et al 2016)

Figure 2. Various agriculture oriented renewable energy products

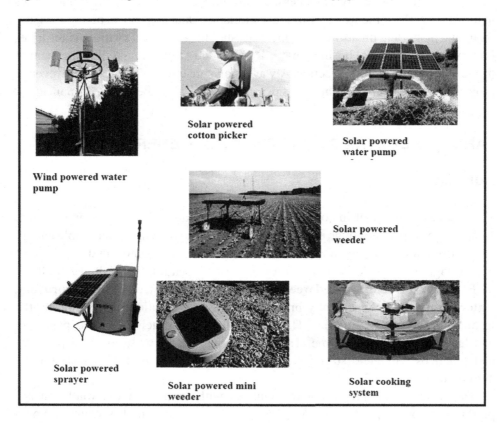

- Public transportation services
- Light commercial vehicle category
- Railways with short distance coverage
- Interlinking waterways
- Two wheelers – battery operated
- Light aviation transport
- Battery powered drone taxis

Entrepreneurs and business thinkers can mitigate the opportunities in this segment, frame policies, device strategies, innovate affordable products. Once the products alternate the conventional fossil fuel powered vehicles, people tend to shift the purchase pattern at the earliest. (Charles Cook 2014)

Manufacturing Sector

For the past hundred plus years industrial revolution has brought immense changes in the world economic system. Some of the prospects include mass production, commercialisation, capitalism and bigger corporates capturing markets. (Renewable energy in Manufacturing, 2014)

Figure 3. Transport sector oriented products

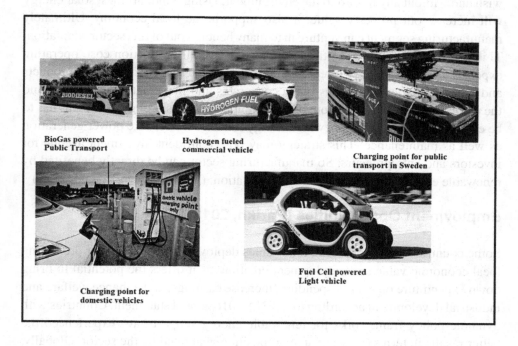

Renewable energy in manufacturing sector consists of huge propagation of benefits. To ensure a sustainable energy in future, renewable energy is the major and available source. We can use solar arrays and wind turbines as the attractive alternative over incumbent energy sources like coal-generated electricity, as solar panels can track the sun and produce energy throughout the day without causing any hazard to the environment. As solar energy is free and available abundantly, it can be used to the industrial sector as a replacement of fossil fuel and greenhouse gas. If we could capture all the sun's energy on Earth for just one hour, we can power the whole world for one full year.

Solar energy usage will decrease the greenhouse gas emissions, particularly carbon dioxide. By shifting to the usage of renewable energy in industrial sector over the greenhouse gases we can reduce its adverse effect on global temperature and climatic changes. As the climatic change contribute to serious environmental changes like weather events, rising sea levels and ecosystem changes which will be a threat to our future generations livelihood.

Renewable energy usage not only saves money, it can also reduce our carbon footprint and improve the environment and health of our world and people which we live.

Renewable energy gives energy Independence; we can use energy as per our wish and without any hazard to the environment. Using wind turbines, solar energy will increase our property value; it also supports the local economy. Ultimately manufacturing segment can venture in to many benefits out of this sector adaptation. This adaptation has the potential to reduce the overall production cost, operating expenses in the long run. Entrepreneurs can devise strategies to innovate products and services that can attract as many corporates and manufacturing units around the world to earn early profits out of the potential business. Long range plans has to be executed for providing renewable energy related services like power generation as well as maintenance. This strategy may pose confident investment avenue for investors and entrepreneurs. So manufacturing sector can be directly benefited by renewable energy implementation and adaptation. (Heymi Bahar, Ronald, 2013)

Employment Opportunities (Parikh, 2019)

Some countries are encouraging renewables deployment as a means of promoting local economic value and employment creation, as it offers the potential to bring down expenditure on energy spending, increase earnings, and enhance welfare and industrial development according to IRENA 2016 annual statement. Countries with dynamic policy frameworks for renewable energy support have experienced the better results in terms of local value proposition generated by the sector. Globally, net job creation in renewables has grown in recent years, particularly in solar PV. The renewables sector created jobs over 9.8 million people as of end-2016 as per the reports of IRENA.

In addition to the employment created in the renewable energy industry, growth in clean energy can create positive economic propelling effects. For example, industries in the renewable power generation supply chain will benefit, and unrelated local businesses will benefit from increased income of households and business earnings. Compared to that of fossil fuel technologies, which are typically mechanized and more capital intensive, the renewable energy industry is comparatively more labour intensive. Solar panels require more manual labours to install them; wind farms need technicians for installation and maintenance. This describes that, on average, more jobs are created for each unit of electricity generated from renewable sources than from fossil fuels and coal powered.

There are even greater scope for new product development engineers, researchers, and designers in the renewable energy field. Technology simplification and affordable process innovation are also the prospective windows for new job seekers in the renewables sector. According to bureau of labour welfare estimates has been reported for steady increase in the job opportunities and employment creation in the next coming decade. From the year 2025 there may be steady requirement of blue collar and maintenance level labour requirement in many countries due to the rapid change in transformation from conventional energy sources to renewables.

With the improving employment criteria and attractiveness, renewable energy may constitute a significant quantum of GDP. Even there may be movement of labour world-wide for huge requirement in technicians in the renewables sector. This movement of labour force can promote better global economic scenario and foreign exchange operations. This shift in labour requirement could also affect the traditional coal and fossil fuel industry.

Educational Institutions

Renewable energy sector may have a huge scope in the coming decades, this boom will pave way for diploma, engineering and technical training courses that are related to this segment. Educational institutions can make use of the technology to bring down their operating cost and keep a note on eco-friendly environment in the campus. The education and non-profit entities are industries in their own momentum; they have a better scope to gain by using renewables to slash operating budgets. Education sector usually does not get top billing as a political priority. Since every penny counts because clean energy is getting more affordable renewables are one of the most potential solutions to tight budgets conditions.

Institutions may design curriculum like renewable energy maintenance, engineering, new product development cells, entrepreneur promoting division, technology business incubators that are relating to renewable energy. Students can be encouraged to bring up possible technology break through, know how, affordable innovations, and alterations in the existing power generating methodologies. During late eighties computers played a vital role in changing the conventional manual accounting and banking scenario. The same kind of outlook can be expected in the transformation phase from coal/fossil fuel powered power generation scenario to renewable energy. Because of the advent of computer transformation, many courses and curriculum were designed by the institutions to meet the demand. Same as that of computer era, renewable energy will also create a huge circulation in the education field. Even technical courses and minimal maintenance courses may also be created for meeting the high demand for renewables labour requirement.

Brazil has been steadily promoting ethanol powered vehicles for domestic and commercial usage for the past six years. This scenario has paved way for new courses in the country for ethanol vehicle maintenance and new product development in the ethanol vehicle segment. In US grow solar program for promoting cooperative power sharing among small scale educational institutions has gained attention of bigger universities. The higher ranked institutions are also looking to transform some of their major energy requirement to renewables base. These universities are also planning to develop courses and part time degrees that are related to renewable energy sector. Even universities are planning to adopt neighbourhood power sharing options for several locations to sort out the excess power usage by the local people.

FEASIBILITY

The entrepreneurs must look in to cost consideration in the primary phase, because the prices of renewable energy modules are still not affordable by the weaker sections of the society. So converting an invention in to a possible innovation in this renewable energy segment would open the doors of new potential market in the near future. The one and only drawback of this segment is the cost of raw materials. Some firm find it difficult to bring down the raw materials outlay due to the prevailing rates in the global market.

Rather than concentrating on the solar and wind energy, young entrepreneurs can frame ideas relating to generation of energy and products from geo thermal and tidal energy which is available abundantly in the environment. They will be supported by eminent investors, if their idea is worthy. Even several governments are ready to take up advice with regard to efficient energy management practices and promote reasonable carbon foot print. Since the business models are changing from traditional/conventional shops to internet and online shopping modes. Customers look for something unique and eye catchy that are relatively useful in the day to day life. (Indra, Bazilian, 2019)

This segment also opens the door for green marketing of several goods which are environment friendly. This is the biggest need of the time in todays' scenario. Renewable energy can be efficiently used for several aspects that are highly beneficial for the society. Even water management can be planned with the use of renewable energy.

With the increased government support and tax benefits for reducing carbon foot print, pollution level; the feasibility of venturing in to the sector seems to be hopeful for young entrepreneurs. Investors can also consider the return on investment on the higher and safer side compared to that of fossil fuels. The excavation and other environmental clearance norms are creating a significant impact on the investors' preference towards fossil fuel, coal and thermal powered foreign direct investments. Reducing the use of existing natural resources also an important advantage in this sector, that provides increased governmental support and subsidies for new entrepreneurs. There are wide varieties of research taking place in European and North American countries for making a technology breakthrough in the renewable energy segment. This segment is also economically better than that of fossil fuel and coal powered avenues. So on these grounds the feasibility criteria of entering in to the renewables sector is justified to be positive.

DIFFICULTIES IN RENEWABLES SECTOR (BARRIERS TO RENEWABLE ENERGY TECHNOLOGIES (2017),

With power always comes fear. Even though there is a huge potential for success in the renewables, draw backs are present in all kinds of business activities in the world. Some of the most serious problems of renewables are listed below. (Meet A Moradiya (2019)

Cost Consideration

While taking up ventures in renewable energy, the most concerned factor is large initial outlay. Obviously this will be the biggest burden of the entrepreneurs in the initial phase of startup. Managing financial resources, planning about the raw materials, strategic logistic evaluation methods can play a supportive hand in reducing this limitation (Economically unviable). So entrepreneurs have to formulate successful business models and cost effective models to penetrate in to the market without much financing difficulties.

Switchover gap

The time gap taken for shifting from conventional energy source to renewable source may affect the operations of the industry. This time gap may bring certain disadvantage to their market position and profit making in the short run. Eminent planning in transition methodology will assist in eliminating difficulties in carrying on with the operations in an effective manner. This is one of the biggest concerns of several multinational corporates who are unwilling to face any temporary pause in their operations.

Reliability

"Nature cannot be predicted", this stands to be a universal truth. The main problem with renewable sector is that it relies much on the nature for generating energy; say it solar, wind, tidal, geothermal, and biomass. Solely depending on the nature for a certain business opportunity makes a critical thinking in the minds of the investors. Any failure in the forecast of renewables will certainly take away the hope of the investing in the industry.

Other Considerations

Renewable energy usages save more money and are considerably good for environment. But some of the technologies in renewables are typically more expensive than traditional energy generation methods.

Renewable energy resources are abundantly available sources but they are not consistent throughout the year. The climatic changes affect its availability in a particular period of the year. During winter season, solar energy cannot be acquired as much as it is required. Therefore, unpredictable weather events disrupt these technologies on the higher scale.

Renewable energy sources have intermittency, so the requirement of storing the energy is highly needed. The storage technology required for this medium is more expensive than the traditional method. Renewable energy options have a drawback relating to collection of energy from specific geographical locations. I.e. wind energy/tidal energy cannot be generated from all locations. Therefore for having effective renewable energy it must have a proper distribution network, so it can be transferred to the needed location. This network of transfer complicates the work of an entrepreneur in the initial phase.

Renewable energy too releases particulates into the air but it is comparatively less than fossil fuel. So, it is not totally free from pollution. I.e. Biomass energy is generated by burning organic matter directly into the atmosphere. This source also emits certain proportion of pollutants. For installing some renewable energy generating technologies like geo thermal and off shore wind mills, the space/land requirement and cost of erecting is comparatively costlier than traditional method. So, it is economically unviable for the entrepreneurs to go with renewable energy resource technology.

Entrepreneur's ultimate aim is to earn profit, but by choosing renewable energy technology the main aim of being an entrepreneur is not accomplished. As the profit earning margin will be comparatively lesser in the initial stages than the entrepreneur who uses traditional (fossil fuel) technology.

Being an entrepreneur whose requirement of energy resources is comparatively lesser than manufacturing companies. So, the lesser requirement needs more cost than using traditional technology. And it's also like gambling, it is totally reliable on nature and weather. I.e. hydro generator needs rain to fill dams to supply flowing water. Likewise for solar and wind energy. Therefore these resources are inconsistent to rely upon.

Being an entrepreneur he cannot afford to get the renewable energy technology like a large scale producer or manufacturing. As entrepreneurs capital input is comparatively lesser than large scale business. So, he cannot spend more on storage of energy, which is more costly than traditional technology.

COUNTRIES THAT ARE LEADING THE WORLD IN RENEWABLE ENERGY (15)

As the urgent need to attend the climate change crisis, rapid change in energy generation has resulted significant increase in renewable energy resources over the decade.

- United Kingdom - wind power - maximum usage by 2019.
- Germany - solar power - 85% of electricity in need is fulfilled with solar power.
- China - owns world's five largest solar and wind turbine manufacturing plants.
- USA - comes second to China in both solar and wind energy.
- India - set 175 - Gig watt (renewable energy) goal by 2022 and 350 GW by 2030.
- Brazil - 76% of their electricity is from renewable energy resources and leader ethanol powered vehicles.
- Uruguay - 95% of their energy supply is renewable.
- Denmark - set goal plan to reach 100% free of fossil fuels by 2050. As of now 50% is from renewable.
- Iceland - Nearly 100% of energy comes from hydropower and geothermal.
- Sweden - have made significant investment in solar, wind energy storage and the use of clean fuel for public transport.
- Costa Rica - majority of its energy usage is from hydroelectric, geothermal, solar and wind power. Also it has set 100% carbon neutral goal for 2021.
- Nicaragua - set goal as 90% energy sources from renewable energy by 2020.
- Morocco - made investment in solar and wind to produce power over one million tons by 2020.

- Kenya - installed continents largest wind farm, invested in geothermal energy also which fulfill more than half of their energy capacity. (IRENA 2017)

CONCLUSION

This chapter holistically answers the questions that are relating to new entrepreneurs entering in to the renewable energy segment. This is not just a business; this is also a global transition. They can be termed as the environmentally responsible entrepreneurs or ENVIPRENEURS. The entrepreneurs who are seriously considering this segment as a cape of good hope can be confidently said that they are on the right track of prosperity. This unit would be an encouraging platform for fostering entrepreneurs who seek some change in the routine world of operations. This will also enable them to consider all other business environment factors before going for startup.

REFERENCES

Armaroli, N., & Balzani, V. (2016). Solar Electricity and Solar Fuels: Status and Perspectives in the Context of the Energy Transition. *Chemistry (Weinheim an der Bergstrasse, Germany)*, 22(1), 32–57. doi:10.1002/chem.201503580 PMID:26584653

Bahar, H., Egeland, J., & Steenblik, R. (2013). *Domestic Incentive Measures for Renewable Energy with Possible Trade Implications*. OECD Trade and Environment Working Papers.

Barriers to renewable energy Technologies. (2017). *Union of Concerned Scientists*.

Cook, C. (2014). Transforming the Transportation Industry with Renewable Energy. *Renewable Energy World*. Retrieved from, https://www.renewableenergyworld. com/2014/09/18/transforming-the-transportation-industry-with-renewable-energy/#gref

11 . Countries leading the charge on Renewable energy. (2019). *Climate council*. Retrieved from https://www.climatecouncil.org.au/11-countries-leading-the-charge-on-renewable-energy/

Delucchi, M. A., & Jacobson, M. Z. (2011). Providing all global energy with wind, water, and solar power, Part II: Reliability, system and transmission costs, and policies. Energy Policy, Elsevier Ltd.

Dillon, J. (2010). *New Transmission Line Reaches Milestone.* Retrieved from https://archive.vpr.org/vpr-news/new-transmission-line-reaches-milestone/

Ellabban, O., Abu-Rub, H., & Blaabjerg, F. (2014). Renewable energy resources: Current status, future prospects and their enabling technology. *Renewable & Sustainable Energy Reviews, 39,* 748–764. doi:10.1016/j.rser.2014.07.113

Renewable Energy and Agriculture: A Natural Fit. (2008). *Union of Concerned Scientists.*

Faunce, Lubitz, Rutherford, MacFarlane, Moore, Yang, Nocera, Moore, Gregory, Fukuzumi, Yoon, Armstrong, Wasielewski, & Styring. (2013). Energy and environment policy case for a global project on artificial photosynthesis. In Energy & Environmental Science. RSC Publishing.

Glassley. (2010). Geothermal Energy: Renewable Energy and the Environment. In *The Way back Machine.* CRC Press.

Global Climate Change. (n.d.). *Vital signs of the planet.* Retrieved from https://climate.nasa.gov/

Global Trends in Sustainable Energy Investment. Analysis of Trends and Issues in the Financing of Renewable Energy and Energy Efficiency in OECD and Developing Countries. (2007) *United Nations Environment Program.* Retrieved from http://wedocs.unep.org/handle/20.500.11822/7958

Heidari, N., & Pearce, J. M. (2016). A Review of Greenhouse Gas Emission Liabilities as the Value of Renewable Energy for Mitigating Lawsuits for Climate Change Related Damages. *Renewable & Sustainable Energy Reviews, 55,* 899–908. doi:10.1016/j.rser.2015.11.025

Hohmeyer, O., & Bohm, S. (2015). Trends toward 100% renewable electricity supply in Germany and Europe: a paradigm shift in energy policies. In *Wiley Interdisciplinary Reviews: Energy and Environment.* Academic Press.

How transportation can run on renewable electricity. (n.d.). *ECOHZ.* Retrieved from https://www.ecohz.com/how-we-work/how-transportation-can-run-renewable-electricity/

Indra, Bazilian, Ilimbek Uulu, Vakulchuk, & Westphal. (2019). The GeGaLo index: Geopolitical gains and losses after energy transition. *Energy Strategy Reviews.*

Isaias, M., Verde Leal, M. L., & Ramos da Silva, J. A. (2004). *Assessment of greenhouse gas emissions in the production and use of fuel ethanol in Brazil.* Secretariat of the Environment, Government of the State of São Paulo. Retrieved from https://www.wilsoncenter.org/sites/default/files/media/documents/event/brazil.unicamp.macedo.greenhousegas.pdf

Jupe, S. C. E., Michiorri, A., & Taylor, P. C. (2007). *Increasing the energy yield of generation from new and renewable energy sources.* Retrieved from https://www.sciencedirect.com/science/article/abs/pii/S0960148105000893

Kaushik. (2011). *Renewable Energy for Sustainable Development.* Springer. Retrieved from https://link.springer.com/article/10.1051/agro/2010029

Khan, M. A. (2007). *The Geysers Geothermal Field, an Injection Success Story - Annual Forum of the Groundwater Protection Council.* Thermal Energy Sources and Application Publication.

Lund, H. (2006). Large-scale integration of optimal combinations of PV, wind and wave power into the electricity supply. *Renewable Energy, 31*(4), 503–515. doi:10.1016/j.renene.2005.04.008

Marketing, S. (2019). *Promoting Your Renewable Energy Purchase.* Urban Grid.

Mathiesen. (2015). Smart Energy Systems for coherent 100% renewable energy and transport solutions. *Applied Energy.*

Mazzucato. (2017). Financing renewable energy: Who is financing what and why it matters. In *Technological forecasting and Social Change.* Elsevier.

Mohammed & Mou. (2019). Analysis of wind speed data and wind energy potential using Weibull distribution in Zagora, Morocco. *International Journal of Renewable Energy Development.*

Moradiya. (2019). The Challenges Renewable Energy Sources Face. *AZO CleanTech.*

Offshore wind test and demonstration facility. (2018). European Offshore Wind Deployment Centre. Retrieved from https://en.wikipedia.org/wiki/European_Offshore_Wind_Deployment_Centre

Parikh, A. (2019). Global Renewable Industry Created 11 Million Job Opportunities in 2018. *MERCOM INDIA.* Retrieved from https://mercomindia.com/irena-11-million-jobs-renewables-2018/

Renewable Energy. (2011). Retrieved from https://en.wikipedia.org/wiki/Renewable_energy

Renewable energy in Manufacturing, A technology Roadmap for Remap 2030. (2014). *International Renewable Energy Agency.*

Running on Renewables. (2018). *Transforming Transportation Through Renewable Technologies.* International Renewable Energy Agency.

Shokri & Heo. (n.d.). Energy Policies to promote Renewable Energy Technologies; Learning from Asian Countries Experiences. *International Association of Exhibitions and Events.*

Shon-Roy, A. W. (2010). Solar Cell Process Costs and Materials. *Renewable Energy World.* Retrieved from https://www.renewableenergyworld.com/2010/11/01/solar-cell-process-costs-and-materials/#gref

Sütterlin, B., & Siegrist, M. (2017). Public acceptance of renewable energy technologies from an abstract versus concrete perspective and the positive imagery of solar power. *Energy Policy, 106,* 356–366. doi:10.1016/j.enpol.2017.03.061

Unwin, J. (2019). *Top five trends in wave power.* Retrieved from https://www.power-technology.com/features/wave-power-energy/

Wiseman, J. (2013). *Post Carbon Pathways.* University of Melbourne.

ADDITIONAL READING

Armaroli, N., & Balzani, V. (2011). *Energy for a Sustainable World – From the Oil Age to a Sun-Powered Future.* Wiley-VCH.

International Energy Agency. (2007). *Renewables in global energy supply: An IEA facts sheet.* OECD.

International Energy Agency. (2011). *Solar Energy Perspectives.* OECD.

Kaltschmitt, M., Streicher, W., & Wiese, A. (2007). *Renewable energy. Technology, economics and environment.* Springer.

REN21 (2009). *Renewables Global Status Report: 2009 Update,* Paris: REN21 Secretariat. IRENA annual reports on renewable energy, 2014 – 2018

KEY TERMS AND DEFINITIONS

IEA: International Energy Agency.

IEA SHC: Solar Heating and Cooling Programme of the International Energy Agency.

INFORSE: International Network for Sustainable Energy.

IPCC: Intergovernmental Panel on Climate Change.

IRENA: International Renewable Energy Agency.

Kw: Kilowatt.

MW: Megawatt.

NEEAP: National Energy Efficiency Action Plan.

NGL: Natural gas liquids.

OECD: Organisation for Economic Co-operation and Development.

PHEV: Plug-in hybrid electric vehicle.

PVC: Photovoltaic cell (solar).

REEEP: Renewable Energy and Energy Efficiency Partnership.

UNEP: United Nations Environment Programme.

UNFCCC: United Nations Framework Convention on Climate Change.

UNO: United Nations Organisation.

VRE: Variable renewable energy.

ZEV: Zero-emission vehicle.

Chapter 10
Information Literacy and the Circular Economy in Industry 4.0

Selma Leticia Capinzaiki Ottonicar
https://orcid.org/0000-0001-6330-3904
Sao Paulo State University (UNESP), Brazil

Jean Cadieux
Université de Sherbrooke (UdeS), Canada

Elaine Mosconi
https://orcid.org/0000-0001-5579-9997
Université de Sherbrooke (UdeS), Canada

Rafaela Carolina da Silva
Sao Paulo State University (UNESP), Brazil

ABSTRACT

Industry 4.0 contributes to the increase in technological production and the use of environmental resources. Because of that, researchers need to discuss circular economy issues in the context of I4.0. To understand the circular economy, people need to know how to access, evaluate, and use the information (information literacy). The purpose of this chapter is to discuss how information literacy has been studied for the development of the circular economy. The methodology implies a review of the literature on circular economy, information literacy, and Industry 4.0. Subsequently, the document connects the information literacy and BNQ21000 standard (Québec) focusing on sustainability. The review showed that there are only a few documents that analyze the circular economy in the context of Industry 4.0. In addition, the information literacy needs to be studied in the circular economy and Industry 4.0 so that managers, students, and researchers can contribute to that revolution in a critical and sustainable way.

DOI: 10.4018/978-1-7998-4882-0.ch010

INTRODUCTION

Industry 4.0 (I4.0), also known as the Fourth Industrial Revolution (4IR), is based on smart technology allowing faster and personalised production of goods. I4.0 is considered a revolution because it changes the means of production and people's lifestyles. I4.0, however, contributes to the increase of technology production and use of environmental resources. Researchers, therefore, need to discuss circular economy issues in the context of I4.0. In order to understand the circular economy, people need to know how to access, evaluate and use information. Intelligent information use occurs through learning. This learning can be considered lifelong learning-as it is useful to professionals and individuals. Lifelong learning is internationally known as information literacy (IL). IL involves learning through information access to allow individuals can think critically.

In order to understand the issues that involve the circular economy in the context of I4.0, people need to become information literate. IL involves a critical discussion about the consequences of I4.0 in society. This critical thinking is fundamental to managers and professionals to allow them to behave in an ethical and sustainable manner.

The purpose of this paper is to discuss how IL has been studied to understand the circular economy development. It, furthermore, develops a framework connecting information literacy and the *Bureau de Normalisation du Quebec's* (BNQ21000) sustainable learning standards of Québec, Canada, so to enable managers can make effective decisions. It also demonstrates how businesses can become more sustainable in the context of I4.0.

The methodology involves a literature review about circular economy, information literacy and I4.0. Additionally, the paper connects IL and BNQ21000 standard (Québec) focusing on sustainability. IL needs to be studied in the context of the circular economy and I4.0, allowing managers, students and researchers to contribute in a critical and sustainable way. Businesses can apply IL in training about the circular economy and find new opportunities in environmental issues.

This paper attempts to connect concepts of Business Management, Sustainability and Information Science. The interdisciplinarity contributes to knowledge construction and helps business into the context of I4.0. Businesses can thus develop economically based on the principles of the circular economy, which promotes growth based on respect for the environment and society.

Industry 4.0 (I4.0) uses smart technologies for faster and personalised of goods and services for customers. It requires new production processes to satisfy changes in people's lifestyles. In addition, the increased use of technologies and intelligence in all business activities has the potential to improve and support circular economy issues in the context of I4.0. In order to understand circular economy benefits for individuals, organisations and society at large people need to know how to access, evaluate and use information about products and services.

Intelligent information use occurs through learning, sometimes lifelong learning, which is useful for professionals and individuals. IL involves a critical discussion about the consequences of I4.0 to all stakeholders, as individuals, organizations and society. Being able to access, evaluate and use information managers and professionals can develop a critical thinking and can make decisions in an ethical and sustainable way. The research question is:

1)   What is the influence of information literacy on the circular economy to support a more sustainable way for Industry 4.0?

The methodology involves a literature review about circular economy and I4.0. Additionally, the paper will explore IL and the BNQ21000 learning standards (Québec) focusing on sustainability. The BNQ21000 is the main focus of this chapter, which is used as a basis of circular economy understanding.

A framework connecting information literacy and BNQ21000 is proposed to help managers and professionals evaluate their understanding about the circular economy in an I4.0 context. The literature reviews and suggests that there are only a few papers discussing the circular economy in the context of I4.0. This interdisciplinary research can help explain the context of I4.0, by allowing businesses to develop economically based on the principles of the circular economy with reference to the environment and society.

BACKGROUND

Information Literacy

Information literacy (IL) is known as a process of lifelong learning and working with means of accessing information (Bruce, 1999; Lloyd, 2017; Belluzzo, 2007). The key point of skills training in our modern society is no longer only access to information but rather the results of its use.

Access to information and transforms it into knowledge does so within an organisation with specific objectives. The information must be of good quality to permit smart learning, and this which is the purpose of the information literacy.

According to Belluzzo and Feres (2015, p.8), information literacy is:

[...] functional literacy within contemporary society, which becomes crucial for each citizen's achievement and full social integration. Its development gives individuals

the ability to access, select, manage, and evaluate the information they need in their professional, social, and personal lives.

In other words, mastery of various types of knowledge and abilities which allow practical real-world interventions. Information literacy changes behaviours and is critical view of the social context. Information literacy has a technical, aesthetic and political aspect (Vitorino and Piantola, 2009). From this perspective, information literacy contributes to education and social inclusion since individuals "learn how to learn" through specific knowledge, attitudes and experiences. Lifelong learning encourages people to become more critical to discuss political, social, cultural, economic and ethical issues. Individuals learn the importance of respecting different points of view. Furthermore, information literacy is fundamental to the development of the circular economy because it helps individuals to think critically about the sustainability.

The *Association of College and Research Libraries* (ACRL, 2014, p. 4) states that "information literacy is the set of integrated abilities encompassing the reflective discovery of information, the understanding of how information is produced and valued, and the use of information in creating new knowledge and participating ethically in communities of learning" (ACRL, 2015, p. 11). As a result of this key, information, literacy enables individuals to understand information quality, which guards them *or* mitigates against misinformation.

When dealing with the volume of data and information that is available today and with the need to produce true meaning information literacy contributes to the development of increasingly qualified and competent professionals who are committed to the search of skills development.

Ethical engagement in society is also part of information literacy. It is also important for sustainability. An ethical person respects other people, animals and the environment, since everything is connected to everything else. Rossetto and Feres (2016, p. 10) created a group to discuss information literacy in a multidisciplinary way and to disseminate information literacy.

As a result of the study the authors (2016, p. 10) explain that:

According to the Mission of the Labirinto do Saber [Labyrinth of Knowledge group], we hope to inspire professionals who work in the management of university libraries, people and communities in general to develop their potential through intelligent access and use of information to construct innovative knowledge in different social reality: the exercise of citizenship, lifelong learning with quality of life, social responsibility, participation and sharing, self-development, ethics and legality, points considered strategic and integral in the dimensions established in sustainability programs.

In 2018 the CILIP (UK Library and Information Association) amplified the concept of information literacy to consider different contexts of learning: *"Information literacy is the ability to think critically and make balanced judgments about any information we find and use. It empowers us as citizens to develop informed views and to engage fully with society"* (CILIP, 2019). Because of that, information literacy is connected to sustainability, since it is a skill that influences individuals, politics and social actions focused on the environment (Nascimento, Moraes, and Paula, 2017).

Information literacy can be used as a strategic tool to help organisations to achieve their goals. It is an integral part of the people management models, which deals specifically in solving problems and decision-making, through the intelligent use of the information.

Industry 4.0 (I4.0)

Industry 4.0 (I4.0), also known as the Fourth Industrial Revolution (4IR), is a means to improve production based on clients needs (Almada-Lobo, 2015; Schwab, 2016). This new means of production involves connected technologies that share data between themselves. The connected technology can help to solve organisational and social problems (Schwab, 2016; Dutton, 2014). The Fourth Industrial Revolution encompasses novel/niche areas which are not normally classified as an industry, such as smart cities, for example.

The connected technologies are artificial intelligence (AI), big data, Internet of things (IoT), cloud computing, additive manufacturing, cyber-physical systems and robots. In I4.0 these technologies provide information quickly and in real time (Dutton, 2014). The production of physical equipment increases. As a consequence, factories may produce more industrial and electronic waste. As natural resources are limited the production of goods without a waste management strategy can lead to pollution and health problems.

According to the United Nations (UN, 2015) guidelines, the lack of waste management hinders sustainably. This requires I4.0 researchers and technology developers to focus on ethical issues of information use. Society needs to become more information literate in order to discuss the consequences of I4.0 and use it for environmental projects. I4.0 technology can promote sustainability to protect ecosystems. The use of renewable energy is an example thereof. Information literacy is a strategic tool, so to enable professionals and citizens can to criticize the unethical use of technology.

Industry 4.0 has been hailed as an opportunity for national economic growth as it involves an enormous production of information and technologies that are more and more interconnected and are able to replace humans in repetitive or manual work (Schwab, 2016). Therefor, the work of human beings will become more intellectual rather than manual creates/invents/anticipates what the machine will do. Humans will work at the strategic and tactical levels, while machines work at operational levels while also being required to carry out certain manual tasks at the tactical level.

Little has been said, however, of the increased production of technological equipment or of the need to correctly reuse or dispose of its wastes. One must not forget to broach the interdisciplinary aspects of sustainability in the fields of Business Management, Engineering, Information Science, and Environment. This research is important to society because it will increase the awareness of environmental issues.

Furthermore, the regulation of strategies for natural resource use, disposal of e-waste, and environmental protection must be considered. Information literacy is a fundamental asset to allow professionals to value ethical and sustainable means of production and the use of smart technologies. With that said, this article aims to discuss how countries can make use of information literacy to participate more critically and sustainably in I4.0.

Circular Economy

The linear model of business is based on the extraction, transformation, production, usage and discarding of goods. This model can be reviewed as is a threat to society because it increases the consumption of natural resources. This influences human lives (UN, 2011) as it creates concern for future generations by creating difficulties for their survival.

The circular economy business model focuses on the economic and environmental issues. This is a sustainable economic model which is "[...] projected to the Earth, instead of focusing on the market, and it respects ecological principles to benefit everyone." (Leitão, 2015, p. 152). The circular economy influences sustainable growth as its intention is to help people in poverty.

The topic of the Circular Economy emerged with a publication of Walter R. Stahel entitled "The product-life factor" in 1982. The paper explains the topic and its impact for waste prevention, job creation and innovation. Furthermore, the paper discusses the useful life of goods through reuse, repair, renewal and recycling processes (Stahel, 1984, 2010). In 2010 the Ellen MacArthur Foundation (Stahel, 1984, 2010) was created in order to disseminate and study the circular economy. This non-profit organisation uses Stahel's ideas (1984, 2010) about renewable energy and elimination of toxic chemical residues. The focus is to remanufacture/recycle goods which were already produced by other businesses.

The circular economy is "[...] a model that optimizes good circulation, maximize natural resources use and minimizes the production of residues. This model allows an increase of the value of the product." (Leitão, 2015, p. 159). According to Martins (2013), the concept of Circular Economy refers to the physiocrats and classical economists, who stated that the accumulation of goods is a luxury. Furthermore, they considered accumulation as a waste rather than a reinvestment in the economic circuit.

Braungart, McDonough and Bollinger (2007) emphasise that biodegradable materials are biological nutrients and that they should be used in manufacturing because they are absorbed by the environment. Synthetic materials damage the soil and nature but can be re-used by other businesses but the residues can sometimes be recycled.

The Circular economy allows businesses to face challenges such as the variation on the price of raw materials and the limitations in the supply chain (Monteiro, 2018). The circular economy enables the company to become more competitive because it reuses/recycles materials, reduces the consumption of energy and reduces the costs of production. The adoption of a circular economy depends on a systemic view of means of production and supply chain. This economy encourages innovation to reduce costs and improve processes. It is believed that the Circular economy is a new model for business to become sustainable and competitive.

The Circular economy is fundamental in the context of I4.0 because organisations can develop smart technology to reduce waste and improve productivity. In order to understand sustainability, circular economy and I4.0, managers and professionals need to become information literate. Quality information is required to enable effective decision-making processes and solving problems ethically. The circular economy context involves the ethical perspective about/regarding the consequences of smart technology to on society.

The Agenda 2030 of the United Nations (UN, 2015) was created to disseminate the relevance of sustainability to countries. This agenda values information access as an important element to the development of the locality. The agenda has seventeen (17) goals to be achieved by countries before the year of 2030.These goals are:

Goal 1. End poverty in all its forms everywhere.

Goal 2. End hunger, achieve food security, improved nutrition and promote sustainable agriculture.

Goal 3. Ensure healthy lives and promote well-being for all at all ages.

Goal 4. Ensure inclusive and equitable quality education and promote lifelong learning opportunities for all.

Goal 5. Achieve gender equality by empowering all women and girls.

Goal 6. Ensure availability and sustainable management of water and sanitation for all.

Goal 7 Ensure access to affordable, reliable, sustainable and modern energy for all.

Goal 8. Promote sustained, inclusive and sustainable economic growth as well as full and productive employment and decent work for all.

Goal 9. Build resilient infrastructure, promote inclusive and sustainable industrialisation and foster innovation.

Goal 10. Reduce inequality within and among countries.

Goal 11. Make cities and human settlements inclusive, safe, resilient and sustainable.

Goal 12. Ensure sustainable consumption and production patterns.

Goal 13. Take urgent action to combat climate change and its impacts.

Goal 14. Conserve and sustainably use the oceans, seas and marine resources for sustainable development.

Goal 15. Protect, restore and promote sustainable use of terrestrial ecosystems, sustainably manage forests, combat desertification, and halt and reverse land degradation and halt biodiversity loss.

Goal 16. Promote peaceful and inclusive societies for sustainable development, provide access to justice for all and build effective, accountable and inclusive institutions at all levels.

Goal 17. Strengthen the means of implementation and revitalise the Global Partnership for Sustainable Development (UN, 2015, p.14).

From this perspective, the BNQ21000 learning standard (created 2012 by the BNQ, the *Neuvaction*, the *Ministère du Développement Économique du Québec* (MDEIE) and the *Chaire Desjardins en gestion du développement durable*) focuses on the management of sustainable development, within manufacturing companies, covering 21 issues grouped under four themes: economic, social, environmental and moral. The 21 micro issues of the organization worked by the BNQ21000 are: 1) mission/vision/values, 2) strategy, 3) ethics, 4) products and services liability, 5) governance, 6) governance, 7) sustainability of the organization, 8) investment practises, 9) purchasing and procurement practices, 10) impact on local development, 11) work conditions, 12) skills development, 13) participation on labour relations, 14) equity, 15) occupational health and safety, 16) management of raw and residual materials, 17) energy management, 18) water management, 19) GHG management, 20) management of other types, like noise, and 21) local environmental impact management. These micro issues are according with the 16 macro principles of the Sustainable Development Act: 1) health and quality of life, 2) equity and social solidarity, 3) environmental protection, 4) economic efficiency, 5) participation and commitment, 6) access to knowledge, 7) subsidiarity, 8) partnership and intergovernmental cooperation, 9) prevention, 10) precautions, 11) protection of cultural heritage, 12) conservation of biodiversity, 13) respect for the support capacity of ecosystems, 14) responsible production and consumption, 15) polluter pay, and 16) internalization of costs (Cadieux, 2017), in order to guide business towards the social project.

The Circular Economy, from the point of view of the micro and macro issues of the BNQ21000 standard, classifies the companies according to five levels of maturity. These responsiveness levels are: 1) somewhat concerned, 2) reactive, 3) accommodating, 4) proactive, and 5) generative, which will guide the management decisions in these organizations.

The sustainable goals of countries that adopt the Agenda 2030 explains that these countries are ready to protect the planet. The focus is to develop sustainable production and consumption of goods and to manage natural resources. The Agenda 2030 protects future generations by taking climate measures (UN, 2015). The countries that accept this agenda have to achieve the goals of sustainability before 2030.

Methodology

This chapter is based on an exploratory, qualitative, and quantitative literature review (Marconi and Lakatos, 2013; Gil, 2002) about information literacy, Industry 4.0, circular economy, and The United Nations Agenda for sustainable development.

According to the authors, the exploratory research aims to obtain familiarity with the study problem. It involves a bibliographic literature review to understand the object of the study. Thus, the exploratory research consists of a deepening and synthesizing technical and conceptual aspects obtained through a bibliographic references and linked to the object of study.

The choice of a qualitative approach resulted from the objectives set for the development of the study, because qualitative research, requires questions and problems arisen from observations in the real world with their dilemmas and issues. They are formulated as hypotheses derived from the theory analyzed.

The literature review generates a quantitative analysis, showing how many documents are found in each issue/category. It is important to say that quantity and quality/qualitative are characteristics which are interrelated. In the development process, gradual quantitative changes generate changes. This transformation is believed to take place by leaps (Gil, 2002).

With respect to literature review, exploratory research is often the first stage of a broader investigation. When the theme chosen is generic, clarification and delimitation become necessary requiring a literature review, discussion with experts and other procedures.

Furthermore, this methodology considers the consequences of I4.0 to the environment. Subsequently, the document connects the information literacy standards and indicators on the BNQ21000 learning standard (Québec) focusing on sustainability.

We focus on the International Agenda 2030, created by the United Nations (thereafter: Agenda 2030) focusing on the objectives 9, 11, 12, 13 and 15. These objectives are related to sustainability for cities and communities, sustainable production and actions to face global warming (UN, 2015). The literature review is relevant because an innovative discussion emerges as it connects both Information Science and Business Management research topics.

RESULTS

The results of this book chapter are based on a discussion about concerning the Agenda 2030 (2015) and the quantitative results of the literature review. These demonstrate a connection between information literacy standards and indicators (Belluzzo, 2007) and the BNQ21000 learning standards for sustainability from Quebec (thereafter BNQ21000). This connection allows the development of indicators which can be used by business to adapt into the circular economy context.

The goal of countries adopting the Agenda 2030 is that they are ready to protect the planet. The focus is to develop sustainable production and consumption of goods and to manage natural resources. The Agenda 2030 protects future generations by implementing climate change measures (UN, 2015).

Countries that accept this agenda must achieve the goals of sustainability before 2030.

The Agenda 2030 (2015) was created to disseminate the relevance of sustainability to countries. This agenda values information access as an important element to development. As previously stated, there are seventeen (17) goals to be achieved before the year 2030.

Sustainability is important because many countries are experiencing problems associated with climate change and a lack of waste management. In this context, the Fourth Industrial Revolution is encouraging organisations to optimise production. The production of goods in I4.0 is based on specific clients' needs (Almada-Lobo, 2015; Schwab, 2016). These new means of production involve interrelated technologies to solve those problems (Schwab, 2016; Dutton, 2014).

Smart technology can consist of Artificial Intelligence (AI), Big Data, Internet of Things (IoT), cloud computing, additive manufacturing, cyber-physical systems and robotization. These I4.0 connected technologies provide data and information in real time to professionals (Dutton, 2014). This can result in managers making fast decisions and solving problems quickly. I4.0 can therefore help improve the quality of manufacturing and services.

This led to an increase in the production of physical equipment, such as robots and drones. Therefore, I4.0 can increase the industrial and electronic waste. Because of that, individuals are worried about the consequences to the environment. Natural resources are limited, and the lack of waste management can prevent organization from complying with the Agenda 2030.

Beyond the respect for the environment, academics are worried about the ethical issues of I4.0, since some organisations are producing smart weapons and robots to participate in wars. Therefore it is believed that society needs to become information literate to evaluate the consequences of smart technology on people and environment. On the other hand, I4.0 technology can be used to protect the environment by using renewable energy.

Organizations can use Agenda 2030 to guide their processes since it values human knowledge. Information literacy creates abilities to adapt to market needs so that organisational learning is fundamental to make decisions and solve in making decisions and solving` problems. Therefore, according to Ottonicar, Valentim and Mosconi (2018), information literacy influences the organization's competitiveness and innovation.

Information literacy can be part of Business Management courses and training in companies that are adapting to the context of I4.0. Information literacy helps professionals to use information and technology in an ethical and sustainable way (Belluzzo, 2007). It is a multidisciplinary topic/approach. The discipline of information literacy has political, aesthetic, technical and ethical perspectives. These perspectives are also known as dimensions (Vitorino and Piantola, 2011).

According to Agenda 2030 (p. 5): "[...] Natural resource depletion and adverse impacts of environmental degradation, including desertification, drought, land degradation, freshwater scarcity and loss of biodiversity, add to and exacerbate the list of challenges which humanity faces. Climate change is one of the greatest challenges of our time and its adverse impacts undermine the ability of all countries to achieve sustainable development. Increases in global temperature, sea-level rise, ocean acidification and other climate change impacts are seriously affecting coastal areas and low-lying coastal countries, including many least developed countries and small island developing States. The survival of many societies, and of the biological support systems of the planet, is at risk."

The dimensions of information literacy contribute to achieving the sustainable development goals of the Agenda 2030. The technical dimension is related to the use of technology (Vitorino and Piantola, 2011). In I4.0, individuals do not perform repetitive work and instead focus on information analysis and knowledge construction (Schwab, 2016). Information literacy can help professionals to use smart technology and develop information analysis.

The aesthetic dimension is related to the way individuals deal with information and express it in a collective context. The political dimension involves the participation of citizens in public decisions and in the transformations of social life. The ethical dimension concerns the responsible use of information (Vitorino and Piantola, 2011).

Information literacy dimensions are relevant in the context of I4.0, so individuals can respect other people and nature.

In the context of I4.0, managers need to use natural resources in a critical and conscious way as humans have damaged the planet. According to Belluzzo (2007) the information literate individual understands ethical, legal, social and economic issues by accessing and using information. Therefore, managers need to be information literate to develop organisational processes respecting the environment.

One aspect of information use is decision-making based on the scarcity of natural resources. Information literate professionals learn to think critically and consider environmental problems such as pollution, water shortage, loss of biodiversity and the increase of temperature. Some academics have been researching information literacy in the context of sustainability. A data search on information literacy in the context of sustainability shows that a total of 264 papers have been published on the topic internationally. This paper includes Base de dados Brasileira de Ciência da Informação (BRAPCI) [Brazilian Database of Information Science], SciELO, Web of Science (WoS) and SCOPUS.

Table 1. Quantitative Results - information literacy and sustainability publications?

Database	Quantity
BRAPCI [Brazilian Database of Information Science]	3
SciELO	0
WoS	15
SCOPUS	206
LISA	40
Total	264

The SciELO database does not contain papers about information literacy and sustainability and SCOPUS and has a total of 206 papers published. Despite being Brazilian, the BRAPCI database is relevant because it includes publications in the Information Science field. Information literacy is well known in Information Science; and needs to be recognised by other fields of research.

Appendix 1 shows the papers retrieved/researched and the respective database. Table 2 illustrates the types of publications in these databases.

Most papers were published as journal articles and only five conference papers were published about regarding information literacy and sustainability. There were twenty-two book reviews and 12 books published about the topic. However, there

Table 2. Type of Publication

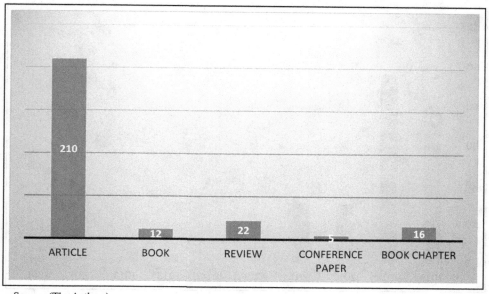

Source: (The Authors)

were no papers published about information literacy in the context of circular economy. Table 3 shows the quantity of publication per year.

There has been an increase of publications about information literacy in sustainability over the years. The literature review considered papers published without time limitation. Table 3 shows that 40 publications out of about 125 were published in 2019, so this topic is achieving a broader audience. This shows how climate change has influenced literature and research over the past years.

SOLUTIONS AND RECOMMENDATIONS

Information literacy has standards and indicators which guide professionals how to access, evaluate and use information. Beyond these standards, individuals can also develop abilities through experience at the workplace. The standards are flexible and can be adapted to many contexts. In this chapter, information literacy standards are set in relation to BNQ 21000. The latter guides professionals to develop sustainable activities at in the work place to improve the management maturity of an enterprise.

The International Federation of Library Association (IFLA) and the Association of College and Research Libraries (ACRL) created standards and indicators of information literacy at higher education facilities/institutions. Regina Belluzzo

Table 3. Quantity of publication per year

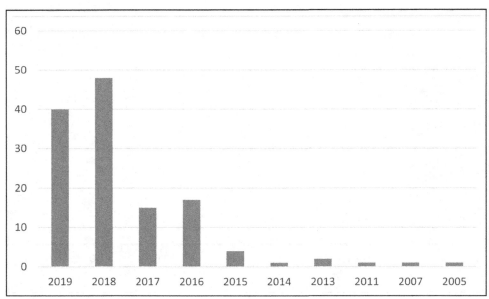

Source: (The Authors)

(2007) a Brazilian researcher adopted those standards at the workplace. As this chapter focuses on the workplace, Belluzzo's information literacy standards (2007) are have been applied.

Standard 1 is connected to information need. Standard 2 guides professionals to access information. Standard 3 demonstrates the relevance of information evaluation. Standard 4 explains the information use in organizations. Standard 5 involves the ability to interpret and understand the context. These levels of information literacy standards are connected to the Environmental topics of BNQ21000.

BNQ21000 guides professionals and organisations to become more mature in terms of sustainability. In this context, the Canadian province of Quebec attempts to achieve a circular economy. These guidelines are useful to guide organisations on how to improve the production process. As a consequence, organisations use renewable energy sources, manage waste and reduce environmental pollution.

BNQ 21000 is based on four dimensions. The first dimension considers transversal topics, such as ethics of a company (mission, vision, values, ethics, governance, responsibility...). The second dimension involves economic topics/issues. The third dimension explains/examines social topics/issues, and the fourth dimension is about environmental topics/issues. It is connected to the circular economy and the sustainable development of organisations. Figure 1 illustrates the connection between information literacy standards and environmental topics/issues.

Table 4. Belluzzo's Information Literacy Standards and Indicators

Standards, indicators and results	Description
Standard 1	Individuals identify the nature and extent of the information need.
Indicator 1.1	Define and recognize information needs.
Result 1.1.1	Identify a research topic or other information need.
Result 1.1.2	Ask proper questions based on information need or research topic.
Result 1.1.3	Use general or specific information sources to increase knowledge about a topic.
Result 1.1.4	Modify information needs or research topics to conclude the focus of the research.
Result 1.1.5	Identify concepts and key words which represent information needs, research topic or question.
Indicator 1.2	Identify a variety of formats and potential information sources.
Result 1.2.1	Identify values and differences between sources in several formats.
Result 1.2.2	Identify the purpose and the kind of information in tendentious sources.
Result 1.2.3	Distinguish primary sources from secondary sources; and recognise their use and their importance to in each field.
Indicator 1.3	Consider the costs and benefits of information acquisition.
Result 1.3.1	Determine the availability of information needs. Take decisions about the research strategy, use of information services and proper/formal media.
Result 1.3.2	Develop a practical planning module and a chronogram adequate to gather information.
Standard 2	Individuals effective access to information.
Indicator 2.1	Select the appropriate research methods or information systems.
Result 2.1.1	Identify the kind of information in a system.
Result 2.1.2	Properly select information retrieval systems to investigate a problem/ topic.
Result 2.1.3	Identify different types of research to find information.
Indicator 2.2	Construct and implement search strategies effectively established.
Result 2.2.1	Develop a research plan appropriate to information retrieval systems and/or research methods.
Result 2.2.2	Identify key words, sentences and synonyms related to information needed.
Result 2.2.3	Select specific vocabulary as a research tool. Identify this vocabulary registered, and execute the research by successfully using proper vocabulary/terms.
Result 2.2.4	Construct and implement research strategy by the use of codes and commands which are proper in tandem with to information retrieval systems.
Result 2.2.5	Use information retrieval systems help and other methods (for example information professionals) to improve their results.
Indicator 2.3	Seek information electronically or with people. Uses a variety of methods.
Result 2.3.1	Use different information retrieval systems in a several formats (printed or digital).
Result 2.3.3	Use several classification plans or other systems to locate information sources and services.
Result 2.3.4	Use online services or specialised people which are available in the organisation to retrieve information needed.
Indicator 2.4	Rework and improves the search strategy.
Result 2.4.1	Evaluate the quantity, quality and relevance of research results to define alternative information systems or research methods.
Result 2.4.2	Identify information gaps which are results of previous research.
Result 2.4.3	Review research strategies and if necessary to gather more information.
Indicator 2.5	Extract, register and manage information and its sources.
Result 2.5.1	Register all information and its sources to retrieve them in for the future.
Result 2.5.2	Understand how to organize and process gathered information.
Result 2.5.3	Distinguish among cited sources. Understand the elements and the correct way to cite different sources based on the rules of patents and intellectual property.
Standard 3	Individuals evaluate information and its sources critically.
Indicator 3.1	Demonstrate knowledge about the information gathered.
Result 3.1.1	Select relevant information based on information sources' ideas.
Result 3.1.2	Reformulate concepts with their own words.
Result 3.1.3	Identify textually information which was redrafted or rephrased.
Indicator 3.2	Apply evaluation criteria to information and its sources.
Result 3.2.1	Analyze and compare information from different sources to evaluate its reliability, validity, accuracy, authority, and points of view.
Result 3.2.2	Analyze the logic of gathered information.
Result 3.2.3	Recognize and describe several aspects of a source, its impacts and value to project/work activity. They also describe trends and impacts related to cultural policy, geographical, historical or timeliness assumptions of the information source.

continued on following page

Table 4. Continued

Standards, indicators and results	Description
Result 3.2.4	Demonstrate the ability to find information about authors and editors who produce technical manuals, proceedings and documents.
Result 3.2.5	Understand and interpret manuals and reports. Manuals and reports are found in several sources and they are also a way to access precise and valid information.
Result 3.2.6	Understand the necessity to verify precise and complete data or facts.
Indicator 3.3	Compare the new knowledge with the previous knowledge to determine the value added, contradictions, or other characteristics of information.
Result 3.3.1	Determine if the gathered information is enough and adequate or if it is necessary to seek more information.
Result 3.3.2	Evaluate if information sources are contradictory.
Result 3.3.3	Compare new information with one's own knowledge and other sources which are considered reliable to the subject.
Result 3.3.4	Select information that brings evidence to the problem, research topic or other information needed.
Standard 4	Individuals use information effectively to reach a goal or a result individually or in a group.
Indicator 4.1	Individuals are capable of synthesizing information to complete a project, activity or task.
Result 4.1.1	Organize information using plans or several structures.
Result 4.1.2	Understand how to use an author's citations, paraphrases or texts to support ideas and arguments. This item is used for writing activities, reports, documents and manuals.
Indicator 4.2	Effectively communicate the results of the projects, activities or work.
Result 4.2.1	Use documentation norms and formats properly to develop a project, activity or work task.
Standard 5	Individuals understand economic, legal and social issues of information use. The access and use information ethically and legally.
Indicator 5.1	Understand the legal, ethical and socio-economic issues which involve information, communication and technology.
Result 5.1.1	Identify and discuss issues related to open access versus private access about/regarding information and communication services.
Result 5.1.2	Understand legal questions about patents and copyright nationally and internationally.
Result 5.1.3	Define and identify examples of patents and brands intellectual property.
Result 5.1.4	Demonstrate knowledge of institutional policy about products and brands. Policies related to intellectual property to investigate a product in business organizations.
Indicator 5.2	Respect laws, rules, institutional policies and guidelines related to information access and information source use.
Result 5.2.1	Use passwords properly to access information sources.
Result 5.2. 2	Respect organization's policy to access information sources.
Result 5.2.3	Preserve information sources, equipment, systems and tools which are available to access and use information.
Result 5.2.4	Know the rules of intellectual property and use them in documents. Understand issues connected to reports, manuals, catalogues which guide products use and processes.
Result 5.2.5	Identify patent elements in different sources and formats. Require authorization to copy texts, images and sounds.
Indicator 5.3	Indicate the information source in the communication of results.
Result 5.3.1	Use style and language appropriate to field.
Result 5.3.2	Identify elements of citation to information sources in different formats. For example, individuals should know how to investigate documents and mention government documents, law and training courses.
Result 5.3.3	Understand norms of documentation which are recommended to a task (for example, product development norms, memorandums and official reports in the organisation).

Source: (Belluzzo, 2007)

The BNQ21000 standard is based on five levels of responsiveness (and corresponds to Belluzzo's model).

- Level 1: the manager is not concerned or not literate about an issue.
- Level 2: the manager is reactive about an issue, he's and trying to get rid of the problem and move on. (Standard 1 and 2 in Belluzzo's model)
- Level 3: the manager has a calculated approach to the problem, he and invests if a form of gain is seen. (Standard 3 in Belluzzo's model)

- Level 4: the manager is in a continuous improving state of mind and proactively addresses problems before they occur. (Standard 4 and 5 in Belluzzo's model)
- Level 5: the manager is a societal generator, and helps its suppliers and customers to become more sustainable. (Standard 5 in Belluzzo's model)

Figure 1. Connection between information literacy standards and environmental themes
Source: (The Authors)

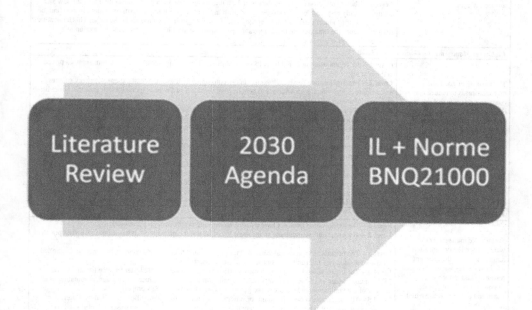

Figure 1 shows that BNQ21000 guides the circular economy in many different topics/issues. The continuous blue arrow indicates that the emphasis is on environmental topics/issues, particularly the sustainable development of businesses in order to achieve a circular economy. However, the other topics/issues of BNQ21000 are equally important. Because of that which, future research can connect information literacy to other topics/issues of BNQ21000. The dotted lines indicate future research opportunities.

The environmental topics focus on six pillars: Raw materials and waste management (4.1), energy management (4.2), water management (4.3), management of Greenhouse Gas Emissions (4.4), management of other forms of pollution (4.5) and management of local environmental impact (4.6). The focus is to help business to follow these

Table 5. Environmental themes of BNQ 21000 learning standard in Québec, Canada

Theme and Issue	
Description	**Levels**
4.1 Raw-Materials and Waste Management – Goals 9, 12 and 15	
The management of raw materials entails setting up a system that manages their controlled use, but also the reduction reuse, recycling, recovery and disposal of waste generated during the product of service life cycle.	**Level 1** – The organisation has no log or no mechanism to monitor the consumption of raw materials and waste management through the production process. **Level 2** – The organisation has undertaken initiatives to reduce the consumption of raw materials and recovery of waste. The organisation does not have a management system for raw materials and waste. **Level 3** – The organisation has a structured management system to optimise the consumption of raw materials, collection and processing of waste and the minimisation of the landfills. It opts for the eco-efficiency of products and values manufacturing by-products (e.g., energy recovery). The organisation has developed indicators to monitor the performance of raw materials and waste. **Level 4** – The efficiency of the organisation's production systems or service creation systems is part of an ongoing improvement process (e.g., ISO 14001, etc.). It develops or funds a programme to reduce the use of raw materials (eco-design, product and service life cycle analysis). **Level 5** – The organisation integrates the eco-design into its business strategy. It constantly looks for new and environmentally responsible replacement materials. It assumes responsibility in terms of materials used and the recycling of its products at the end of their life cycle. It encourages its suppliers to do the same. This innovative strategy enables the organisation to put forward new business models in its business activity section (e.g., dematerialisation of products).
4.2 Energy Management – Goals 7, 12, 13 and 15	
The purpose of good energy management is to reduce energy consumption costs and its environmental impact without necessarily compromising comfort or the level of production of the organisation. This is called energy efficiency. Good strategies make the organisation more productive and less vulnerable to changes in energy supply costs.	**Level 1** – the organisation does not track its energy bills. At best, it only seeks to benefit from supplies priced at the best rate. **Level 2** – The organisation partly follows its energy consumption. It uses the least expensive energy sources and accepts energy suppliers invitations to benefit from subsidies of financial incentives for potential sporadic measures of energy efficiency. **Level 3** – The organisation conducts an energy audit and has a management system to properly and efficiently monitor its energy consumption at different points. It adopts eco-efficiency practises and draws up a list of measures that would enable it to reduce its energy costs, and it stays informed of available subsidies and financial incentives. **Level 4** – The organisation maintains an energy efficiency measures plan. Energy management is part of the ongoing improvement process (eco-efficiency, research and development, eco-design). Eco-design approaches are part of the development plan for its facilities and its products and services. It favours, in particular, energy-efficient technologies, renewable energy sources or alternative energy sources. **Level 5** – The organisation considers energy an important part of its environmental footprint. It demonstrates to its stakeholders its pro-activity in and commitment to sustainable development. It is in the vanguard and adopts innovative technologies combining energy storage with renewable or alternative energy sources.
4.3 Water Management – Goal 13, 14 and 15	
Sustainable management of water within the organisation aims to improve the efficient use of water resources (essential resource) and reduce sources of contamination of running water and groundwater (shared resource)	**Level 1** – The organisation does not have a log or monitoring mechanism on the subject. **Level 2** – The organisation maintains an informal log of its water consumption. It has water-use saving practices in place. **Level 3** – The organisation has a water-use savings program and manages its wastewater (subject to controlled release of wastewater and runoff) and raises employees' awareness. **Level 4** – The organisation has a programme for efficient water management: water balance for all services (water intake, water use, water consumption), adaptation of processes to reduce water usage, elimination of all sources of contamination and diffuse in the ground and on the organisation's property. **Level 5** – The organisation has a program for water regeneration: process modification to reduce water consumption, reuse of water that is slightly contaminated or treated within the organisation, rehabilitation of impermeable surfaces to slow and filter runoff.
4.4 Management of Greenhouse Gas Emission (GHG) – Goals -7, 9, 12, 13 and 15	
This issue seeks to identify actions and initiatives taken by the organisation to reduce GHG emission. It focuses primarily on facility emissions (building, machinery and processes) and transport emissions (employees, supply and distribution).	**Level 1** – The organisation does not have information on the quantities of GHG generated in its daily activities. **Level 2** – The organisation has put in place specific actions to reduce GHG emissions associated with its activities. **Level 3** – The organisation has a partial inventory of its GHG emissions (direct and a few indirect sources). It has a targeted a project to reduce GHG emissions, which also represents a reduction in activity-related costs. **Level 4** – The organisation produces a full-carbon assessment (raw materials, manufacturing processes, transportation of employees, etc.). The organisation seeks innovation, taking into account the reduction of GHG emissions. It has also targeted several reduction projects requiring more effort to implement (e.g., change in technology and logistics, transportation of employees). **Level 5** – The organisation is a leader in GHG management. It constantly seeks new reduction opportunities from a product and service life cycle perspective, thus encouraging all of its stakeholder to make an effort to manage their GHG emissions. As a leader, it commits itself to an emission offsetting process and works towards carbon neutrality.
4.5 Management of other forms of pollution – Goal 9, 14 and 15	

continued on following page

Table 5. Continued

Theme and Issue	
Description	**Levels**
	4.1 Raw-Materials and Waste Management – Goals 9, 12 and 15
This issue takes into account all other forms of pollution: soil, air, and noise nuisance, ardour/ odour nuisance or volatile (volatile organic compounds (VOC), dust).	**Level 1** – The organisation does not have a log or monitoring mechanisms on the subject. **Level 2** – The organisation has knowledge of past events such as accidental or regular dumping and complains about odours or noise. A few corrective measures were applied to reduce (even eliminate) the occurrence of incidents. **Level 3** – The organisation has a pollution-management plan and has detailed documentation on the organisation's pollution sources. Facility inspections are conducted at regular intervals. **Level 4** – The organisation seeks innovation and has a program for cleaning up historically contaminated soil and water. This program goes beyond the standards of regulatory compliance. Proactive measures are implemented in order to reduce noise, odour and volatile pollution. **Level 5** – The organisation invests in change in technology or in production techniques to avoid emissions of pollutants (soil, air) and other nuisances (odour, noise) at the source for the local environment. It works together with relevant stakeholders or experts to reduce its environmental impact.
	4.6 Management of the local environment impacts – Goals - 9, 13, 14 and 15
This issue assesses certain actions taken by the organisation aimed at reducing its local environmental footprint.	**Level 1** – The organisation does not have a log or monitoring mechanisms on the subject. **Level 2** – The organisation has a partial knowledge of the pollutants that have an environmental impact on its actions and activities. **Level 3** – The organisation studies and documents the impacts of its activities and carries out initiatives, work, or assignments to lessen the impact of its activities on the environment. **Level 4** – The organisation is part of an offsetting logic. It listens and favours partnerships with the local communities in order to preserve the environment and bio-diversity. **Level 5** – The organisation is forward thinking and protects bio-diversity. It initiates and carries out projects that strive to preserve lasting bio-diversity or restore the environment in its region.

Source: (BNQ, 2011, p. 38-39)

steps in order to become more sustainable (BNQ, 2011). Each of those levels are associated with information literacy standards and indicators, since professionals need to access, evaluate and use information daily for work at a circular economy company.

The interrelation between information literacy and environmental topics demonstrates that new indicators are required for businesses and organisations to develop processes in a circular economy context. In every level of progression in the BNQ21000, professionals need to access another level of quality information to make effective decisions.

The overall interpretation of these standards demonstrates the following:

Standard 1 - Professionals identify the nature and extent of the information needed. They access information about the relevance of sustainability of society. They focus the management of raw materials, waste, energy, greenhouse gas emissions, as well as other forms of pollution and evaluates the impacts on the local environment.

Standard 2 – Professionals access required information effectively. They identify potential sources of information. They make a distinction between digital technology, analogue documents and smart technology. They know how to use artificial intelligence and big data algorithms. They know how to access cloud computing and other systems to find information.

Standard 3 – Individuals evaluate information and its sources critically. They filter information to gather the most useful to their needs. They verify the quality of information and identify unreliable or false information. They are capable of interpreting information critically and understanding the ideology behind information sources.

Standard 4 – Professionals use information effectively to reach a goal or a result individually or in a group. They use information to feed the system about raw materials and waste management. They use information to innovate and find good strategies for renewable energy. They solve problems related to GHG emissions and the use of water. They identify other forms of pollution and make decisions to avoid damaging the environment (learning company).

Standard 5 – Professionals understand economic, legal and social issues of information use. As well as accessing and using information ethically and legally. They implement actions to recycle and recover raw materials and water. They understand the consequences of human impacts on bio-diversity. They focus on the reduction of energy consumption to make more profit. They reduce environmental pollution and develop partnerships with the supply chain to reduce GHG emissions and other forms of pollution. They understand the importance of information access, evaluation and use, to manage resources effectively (learning societal company).

FUTURE RESEARCH DIRECTIONS

Future research can apply the connection between information literacy standards and indicators (Belluzzo, 2007) and BNQ21000. This model is flexible and can be adapted to different organisations in the context of the circular economy within the Agenda 2030.

There are very few publications on information literacy in the context of the circular economy, leaving space for more academic research.

Information literacy can be applied to courses such as engineering, business management and sustainability. The focus is to enable students to access, evaluate and use information ethically and intelligently and to understand the consequences of industrial production and I4.0 technology to society.

Circular economy allows organisations to become partners and complement their production processes in a sustainable way. Industry is fundamental in the context of I4.0, since it encourages the production of technology such as robots and devices. Unfortunately, I4.0 can increase industrial waste, thereby damaging the environment.

Therefore, academics and professionals should redirect their actions in context of I4.0 in a more sustainable way. Research needs collaborative approaches in order to minimise the impact of economic growth to nature.

CONCLUSION

Information literacy applied to courses in the field of business management and information science is crucial to organisations adapting to the context of I4.0. Information literacy focused on the circular economy contributes to professional education and sustainable practices. Business needs to respect the environment, so future generations can survive in a safe place.

Information literacy helps professionals, managers and individuals to use information and smart technology ethically. The ethical aspects of information literacy involve the sustainable use of resources and the achievement of Agenda 2030.

Information literacy standards and indicators as well as BNQ21000 contribute to business ethics and the sustainability of organisations. Furthermore, BNQ21000 can be adapted and used in different contexts for guiding organisations to operate in the circular economy. This standard helps us to become more mature, to value the environment and to understand the consequences of pollution on society.

Individuals live in an era of change, which requires them to reinvent themselves in order to survive. Lifelong learning is fundamental to every aspect of human life and to the responsible growth of businesses. People and organisations need to be ready to compete ethically, while respecting the environment.

In conclusion, information literacy has been studied for the development of circular economy, and connecting it with learning standards, in order to promote sustainability for companies in the context of I4.0. From this perspective, critical literacy promotes necessary incentives to achieve the goals of Agenda 2030, by working with sustainability, digital literacy, economic growth and focusing on the environment of the circular economy.

The interdisciplinarity among Business Management, Sustainability and Information Science contributes to knowledge construction and helps business to develop a sustainable economy in their organizations. Information literacy standards and indicators, along with environmental themes of the BNQ 21000 learning standard, therefore, contribute to the development of a circular economy in the context of I4.0.

REFERENCES

Almada-Lobo, F. (2015). The Industry 4.0 revolution and the future of Manufacturing Execution Systems (MES). *Journal of Innovation Management*, *3*(4), 16–21. doi:10.24840/2183-0606_003.004_0003

Association of College and Research Libraries. (2014). *First part of the draft framework for information literacy for higher education.* Retrieved on 2019/03/20 from: http://acrl.ala.org/ilstandards/wp-content/uploads/2014/02/Framework-for-IL-for-HE-Draft-1-Part-1.pdf

Belluzzo, R. C. B. (2007). *Construção de mapas: desenvolvendo competências em informação e comunicação.* Cá Entre Nós.

Belluzzo, R. C. B., & Feres, G. G. (2015). Competência em informação, redes de conhecimento e as metas educativas para 2021: reflexões e inter-relações. In Redes de conhecimento e competência em informação: interfaces da gestão, mediação e uso da informação/organização. Rio de Janeiro: Interciência.

Braungart, M., Mcdonough, W., & Bollinger, A. (2007). Cradle-to-cradle design: creating healthy emissions: a strategy for eco-effective product and system design. *Journal of Cleaner Production*, *15*(13-14), 1337–1348. doi:10.1016/j.jclepro.2006.08.003

Cadieux, J. (2017). The BNQ21000 standard: the management of sustainable development: from learning to audit. *WIT Transactions on Ecology and The Environment, 226.* Retrieved on 2020/02/24 from: https://www.researchgate.net/publication/320220750_THE_BNQ21000_STANDARD_THE_MANAGEMENT_OF_SUSTAINABLE_DEVELOPMENT_-_FROM_LEARNING_TO_AUDIT

Dutton, W. H. (2014). Putting things to work: Social and policy challenges for the Internet of things. *Info*, *16*(3), 1–21. doi:10.1108/info-09-2013-0047

Ellen Macarthur Foundation. (2012). *Towards the circular economy 1: economic and business rationale for an accelerated transition.* Cowes: Ellen MacArthur Foundation.

Gil, A. C. (2002). *Como elaborar projetos de pesquisa.* Atlas.

Leitão, A. (2015). Economia Circular: uma nova filosofia de gestão para o séc. XXI. *Portuguese Journal of Finance, Management and Accounting, 1*(2), 149-171. Retrieved on 2019/05/05 from: http://u3isjournal.isvouga.pt/index.php/PJFMA/article/view/114/52

Marconi, M. A., & Lakatos, E. M. (2013). *Técnicas de pesquisa.* Atlas.

Martins, N. (2013). *The Cambridge revival of political economy.* Routledge. doi:10.4324/9781315883915

Monteiro, M. (2018). Economia Circular. *Empreendorismo Start&Go, 20.* Retrieved from: https://www.startandgo.pt/pubs/startgo20.pdf

Nascimento, F. G. F. B., Moraes, M. L., & Paula, R. P. S. (2017). *Anais do Congresso Brasileiro de Biblioteconomia.* Documentação e Ciência da Informação, Fortaleza, FEBAB. Retrieved on 2019/01/29 from: https://portal.febab.org.br/anais/article/viewFile/1695/1696

Norme BNQ 21000. Développement durable – Guide d'application des principes de la Loi sur le développement durable dans la gestion des entreprises et des autres organisations. (n.d.). Retrieved on 2019/02/24 from: https://www.bnq21000.qc.ca/guide-bnq-21000/description/

Rossetto, M., Belluzzo, R. C. B., & Feres, G. G. (2016). *A competência em informação (CoInfo) como recurso didático pedagógico e institucional: o Website Labirinto do saber como fonte de informação, de pesquisa e práticas.* Retrieved on 2019/02/24 from: https://repositorio.usp.br/item/002789636

Schwab, K. (2016). *The fourth industrial revolution.* Crown Business.

Stahel, W. R. (1984). The product-life factor. In An inquiry into the nature of sustainable societies, the role of the private sector. Houston: The Mitchell Prizes.

Stahel, W. R. (2010). *The performance economy.* Palgrave McMillan.

United Nations. (2015). *Transforming our world: the 2030 Agenda for Sustainable Development.* Retrieved on 2020/02/20 from: https://www.un.org/ga/search/view_doc.asp?symbol=A/RES/70/1&Lang=E

Vitorino, E. V., & Piantola, D. (2009). Competência informacional: bases históricas e conceituais: construindo significados. *Ciência da Informação, Brasília, 38*(3), 130–141.

ADDITIONAL READING

Cargas, S., Williams, S., & Rosenberg, M. (2017). An approach to teaching critical thinking across disciplines using performance tasks with a common rubric. *Thinking Skills and Creativity*, *26*, 24–37. doi:10.1016/j.tsc.2017.05.005

Elder, L., & Paul, R. (2010). Critical Thinking: Competency Standards Essential for the Cultivation of Intellectual Skills, Part 1. *Journal of Developmental Education*, *34*(2), 38–39.

Fahim, M., & Masouleh, N. S. (2012). Critical Thinking in Higher Education: A Pedagogical Look. *Theory and Practice in Language Studies*, *2*(7), 1370–1375. doi:10.4304/tpls.2.7.1370-1375

Hodgson, G. (2005). Institutions and economic development: constraining, enabling and reconstituting. In G. Dymski & S. De Paula (Eds.), *Reimagining Growth: towards a Renewal of Development Theory* (pp. 88–95). Zed Books.

Jackson, T. (2009). *Prosperity without Growth. Economics for a Finite Planet.* Earthscan. doi:10.4324/9781849774338

Murawski, L. M. (2014). Critical Thinking in the Classroom...and Beyond. *The Journal of Learning in Higher Education*, *10*(1), 25–30.

Paul, R., & Elder, L. (2016). *Critical thinking: concepts and tools. Lanhand.* Rowman & Littlefield.

Woollard, R. F., & Ostry, A. S. (2000). *Fatal Consumption: Rethinking Sustainable Development.* UBC Press.

KEY TERMS AND DEFINITIONS

Circular Economy: Circular economy is a concept of Economy focused on sustainable development of business and society.

Critical Thinking: Critical thinking is the ability to think critically about information.

Industry 4.0: I4.0 is the new digital disruption that is focused on the connection of smart technology.

Information Literacy: Information Literacy is the ability to access, evaluate and use information critically.

Information Literacy Standards and Indicators: Standards that help to use information literacy in practice.

Information Science: It is a scientific field that studies information in many contexts. It is considered as a multi, inter and transdisciplinary field.

Information Use: It is the result of information access, for example: decision-making, problem solving, innovation and learning.

Knowledge Construction: Knowledge construction is the ability to learn from information. Information interpretation.

Sustainability: It is a social, economic, and political process based on the use of resources in a sustainable way.

Chapter 11
When Ethics Meets Technology

Tamar Apel Campo
CimeH Institute, Israel

ABSTRACT

Two conceptual platforms meet in the use of technologies: the technological milieu and the ethical principles that underlie every human action. The interface, called "use," imposes a change of attitude in the behavior developed by humankind throughout centuries of mental evolution. This interface connects the two platforms although this is invisible to the naked eye. Using complex system analysis, it is possible to identify the components of the two platforms and understand the influences of their characteristics, providing a meaningful perspective of how technologies can contribute to the development of a secure and positive society in the future. The development and use of technologies can influence the developer/user in a positive or damaging way. Neuroscience's contributions point in this direction. The concern for the welfare of people affected by technologies is a must in the next era. The author intends to prove in an extensive way that for safety, ethic regulations should be considered for industry, health, and education.

INTRODUCTION

Putting ethics with technology is probably as ludicrous as rubbing soap on the keys of a piano to enhance the performance of the pianist. Ethics is not soap on the keys of technology. The metaphor presents an absurd situation based on the qualities of the soap, the needs of the pianist and the characteristics of the ivory piano keys. They combine to attain the principal objective of the actions: a smooth movement of hands on the keyboard. This results in a perfect concerto.

DOI: 10.4018/978-1-7998-4882-0.ch011

This idealistic thought is difficult to contradict under the circumstances posed. Yet, it would be difficult to convince Krystian Zimmerman, the virtuous Polish pianist, when playing Beethoven's Piano Concerto No. 2, to accept this proposal. Not because of the disgusting touch of soap, but because the soap would prevent him from hitting the keys with enough strength to present the chords in their real intensity. To avoid this conflict, soap is not rubbed on the keys of the piano in spite of its possible contribution to enhance a smooth movement of the pianist' fingers.

In a parallel dimension, despite the positive influence that ethics can have on the use and development of technology, this connection could generate a conflict for many of the technological creations today. Just as soap is not rubbed on pianos, ethics is not normally included in technological matters.

This comfortable position needs to be reviewed.

POINT OF VIEW

The management of human affairs requires social skills, knowledge of topics involved and mastery of principles ruling the system. This triad has enabled army people to win wars, citizens to become presidents of their countries, infrastructure companies to install water lines and teachers to survive in the educational environment. This consensus is no longer strong enough to continue doing the work, or as marketing people say, deliver the goods. The scope of action of human affairs is now broader, challenging the boundaries of the visible and knowledgeable. The advances in the computer industry had the effect of redesigning old machines as computer-based devices, and presented many new human performance issues that were not readily addressed by existing theories. (Guastello, 2013). The ability to move from and into the micro and the macro is now a fact. The enthusiasm that this movement creates spreads like ocean waves from one level and sector of society to another. Not only a wave, but a tsunami.

The SKP (social skills, knowledge, principles) triad that has been guiding our lives successfully, standing on an invisible and powerful platform of silent acceptance of actions until now, is no longer capable of supplying the understanding required by the new situation, which is approaching quickly in the form of the Fourth Industrial Revolution (4IR). To maintain its ruling position, the SKP triad needs to adapt itself to a changing and dynamic environment where strong forces coming from financial, political and environmental fields based on technological wisdom are activated. The movement from an industrial era to a new one requires more sophisticated patterns of management, if it wants to serve society properly.

One important landmark in this trajectory is the global climate crisis and the Corona pandemic. What we were not willing to accept formerly is brought loud and clear in the form of a powerful global expression. This "what" can be the guiding point for decision makers, leading to the next inevitable stage: accepting complex system theory as a methodology to find answers to phenomena that cannot be reduced by science from the whole to its parts like in medicine, education or transportation. Medicine can treat a headache with a pill that would reduce the pain without inquiring on the cause. Education can get children to sit in their chairs for hours without providing enough space to move according to their needs. Transportation industry can produce cars without considering their effect on traffic and pollution.

A reductionist point of view enables a limited mapping of the components of the situations and phenomena, providing a limited and temporal solution to the problem. The worst thing about this perspective is that upon implementation, the provided solutions cause greater problems. This increase of problems creates insolvable impacts on society with repercussion on the welfare of mental health of living beings, augmented tension and stress, fat people looking for food as pleasure compensation, children connected to screens instead of enjoying the company of their parents. Technology and artificial intelligence add complexity to the situation. An elderly person with visual impairment can wear audio glasses that can read the text of the book, a missile can be targeted accurately to hit the apartment in the third floor of a building, toddlers can stay home alone while cameras transmit their actions to parents working miles away. Technology can be used in beneficial and non-beneficial manners. The dilemma of the use, if it exists, calls for a review of the ethical dimensions involved, those that people decide to activate.

MOVING INTO THE PENUMBRA

Alexis Carrel, 1912 Nobel Laureate in the field of medicine was aware already in 1935 of the tremendous importance that our mental attitude has in the understanding of social phenomena and the value of the ideas required in this process. *Neither prosperity nor war will solve the problems of modern society. Like sheep at the approach of a storm, civilized humanity vaguely feels the presence of danger. And we are driven by anxiety toward the ideas that deal with the mystery of our ills.* (Carrel, 1939: 2).

Interestingly enough, humankind has invested since ancient times more effort in the development of technology than in the development of techniques that could help to improve the understanding of its mental performance. The outer world was and still is far more accessible than the inner world of people. One invention follows the other: wheel, cart, knife, gun, car, plane, phone, and computer. Each invention was a proclamation of the power of human beings over nature; of our marvelous ability to identify problems and solve them (as long as they were defined in a clear and understandable format).

Medicine solves problems of heart failure using the technology of cardiac catheterization. Education solves problems related to students' attention with the use of computers in schools. Cosmetics uses laser beams for facial skin treatments. The list is long. The success in this direction has been larger than expected. The connection between a situation that can be solved mechanically and its solution falls in an area where thought has been trained to act. For centuries, the concrete materialist world manifested itself in clear and strong tones, from the wheel to the spacecraft and it will continue to do so if we maintain the same point of view, the same attitude toward the surroundings and ourselves. One reason for this attitude is that our mind is so constructed as to delight in contemplating simple facts. (Carrel, 1939).

We can speculate in one or other direction, since our knowledge of people's mind is so incomplete. Our contribution can only come from awareness of the limitation of this knowledge, adding the intention to seek ways to upgrade the implementation of mental abilities that go beyond the concrete observable and measurable world. To be sure, this does not mean going into a spiritual trance or fasting until enlightenment is attained. Enlarging the planes of the human action scenario means giving place for the thinkable ethical principles that come with every human act to manifest themselves. This place has to be moved from the penumbra to the place where the rays of human concern for moral and ethical principles can be applied. This is not an easy task.

BRINGING ETHICS INTO THE SCHEME

The essence of moral and ethical principles is a subtle one. It emerges from philosophical premises which in more than one occasion can display more questions than answers, more confusion than certitude. Even so the discussion of what is ethics cannot be overlooked. Varela challenges us with his declaration in the beginning of his book *Ethical Know-How* saying that "Ethics is closer to wisdom than to reason, closer to understanding what is good than to correctly adjudicating particular situations" (Varela, 1999:3).

This opening statement points clearly to the problematic situation we are involved with. The confusion around the meaning of ethics is waiting for clarification. Are we speaking of knowing what or knowing how? Or maybe it is a differentiation that minimizes itself when ethical concerns are involved? Varela differentiates between "thinking about" and "doing of". This is not enough to explain what ethics deals with but it can demonstrate the relationship between human actions and thoughts about the actions. These are not thoughts regarding planning, evaluation of consequences or marketing. These are thoughts that relate to the moral responsibility of actions undertaken.

Ethics is related to the evaluation of people's actions. Such evaluation has been done since ancient times and continues to be present today. Sometimes it is implemented by the system, such as laws reinforcing economic benefits for low class families, accessibility for people with disabilities or caretakers for special education students. A cooperative feeling of group responsibility is enhanced through the administration of public resources emerging from what we can call ethical principles. The *what* connects with the *how* through visible and implementable rules and regulations. Yet, we should not forget that slavery was publically accepted not so many years ago and prostitution is still legally approved all around the world. Cooperation and administration are not always part of the ethical circle.

Without interfering with the great work that philosophers have done elucidating ethics, it would be of great benefit to accept that the only reason ethics exists is because people make mistakes, harming themselves and others. The study of ethics is bound to explain the way that mistakes can be avoided. Not mistakes such as buying the wrong type of bread, but mistakes in taking the wrong action when speaking, thinking or doing. Such wrong actions can be measured according to two parameters: the inner feeling of the doer and the consequences of the action.

Ethics can be known through awareness of the existence of a value dimension in the action. Ethics cannot be taught or explained. The ethic postulate can be claimed, defended or contradicted through reasoning based on logic but only for the sake of "making a point". The ethic truth embedded in the action stands by itself, even if not accepted, irradiating its qualities without needing defense.

Ethics is the normative expression of the invisible foundations of values which lead people to act, unrelatedly to the object of their action. The ethical principles guide the doers in their interaction with their environment, independently of the time parameter. The now action can activate the other now and after. In both cases, the doer influences the other. The relationship between one person and another can originate from direct or indirect connection. Drawing from Martin Buber's writings, the direct connection implies a living dialogical event involving responsive voices (I-Thou) which differs from situations where the indirect connection presumes that a single perspective expands the realm of the same and objectifies all otherness (I-It) (Wegerif & Major, 2019). The relationship between I and Thou or I and It demands respect precisely because they are strangers to I, whoever it is. If we switch from I-It mode to I-Thou mode, we find that these terms, technology, education and humanity do not so much refer to substantive areas of a reality already "out there", but to orientations that we can take up and that shape our ways of thinking and of being. Building on Buber's approach, Wegerif & Major argue that constructive dialogue with technology is not only possible, but essential, taking the form of opening a dialogic space, (Buber's "das Zwischen" or the "space of the 'in-between'") which to their opinion has heterogenically manifestations depending primarily on the mediating technology (Wegerif & Major, 2019: 109).

The existing tension between ethical and non-ethical actions is a theoretical fact. In reality we live in a patriarchal society where authority and control trap all theories in the appropriation of truth and transform them into instruments of domination through the justification of control of the other for the sake of a superior good (Maturana in Eisler, 1991: xiv). The degree of the tension rises proportionally to the relationship between individuals and organizations. Individual human beings are bound to take infinite decisions during their lifetimes in either way, ethical or non-ethical. In the first case, awareness of moral responsibility is present. In the second case it can be or not. If it is present and the action taken contradicts it, the individual chooses the harming position, ignoring themselves and the other. Frankfurt explains this situation using the terminology "the principle of alternate possibilities" which states "that a person is morally responsible for what he has done only if he could have done otherwise" (Frankfurt, 1969: 829). This interesting perspective fails to provide a solution when coercion or threat are present but it opens a wide range of opportunities for being morally responsible when the choice is given. These are the critical situations that we want to explore in this time, when technology is leading the way, unaware of the ethical consequences for society's welfare.

THE ENTRANCE OF CYBERNETICS

After World War II, mathematician and philosopher Norbert Wiener, and Mexican physiologist Arturo Rosenblueth, started developing systems that could establish communication between people and technology, cybernetics. Working with engineers and medical doctors they developed devices that could replace a lost sensory mode, thus creating a breakthrough towards the connection between people and machines. Wiener moved from the implementation of mathematical theories that would be able to predict anti-aircraft fire during the war to the elaboration of stronger connections between high technologies and people in "a human – rather than the inhuman use", (Wiener,1989) as he used to say. This approach requires an objective point of view based on the following:

1) The ability to identify linking points between technology and humanity.
2) The commitment to activate moral and ethical principles in every action.
3) The understanding that machines are products of people's creation.
4) The possibility to take decisions beneficial to those involved in the situation.

These four premises, sequenced from the simplest to the more complex, are components required in the practical implementation of an attitude that can supervise human actions when using technologies, from the hammer up to the thinking robot. For each of the four premises pre-requisites and consequences apply, widening the scope of their existence, linking philosophy with practical activities. They present an ordered protocol of activation of rational considerations embedded in a very subtle plane of human existence: awareness. None of this premises can take place without consciousness of the role of the human being in life.

Cybernetics' impact on society is widely recognized, changing priorities, methodologies and communication features. In many cases, the *what* is more important than the *how*. What to eat is more important than how food was produced. What to learn is more important than how that learning is done. What cures sickness is more important than how the sickness is cured.

The technological approach conveying immediate results for almost every action done has permeated the tissue of human common sense, changing patience to impatience, problem-solving to trouble-shooting, commerce to marketing and so on. But, on the other side, technologies have provided uncountable numbers of solutions for important activities in society: Safe piloting of planes, use of solar cookers in Africa, support for weak hearts, communication with phones and computers, calculators, sound and light entertainment accessories, behavioral training through computerized programs and many others. Every day and hour a new app is climbing the stage, receiving hundreds of "likes".

Order and chaos combine constantly in a dynamic feature that makes it impossible to discern which is which. In this chaos-order millieu we need to identify which is which and how they manifest in practical situations, since we are aware that new relations between people and machines emerge at an exponential pace. We speak of assistive technology versus adaptive technology and we attach a definition to each of these creations. Assistive technology is thus considered as items or equipment used to improve functional capabilities of living beings with disabilities and adaptive technology is considered as electronic and technology information access (Forman, 2007). In this case, technology is extremely useful to supply needs of living beings that for some reason cannot perform in their natural capacities. Who will be using these technological facilities? Will it be those that need them or those that can afford them? How is society going to take the right action for their welfare?

We also speak of digital humanities, trying to understand what this new discipline is. Wikipedia provides the following explanation: *Digital humanities (DH) is an area of scholarly activity at the intersection of computing or digital technologies and the disciplines of the humanities. It includes systematic use of digital resources in the humanities, as well as the analysis of their application*" (Wikipedia, 2020).

Two search results mentioned in the cited web page need to be taken in account:

1) Digital Humanities both employs technology in the pursuit of humanities research and subjects technology to humanistic questioning and interrogation, often simultaneously.

2) The printed word is no longer the main medium for knowledge production and distribution.

Are we comfortable with these two? What questions are we posing to technology? Do we accept the second one as complete truth, or are they worth some research and discussion? Can the two declarations co-exist concurrently?

One of the major manifestations of technology is found in the field of education. Not only the use of smart teaching boards and computers, calculators and tablets in the classroom, but also the invisible aspect of no-teacher programs. MOOC (Massive Open Online Courses) format is conquering the international scene. Access to information, here and now, is easy and manageable by the student. There is no need to connect to the teacher's method and syllabus. Whenever and wherever the student wants, the knowledge can be distilled from internet sites. Students rely on this system. The only limitation is the ability to communicate with the electronic media.

Imitating the marketing methodology, personalization in education took place, not only delivering information but also offering updates of students' enrolments, deadlines or other educational materials that contributed to their learning (Ashman et Al., 2014). Another aspect that needs to be taken into account is that personalization has a bidirectional feature embedded in Web 2.0 systems developed today, including interaction and responsiveness. The responsiveness component enables the system to recognize users' needs, direct them to the right information (Brusilovsky, 2001), improve learning outcomes (Brusilovsky, 2003) and increase the speed of learning (Boyle, 1994). There is more to it when we dig deeper in the issue. Personalization of e-learning can offer students the kind of content that matches their preferred learning modality, assuming that in such conditions the learning will be achieved more easily. The benefits of e-learning on this side of the coin are enormous.

The problems start when we look at the other side of the coin. Personalization means that in a systematic way, the actions of the user of the technology will be recorded and incorporated into a virtual reservoir where this data will be taken care of, sorted and matched to previously prepared elements corresponding to defined parameters. (Sullins, 2019). This eliminates privacy. The stimuli–response Skinnerian protocol will supply the "personalized" responses to some of the actions. Others will lead to escalated bodies of knowledge where modulated analysis will confirm or reject the prepared diversified online trajectory. The user of the technology surrenders to the technological maneuvers underlying its use. Technology has the ability to get information on the user quickly, constantly and invisibly. Not only what the user is doing, but how. How long does it take to reply? From where to where did they go? How accurate were the searches? Etc. It also has the ability to decide which information is relevant to serve objectives defined by economic and commercial interests.

Information on how you can use the system in order to learn better and how you can maintain your private interests locked in your minds' vault is not displayed as it should be. Is this an ethical failure of the management of the site or is it part of the web culture that uses personalization to learn about the user and manipulate their actions? When is the user asked for permission to have their movement followed? This permission is asked when the user enters the site, in a very polite modality: cookies are offered. Indeed, web developers coined the term intelligently. "We use cookies to personalize content and ads, to provide social media features and to analyse our traffic. We also disclose information about your use of our site with our social media, advertising and analytics partners. Additional details are available in our cookie policy ..." Who wants to reject a properly served invitation? The "cookies" will enable the website owner to *personalize* the use. This is one of the pitfalls in the personalization process. If there is a possibility of harming the user/student/learner when using e-learning technologies, should we stop its implementation until the harmful situations are solved? Should we consider ethical elements in this issue or are they not in the scope of this technology?

The dilemma between traditional education and technology-based education reaches the universities at times when there is an increment in online training courses that not only supply the contents of the course but also provide video conference facilities and a cooperative international infrastructure that enables students from all around the world to participate in – or review later – classes of courses. Libraries are being digitized in great quantities. Education moves towards computerization at a great pace and it spreads horizontally and vertically towards other levels of education.

Industry is a great consumer of cybernetics, providing the perfect scenario for technology to manifest itself. From the design of chain production protocols up to camera surveillance and minimizing energy costs through customers' engagement, technology is the perfect servant for industrialized production. The simple motto "less for more" strongly guides the actions of entrepreneurs, production designers and investors. The mass production idea overflows the boundaries of the industry permeating silently into society. "More" is a need. "Less" is the source.

Is this simple outcome, which seems so natural today, a topic that should be studied or considered at some time? How much understanding is required from those using the technological tools in order to feel "comfortable" with them? Do I need to know what is happening when I switch the lights on in my home using a mechanical wall switch or is it good enough that I know that it puts the lights on in my room? If I don't get the explanation, does this mean that I am not a worthy intelligent person? Is this situation the same when I use a "smart-home" device to put the lights on? Does this happen in industry too? How much does the operator of the management device need to know in order to be responsible for activating it? Does this disqualify some potential candidates from the job? How does this requisite influence social status and financial position of members of society? Should we avoid asking ourselves these questions?

JOINING ROUTES

There can be a tangent point between ethics and technology which is visible and researchable only under one condition: moving to an angle where moral and ethical considerations are visible. This movement requires a continuous effort from those willing to see it. Those willing to move to a place where the components involved in the phenomena will be taken into consideration, will be able to see the tangent point.

This situation was seen by scientists Marvin Minsky (1968) and Raymond Kurzweil (1987) who wrote about the relations between human beings and artificial intelligence, refining the emergent concept of *transhumanism*. The increasing development of technological applications in human dimensions moved philosophers Nick Bostrom and David Pearce to find the World Transhumanist Association (WTA), an NGO that advocates the recognition of transhumanism as a legitimate movement of scientific and socio-political research (Tárraga, 2017:95).

The WTA provided an inclusive definition of transhumanism: *The study of the ramifications, promises and potential dangers of technologies that will allow us to overcome human limitations fundamentals and related study of the ethical issues involved in the development and use of such technologies.* (Tarraga, 2017:93) The acceptance of this definition compels us to move to an angle where new parameters are included in the relationship between technology and people. The ethical component in the definition is not a philosophical subject for discussion but an element that has to be included when taking the actions stated when using technologies. Two important branches of the technological spectrum appear in the definition: development and use. According to the definition, the construct "people-machine" will be studied for the identification of those characteristics that are ethically acceptable in a normative caring society, both during the development and the use of the technological products. Yet, the main argument for this group remains the priority given to the improvement of human performance using technological features. In simple words: "Transhumanism suggests supporting new technologies without ethical limitations." (Tarraga, 2017:96)

The two platforms, the technological milieu and the ethical principles that underlie every human action meet in the interface called "use" in a very clear and specific way through the understanding that technologies have two poles that are connected.

The "designer" pole and the "user" pole. Technology designers usually benefit from their creation. Users not always do. One of the most common examples is the use of smartphones by young adults which might influence Acute Acquired Comitant Esotropia (a kind of strabismus) development in adolescents (Lee et al., 2016). The distance between the two poles invites a third component to act: The intelligent use of technology. Questioning the definition of "intelligent use" is the responsibility of ethics which cannot remain anonymous in those situations.

The development and the use of technologies in a responsible manner is the real importance of its presence, enhancing a byproduct which influences the developer/user in a positive or damaging way. Neuroscience research can contribute to the evaluation of consequences of the use of technological devices which will help to avoid the parsimony of accepting unknown consequences of their use. The concern for the welfare of those in contact with technologies is a must in the next era.

One field that we have overlooked is the economical one. What are the economic consequences of the use of technology? How is the financial resource of society divided in this 4IR? Does the distribution of wealth accumulated by successful technological startups contribute to diminish poverty, or should we look to the other side when the differences in income numbers are showing? What is the tradeoff between developing more and more intelligent devices that serve society and the impact it has in economy models? Will artificial intelligent devices supply answers on how the lower classes in society will have access to their benefits? Or will they be limited to those that can afford them? Is governmental regulation going to take care of the establishment of equal benefits for people independently of their bank account?

Using complex system analysis, it could be possible to identify the components of the new situation that will emerge from the use of technologies by and for human beings. For this purpose, Edgar Morin's conception of complexity, sustaining the necessity for complexification rather than reduction in order to make phenomena intelligible, can be of great value (Eriksson, 1997). An objective description of the components, relations and influences in any dynamic structure is considered by Morin as a principle that has to be implemented in complex system analysis: *To conceive the principle of complexity, it is not sufficient to associate the antagonistic ideas in a concurrent and complementary way. The very character of the association also has to be considered: organization that transforms each of the terms in the process of looping.* (Morin 1977:381). The outcome of the former is none other but the inclusion of ethics as a permanent component in the modelling practices of organizations active in the 4IR.

THE FINAL CHORD

4IR technologies can increase efficiency and safety, eliminate poverty and reduce inequality if economy strategies will be applied in that direction. Revealing the existence of the ethic platform and getting to know the components embedded in it will transform blind users of technology into open eyed clients who can take proper decisions to assure that efficiency is understood in all its dimensions, as well as safety. In other words, it is of high necessity and importance that provision of means to recognize the invisible and subtle components of technological entities interacting with people and the environment applied, so as to be on the "supporting" side of existence and not on the "destroying" side.

Once developed, technology follows a self-sustaining evolutionary path with the dynamic that whatever can be developed must be developed. Technology is influencing the environment industrially and socially. It is not possible to isolate one from the other. Industrial technologies are used by people, developed by people and serve people. not only privately but also organizational-wise. The implications of the use of technology in organizations have been mentioned with a worried tone by Markus and Robey. Building on the work of Jeffrey Pfeffer's on Organization Theories, (Pfeffer, 1982) they stated that after reviewing causal analysis of the organization-technology behavior it appears that there exists and emergent perspective due to which *organizational change emerges from an unpredictable interaction between information technology and its human and organizational users.* (Markus, 1988:585). Once more the ethical conundrum uprising from the use of technology requires our attention.

Limiting the boundaries of technology application to outputs and investments creates a non-realistic model of the forces involved. These forces are basically commercial and have to be identified in order to assure they will serve the overall purpose the leaders of society have to consider and follow: physical and mental welfare of living beings. Evaluation of outcomes from an ethical point of view is required.

This brings us to a new level of discussion: the leadership of society. The 4IR is an offspring of people's need to organize time. Categories help with this organization. Thus we create boundaries in time that do not really exist and we speak about the Agricultural Revolution, the Technological Revolution and so on. What really happens is that there is an evolving movement of people's thought, from primitive to sophisticated, from very concrete to more abstract. A landscape was a landscape to be seen, then it was drawn, then it was photographed, then it was created in a screen. From real to virtual. Following the thoughts… abstract and untouchable too. This lead the way for action.

We are running so fast that we are not able to remember how it started and what guided us. The suggestion is clear: the imperative and crucial agenda for the 4IR time is clear and loud. Stop. Not the production or the development. Stop momentarily the *doing* in order to think about what technological industry does. Stop in order to introduce the ideas that will produce benefit for those involved in the use. Stop so that you can invest in a world-wide ethical forum that can study, research and formulate ethical global principles preparing society for this era. Stop to provide the proper educational means to protect the people developing and using the technology. "Regarding human identity, a relationship between humans and non-human organisms is generated as an assembly of a subject-system in the post humanist era. In education, this revolution modifies teaching and learning processes, methods, educational technologies and curricula. (Fabela, 2018:7) *It is, from our point of view, a scientific-industrial revolution and a radical change of paradigm, because it involves nothing less than a transformation of humanity.* (Schwab, 2017, p.13). It is a new way of seeing, living and understanding reality, of relating to others, of living in the world and in the universe.

The fundamentals are based on the union of intelligently evaluated production systems in all stages of the development of a product or process, in order to generate impact and benefit in efficiency and productivity. There are four elements on which the 4IR is based: instantaneity, virtualization, decentralization and modularization. The changes that are taking place have been classified by the World Economic Forum in categories relevant to society development. The technological risks appear to be on two polar extremes: increasing use of cybernetics by society and cyber-attacks. Both are not surprising at all. They emerge from a poor ethical oriented society management growing from destructive education and ignoring the needs and capacities of the human being (WEFORUM, 2017).

This drives us to understand that we have to add a new dimension to our concerns in the 4IR. The bioethic dimension that has been integrated in the last century in science to monitor scientific experiments has to be included in the actions in the technological plane. Moving, back and forth, from a philosophical concern to a practical one is not a luxury that we can choose not to invest in. It is a pre-requisite for the implementation of guidelines that will take into account the invisible influence of technology in the physical brain construct as pointed out by neuroscience researchers.

As Pascuale Leone and others mention: "The brain, as the source of human behavior, is by design molded by environmental changes and pressures, physiologic modifications, and experiences... changes in the input of any neural system, or in the targets or demands of its efferent connections, lead to system plasticity" (Pascuale Leone, Amedi, Fregni, Merabet, 2005). The human brain is a treasure that needs to be guarded.

The use of Artificial Intelligence and sophisticated and non-sophisticated technologies modify the brain not only in the neuroscience lab. The emission of induced electromagnetic vibrations by electronic devices designed by human beings will continuously be received, in an unconscious manner by the whole environment. Trees, animals, human beings will be more predisposed to connect with and thus be influenced by. (Tanim, 2016) This process is not new. It has been taking place and has been a source of interest for researches in this field in the last fifteen years. These researchers fall dichotomically in two categories: those that claim that their work has not supplied any clear conclusions regarding the relationship between the activation of the electromagnetic fields and its consequences on the health of living beings, and those that present the opposite position, claiming that either there is a clear evidence of influence or there is no influence at all.

A comprehensive report submitted by an independent advisory group in April 2012 to the Health Protection Agency in the UK dealing with health effects from radiofrequency electromagnetic field presents a clear picture of the situation: "Although a substantial amount of research has been conducted in this area, there is no convincing evidence that Radio Frequency field exposure below guideline levels causes health effects in adults or children". They also add: "It is clear that radio frequency sources give rise to electric and magnetic fields and these fields in turn can induce currents or raise temperature inside the human body."

The situation is different in industry, or what Valentina et al. call "production spaces". *It is noticed that the presence of electromagnetic fields of low frequency has a negative influence on cardio-vascular system of workers, observing a pulse reducing, a change of ECG, a decrease of visual and auditory reception power and a showing up of tiredness state.* (Valentina et al., 2010: 4).

If we want to care for human beings: *We have to rewire the tech industry's culture if ethics is ever to become a priority. We urgently need all the thoughtful technologists we can get; people who care enough to make a difference, who are curious and inclusive enough to navigate this crucial industry towards better futures.* (Bowles, 2018: 197,206)

KIaus Schwab, Founder and Executive Chairman of the World Economic Forum points, *In the end, it all comes down to people and values. We need to shape a future that works for all of us by putting people first and empowering them. In its most pessimistic, dehumanized form, the Fourth Industrial Revolution may indeed have the potential to "robotize" humanity and thus to deprive us of our heart and soul. But as a complement to the best parts of human nature—creativity, empathy, stewardship—it can also lift humanity into a new collective and moral consciousness based on a shared sense of destiny. It is incumbent on us all to make sure the latter prevails"* (Schwab, 2016:8).

The complex environment where living beings are moving requires more than research on the influences of electromagnetism on their constitution. We need to prove in an extensive way that for our safety, ethic regulations should be considered and implemented following a precise protocol as a routine for industry, health and educational fields.

REFERENCES

Ashman, H., Brailsford, T., Cristea, A. I., Sheng, Q. Z., Stewart, C., Toms, E. G., & Wade, V. (2014). The ethical and social implications of personalization technologies for e-learning. *Information & Management, 51*(6), 819–832. doi:10.1016/j. im.2014.04.003

Bowles, C. (2018). *Future Ethics*. NowNext Press.

Boyle, C., & Encarnación, A. O. (1994). MetaDoc: An adaptive hypertext reading system. *User Modeling and User-Adapted Interaction, 4*(1), 1–19. doi:10.1007/ BF01142355

Brusilovsky, P. (2001). Adaptive Hypermedia. User Modeling and User-Adapted Interaction, 11(1-2), 87–110. doi:10.1023/A:1011143116306

Brusilovsky, P. (2003). Adaptive navigation support in educational hypermedia: The role of student knowledge level and the case for meta-adaptation. *British Journal of Educational Technology, 34*(4), 487–497. doi:10.1111/1467-8535.00345

Carrel, A. (1939). *Man, The Unknown*. Harper & Brothers.

Eisler, R. (1991). *El Cáliz y la Espada. Nuestra Historia, nuestro Futuro*. Editorial Cuatro Vientos.

Ellul, J. (1964). *The Technological Society*. Knopf.

Eriksson, D. (1997). A principal exposition of Jean-Louis Le Moigne's systemic theory. *Cybernetics & Human Knowing, 4*(2–3), 33–77. http://citeseerx.ist.psu.edu/ viewdoc/download?doi=10.1.1.127.1115&rep=rep1&type=pdf

Fabela, A. M. R., & Pedroza Flores, R. (2018). Retos de la formación profesional del diseñador industrial en la Cuarta Revolución Industrial (4RI). In Revista Iberoamericana para la Investigación y el Desarrollo Educativo (Vol. 8). doi:10.23913/ ride.v8i16.330

Forman, T. (2007). *Assessing for Adaptive Technology Needs*. Slide Presentation, Texas A&M University.

Frankfurt, G. G. (1969). Alternate Possibilities and Moral Responsibility. *The Journal of Philosophy*, *66*(23), 829–839. doi:10.2307/2023833

Guastello, S. J. (1995). *Chaos, catastrophe, and human affairs*. Lawrence Erlbaum Associates, Publishers.

Lee, H. S., Park, S. W., & Heo, H. (2016). Acute acquired comitant esotropia related to excessive Smartphone use. *BMC Ophthalmology*, *16*(1), 37. doi:10.118612886-016-0213-5 PMID:27061181

Markus, M. L., & Robey, D. (1988). Information Technology and Organizational Change: Causal Structure in Theory and Research. *Management Science*, *34*(5), 583–598. doi:10.1287/mnsc.34.5.583

Morin, E. (1977). *La Méthode La Nature de la Nature*. Editions du Seuil.

Pascual-Leone, A., Amedi, A., Fregni, F., & Merabet, L. B. (2005). The Plastic Human Brain Cortex. *Annual Review of Neuroscience*, *28*(1), 377–401. doi:10.1146/annurev.neuro.27.070203.144216

Pfeffer, J. (1982). Organizations and Organization Theory. Pacific Sociological Rev., 20, 241-261.

Schwab, K. (2016). *The Fourth Industrial Revolution : what it means, how to respond*. Retrieved from https://www.weforum.org/agenda/2016/01/the-fourth-industrial-revolution-what-it-means-and-how-to-respond/# 24.4.20

Schwab, K. (2017). *La Cuarta Revolución Industrial*. Ciudad de México.

Sullins, J. (2019). Information Technology and Moral Values. Stanford Encyclopedia of Philosophy Archive, (Summer), 1–52.

Tanim, M. M. Z. (2016). *Electromagnetic Radiation and Human Health*. Electromagnetic Radiation and Human Health; doi:10.13140/RG.2.2.13195.28962

Tarraga Albacete, F. (2017). *Ventajas y Desventajas pedagógicas en torno a la irrupción de las NTICX* (Tesis Doctoral). Universidad de Castilla La Mancha, Albacete.

Valentina, S. E., Cristiana-Zizi, R., Elena, C., & Poinescu, A. A. (2010). *Electromagnetic Pollution of Environment*. Academic Press.

Varela, F. J. (1999). *Ethical know-how: Action, wisdom, and cognition*. Stanford University Press.

Velázquez Fernández, H. (2009). Transhumanismo, Libertad e Identidad Humana. *Themata. Revista de Filosofia.*, *41*, 577–590.

WEF. (2017). Retrieved from https://www.weforum.org/reports/the-global-risks-report-2017 3.4.2020

Wegerif, R., & Major, L. (2019). *Buber, educational technology, and the expansion of dialogic space subjectivity in which two separate consciousnesses engage.* Academic Press.

Wikipedia. (2020). *Digital Humanities.* Retrieved from: https://en.wikipedia.org/wiki/Digitalhumanities

Compilation of References

11 . Countries leading the charge on Renewable energy. (2019). *Climate council*. Retrieved from https://www.climatecouncil.org.au/11-countries-leading-the-charge-on-renewable-energy/

A Short History of the Fourth Industrial Revolution. (n.d.). *IoT World Today*. Retrieved May 15, 2020, from https://iotworldtoday.com/2016/11/02/short-history-fourth-industrial-revolution/

ABET. (2015). *Criteria for accrediting engineering programs.* Engineering Technology Accreditation Commission. Retrieved from https://www.abet.org/wp-content/uploads/2015/04/criteria-eac-2010-2011.pdf

Ackermann, M. (2015). *Reporting and Big Data. Big Data as one megatrend of industry 4.0 and the impacts on controlling.* GRIN Verlag.

AdditiveG. E. (2018). Retrieved from https://www.ge.com/additive/blog/new-manufacturing-milestone-30000-additive-fuel-nozzles

Aguayo-Torres, M. C., Gómez, G., & Poncela, J. (2015). *Wired/Wireless Internet Communications: 13th International Conference, WWIC 2015, Malaga, Spain, May 25-27, Revised Selected Papers.* Malaga: Springer.

Akbar, M. A., Rashid, M. M., & Embong, A. H. (2018). Technology Based Learning System in Internet of Things (IoT) Education. In *7th International Conference on Computer and Communication Engineering (ICCCE)* (pp. 192-197). Kuala Lumpur, Malaysia: IEEE. 10.1109/ICCCE.2018.8539334

Ake, K., Clemons, J., Cubine, M., & Lilly, B. (2016). Information Technology for Manufacturing: Reducing Costs and Expanding Capabilities (Illustrated ed.). Boca Raton: CRC Press.

Alao, A. (2019). *How telecentres contribute to women empowerment in rural communities: Case of Western Cape, South Africa* (Doctoral dissertation). Faculty of Commerce.

Alao, A., Lwoga, T. E., & Chigona, W. (2017, May). Telecentres use in rural communities and women empowerment: Case of Western Cape. In *International Conference on Social Implications of Computers in Developing Countries* (pp. 119-134). Springer. 10.1007/978-3-319-59111-7_11

Aldersey-Williams, H. (2011). *The new tin ear: Manufacturing, materials and the rise of the user-maker. RSA Design Projects.* RSA.

Almada-Lobo, F. (2016). The Industry 4.0 revolution and the future of Manufacturing Execution Systems (MES). *Journal of Innovation Management, 3*(4), 16–21. doi:10.24840/2183-0606_003.004_0003

Amesheva, I., Clark, A., & Payne, J. (2019). Financing for Youth Entrepreneurship in Sustainable Development. *Sustainable Development Goals: Harnessing Business to Achieve the SDGs through Finance, Technology, and Law Reform,* 253-273.

Anderson, T. (2008). *Disruptive, Online Education to Go Main Stream.* Virtual Canuck blog entry.

Anderson, T., & Wark, N. (2004). Why Do Teachers Get to Learn the Most?: A Case Study of a Course Based on Student Creation of Learning Objects. *E-Journal of Instructional Science and Technology.*

Anderson, C. (2012). *Makers: The next industrial revolution.* Crown Business.

Andriole, S. J. (2017). *Five myths about digital transformation.* Academic Press.

Anton, P. S., Silberglith, R., & Schveeder, J. (2011). *The Global Technology Revolution Bio/Nano/Materials Trends and their Synergies with Information Technology.* RAND.

Anton, P. S., Silberglith, R., & Schveeder, J. (2011). *The Global Technology Revolution Bio/Nano/Materials Trends and Their Synergies with Information Technology.* RAND.

Armaroli, N., & Balzani, V. (2016). Solar Electricity and Solar Fuels: Status and Perspectives in the Context of the Energy Transition. *Chemistry (Weinheim an der Bergstrasse, Germany), 22*(1), 32–57. doi:10.1002/chem.201503580 PMID:26584653

Arnaud, M. (2017). *Detroit: The dream is now: The design, art, and resurgence of an American city.* Abram Books.

Ashman, H., Brailsford, T., Cristea, A. I., Sheng, Q. Z., Stewart, C., Toms, E. G., & Wade, V. (2014). The ethical and social implications of personalization technologies for e-learning. *Information & Management, 51*(6), 819–832. doi:10.1016/j.im.2014.04.003

Association of College and Research Libraries. (2014). *First part of the draft framework for information literacy for higher education.* Retrieved on 2019/03/20 from: http://acrl.ala.org/ilstandards/wp-content/uploads/2014/02/Framework-for-IL-for-HE-Draft-1-Part-1.pdf

Atkinson, P. (2011). Orchestral manoeuvres in design. In Open Design Now. Amsterdam: BIS.

Attwood, H. E. (2014). *Researching QoL change from ICT training, access and use at South African telecentres: empowerment through participatory research* (Doctoral dissertation).

Attwood, H., Diga, K., Braathen, E., & May, J. (2013). Telecentre functionality in South Africa: Re-enabling the community ICT access environment. *The Journal of Community Informatics, 9*(4).

Atzori, L., Iera, A., & Morabito, G. (2010). The Internet of Things: A survey. *Computer Networks, 54*(15), 2787–2805. doi:10.1016/j.comnet.2010.05.010

Avdjiev, S., Bruno, V., Koch, C., & Shin, H. S. (2019). The dollar exchange rate as a global risk factor: Evidence from investment. *IMF Economic Review*, *67*(1), 151–173. doi:10.105741308-019-00074-4

Ayentimi, D. T., & Burgess, J. (2019). Is the fourth industrial revolution relevant to sub-Sahara Africa? *Technology Analysis and Strategic Management*, *31*(6), 641–652. doi:10.1080/095373 25.2018.1542129

Bahar, H., Egeland, J., & Steenblik, R. (2013). *Domestic Incentive Measures for Renewable Energy with Possible Trade Implications*. OECD Trade and Environment Working Papers.

Bakhshalipour, V., Sareshkeh, S. K., & Azizi, B. (2019). The effect of the use of information and communication technology skills with empowerment indicators on staff in the Ministry of Sports and Youth of Islamic Republic of Iran (Case Study in Youth and Sports General Directorate of Guilan Province). *Arquivos de Ciências do Esporte*, *6*(3). Advance online publication. doi:10.17648/aces.v6n3.2938

Balachandran, B. M., & Prasad, S. (2017). *Challenges and benefits of deploying big data analytics in the cloud for business intelligence*. Academic Press.

Balogun, J., Hope Hailey, V., & Gustafsson, S. (2015). Exploring Strategic Change (4th ed.). Academic Press.

Balouza, M. (2019). The Impact of Information and Communication Technologies on the Human Development in the Gulf Cooperation Council Countries: An Empirical Study. *Management Studies and Economic Systems*, *4*(2), 79–113.

Barriers to renewable energy Technologies. (2017). *Union of Concerned Scientists*.

Bartodziej, C. J. (2017). *The Concept Industry 4.0: An Empirical Analysis of Technologies and Applications in Production Logistics*. Springer. doi:10.1007/978-3-658-16502-4

Baskarada, S., & Koronios, A. (2012). Exploring the Effects of Enterprise Instant Messaging Presence Information on Employee Attendance in a Distributed Workforce: An Ethnographic Study of a Large Professional Services Organization. *International Journal of e-Collaboration*, *8*(3), 1–18. doi:10.4018/jec.2012070101

Becker, L. (2012). Design, ethics and group myopia. In E. Felton, O. Zelenko, & S. Vaughan (Eds.), *Design and ethics: Reflections on practice*. Routledge.

Bell, E., Bryman, A., & Harley, B. (2018). *Business research methods*. Oxford University Press.

Belluzzo, R. C. B., & Feres, G. G. (2015). Competência em informação, redes de conhecimento e as metas educativas para 2021: reflexões e inter-relações. In Redes de conhecimento e competência em informação: interfaces da gestão, mediação e uso da informação/organização. Rio de Janeiro: Interciência.

Belluzzo, R. C. B. (2007). *Construção de mapas: desenvolvendo competências em informação e comunicação*. Cá Entre Nós.

Benedict, K. (2016). *The Work Ahead 40 months of Hyper - Digital Transformation.* The Center for Future Work.

Benefits of Industry 4.0 - SL Controls. (2018). *SL Controls.* https://slcontrols.com/benefits-of-industry-4-0/

Benias, N., & Markopoulos, A. (2017). A review on the readiness level and cyber-security challenges in Industry 4.0. *South Eastern European Design Automation, Computer Engineering, Computer Networks and Social Media Conference (SEEDA-CECNSM)*, 1-5.

Bergmann, J., & Sams, A. (2012). *Flip Your Classroom: Reach every student in every class every day* (1st ed.). ISTE.

Bhojaraju, G. (2005). Knowledge Management: Why we need it for corporates. *Malaysian Journal of Library and Information Science, 10*(2), 37–50.

Binedell, N. (2015). The Fingers of the strategist. *Fingers of the Strategist,* (11), 14-15.

Bi, Z., Xu, L. D., & Wang, C. (2014). Internet of Things for enterprise systems of modern manufacturing. *IEEE Transactions on Industrial Informatics*, 1537–1546.

Blayone, T. J., Mykhailenko, O., van Oostveen, R., Grebeshkov, O., Hrebeshkova, O., & Vostryakov, O. (2018). Surveying digital competencies of university students and professors in Ukraine for fully online collaborative learning. *Technology, Pedagogy and Education, 27*(3), 279–296. doi:10.1080/1475939X.2017.1391871

Bloem, J., Van Doorn, M., Duivestein, S., Excoffier, D., Maas, R., & Van Ommeren, E. (2014). The fourth industrial revolution. *Things Tighten, 8.*

Boag, P. (2013). *So you want to write a Digital Strategy? Smashing Magazine.*

Boisit, M. (1998). *Knowledge Assets: Securing Competitive Advantage in the Information Economy.* OUP Oxford.

Bolton, T., Goosen, L., & Kritzinger, E. (2020a, March 8). Security Aspects of an Empirical Study into the Impact of Digital Transformation via Unified Communication and Collaboration Technologies on the Productivity and Innovation of a Global Automotive Enterprise. Communications in Computer and Information Science, 1166, 99-113. doi:10.1007/978-3-030-43276-8_8

Bolton, A., Goosen, L., & Kritzinger, E. (2016). Enterprise Digitization Enablement Through Unified Communication and Collaboration. In *Proceedings of the Annual Conference of the South African Institute of Computer Scientists and Information Technologists.* Johannesburg: ACM. 10.1145/2987491.2987516

Bolton, A., Goosen, L., & Kritzinger, E. (2020b). Unified Communication Technologies at a Global Automotive Organization. In D. B. Khosrow-Pour (Ed.), *Encyclopedia of Organizational Knowledge, Administration, and Technologies.* IGI Global Hershey, PA, USA: . doi:10.4018/978-1-7998-3473-1

Booi, S. L., Chigona, W., Maliwichi, P., & Kunene, K. (2019, May). The Influence of Telecentres on the Economic Empowerment of the Youth in Disadvantaged Communities of South Africa. In *International Conference on Social Implications of Computers in Developing Countries* (pp. 152-167). Springer. 10.1007/978-3-030-18400-1_13

Bordignon, D. (2017). The exponential digital world. *Dimension Data Australia*, 1-67.

Botha, J.-A., & Coetzee, M. (2016, June). The influence of biographical factors on adult learner self-directedness in an open distance learning environment. *The International Review of Research in Open and Distributed Learning*, *17*(4), 242–263. doi:10.19173/irrodl.v17i4.2345

Bowles, C. (2018). *Future Ethics*. NowNext Press.

Boyle, C., & Encarnación, A. O. (1994). MetaDoc: An adaptive hypertext reading system. *User Modeling and User-Adapted Interaction*, *4*(1), 1–19. doi:10.1007/BF01142355

Bozzoli, B. (2019). *The ANC vs the Fourth Industrial Revolution - OPINION | Politicsweb*. Retrieved Sept 25, 2019, from https://www.politicsweb.co.za/opinion/the-anc-vs-the-fourth-industrial-revolution

Braungart, M., Mcdonough, W., & Bollinger, A. (2007). Cradle-to-cradle design: creating healthy emissions: a strategy for eco-effective product and system design. *Journal of Cleaner Production*, *15*(13-14), 1337–1348. doi:10.1016/j.jclepro.2006.08.003

Breazeal, C. (2002). *Designing Sociable Robots*. MIT Pres.

Bregman, R. (2017). *Utopia for realists*. Bloomsbury.

Bressan, B. (2014). From Physics to Daily Life: Applications in Informatics, Energy, and Environment (Illustrated ed.). Hoboken: John Wiley & Sons.

Brettel, M., Friederichsen, N., Keller, M., & Rosenberg, M. (2014). How Virtualization, Decentralization and Network Building Change the Manufacturing Landscape: An Industry 4.0 Perspective. *World Academy of Science. Engineering and Technology International Journal of Information and Communication Engineering*, *8*(1), 37–44.

Brown, T. (2009). *Change by design: How design thinking transforms organisations and inspires innovation*. Harper Business.

Brush, K. (2012). *The Power of One: You're the Boss*. Scotts Valley: CreateSpace Independent Publishing Platform.

Brusilovsky, P. (2001). Adaptive Hypermedia. User Modeling and User-Adapted Interaction, 11(1-2), 87–110. doi:10.1023/A:1011143116306

Brusilovsky, P. (2003). Adaptive navigation support in educational hypermedia: The role of student knowledge level and the case for meta-adaptation. *British Journal of Educational Technology*, *34*(4), 487–497. doi:10.1111/1467-8535.00345

Brynjolfsson, E., McAfee, A., & Spence, M. (2014). New world order: Labor, capital, and ideas in the power law economy. *Foreign Affairs, 93*(4), 44–53.

Cadieux, J. (2017). The BNQ21000 standard: the management of sustainable development: from learning to audit. *WIT Transactions on Ecology and The Environment, 226*. Retrieved on 2020/02/24 from: https://www.researchgate.net/publication/320220750_THE_BNQ21000_STANDARD_THE_MANAGEMENT_OF_SUSTAINABLE_DEVELOPMENT_-_FROM_LEARNING_TO_AUDIT

Caiado, R. G. G., Leal Filho, W., Quelhas, O. L. G., de Mattos Nascimento, D. L., & Ávila, L. V. (2018). A literature-based review on potentials and constraints in the implementation of the sustainable development goals. *Journal of Cleaner Production, 198*, 1276–1288. doi:10.1016/j.jclepro.2018.07.102

Cakula, S., & Salem, A. B. M. (2011), Analogy-Based Collaborative Model for e-Learning. *Proceedings of the Annual International Conference on Virtual and Augmented Reality in Education*, 98-105.

Calitz, A. P., Greyling, J. H., & Cullen, M. D. (2014). *South African industry ICT graduate skills requirements*. Southern African Computer Lecturers' *Association*.

Calitz, A. P., Poisat, P., & Cullen, M. (2017). The future African workplace: The use of collaborative robots in manufacturing. *SA Journal of Human Resource Management, 15*(1), 1–11. doi:10.4102ajhrm.v15i0.901

Cameron, N. (2017). *Will robots take your job?* Polity.

Carrel, A. (1939). *Man, The Unknown*. Harper & Brothers.

Carte, T., & Chidambaram, L. (2004). A Capabilities-Based Theory of Technology Deployment in Diverse Teams: Leapfrogging the Pitfalls of Diversity and Leveraging Its Potential with Collaborative Technology. *Journal of the Association for Information Systems, 5*(11-12), 448–471. doi:10.17705/1jais.00060

Caruso, L. (2018). Digital innovation and the fourth industrial revolution: Epochal social changes? *AI & Society, 33*(3), 379–392. doi:10.100700146-017-0736-1

Cascio, W. (2000). Managing a virtual workplace. *The Academy of Management Executive, 14*(3), 81–90. doi:10.5465/ame.2000.4468068

Chappell, D. (2015). *Introducing Azure Machine Learning. In A Guide for Technical Professionals*. Microsoft Corporation.

Charter, M. (2018). Introduction. In M. Charter (Ed.), *Designing for a circular economy*. Routledge. doi:10.4324/9781315113067-1

Cheruvalath, R. (2019). Does studying 'ethics' improve engineering students' meta-moral cognitive skills? *Science and Engineering Ethics, 25*, 583–596. doi:10.100711948-017-0009-x

Chetty, J., & Barlow-Jones, G. (2012, June 26). The Effects of a Social Constructivist Pedagogy on At-Risk Students Completing a Computer Programming Course at a Post-secondary Institution. In *Proceedings of World Conference on Educational Multimedia, Hypermedia and Telecommunications* (pp. 1914 - 1919). Denver: Association for the Advancement of Computing in Education.

Chitla, A. (2012). Impact of Information and Communication Technology on Rural India. *IOSR Journal of Computer Engineering*.

Christensen, C. M., & Raynor, M. E. (2003). *The Innovator's Solution: Creating and Sustaining Successful Growth*. Harvard University Press.

Christiansen, H.-M. (2007). Meeting the Challenge of Communication in offshore software development. In B. Meyer, & M. Joseph (Eds.), *International Conference on Software Engineering Approaches for Offshore and Outsourced Development* (pp. 19-26). Berlin: Springer. 10.1007/978-3-540-75542-5_2

Chun, M. (2010). Taking Teaching to (Performance) Task: Linking Pedagogical and Assessment Practices. *Change: The Magazine of Higher Learning*, *42*(2), 22–29. doi:10.1080/00091381003590795

Codrington, G. T., & Grant-Marshall, S. (2011). *Mind the gap* (2nd ed.). Penguin Books.

Colby, A., & Sullivan, W. (2008). Ethics teaching in undergraduate engineering education. *Journal of Engineering Education*, *97*(3), 327–338. Advance online publication. doi:10.1002/j.2168-9830.2008.tb00982.x

Conlan, E. & Zandvoort, H. (2011). Broadening ethics teaching in engineering: Beyond the individualistic approach. *Science Engineering Ethics*, *17*, 217-232. doi 10.100%11948-010-9305-?

Cook, C. (2014). Transforming the Transportation Industry with Renewable Energy. *Renewable Energy World*. Retrieved from, https://www.renewableenergyworld.com/2014/09/18/transforming-the-transportation-industry-with-renewable-energy/#gref

Correa, T., Pavez, I., & Contreras, J. (2018). Digital inclusion through mobile phones?: A comparison between mobile-only and computer users in internet access, skills and use. *Information Communication and Society*, 1–18. doi:10.1080/1369118X.2018.1555270

Crawford, K. (1996). Vygotskian approaches in human development in the information era. *Educational Studies in Mathematics*, *31*(1-2), 43–62. doi:10.1007/BF00143926Das, S., Day, A., Pal, A., & Roy, N. (2015). Applications of Artificial Intelligence in Machine Learning. *International Journal of Computers and Applications*, *115*(9).

Creswell, J. W. (2014). *Research design qualitative, quantitative, and mixed methods approaches* (4th ed.). SAGE Publications, Inc.

Creswell, J. W. (2014). *Research Design: Qualitative, quantitative and mixed methods approaches*. SAGE Publications, Inc.

Cronin, P., Ryan, F., & Coughlan, M. (2008). Undertaking a literature review: A step-by-step approach. *British Journal of Nursing (Mark Allen Publishing)*, *17*(1), 38–43. doi:10.12968/bjon.2008.17.1.28059 PMID:18399395

Crosby, M., Pattanayak, P., Verma, S., & Kalyanaraman, V. (2016). *Blockchain technology: Beyond bitcoin.* Academic Press.

Cross, J. R., Frazier, A. D., Kim, M., & Cross, T. L. (2018). A comparison of perceptions of barriers to academic success among high-ability students from high- and low-income groups: Exposing poverty of a different kind. *Gifted Child Quarterly*, *62*(1), 111–129. doi:10.1177/0016986217738050

D'Souza, U. J., & Mudin, D. K. (2018, January). Industrial Revolution 4.0: Role of Universities. *Borneo Journal of Medical Sciences*, *12*(1), 1–2.

Daurer, S., Molitor, D., Spann, M., & Manchanda, P. (2016). *Consumer Search Behavior on the Mobile Internet: An Empirical Analysis.* Michigan Ross School of Business.

David, J., & Surmaya, T. (2005). A Best Process Approach for Using ICTs in Development. Intermediate Technology Development Group. The Schumacher Centre for Technology and Development. *IRFD World Forum on Information Society – Tunis 2005*.

De Vaus, D. (2014). *Surveys in social research* (M. Bulmer, Ed.; 6th ed.). Routledge.

Dekker, D., & Rutte, C. (2007). Effective Versus Ineffective Communication Behaviours in Virtual Teams. In *Proceedings of the 40th IEEE Hawaii International Conference on System Sciences* (p. 41). Waikoloa: IEEE.

Delucchi, M. A., & Jacobson, M. Z. (2011). Providing all global energy with wind, water, and solar power, Part II: Reliability, system and transmission costs, and policies. Energy Policy, Elsevier Ltd.

De-Mauro, A., Greco, M., & Grimaldi, M. (2014). What is big data? A consensual definition and a review of key research topics. *AIP Conference Proceedings*, *1644*(1), 97–104.

DFID. (2005). *The economic impact of telecommunication on rural livelihood and poverty reduction.* Available: www.livelihoods.org

Diegel, O., Nordin, A., & Motte, D. (2019). *A practical guide for design for additive manufacturing.* Springer. doi:10.1007/978-981-13-8281-9

Dillon, J. (2010). *New Transmission Line Reaches Milestone.* Retrieved from https://archive.vpr.org/vpr-news/new-transmission-line-reaches-milestone/

Discover industry 4.0 in manufacturing with HARTING. (n.d.). Retrieved May 15, 2020, from http://harting.com/IT/en-gb/topics/industry-40

Dogo, E. M., Salami, A. F., Aigbavboa, C. O., & Nkonyana, T. (2019). Taking cloud computing to the extreme edge: A review of mist computing for smart cities and industry 4.0 in Africa. In *Edge Computing* (pp. 107–132). Springer. doi:10.1007/978-3-319-99061-3_7

Duncombe, R. A. (2014). Understanding the impact of mobile phones on livelihoods in developing countries. *Development Policy Review*, *32*(5), 567–588. doi:10.1111/dpr.12073

Dutton, W. H. (2014). Putting things to work: Social and policy challenges for the Internet of things. *Info*, *16*(3), 1–21. doi:10.1108/info-09-2013-0047

Easterby-Smith, M., Thorpe, R., & Jackson, P. R. (2012). Management research. *Sage*.

EDUCAUSE. (2019). *Horizon Report Preview*. Retrieved from https://er.educause.edu/articles/2010/3/the-role-of-disruptive-technology-in-the-future-of-higher-education

Ehlers, U.-D. (2019). Future Skills and Higher Education "Future Skill Readiness". In *European Distance and E-Learning Network (EDEN) Annual Conference Proceedings* (pp. 85-96). Bruges, Belgium: EDEN.

Einhorn, S. (2012). *Micro-Worlds, Computational Thinking, and 21st Century Learning*. White Paper, Logo Computer Systems Inc.

Eisler, R. (1991). *El Cáliz y la Espada. Nuestra Historia, nuestro Futuro*. Editorial Cuatro Vientos.

Ellabban, O., Abu-Rub, H., & Blaabjerg, F. (2014). Renewable energy resources: Current status, future prospects and their enabling technology. *Renewable & Sustainable Energy Reviews*, *39*, 748–764. doi:10.1016/j.rser.2014.07.113

Ellen Macarthur Foundation. (2012). *Towards the circular economy 1: economic and business rationale for an accelerated transition*. Cowes: Ellen MacArthur Foundation.

Ellul, J. (1964). *The Technological Society*. Knopf.

Eriksson, D. (1997). A principal exposition of Jean-Louis Le Moigne's systemic theory. *Cybernetics & Human Knowing*, *4*(2–3), 33–77. http://citeseerx.ist.psu.edu/viewdoc/download?doi=10.1.1.127.1115&rep=rep1&type=pdf

Errasti, A. (2013). *Global Production Networks: Operations Design and Management* (2nd ed.). CRC Press.

Eşkinat, R. (2016). The Importance of Digital Technologies for Sustainable Development. *Inclusive and Sustainable Development and the Role of Social and Solidarity Economy, 106*.

eTransform Africa. (2012). *The transformational use of information and communication technologies in Africa*. The World Bank and the African Development Bank, with the support of the African Union.

Evans, G. (2019). 10 Years of Learning Design at The Open University: Evolution, Findings and Future Direction. In *European Distance and E-Learning Network (EDEN) Annual Conference Proceedings* (pp. 341-346). Bruges, Belgium: EDEN.

Eynon, R., & Geniets, A. (2016). The digital skills paradox: How do digitally excluded youth develop skills to use the internet? *Learning, Media and Technology*, *41*(3), 463–479. doi:10.1080/17439884.2014.1002845

Fabela, A. M. R., & Pedroza Flores, R. (2018). Retos de la formación profesional del diseñador industrial en la Cuarta Revolución Industrial (4RI). In Revista Iberoamericana para la Investigación y el Desarrollo Educativo (Vol. 8). doi:10.23913/ride.v8i16.330

Faunce, Lubitz, Rutherford, MacFarlane, Moore, Yang, Nocera, Moore, Gregory, Fukuzumi, Yoon, Armstrong, Wasielewski, & Styring. (2013). Energy and environment policy case for a global project on artificial photosynthesis. In Energy & Environmental Science. RSC Publishing.

Fernández-Sanz, L., Gómez-Pérez, J., & Castillo-Martínez, A. (2017). e-Skills Match: A framework for mapping and integrating the main skills, knowledge and competence standards and models for ICT occupations. *Computer Standards & Interfaces*, *51*, 30–42. doi:10.1016/j.csi.2016.11.004

Fink, A. (2016). *How to conduct surveys: A step-by-step guide* (6th ed.). SAGE.

Forman, T. (2007). *Assessing for Adaptive Technology Needs*. Slide Presentation, Texas A&M University.

Frankfurt, G. G. (1969). Alternate Possibilities and Moral Responsibility. *The Journal of Philosophy*, *66*(23), 829–839. doi:10.2307/2023833

Fuad-Luke, A. (2009). *Design activism: Beautiful strangeness for a sustainable world*. Earthscan.

Future technologies will drive Industry 4.0. (n.d.). *World Economic Forum*. Retrieved May 15, 2020, from https://www.weforum.org/agenda/2019/01/future-technologies-will-drive-industry-4-0/

Germany. (2019). *GTAI - Industrie 4.0 – What is it? Gtai.De*. https://www.gtai.de/GTAI/Navigation/EN/Invest/Industries/Industrie-4-0/Industrie-4-0/industrie-4-0-what-is-it.html

Gershenfeld, N. (2005). *Fab: The coming revolution on your desktop – from personal computing to personal fabrication*. Basic Books.

Ghosh, A. (2011). Initiatives in ICT for Rural Development: An Indian Perspective. Global Media Journal: Indian Edition, 2(2).

Giannakopoulos, A. (2012). *Problem solving in academic performance: A study into critical thinking and mathematics content as contributors to successful application of knowledge and subsequent academic performance* (Ph.D. Thesis). University of Johannesburg, South Africa.

Gil, A. C. (2002). *Como elaborar projetos de pesquisa*. Atlas.

Gilchrist, A. (2016). Introducing Industry 4.0. In Industry 4.0. Apress.

Gilchrist, A. (2016). *Industry 4.0: The Industrial Internet of Things*. Apress. doi:10.1007/978-1-4842-2047-4

Glassley. (2010). Geothermal Energy: Renewable Energy and the Environment. In *The Way back Machine*. CRC Press.

Global Climate Change. (n.d.). *Vital signs of the planet*. Retrieved from https://climate.nasa.gov/

Global Trends in Sustainable Energy Investment. Analysis of Trends and Issues in the Financing of Renewable Energy and Energy Efficiency in OECD and Developing Countries. (2007) *United Nations Environment Program*. Retrieved from http://wedocs.unep.org/handle/20.500.11822/7958

Göll, E., & Zwiers, J. (2019). Technological Trends in the MENA Region: The Cases of Digitalization and Information and Communications Technology (ICT). *MENARA, 206*.

Goosen, L., & Van Heerden, D. (2013b). Project-Based Assessment Influencing Pass Rates of an ICT Module at an ODL Institution. In E. Ivala (Ed.), *Proceedings of the 8th International Conference on e-Learning* (pp. 157-164). Cape Town: Academic Conferences and Publishing.

Goosen, L., & Van Heerden, D. (2015). e-Learning Management System Technologies for Teaching Programming at a Distance. In C. Watson (Ed.), *Proceedings of the 10th International Conference on e-Learning (ICEL)* (pp. 116-126). Nassua: Academic Conferences and Publishing International. Retrieved from https://scholar.google.co.za/scholar?oi=bibs&cluster=162553269 38393691479&btnI=1&hl=en

Goosen, L., & Van Heerden, D. (2016). e-Learning Environment Tools to Address Online and Open Distance Education Context Challenges. In R. M. Idrus, & N. Zainuddin (Ed.), *Proceedings of the 11th International Conference on e-Learning (ICEL)* (pp. 275 - 284). Kuala Lumpur, Malaysia: Academic Conferences and Publishing International.

Goosen, L., & Van Heerden, D. (2017). Beyond the Horizon of Learning Programming with Educational Technologies. In U. I. Ogbonnaya, & S. Simelane-Mnisi (Ed.), *Proceedings of the South Africa International Conference on Educational Technologies* (pp. 78 - 90). Pretoria: African Academic Research Forum.

Goosen, L., & Naidoo, L. (2014). Computer Lecturers Using Their Institutional LMS for ICT Education in the Cyber World. In C. Burger, & K. Naudé (Ed.), *Proceedings of the 43rd Conference of the Southern African Computer Lecturers' Association (SACLA)* (pp. 99-108). Port Elizabeth: Nelson Mandela Metropolitan University.

Goosen, L., & Van Heerden, D. (2013a). Project-based learning and assessment of an IT module in an ODL context. *South African Journal of Higher Education, 27*(6), 1430–1443.

Goosen, L., & Van Heerden, D. (2018). Assessment of Students in Higher Education – Information and Communication Technology Tools and Tips. *Progressio, 40*(1). doi:10.25159/0256-8853/4706

Goosen, L., & Van Heerden, D. (2019a). Promoting Research-Based Opportunities for First Year Programming Learners: Relevant and Quality Information Technology Education. In N. Govender, R. Mudaly, T. Mthethwa, & A. Singh-Pillay (Ed.), *Proceedings of the 27th Conference of the Southern African Association for Research in Mathematics, Science and Technology Education (SAARMSTE)* (pp. 215 - 228). Durban: University of KwaZulu-Natal.

Goosen, L., & Van Heerden, D. (2019b). Student Support for Information and Communication Technology Modules in Open Distance Environments: Towards Self-Directed Learning. In M. M. Van Wyk (Ed.), *Student Support Toward Self-Directed Learning in Open and Distributed Environments* (pp. 26–58). IGI Global Hershey, PA, USA. doi:10.4018/978-1-5225-9316-4.ch002

Gore, A. (2013). *The future: Six drivers for global change*. WH Allen.

Green, A., de Hoyos, M., Barnes, S. A., Owen, D., Baldauf, B., & Behle, H. (2013). *Literature Review on Employability, Inclusion and ICT, Part 1: The Concept of employability, with a specific focus on young people, older workers and migrants* (No. JRC75518). Joint Research Centre (Seville site).

Greenfield, A. (2017). *Radical technologies: The design of everyday life*. Verso.

Gross, A.-K. (2019, May). *Sub-Saharan Africa and the 4th Industrial Revolution: Technological Leapfrogging as a Strategy to enhance Economic Growth?* (Master's Thesis). Lund University.

Gruman, G. J. I. (2016). *What digital transformation really means*. Academic Press.

Guastello, S. J. (1995). *Chaos, catastrophe, and human affairs*. Lawrence Erlbaum Associates, Publishers.

Haldane, A. G. (2019, May 22). *The Third Sector and the Fourth Industrial Revolution*. Retrieved from Pro Bono Economics Annual Lecture: https://www.probonoeconomics.com/sites/default/files/files/Andy%20Haldane%20-%20Pro%20Bono%20Economics%20Annual%20Lecture%20%282019%29_0.pdf

Hallberg, D., Kulecho, M., Kulecho, A., & Okoth, L. (2011). Case studies of Kenyan digital villages with a focus on women and girls. *Journal of Language, Technology & Entrepreneurship in Africa*, *3*(1), 255–273.

Halpern, D. (2003). *Thought and knowledge: An introduction to critical thinking* (4th ed.). Earlbaum.

Hamilton, M., Carbone, A., Gonsalvez, C., & Jollands, M. (2015, January). Breakfast with ICT Employers: What do they want to see in our graduates? *Proceedings of the 17th Australasian Computing Education Conference (ACE 2015)*, *27*(1), 30.

Hargittai, E., Piper, A. M., & Morris, M. R. (2018). From internet access to internet skills: Digital inequality among older adults. *Universal Access in the Information Society*, 1–10.

Heavin, C., & Power, D. J. (2018). *Challenges for digital transformation–towards a conceptual decision support guide for managers*. Academic Press.

Heeks, R. (2010). Do information and communication technologies (ICTs) contribute to development? *Journal of International Development*, *22*(5), 625–640. doi:10.1002/jid.1716

Heidari, N., & Pearce, J. M. (2016). A Review of Greenhouse Gas Emission Liabilities as the Value of Renewable Energy for Mitigating Lawsuits for Climate Change Related Damages. *Renewable & Sustainable Energy Reviews*, *55*, 899–908. doi:10.1016/j.rser.2015.11.025

Heimans, J., & Timms, H. (2018). *New power: How power works in our hyperconnected world – and how to make it work for you*. Macmillan.

Helbing, D. (2019). Societal, economic, ethical and legal challenges of the digital revolution: From big data to deep learning, artificial intelligence, and manipulative technologies. In *Towards Digital Enlightenment* (pp. 47–72). Springer. doi:10.1007/978-3-319-90869-4_6

Hendrix, C. S., & Kang, S. (2019). *19-10 Keeping Up with the Future: Upgrading Forecasts of Political Instability and Geopolitical Risk.* Academic Press.

Hess, J., & Fore, G. (2018). A systematic literature review of US engineering ethics interventions. *Science and Engineering Ethics*, *24*, 551–583. doi:10.100711948-017-9910-6 PMID:28401510

Hilbert, M. (2011, November). Digital gender divide or technologically empowered women in developing countries? A typical case of lies, damned lies, and statistics. *Women's Studies International Forum*, *34*(6), 479–489. doi:10.1016/j.wsif.2011.07.001

Hodges, A. (2012). *Alan Turing: The Enigma (The Centenary Edition).* Princeton University Press. doi:10.1515/9781400844975

Hohmeyer, O., & Bohm, S. (2015). Trends toward 100% renewable electricity supply in Germany and Europe: a paradigm shift in energy policies. In *Wiley Interdisciplinary Reviews: Energy and Environment.* Academic Press.

Holmes, W., Bialik, M., & Fadel, C. (2019). *Artificial Intelligence in Education - Promises and Implications for Teaching and Learning.* Center of Curriculum Redesign.

How transportation can run on renewable electricity. (n.d.). *ECOHZ.* Retrieved from https://www.ecohz.com/how-we-work/how-transportation-can-run-renewable-electricity/

Hrastinski, S. (2008). The potential of synchronous communication to enhance participation in online discussions: A case study of two e-learning courses. *Information & Management*, *45*(7), 499–506. doi:10.1016/j.im.2008.07.005

Hunsaker, A., & Hargittai, E. (2018). A review of Internet use among older adults. *New Media & Society*, *20*(10), 3937–3954. doi:10.1177/1461444818787348

Indra, Bazilian, Ilimbek Uulu, Vakulchuk, & Westphal. (2019). The GeGaLo index: Geopolitical gains and losses after energy transition. *Energy Strategy Reviews.*

Industrial | Industry 4.0 | TI.com. (2020). http://www.ti.com/applications/industrial/industry-4-0.html

Industries 4.0. (2019). *Fraunhofer-Gesellschaft.* https://www.fraunhofer.de/en/research/fields-of-research/production-supply-of-services/industry-4-0.html

Industry 4.0 - the Nine Technologies Transforming Industrial Production. (n.d.). Retrieved May 15, 2020, from https://www.bcg.com/en-in/capabilities/operations/embracing-industry-4.0-rediscovering-growth.aspx

Industry 4.0 | Advantages Engineering Execs Can't Ignore. (n.d.). Retrieved May 15, 2020, from https://www.autodesk.com/industry/manufacturing/resources/engineering-leadership/industry4-0-efficiency-gains-cant-ignore

Industry 4.0 and the Industrial Internet of Things. (n.d.). *Atos*. Retrieved May 15, 2020, from https://atos.net/en/solutions/industry-4-0-the-industrial-internet-of-things

Industry 4.0. (n.d.). *Roland Berger*. Retrieved May 15, 2020, from https://www.rolandberger.com/en/Insights/Global-Topics/Industry-4.0/

Industry 4.0: Optimize Operations & Shape Future Innovation | PTC. (2019). https://www.ptc.com/en/solutions/digital-manufacturing/industry-4-0

Isaias, M., Verde Leal, M. L., & Ramos da Silva, J. A. (2004). *Assessment of greenhouse gas emissions in the production and use of fuel ethanol in Brazil.* Secretariat of the Environment, Government of the State of São Paulo. Retrieved from https://www.wilsoncenter.org/sites/default/files/media/documents/event/brazil.unicamp.macedo.greenhousegas.pdf

Johnsen, H. C. (2014). *The new natural resource: Knowledge development, society and economics.* Ashgate Publishing, Ltd.

Jupe, S. C. E., Michiorri, A., & Taylor, P. C. (2007). *Increasing the energy yield of generation from new and renewable energy sources.* Retrieved from https://www.sciencedirect.com/science/article/abs/pii/S0960148105000893

Kaldero, N. (2018). *Data Science for Executives: Leveraging Machine Intelligence to Drive Business ROI.* Lioncrest Publishing.

Kamel, S. (2010, October). The evolution of the ICT sector in Egypt–Partnership4Development. In *International Business Information Management Association (IBIMA) Conference on Innovation and Knowledge Management in Twin Track Economies: Challenges and Opportunities.* International Business Information Management Association (IBIMA).

Kane, G. C., Palmer, D., Phillips, A. N., Kiron, D., & Buckley, N. (2015). Strategy, not technology, drives digital transformation. MIT Sloan Management Review, 14.

Kanniappan, J., & Rajendrin, B. (2017). Privacy and the Internet of Things. In I. Lee (Ed.), *The Internet of Things in the Modern Business Environment* (pp. 94–106). IGI Global. doi:10.4018/978-1-5225-2104-4.ch005

Kaplan, R. S., & Norton, D. P. (2008). *The execution premium: Linking strategy to operations for competitive advantage.* Harvard Business Press.

Karim, R. A., Abu, A. G., Adnan, A. H., & Suhandoko, A. D. (2018). The Use of Mobile Technology in Promoting Education 4.0 for Higher Education. *Advanced Journal of Technical and Vocational Education*, 2(3), 34–39.

Katz, R., & Koutroumpis, P. (2012, May 29). *Measuring Socio-Economic Digitization: A Paradigm Shift.* Retrieved October 24, 2016, from https://ssrn.com/abstract=2070035

Kaushik. (2011). *Renewable Energy for Sustainable Development.* Springer. Retrieved from https://link.springer.com/article/10.1051/agro/2010029

Kayisire, D., & Wei, J. (2016). ICT adoption and usage in Africa: Towards an efficiency assessment. *Information Technology for Development, 22*(4), 630–653. doi:10.1080/02681102.2015.1081862

Kazimoglu, C., Kiernan, M., Bacon, L., & MacKinnon, L. (2011). Understanding Computational Thinking Before Programming: Developing Guidelines for the Design of Games to Learn Introductory Programming Through Game-Play. *International Journal of Game-Based Learning, 1*(3), 30–52. doi:10.4018/ijgbl.2011070103

Kellner, T. (2019). Mad props: Why GEs new catalyst turboprop engine is turning heads. *GE Additive Reports.* Retrieved from https://www.ge.com/reports/mad-props-ges-new-catalyst-turboprop-engine-turning-heads/

Khan, M. A. (2007). *The Geysers Geothermal Field, an Injection Success Story - Annual Forum of the Groundwater Protection Council.* Thermal Energy Sources and Application Publication.

Kim, K., & Wang, C. (2011). Enterprise VOIP in Fixed Mobile Converged Networks. In L. Weisi, D. Tao, J. Kacprzyk, Z. Li, E. Izquierdo, & H. Wang (Eds.), *Multimedia Analysis, Processing and Communications. Studies in Computational Intelligence* (Vol. 346, pp. 585–621). Springer. doi:10.1007/978-3-642-19551-8_22

Kirlidog, M., van der Vyver, C., Zeeman, M., & Coetzee, W. (2018). Unfulfilled need: Reasons for insufficient ICT skills in South Africa. *Information Development, 34*(1), 5–19. doi:10.1177/0266666916671984

Klein, G. (2017). *Seeing what others don't: The remarkable ways we gain insights.* Nicholas Brealey Publishing.

Klir, G. J., & Folger, T. A. (1988). *Fuzzy Sets, Uncertainty and Information.* Prentice-Hall.

Koutroumpis, P. (2009). The economic impact of broadband on growth: A simultaneous approach. *Telecommunications Policy, 33*(9), 471–485. doi:10.1016/j.telpol.2009.07.004

Kranz, M. (2016). *Building the Internet of Things: Implement new Business Models, Disrupt Competitors, Transform Your Industry.* John Wiley & Sons.

Kryvinska, N., Auer, L., & Strauss, C. (2009). The Place and Value of SOA in Building 2.0-Generation Enterprise Unified vs. Ubiquitous Communication and Collaboration Platform. In *The Third IEEE International Conference on Mobile Ubiquitous Computing Systems, Services and Technologies (UBICOMM 2009).* 1, pp. 305-310. Sliema, Malta: IEEE. 10.1109/UBICOMM.2009.52

Kuaban, G. S., Czekalski, P., Molua, E. L., & Grochla, K. (2019, June). An Architectural Framework Proposal for IoT Driven Agriculture. In *International Conference on Computer Networks* (pp. 18-33). Cham: Springer. 10.1007/978-3-030-21952-9_2

Lage, M. G., Platt, G. J., & Tregla, M. (2000). Inverting the classroom: A gateway to create an inclusive learning environment. *The Journal of Economic Education, 31*(1), 30–43. doi:10.1080/00220480009596759

Lamprini, K., & Bröchler, R. (2018). How collaborative innovation and technology in educational ecosystem can meet the challenges raised by the 4th industrial revolution. *World Technopolis Review, 7*(1), 2–14.

Lanius, R., & McCurdy, H. (2008). *Robots in Space: Technology, Evolution, and Interplanetary Travel.* Baltimore: Johns Hopkins University Press.

Le Merlus, L. (2019, December 16). Formnext 2019: A lot of new players, but where is the business value? *3D Print.com.* Retrieved from https://3dprint.com/261368/formnext-2019-a-lot-of-new-players-but-where-is-the-business-value/

Leake, D. (2015). Problem Solving and Reasoning: Case-Based. In J. D. Wright (Ed.), *International Encyclopedia of the Social and Behavioral Sciences* (2nd ed., pp. 56–60). Elsevier. doi:10.1016/B978-0-08-097086-8.43075-8

Leduff, C. (2014). *Detroit: An American autopsy.* Penguin.

Ledwith, M. (2020). *Community development: A critical approach.* Policy Press.

Lee, I., & Shin, Y. J. (2019). *Machine learning for enterprises: Applications, algorithm selection, and challenges.* Academic Press.

Lee, J., & Behrad Bagheri, H.-A. K. (2015). A cyber-physical systems architecture for industry 4.0-based manufacturing systems. *Manufacturing Letters, 1*(3), 18-23.

Lee, H. S., Park, S. W., & Heo, H. (2016). Acute acquired comitant esotropia related to excessive Smartphone use. *BMC Ophthalmology, 16*(1), 37. doi:10.118612886-016-0213-5 PMID:27061181

Lee, J., Lim, C., & Kim, H. (2017). Development of an instructional design model for flipped learning in higher education. *Educational Technology Research and Development, 65*(2), 427–453. doi:10.100711423-016-9502-1

Leitão, A. (2015). Economia Circular: uma nova filosofia de gestão para o séc. XXI. *Portuguese Journal of Finance, Management and Accounting, 1*(2), 149-171. Retrieved on 2019/05/05 from: http://u3isjournal.isvouga.pt/index.php/PJFMA/article/view/114/52

Lele, S. M. (1991). Sustainable development: A critical review. *World Development, 19*(6), 607–621. doi:10.1016/0305-750X(91)90197-P

Letaba, T. P., Pretorius, M. W., & Pretorius, L. (2018). Innovation profile from the perspective of technology roadmapping practitioners in South Africa. *South African Journal of Industrial Engineering, 29*(4), 171–183. doi:10.7166/29-4-1919

Levin, R. (2018). Building a people-centred, people-driven public service and administration culture in Africa for youth empowerment and development. *Africa Journal of Public Sector Development and Governance*, *1*(1), 34–45.

Libbrecht, P., & Goosen, L. (2016). Using ICTs to Facilitate Multilingual Mathematics Teaching and Learning. In R. Barwell, P. Clarkson, A. Halai, M. Kazima, J. Moschkovich, N. Planas, & M. Villavicencio Ubillús (Eds.), *Mathematics Education and Language Diversity* (pp. 217–235). Springer. doi:10.1007/978-3-319-14511-2_12

Li, G., Hou, Y., & Wu, A. (2017). Fourth Industrial Revolution: Technological drivers, impacts and coping methods. *Chinese Geographical Science*, *27*(4), 626–637. doi:10.100711769-017-0890-x

Lincoln, Y. S., Lynham, S. A., & Guba, E. G. (2011). *Paradigmatic controversies, contradictions, and emerging confluences, revisited*. Academic Press.

Lipson, H., & Kurman, M. (2013). *Fabricated: The new world of 3D printing, the promise and peril of a machine that can make (almost) anything*. John Wiley and Sons.

Liu, J., & Wang, L. (2010). Computational Thinking in Discrete Mathematics. *IEEE 2nd International Workshop on Education Technology and Computer Science*, 413-416.

Lloyd, H. (2015). *Marketing Essentials, Tech and Design*. Harrison James Co.

Lochlainn, C. M., Mhichíl, M. N., Beirne, E., & Brown, M. (2019). Back to the Future, the Learner Strikes back: Feedback and Reflection as key Elements in MOOC re-design. In *European Distance and E-Learning Network (EDEN) Annual Conference Proceedings* (pp. 365-372). Bruges, Belgium: EDEN.

Loh, R. S. M., & Lim, S. S. (2019). *Youth Digital Culture*. The International Encyclopedia of Media Literacy. doi:10.1002/9781118978238.ieml0245

Lom, M., Pribyl, O., & Svitek, M. (2016, May). Industry 4.0 as a part of smart cities. In *Smart Cities Symposium Prague (SCSP)* (pp. 1-6). Prague: IEEE. 10.1109/SCSP.2016.7501015

Loo, S. (2012). Design-ing ethics. In E. Felton, O. Zelenko, & S. Vaughan (Eds.), *Design and ethics: Reflections on practice* (pp. 10–19). Routledge.

Loy, J. (2015). The future for design education: Preparing the design workforce for additive manufacturing. *International Journal of Rapid Manufacturing*, *5*(2), 199–212. doi:10.1504/IJRAPIDM.2015.073577

Lund, H. (2006). Large-scale integration of optimal combinations of PV, wind and wave power into the electricity supply. *Renewable Energy*, *31*(4), 503–515. doi:10.1016/j.renene.2005.04.008

Maddux, C. D., & Lamont Johnson, D. (2005). Type II Applications of Technology in Education. *Computers in the Schools*, *22*(1 & 2), 1–5. doi:10.1300/J025v22n01_01

Ma, J. K. H., Vachon, T. E., & Cheng, S. (2019). National income, political freedom, and investments in R&D and education: A comparative analysis of the second digital divide among 15-year-old students. *Social Indicators Research, 144*(1), 133–166. doi:10.100711205-018-2030-0

Manalo, J. A. IV, Pasiona, S. P., Bautista, A. M. F., Villaflor, J. D., Corpuz, D. C. P., & Biag-Manalo, H. H. M. (2019). Exploring youth engagement in agricultural development: The case of farmers' children in the Philippines as rice crop manager infomediaries. *Journal of Agricultural Education and Extension, 25*(4), 1–17. doi:10.1080/1389224X.2019.1629969

Manu, A. (2015). *Value Creation and the Internet of Things*. Gower.

Marconi, M. A., & Lakatos, E. M. (2013). *Técnicas de pesquisa*. Atlas.

Marketing, S. (2019). *Promoting Your Renewable Energy Purchase*. Urban Grid.

Markus, M. L., & Robey, D. (1988). Information Technology and Organizational Change: Causal Structure in Theory and Research. *Management Science, 34*(5), 583–598. doi:10.1287/mnsc.34.5.583

Marr, B. (2017). *Data Strategy: How to Profit from a World of Big Data, Analytics and the Internet of Things*. Kogan Page Publishers.

Martins, N. (2013). *The Cambridge revival of political economy*. Routledge. doi:10.4324/9781315883915

Marumo, P. O., & Sebolaaneng, M. E. (2019). Assessing the state of youth unemployment in South Africa: A discussion and examination of the structural problems responsible for unsustainable youth development in South Africa. *Gender & Behaviour, 17*(3), 13477–13485.

Mathiesen. (2015). Smart Energy Systems for coherent 100% renewable energy and transport solutions. *Applied Energy*.

Mathiyalakan, S. (2006). VOIP Adoption: Issues & Concerns. *Communications of the IMMA, 6*(2), 19–24.

Matthews, J. (2013). *Encyclopedia of Environmental Change* (Vol. 1). Sage.

Mazibuko, S., Hart, T., Mogale, M., Mohlakoana, N., & Aliber, M. (2008). Baseline information on technology-oriented initiatives in rural areas to promote economic development. Academic Press.

Mazzucato. (2017). Financing renewable energy: Who is financing what and why it matters. In *Technological forecasting and Social Change*. Elsevier.

McConnell, T., Parker, J., Eberhardt, J., Koehler, M., & Lunderberg, M. (2013). Virtual professional learning communities: Teachers' perceptions of virtual versus face-to-face professional development. *Journal of Science Education and Technology, 22*(3), 267–277. doi:10.100710956-012-9391-y

Mckenzie, S., Coldwell-Neilson, J., & Palmer, S. (2017). Career aspirations and skills expectations of undergraduate IT students: are they realistic? In *HERDSA 2017: Research and development in higher education: curriculum transformation: Proceedings of the 40th HERDSA Annual International Conference* (pp. 229-240). Higher Education Research and Development Society of Australasia.

McKinley, J. (2015). Critical argument and writer identity: Social constructivism as a theoretical framework for EFL academic writing. *Critical Inquiry in Language Studies, 12*(3), 184–207. doi:10.1080/15427587.2015.1060558

Meffert, J., & Swaminathan, A. (2018). *Leadership and the urgency for digital transformation.* Academic Press.

Meiers, M. (2017). *Teacher Professional Learning, Teaching Practice and Student Learning Outcomes: Important Issues.* . doi:10.1007/1-4020-4773-8_27

Mell, P., & Grance, T. (2011). *The NIST definition of cloud computing.* Academic Press.

Merkel, S., Heinze, R. G., Hilbert, J., & Naegele, G. (2019). Technology for all. In The Future of Ageing in Europe (pp. 217-253). Palgrave Macmillan. doi:10.1007/978-981-13-1417-9_8

Messer, N., & Townsley, P. (2003). *Local institutions and livelihoods: guidelines for analysis.* Food & Agriculture Org.

Michael, O. I., & Samson, A. J. (2014). The impact of information and communication technology on youth and its vocational opportunities in Nigeria. *Journal of Good Governance and Sustainable Development in Africa, 2*(1).

MIT Sloan Management Review. (n.d.). Retrieved from https://sloanreview.mit.edu/projects/reshaping-business-with-artificial-intelligence/

Mkhize, P., Mtsweni, E. S., & Buthelezi, P. (2016, April). Diffusion of innovations approach to the evaluation of learning management system usage in an open distance learning institution. *The International Review of Research in Open and Distributed Learning, 17*(3), 295–312. doi:10.19173/irrodl.v17i3.2191

Mohamed, M. (2018). Challenges and benefits of Industry 4.0: An overview. *International Journal of Supply and Operations Management, 5*(3), 256–265.

Mohammed & Mou. (2019). Analysis of wind speed data and wind energy potential using Weibull distribution in Zagora, Morocco. *International Journal of Renewable Energy Development.*

Mohammed, A. (2007). Work together any place, any time. *Computer Weekly*, 38–40.

Molema, T. M., & Quan-Baffour, K. P. (2019). Participation in the Acet Programmes in Mashashane-Maraba Area of Limpopo Province: Gender Discriminatory? *Rethinking Teaching and learning in the 21st Century, 355.*

Monteiro, M. (2018). Economia Circular. *Empreendorismo Start&Go, 20*. Retrieved from: https://www.startandgo.pt/pubs/startgo20.pdf

Moor, J. (2006). The Dartmouth College Artificial Intelligence Conference: The Next Fifty years. *AI Magazine, 27*(4), 87–91.

Moradiya. (2019). The Challenges Renewable Energy Sources Face. *AZO CleanTech.*

Moreno, M., & Charnley, F. (2016). Can Re-distributed Manufacturing and Digital Intelligence Enable a Regenerative Economy? An Integrative Literature Review. In R. Setchi, R. Howlett, Y. Liu, & P. Theobald (Eds.), *Sustainable Design and Manufacturing 2016* (pp. 563–577). Springer. doi:10.1007/978-3-319-32098-4_48

Morin, E. (1977). *La Méthode La Nature de la Nature*. Editions du Seuil.

Morrison, L. (2019). Situating moral agency: How postphenomenology can benefit engineering ethics. *Science and Engineering Ethics*. Advance online publication. doi:10.100711948-019-00163-7 PMID:31792776

Morse, S., & McNamara, N. (2013). *Sustainable livelihood approach: A critique of theory and practice*. Springer Science & Business Media. doi:10.1007/978-94-007-6268-8

Mutula, S. M., & Van Brakel, P. (2007). ICT skills readiness for the emerging global digital economy among small businesses in developing countries. *Library Hi Tech, 25*(2), 231–245. doi:10.1108/07378830710754992

Myerson, J., & Makepeace, J. (1995). *Makepeace: Spirit of adventure in craft and design*. Conran Octopus.

Nascimento, F. G. F. B., Moraes, M. L., & Paula, R. P. S. (2017). *Anais do Congresso Brasileiro de Biblioteconomia*. Documentação e Ciência da Informação, Fortaleza, FEBAB. Retrieved on 2019/01/29 from: https://portal.febab.org.br/anais/article/viewFile/1695/1696

Neuman, W. L. (2013). *Social research methods: Qualitative and quantitative approaches*. Pearson education.

Nick, G. A., & Pongrácz, F. (2016). Hungarian Smart Cities Strategies Towards Industry 4.0. *Industry 4.0, 1*(2), 122-127.

Norme BNQ 21000. Développement durable – Guide d'application des principes de la Loi sur le développement durable dans la gestion des entreprises et des autres organisations. (n.d.). Retrieved on 2019/02/24 from: https://www.bnq21000.qc.ca/guide-bnq-21000/description/

Nourani, C. F. (2017). *Ecosystems and Technology: Idea Generation and Content Model Processing: Innovation Management and Computing*. CRC Press.

O'Brien, M. N., Lin, H.-X., Girard, M., Olvera de la Cruz, M., & Mirkin, C. A. (2016). *Programming colloidal crystal habit with anisotropic nanoparticle building blocks and DNA bonds*. Academic Press.

O'Leary, Z. (2017). The essential guide to doing your research project. *Sage (Atlanta, Ga.)*.

Offshore wind test and demonstration facility. (2018). European Offshore Wind Deployment Centre. Retrieved from https://en.wikipedia.org/wiki/European_Offshore_Wind_Deployment_Centre

Ohei, K. N., Brink, R., & Abiodun, A. (2019). Information and Communication Technology (ICT) graduates and challenges of employability: A conceptual framework for enhancing employment opportunities in South Africa. *Gender & Behaviour, 17*(3), 13500–13521.

Oleksandr Shkabura. (2019). *The Main Benefits and Challenges of Industry 4.0 Adoption in Manufacturing.* https://www.infopulse.com/blog/the-main-benefits-and-challenges-of-industry-4-0-adoption-in-manufacturing/

Olivier, M. (2009). *Information Technology research: A practical guide for Computer Science and Informatics* (3rd ed.). Van Schaik.

Oye, N. D., Inuwa, I., & Shakil, A. M. (2011). Role of information communication technology (ICT): Implications on unemployment and Nigerian GDP. *Journal of International Academic Research, 11*(1), 9–17.

Özdemir, V., & Hekim, N. (2018). Birth of industry 5.0: Making sense of big data with artificial intelligence, "the internet of things" and next-generation technology policy. *OMICS: A Journal of Integrative Biology, 22*(1), 65–76. doi:10.1089/omi.2017.0194 PMID:29293405

Paganetto, L., & Scandizzo, P. (2016). Industrial Policy, Investment and Green Growth. In L. Paganetto (Ed.), *Stagnation Versus Growth in Europe: Capitalism in the 21st Century* (pp. 87–101). Springer.

Pande, R., & van der Weide, T. P. (2012). *Globalization, technology diffusion and gender disparity: Social impacts of ICTs*. Information Science Reference. doi:10.4018/978-1-4666-0020-1

Pandey, P., & Zheng, Y. (2019, May). Unpacking Empowerment in ICT4D Research. In *International Conference on Social Implications of Computers in Developing Countries* (pp. 83-94). Springer.

Parikh, A. (2019). Global Renewable Industry Created 11 Million Job Opportunities in 2018. *MERCOM INDIA.* Retrieved from https://mercomindia.com/irena-11-million-jobs-renewables-2018/

Parkinson, S., & Ramirez, R. (2007). Using a Sustainable Livelihoods Approach to Assessing the Impact of ICTs in Development. *The Journal of Community Informatics, 2*(3). http://jat.gws.uky.edu/index.php/ciej/article/view/310

Pascual-Leone, A., Amedi, A., Fregni, F., & Merabet, L. B. (2005). The Plastic Human Brain Cortex. *Annual Review of Neuroscience, 28*(1), 377–401. doi:10.1146/annurev.neuro.27.070203.144216

Paulin, A. (2017). Data Traffic Forecast in Health 4.0. In C. Thuemmler & C. Bai (Eds.), *Health 4.0: How Virtualization and Big Data are Revolutionizing Healthcare* (pp. 39–52). Springer. doi:10.1007/978-3-319-47617-9_3

Pei, E., Monzon, M., & Bernard, A. (Eds.). (2018). *Additive manufacturing – developments in training and education*. Springer.

Penprase, B. E. (2018). The Fourth Industrial Revolution and Higher Education. In N. Gleason (Ed.), *Higher Education in the Era of the Fourth Industrial Revolution*. doi:10.1007/978-981-13-0194-0_9

Pereira, T., Barreto, L., & Amaral, A. (2017). Network and information security challenges within Industry 4.0 paradigm. *Procedia Manufacturing*, *13*, 1253–1260. doi:10.1016/j.promfg.2017.09.047

Pfeffer, J. (1982). Organizations and Organization Theory. Pacific Sociological Rev., 20, 241-261.

Pinheiro, P., Santos, R., & Barbosa, R. (2018). Industry 4.0 Multi-agent System Based Knowledge Representation Through Blockchain. In *International Symposium on Ambient Intelligence* (pp. 331-337). Springer.

Pinker, S. (2018). *Enlightenment now: The case for reason, science, humanism and progress*. Penguin.

Ponelis, S. R., & Holmner, M. A. (2015). ICT in Africa: Enabling a better life for all. *Information Technology for Development*, *21*(1), 1–11. doi:10.1080/02681102.2014.985521

Porcaro, G. (2016). Internet, Policy and Politics in the Era of the Industrial. In Porcaro, J. Klewes, D. Popp, & M. Rost-Hein (Eds.), Out-thinking Organizational Communications: The Impact of Digital Transformation (pp. 51-61). New York: Springer.

Porter, M. E., & Millar, V. E. (1985, July). How information gives you competitive advantage. Harvard Business Review.

Porter, M. E. (2008). The five competitive forces that shape strategy. *Harvard Business Review*, *86*(1), 25–40. PMID:18271320

Porter, M. E., & Heppelmann, J. E. (2015). How smart, connected products are transforming companies. *Harvard Business Review*, *93*(10), 96–114.

Pullin, G. (2009). *Design meets disability*. MIT Press.

Pyle, D., & San Jose, C. J. M. Q. (2015). *An executive's guide to machine learning*. Academic Press.

Radziwon, A., Bilberg, A., Bogers, M., & Madsen, E. (2014). The smart factory: Exploring adaptive and flexible manufacturing solutions. *Procedia Engineering*, *69*, 1184–1190. doi:10.1016/j.proeng.2014.03.108

Rakodi, C. (2014). A livelihoods approach–conceptual issues and definitions. In *Urban livelihoods* (pp. 26–45). Routledge.

Redwood, B., Schoffer, F. Garret, B. & Debicki, T. (2017). *The 3D printing handbook: Technologies, design and applications*. Amsterdam: 3D Hubs B.V.

Reid, S. (2011). The Momentum of the Technology of the Classroom. In *Adaptation, Resistance and Access to Instructional Technologies: Assessing Future Trends In Education* (pp. 316–331). IGI Global. doi:10.4018/978-1-61692-854-4.ch018

Reimer, K., & Taing, S. (2009). Unified Communications. *Business & Information Systems Engineering*, *1*(4), 326–330. doi:10.100712599-009-0062-3

Renewable Energy and Agriculture: A Natural Fit. (2008). *Union of Concerned Scientists.*

Renewable energy in Manufacturing, A technology Roadmap for Remap 2030. (2014). *International Renewable Energy Agency.*

Renewable Energy. (2011). Retrieved from https://en.wikipedia.org/wiki/Renewable_energy

Rifkin, J. (2011). *The Third Industrial Revolution: How Lateral Power is Transforming Energy, the Economy and the World.* Palgrave - McMillan.

Rifkin, J. (2014). *The Zero Marginal Cost Society: The Internet of Things, the Collaborative Commons and the Eclipse of Capitalism.* St. Martins Press.

Rochet, L. (2017). *Leading digital transformation at L'Oreal.* SAID Oxford Business School.

Roco, M. C. (2011). *The long view of nanotechnology development: the National Nanotechnology Initiative at 10 years.* Springer.

Ross, J. W., Sebastian, I., Beath, C., Mocker, M., Moloney, K., & Fonstad, N. (2016). *Designing and executing digital strategies.* Academic Press.

Rossetto, M., Belluzzo, R. C. B., & Feres, G. G. (2016). *A competência em informação (CoInfo) como recurso didático pedagógico e institucional: o Website Labirinto do saber como fonte de informação, de pesquisa e práticas.* Retrieved on 2019/02/24 from: https://repositorio.usp.br/item/002789636

Rouse, M. (2017). *What is fourth industrial revolution?* Retrieved Sept 25, 2019, from https://whatis.techtarget.com/definition/fourth-industrial-revolution

Running on Renewables. (2018). *Transforming Transportation Through Renewable Technologies.* International Renewable Energy Agency.

Ryan, C. (2004). *Digital eco-sense: Sustainability and ICT – a new terrain for innovation.* Melbourne: Lab 3000.

Saad, M. S. M., & Majid, I. A. (2014). Employers' perceptions of important employability skills required from Malaysian engineering and information and communication technology (ICT) graduates. *Global Journal of Engineering Education*, *16*(3), 110–115.

Sabia, J. J. (2015). Do minimum wages stimulate productivity and growth? *IZA World of Labor*, (221).

Sachs, J. D. (2015). *The age of sustainable development.* Columbia University Press. doi:10.7312ach17314

Sachs, J. D., Schmidt-Traub, G., Mazzucato, M., Messner, D., Nakicenovic, N., & Rockström, J. (2019). Six Transformations to achieve the Sustainable Development Goals. *Nature Sustainability, 2*(9), 805–814. doi:10.103841893-019-0352-9

Sadiq, A. M., & Mohammed, M. (2015). The role of information and communication technology (ICT) in providing job opportunities for youth in the developing world. *Journal of Emerging Trends in Engineering and Applied Sciences, 6*(7), 174–179.

Safiullin, A., Krasnyuk, L., & Kapelyuk, Z. (2019, March). Integration of industry 4.0 technologies for "smart cities" development. *IOP Conference Series. Materials Science and Engineering, 497*(1), 012089. doi:10.1088/1757-899X/497/1/012089

Sainato, M. (2019). Revealed: Amazon touts high wages while ignoring issues in its warehouses. *The Guardian.* Retrieved from https://www.theguardian.com/technology/2019/aug/06/amazon-workers-minimum-wage-injuries-working-conditions

Salem, A.-B.M., & Parusheva, S. (2018), Exploiting the Knowledge Engineering Paradigms for Designing Smart Learning Systems. *Eastern-European Journal of Enterprise Technologies, 2*(92), 38-44.

Salem, A.-B. M. (2019). Computational Intelligence in Smart Education and Learning. In *Proceedings of the International Conference on Information and Communication Technology in Business and Education,* (pp. 30-40). University of Economics.

Salem, A.-B. M., & Nikitaeva, N. (2019), Knowledge Engineering Paradigms for Smart Education and Smart Learning Systems. *Proceedings of the 42nd International Convention of the MIPRO Croatian Society,* 1823-1826. 10.23919/MIPRO.2019.8756685

Salkin, C., Oner, M., Unstundag, A., & Cevikcan, E. (2018). A Conceptual Framework for Industry 4.0. In A. Ustundag & E. Cevikcan (Eds.), *Industry 4.0: Managing The Digital Transformation* (pp. 3–22). Springer. doi:10.1007/978-3-319-57870-5_1

Sarathy, R., & Robertson, C. J. (2003). Strategic and ethical considerations in managing digital privacy. *Journal of Business Ethics, 46*(2), 111–126. doi:10.1023/A:1025001627419

Scanlon, M., Jenkinson, H., Leahy, P., Powell, F., & Byrne, O. (2019). 'How are we going to do it?' An exploration of the barriers to access to higher education amongst young people from disadvantaged communities. *Irish Educational Studies, 38*(3), 343–357. doi:10.1080/0332331 5.2019.1611467

Schmidt, R., Mohrin, M., Harting, R.-C., Reichstein, C., Neumaier, P., & Jozinovic, P. (2015). Industry 4.0 Potentials for Creating Smart Products: Empirical Research Results. In W. Abramowicz (Ed.), *Business Information Systems: 18th International Conference, BIS 2015, Poznań, Poland, June 24-26, 2015, Proceedings* (pp. 16-25). New York: Springer. 10.1007/978-3-319-19027-3_2

Schneider, F., & Friesinger, G. (2011). The digital reformulation of the relationship of mind and matter. In G. Friesingerl, J. Grenzfurthner, & T. Ballhausen (Eds.), *Mind and Matter: Comparative Approaches towards Complexity* (p. 20). Transaction Publishers. doi:10.14361/transcript.9783839418000.11

Scholz, R., Yarime, M., & Shiroyama, H. (2018). Global leadership for social design: Theoretical and educational perspectives. *Sustainability Science, 13*(2), 447–464. doi:10.100711625-017-0454-0

Schwab, K. (2015). *The Fourth Industrial Revolution.* Retrieved from https://www.weform.org/press/2015/fourth-industrial-revolution

Schwab, K. (2016). *The Fourth Industrial Revolution : what it means, how to respond.* Retrieved from https://www.weforum.org/agenda/2016/01/the-fourth-industrial-revolution-what-it-means-and-how-to-respond/# 24.4.20

Schwab, K. (2016). *The Fourth Industrial Revolution.* Crown Publishing Group.

Schwab, K. (2017). *La Cuarta Revolución Industrial.* Ciudad de México.

Schwab, K. (2017). *The fourth industrial revolution.* Currency.

Sebastian, I. M., Ross, J. W., Beath, C., Mocker, M., Moloney, K. G., & Fonstad, N. O. (2017). How Big Old Companies Navigate Digital Transformation. *MIS Quarterly Executive.*

Seldon, A., & Abidoye, O. (2018). *The fourth education revolution: will artificial intelligence liberate or infantilise humanity?* The University of Buckingham Press.

Semutenga, E., Aquarius, I., & Ssengendo, L. (2019). *ICT for Youth Employability.* Academic Press.

Shahroom, A., & Hussin, N. (2018). Industrial revolution 4.0 and education. *International Journal of Academic Research in Business and Social Sciences, 8*(9), 314–319. doi:10.6007/IJARBSS/v8-i9/4593

Shariat-Zadeh, N., Lundholm, T., Lindberg, L., & Franzén-Sivard, G. (2016). Integration of digital factory with smart factory based on Internet of Things. *26th CIRP Design Conference, 50*, 512-517.

Sharma, K. (2016). *Overview of Industrial Process Automation* (2nd ed.). Elsevier.

Sharma, P. (2019). Digital Revolution of Education 4.0. *International Journal of Engineering and Advanced Technology, 9*(2).

Shetty, A. D. (2017). E-Commerce Industry Significant Factor for the Growth of Indian Economy. *Asian Journal of Research in Social Sciences and Humanities, 7*(4), 177–183. doi:10.5958/2249-7315.2017.00275.1

Shiroishi, Y., Uchiyama, K., & Suzuki, N. (2019). Society 5.0: For human security and well-being, Cyber-physical systems. Hitachi Research and Development Group.

Shokri & Heo. (n.d.). Energy Policies to promote Renewable Energy Technologies; Learning from Asian Countries Experiences. *International Association of Exhibitions and Events.*

Shon-Roy, A. W. (2010). Solar Cell Process Costs and Materials. *Renewable Energy World.* Retrieved from https://www.renewableenergyworld.com/2010/11/01/solar-cell-process-costs-and-materials/#gref

Silic, M., & Back, A. (2016). Factors driving unified communications and collaboration adoption and use in organizations. *Measuring Business Excellence, 20*(1), 21–40. doi:10.1108/MBE-05-2015-0026

Silic, M., Back, A., & Sammer, T. (2014). Employee Acceptance and Use of Unified Communications and Collaboration in a Cross Cultural Environment. *International Journal of e-Collaboration, 10*(2), 1–19. doi:10.4018/ijec.2014040101

Skobelev, P. O., & Borovik, S. Y. (2017). On the way from Industry 4.0 to Industry 5.0: from digital manufacturing to digital society. *Industry 4.0, 2*(6), 307-311.

Slade, S., & Prinsloo, P. (2015). Stemming the flow: Improving retention for distance learning students. In *European Distance and E-Learning Network (EDEN) Annual Conference Proceedings.* Barcelona: EDEN. Retrieved from http://www.eden-online.org/system/files/Book%20of%20 Abstracts EDEN%202015%20Annual%20Conference Barcelona.pdf

Small, L. A. (2007). The sustainable rural livelihoods approach: A critical review. *Canadian Journal of Development Studies. Canadian Journal of Development Studies, 28*(1), 27–38. doi :10.1080/02255189.2007.9669186

Sondhi, R. (2008). Total strategy (3rd ed.). BMC Global Services Publications.

Song, H., Rawat, D., Jeschke, S., & Brecher, C. (2016). *Cyber-physical Systems: Foundations, Principles and Applications.* Morgan Kaufmann.

Stahel, W. R. (1984). The product-life factor. In An inquiry into the nature of sustainable societies, the role of the private sector. Houston: The Mitchell Prizes.

Stahel, W. R. (2010). *The performance economy.* Palgrave McMillan.

Stanford 2025. (n.d.). *Learning and Living at Stanford – An Exploration of Undergraduate Experiences in the Future.* http://www.stanford2025.com/

Statistics SA. (2018). *Youth unemployment still high in Q1: 2018.* Statistics South Africa.

Statistics SA. (2019). *Statistical release P0211: Mid-year population estimates 2019.* Statistics South Africa. Available: http://www.statssa.gov.za/publications/P0211/P02111stQuarter2019

Straub, E. T. (2009). Understanding technology adoption: Theory and future directions for informal learning. *Review of Educational Research, 79*(2), 625–649. doi:10.3102/0034654308325896

Sullins, J. (2019). Information Technology and Moral Values. Stanford Encyclopedia of Philosophy Archive, (Summer), 1–52.

Sutopo, W. (2019, April). The Roles of Industrial Engineering Education for Promoting Innovations and Technology Commercialization in the Digital Era. *IOP Conference Series. Materials Science and Engineering, 495*(1), 012001. doi:10.1088/1757-899X/495/1/012001

Sütterlin, B., & Siegrist, M. (2017). Public acceptance of renewable energy technologies from an abstract versus concrete perspective and the positive imagery of solar power. *Energy Policy, 106*, 356–366. doi:10.1016/j.enpol.2017.03.061

Taber, K. S. (2011). Constructivism as educational theory: Contingency in learning, and optimally guided instruction. In J. Hassaskhah (Ed.), *Educational Theory*. Nova Science Publishers.

Taipale, S., Vincent, J., Sapio, B., Lugano, G., & Fortunati, L. (2015). Introduction: Situating the Human in Social Robots. In *Social Robots from a Human Perspective* (pp. 1–17). Springer. doi:10.1007/978-3-319-15672-9_1

Talbot, P., & Bizzell, B. (2016). Teaching, Technology, and Transformation. In *Educational Leaders without Borders* (pp. 83–104). Springer. doi:10.1007/978-3-319-12358-5_4

Tanim, M. M. Z. (2016). *Electromagnetic Radiation and Human Health*. Electromagnetic Radiation and Human Health; doi:10.13140/RG.2.2.13195.28962

Tankelevcience, L., & Damasevicius, F. (2009). Characteristics for Domain Ontologies for Web Based Learning and their Applications for Quality Evaluation. *Informatics in Education, 8*(1), 131–152.

Tarraga Albacete, F. (2017). *Ventajas y Desventajas pedagógicas en torno a la irrupción de las NTICX* (Tesis Doctoral). Universidad de Castilla La Mancha, Albacete.

Tashakkori, A., & Teddlie, C. (2010). *Sage handbook of mixed methods in social & behavioral research* (2nd ed.). Sage. doi:10.4135/9781506335193

Tavani, H. T. (2011). *Ethics and Technology: Controversies, Questions, and Strategies for Ethical Computing*. John Wiley & Son.

The Chronicle of Higher Education (n.d.). Retrieved from https://www.chronicle.com/article/How-AI-Is-Infiltrating-Every/243022'

The Practical Application of Industry 4.0. (2015). *Automation World*. https://www.automationworld.com/article/technologies/motion-control-systems/practical-application-industry-40

The-Digital-Enlightment-Forum. (2016). *Security for the Digital World Within an Ethical Framework*. IOS Press.

Thramboulidis, K., Vachtsevanou, D. C., & Solanos, A. (2018). *Cyber-Physical Microservices: An IoT-based Framework for Manufacturing Systems*. arXiv preprint arXiv:1801.10340

Toffler, A. (1980). *The third wave*. Bantam Books.

Tondi, P. (2019, March). The significance of Indigenous Knowledge Systems (IKS) for Africa's socio-cultural and economic development in the dawn of the Fourth Industrial Revolution (4IR). *Journal of Gender, Information and Development in Africa (JGIDA), 8*(Special Issue 1), 239-245.

Top 5 things to know about Industry 4.0. (n.d.). *TechRepublic*. Retrieved May 15, 2020, from https://www.techrepublic.com/article/top-5-things-to-know-about-industry-4-0/

Tripathi, K. (2015). Optimizing Operational and Migration Cost in Cloud Paradigm (OOMCCP). In P. Sharma, P. Banerjee, J.-P. Dudeja, P. Singh, & R. K. Brajpuriya (Eds.), *Making Innovations Happen* (p. 89). Allied Publishers.

Tsai, M.-J., Wang, C.-Y., & Hsu, P.-F. (2019). Developing the computer programming self-efficacy scale for computer literacy education. *Journal of Educational Computing Research, 56*(8), 1345–1360. doi:10.1177/0735633117746747

Tylor, E. B. (1871). Primitive Culture: Researches Into the Development of Mythology, Philosophy, Religion, Art, and Custom (Vol. 1). London: John Murray.

UN General Assembly. (2015). *Sustainable development goals. SDGs, transforming our world: The 2030.* Author.

United Nations Development Programme (Kenya). (2001). *Kenya Human Development Report.* United Nations Development Programme.

United Nations. (2015). *Transforming our world: the 2030 Agenda for Sustainable Development.* Retrieved on 2020/02/20 from: https://www.un.org/ga/search/view_doc.asp?symbol=A/RES/70/1&Lang=E

Unwin, J. (2019). *Top five trends in wave power.* Retrieved from https://www.power-technology.com/features/wave-power-energy/

Valentina, S. E., Cristiana-Zizi, R., Elena, C., & Poinescu, A. A. (2010). *Electromagnetic Pollution of Environment.* Academic Press.

Van Heerden, D., & Goosen, L. (2019). Assessments Used in an Open Distance e-Learning Environment to Promote Self-Directed Learning. In R. Ørngreen, M. Buhl, & B. Meyer (Ed.), *Proceedings of the 18th European Conference on e-Learning (ECEL 2019)* (pp. 593 - 602). Copenhagen: Academic Conferences and Publishing International Limited. doi:10.34190/EEL.19.003

Van Heerden, D., & Goosen, L. (2012). Using Vodcasts to Teach Programming in an ODL Environment. *Progressio, 34*(3), 144–160.

Varela, F. J. (1999). *Ethical know-how: Action, wisdom, and cognition.* Stanford University Press.

Velázquez Fernández, H. (2009). Transhumanismo, Libertad e Identidad Humana. *Themata. Revista de Filosofía., 41,* 577–590.

Ventola, L. (2014). Mobile devices and apps for health care professionals: Uses and benefits. *P&T*, *39*(5), 356–364. PMID:24883008

Vestager, M. (2016). *Big Data and Competition - European Data Commisioner Speech to EDPS-BEUC Conference, 29 September 2016.* Brussels: European Commission. Retrieved Jan 10th, 2017, from https://ec.europa.eu/commission/2014-2019/vestager/announcements/big-data-and-competition_en

Vezzoli, C., & Manzini, E. (2008). *Design for environmental sustainability.* Springer.

Vinichenko, M. V., Makushkin, S. A., Melnichuk, A. V., Frolova, E. V., & Kurbakova, S. N. (2016). Student employment during college studies and after career start. *International Review of Management and Marketing*, *6*(5S).

Vitorino, E. V., & Piantola, D. (2009). Competência informacional: bases históricas e conceituais: construindo significados. *Ciência da Informação, Brasília*, *38*(3), 130–141.

Vollenweider, M. (2016). *Mind+Machine: A Decision Model for Optimizing and Implementing Analytics.* John Wiley & Sons.

Voskoglou, M. Gr. (2017b). Finite Markov Chain and Fuzzy Logic Assessment Models: Emerging Research and Opportunities. Createspace Independent Publishing Platform (Amazon).

Voskoglou, M. G. (2008). Case-Based Reasoning: A Recent Theory for Problem-Solving and Learning in Computers and People. *Communications in Computer and Information Science*, *19*, 314–319. doi:10.1007/978-3-540-87783-7_40

Voskoglou, M. G. (2011). Problem Solving from Polya to Nowadays: A Review and Future Perspectives. In R. V. Nata (Ed.), *Progress in Education* (Vol. 22). Nova Science Publishers.

Voskoglou, M. G. (2016). Problem solving in the forthcoming era of the third industrial revolution. *International Journal of Psychological Research*, *10*(4), 361–380.

Voskoglou, M. G. (2016). Problem-solving in the forthcoming era of the third industrial revolution. *International Journal of Psychological Research*, *10*(4), 361–380.

Voskoglou, M. G. (2017a). An Absorbing Markov Chain Model for Case-Based Reasoning. *International Journal of Computers*, *2*, 99–105.

Voskoglou, M. G. (2019a). Communities of practice for teaching and learning mathematics. *American Journal of Educational Research*, *7*(6), 186–191. doi:10.12691/education-7-6-2

Voskoglou, M. G. (2019b). An Application of the "5 E's" Instructional Treatment for Teaching the Concept of Fuzzy Set. *Sumerianz Journal of Education. Linguistics and Literature*, *2*(9), 73–76.

Voskoglou, M. G. (2019c). Generalizations of Fuzzy Sets and Relative Theories. In M. Voskoglou (Ed.), *An Essential Guide to Fuzzy Systems* (pp. 345–353). Nova Science Publishers.

Voskoglou, M. Gr. & Buckley, S. (2012). Problem Solving and Computers in a Learning Environment. *Egyptian Computer Science Journal*, *36*(4), 28–46.

Voskoglou, M. Gr. & Salem, A-B. M. (2014). Analogy-Based and Case-Based Reasoning: Two Sides of the Same Coin. *International Journal of Applications of Fuzzy Sets and Artificial Intelligence*, *4*, 5–51.

Waema, T. M., & Miroro, O. O. (2014). Access and use of ICT and its contribution to poverty reduction in Kenya. ICT pathways to poverty reduction: Empirical evidence from East and Southern Africa, 102-131. doi:10.3362/9781780448152.005

Wall, M. (2016). Challenger disaster 30 years ago shocked the world, changed NASA. *Space.com.* Retrieved from https://www.space.com/31760-space-shuttle-challenger-disaster-30-years.html

Walling, O. (2015). Beyond ethical frameworks: Using moral experimentation in the engineering ethics classroom. *Science and Engineering Ethics*, *21*(6), 1637–1656. doi:10.100711948-014-9614-0 PMID:25431220

WEF. (2017). Retrieved from https://www.weforum.org/reports/the-global-risks-report-2017 3.4.2020

Wegerif, R., & Major, L. (2019). *Buber, educational technology, and the expansion of dialogic space subjectivity in which two separate consciousnesses engage.* Academic Press.

Wenger, E. (1998). *Communities of Practice: Learning, Meaning, and Identity.* Cambridge University Press, UK. doi:10.1017/CBO9780511803932

Westerman, G., Bonnet, D., & McAfee, A. (2014). *The nine elements of digital transformation.* Academic Press.

Westkämper, E. (2013). *Towards the Re-Industrialization of Europe: A Concept for Manufacturing for 2030.* Springer Science & Business Media.

Wieser, M. (1991). The computer for the 21st century. *Scientific American*, *265*(3), 94–104. doi:10.1038cientificamerican0991-94 PMID:1675486

Wikipedia. (2020). *Digital Humanities.* Retrieved from: https://en.wikipedia.org/wiki/Digitalhumanities

Wing, J. M. (2006). Computational thinking. *Communications of the ACM*, *49*(3), 33–35. doi:10.1145/1118178.1118215

Wiseman, J. (2013). *Post Carbon Pathways.* University of Melbourne.

Wohlers. (2019). *Wohlers report: 3D printing and additive manufacturing, State of the Industry.* Wohlers. https://wohlersassociates.com/2019report.htm

World Bank. (2008b). *Understanding Poverty report.* Available: http://web.worldbank.org/wbsite/external/topics/extpoverty0contentmdk:20153855~menupk:373757~page:148956~pipk:216618~thesitepk:336992,00.Html

World Bank. (2012). *Information, Communication Technologies, and infoDev (Program) (2012) Information and Communications for Development 2012: Maximizing Mobile.* World Bank Publications.

World Economic Forum (WEF) Asian Development Bank (ADB). (2017). *ASEAN 4.0: what does the Fourth Industrial Revolution mean for regional economic integration?* Geneva: World Economic Forum.

World Economic Forum. (2016, January). The future of jobs: Employment, skills and workforce strategy for the fourth industrial revolution. In *Global Challenge Insight Report.* Geneva: World Economic Forum. Retrieved from https://www.voced.edu.au/content/ngv:71706

World Economic Forum. (2017). *Accelerating Workforce Reskilling for the Fourth Industrial Revolution: An agenda for Leaders to Shape the Future of Education, Gender and Work.* Geneva: World Economic Forum. Retrieved from https://www.voced.edu.au/content/ngv:77198

Wu, Q., Ding, G., Xu, Y., Feng, S., Du, Z., Wang, J., & Long, K. (2014). Cognitive internet of things: A new paradigm beyond connection. *IEEE Internet of Things Journal, 1*(2), 129–143. doi:10.1109/JIOT.2014.2311513

Xu, L. D., Xu, E. L., & Li, L. (2018). Industry 4.0: State of the art and future trends. *International Journal of Production Research, 56*(8), 2941–2962. doi:10.1080/00207543.2018.1444806

Yato, S. (2019). Japan pushing ahead with Society 5.0 to overcome chronic social challenges. *UNESCO.* https://en.unesco.org/news/japan-pushing-ahead-society-50-overcome-chronic-social-challenges

Zadeh, L. A. (1965). Fuzzy Sets. *Information and Control, 8*(3), 338–353. doi:10.1016/S0019-9958(65)90241-X

Zelenika, I., & Pearce, J. M. (2013). The Internet and other ICTs as tools and catalysts for sustainable development: Innovation for 21st century. *Information Development, 29*(3), 217–232. doi:10.1177/0266666912465742

Zelenko, O., & Felton, E. (2012). Framing design and ethics. In E. Felton, O. Zelenko, & S. Vaughan (Eds.), *Design and ethics: Reflections on practice.* Routledge.

Zezulka, F., Marcon, P., Vesely, I., & Sajdl, O. (2016). Industry 4.0–An Introduction in the phenomenon. *IFAC-PapersOnLine, 49*(25), 8–12. doi:10.1016/j.ifacol.2016.12.002

Zhang, Y., Min, Q., & Wu, L. (2008). GVTs Communication Management: A Conceptual Model. *IEEE Service Operations and Logistics and Informatics, 1*, 583–587.

Zhang, Y., & Tao, F. (2016). *Optimization of Manufacturing Systems Using the Internet of Things.* Elsevier.

Zhou, K., Liu, T., & Zhou, L. (2015). Industry 4.0: Towards future industrial opportunities and challenges. In *2015 12th International conference on fuzzy systems and knowledge discovery (FSKD)* (pp. 2147-2152). IEEE.

About the Contributors

Sheryl Beverley Buckley is an Academic Associate in the School of Computing at the University of South Africa (UNISA). Her passion ranges from Knowledge sharing in communities of practice, Knowledge management, E-Learning, Learning organizations, Management fundamentals, Business Intelligence and Communities of practice to mention a few. Sheryl has presented and published research papers locally and internationally and is a member of a number of professional organisations.

* * *

Abiodun Alao obtained her Doctor of Philosophy in Information Systems at the University of Cape Town. She has been an active researcher and teaching fellow at various South African Universities. Abiodun is passionate about research and is keen to demonstrate her academic capabilities the Information Systems field. She is currently a research fellow at the University of Johannesburg where she derives great joy working on projects and mentoring learners Information and Communication Technology skills.

Tamar Apel Campo is an independent researcher based in Israel involved in the development and implementation of ethical based pedagogics. The fundamental contribution of the research conducted in the framework of the CimeH Institute under her guidance is the Let's Track Math methodology which enables the activation of a non-interventional and respectful inquiry in mathematics' learning processes, moving from a two to a three dimensional model of research.

Anthony Bolton is a PhD candidate in the School of Computing at the University of South Africa. He is also Chief Information Officer (CIO) and Chief Technical Officer (CTO) Global Telecom, End User Infrastructure & Services, Immersive Technology Development and Engineering at General Motors in Ireland.

Roelien Brink is a senior lecturer and researcher at the Department of Applied Information Management, University of Johannesburg. She holds a PhD (University of Johannesburg, South Africa), with the focus on information management for the work-integrated learning process. She is the chair of research committee, co-editor of the African Journal for Work-Based Learning, an Exco and board member of Southern African Society for Cooperative Education (SASCE). She is the Vice Chair Africa on the International Research group for World Association for Cooperative Education (WACE) - Research for work-integrated learning, She was part of the advisory board for the World Association for Cooperative Education (WACE) Second International Research Symposium 2016. She is also part of the international review team for the WACE 2nd International Research Symposium and WACE 20th World Conference. Her research interests focus on e-assessment, work-integrated learning, information systems, information communication and technology for development. I am in the cluster information communication and technology for development (ICT4D) and currently supervising students in Omni Channels, E-commerce, Cashless Economy, Digitized displacement in socio-economic displacement of individuals in emerging economies, Learning Management Systems in HEIs.

Jean Cadieux, as a mathematician, is a specialist in data analysis and modelling (learning machine, predictive modeling, data mining, ...). As a professor at the École de gestion de l'Université de Sherbrooke, he conducts his research in the field of sustainable development where he was the architect of the BNQ21000 Standard for Sustainable Development Management. This standard from the Bureau de Normalisation du Québec offers companies a self-assessment and enables them to integrate sustainable development into their management practices. For the renewal of the standard, it proposes to integrate 4.0, digital shift and business intelligence.

Kesavan Dhanapal worked as Credit manager at City Union Bank for 5 years, Business analyst at Client Digital India Ltd, Published 20 high rated journals, Published a book on Entrepreneurship Development.

Garth Gaffley has combined private sector and academic expertise, in strategy, brand marketing, social media marketing, customer management, logistics and supply chain management, e-commerce, data management, digital strategy, digital transformation and migration. He holds numerous degrees BSc (Chemistry and Geology) from UCT, BCom (Economics and Business Economics), BCom Hons (Marketing), and Advanced Executive Program (AEP) all from UNISA, MBA from Henley Business School and in May 2020 will submit a dissertation for the qualification of Doctor of Business Administration through UKZN. He served on the academic board of Henley business school from 2007 to 2011 and was recipient of the class medal for the AEP program and the class awards for Finance and IT modules at Henley. Private sector experience has spanned over twenty years in diverse fields, initially in technical capacities in mining, heavy industry and manufacturing moving into packaging and consumer goods (FMCG) sectors in sales and marketing roles. Entrepreneurial endeavours led to establishing a management consultancy in 2000 providing strategic marketing, brand, category, and route to market service solutions for clients both local and international in the Pharmaceutical (OTC), FMCG, Retail, Manufacturing, and IT sectors. Current consulting activities encompass the outsourced marketing of digital platforms for several IT service providers, digital transformation and data management projects and academic development through Doctoral studies at UKZN.

Leila Goosen is a full professor in the Department of Science and Technology Education of the University of South Africa. Prof. Goosen was an Associate Professor in the School of Computing, and the module leader and head designer of the fully online signature module for the College for Science, Engineering and Technology, rolled out to over 92,000 registered students since the first semester of 2013. She also supervises ten Masters and Doctoral students, and has successfully completed supervision of more than 70 students at postgraduate level. Previously, she was a Deputy Director at the South African national Department of Education. In this capacity, she was required to develop ICT strategies for implementation. She also promoted, coordinated, managed, monitored and evaluated ICT policies and strategies, and drove the research agenda in this area. Before that, she had been a lecturer of Information Technology (IT) in the Department for Science, Mathematics and Technology Education in the Faculty of Education of the University of Pretoria. Her research interests have included cooperative work in IT, effective teaching and learning of programming and teacher professional development.

Elmarie Kritzinger joined the University of South Africa's College of Science, Engineering and Technology (CSET) in 2000 and currently holds the position of Professor in the School of Computing. Prof Kritzinger completed her PhD in 2006 and Post Graduate Certificate in Education in 2012. She is currently enrolled for her Master's in Education (Online Technology). Her research primarily focuses on Cyber Safety awareness, training and education for school learners, teachers and schools. The main aim is to establish and promote social responsibilities within communities to establish and grow a cyber-safety culture within South Africa. Prof Kritzinger has established herself as a mature researcher and has published in accredited national and international journals, contributed to a chapter in a book and presented at peer-reviewed conferences across the globe. Prof Kritzinger currently hold a NRF C3 rating within her research field.

Jennifer Loy is Professor of Additive Manufacturing Engineering at Deakin University in Geelong, Australia. Jennifer has a background in Industrial Design, with a specialisation in digital technologies. Her research interests are in design for additive manufacturing, with a particular focus on medical and health products. Jennifer is an adjunct professor with the Menzies Health Institute in Queensland. Her work includes product design and development, workforce evolution and training and supply chain management.

Andeep Mathur is a propelling and energetic academician, having PhD CSE with 13+ years of experience, along with multiple skill sets. He has published several papers in numerous reputed journals. Author have been continuously contributed to distinctive Research & academics teams at national and International level. Furthermore, he has a patent on C2MC. His research areas are Data analytics, Data modelling & IoT.

Elaine Mosconi is Associate Professor at École de Gestion, Université de Sherbrooke (UdeS). Responsible for the graduate program in management and manufacturing intelligence. Researcher associated with the Research Pole in Strategic and Multidimensional Business Intelligence (PRISME). Her future research is motivated by topics relating to integrated information management and business technologies related to decision-making performance in value creation networks, knowledge management, decision support systems and business intelligence.

Selma Ottonicar is a Ph.D. Candidate at Sao Paulo State University UNESP (Marilia campus) in the Information Science Postgraduate Program (PPGCI). Online Tutor at Brazilian Association of Information Science (ABECIN). She holds a Masters in Information Science from UNESP where she received a CAPES scholarship. She is a member of the Information, Knowledge and Organizational Intelligence research group at UNESP and a member of the IntelliLab research group at Université de Sherbrooke (UdeS), Canada. She is also a member of Information Literacy and Archiving Science at Federal University of Para (UFPA). She holds a Business Management Technologist degree from the Faculty of Technology (FATEC) where she did her scientific initiation. She was an English teaching assistant at FATEC because of her language skills, and she received a Certificate of Excellence for her transcript of records at FATEC. She has received eight awards which allowed her to improve her professional development. She was chosen among the 20 students who had the best grades in Sao Paulo State to study Spanish in Argentina in 2013. This scholarship was provided by the Government of Sao Paulo State and Centro Paula Souza. She received two Canadian scholarships to work as an intern at Université de Sherbrooke (UdeS), The Future Leaders of America Program (ELAP) from the

Federal Government of Canada and the Funds de Recherche du Québec - Nature et Technologies (FRQNT) in 2nd place. Furthermore, her proposal was chosen by CAPES student exchange scholarship (Brazil) to collect data in Canada. She has experience with teaching and research, and she is interested in Information Literacy, Competitive Intelligence, Competitive Advantage, Small Businesses, Clusters, Information and Knowledge Management. Her focus is to develop interdisciplinary research between Information Science and Business Management.

Theunis Pelser has proven expertise in disciplines involving strategy, marketing and technology management. He holds the degrees BCom, BCom (Hons), MCom (Marketing) and a PhD in Strategic Management focusing on strategic management of technology and innovation, all from the Potchefstroom University. Professor Theuns Pelser was appointed at University KwaZulu-Natal from 1 April 2015 as the Dean and Head of School for the Graduate School of Business and Leadership. He is currently a Strategy Professor in the School. Prior to his appointment, he was the Director of the Graduate School of Business and Government Leadership, North-West University. Before that, he was the Head of Regenesys Business School (RBS) and Strategy Manager at Sasol. Prof Theuns had published more than 70 academic peer-reviewed papers and supervised 40 masters and doctoral students that resulted in the conferring of degrees. He is a member of the South African Journal of Business Management (SAJBM): Editorial Advisory Board. He received two best paper awards during the last four years, at international peer-reviewed conferences.

Rafaela Silva is a Master in Information Science by the Post-Graduate Program in Information Science of Unesp Marilia, in the line of Research Management, Mediation and Information Use, were received FAPESP scholarship. Member of the Information, Knowledge and Organizational Intelligence (ICIO) Research Group. She has done research internship at Robert Gordon University, Scotland, United Kingdom (September to December 2016). Specialization in Institutional Educational Psychology by FUNDEPE, Marilia/SP. Graduated in Librarianship, where also received FAPESP scholarship. Currently she is dedicated to scientific research, working mainly in the interdisciplinarity of themes: Hybrid libraries; Public libraries; Information management; and Development of community. ORCID: http://orcid.org/0000-0001-9684-0327.

Dalize van Heerden is a lecturer within the School of Computing at the University of South Africa. She started working for UNISA in 1999 and has been teaching programming modules ever since. Her main research interests include e-learning, m-learning and technology-enhanced learning.

Index

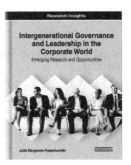

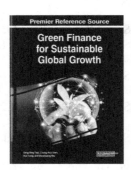

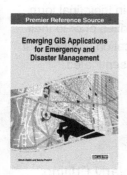

IGI Global Proudly Partners With eContent Pro International

Receive a 25% Discount on all Editorial Services

Editorial Services

IGI Global expects all final manuscripts submitted for publication to be in their final form. This means they must be reviewed, revised, and professionally copy edited prior to their final submission. Not only does this support with accelerating the publication process, but it also ensures that the highest quality scholarly work can be disseminated.

English Language Copy Editing

Let eContent Pro International's expert copy editors perform edits on your manuscript to resolve spelling, punctuaion, grammar, syntax, flow, formatting issues and more.

Scientific and Scholarly Editing

Allow colleagues in your research area to examine the content of your manuscript and provide you with valuable feedback and suggestions before submission.

Figure, Table, Chart & Equation Conversions

Do you have poor quality figures? Do you need visual elements in your manuscript created or converted? A design expert can help!

Translation

Need your documjent translated into English? eContent Pro International's expert translators are fluent in English and more than 40 different languages.

Email: customerservice@econtentpro.com   **www.igi-global.com/editorial-service-partners**